PIONEER HISTORY OF
ORLEANS COUNTY, NEW YORK

PIONEER HISTORY

OF ORLEANS COUNTY, NEW YORK

ARAD THOMAS

ISBN: 979-8-89416-005-4 (paperback)
ISBN: 979-8-89416-028-3 (hardcover)
ISBN: 979-8-89416-000-9 (audiobook)
ISBN: 979-8-89416-001-6 (epub)
ISBN: 979-8-89416-003-0 (pdf)

Other languages available.
Visit *pioneerhistory.us* for more information.

This book is part of a series:
Pioneers of Orleans County, NY
Pioneer History of Orleans County, New York (vol1)
*Pioneer Handbook: Mastering Frontier Life
in Orleans County, New York* (vol2)
Pioneer Cookbook: Wilderness Recipes of Orleans County (vol3)

Visit *folk.studio* for other works.

CONTENTS

ZENAS F. HIBBARD; WILLIAM TANNER; ROSWELL S. BURROWS; WILLIAM PENNIMAN; JESSE MASON; STEPHEN B. THURSTON; RUFUS HALLOCK; JONATHAN CLARK; OLIVER BENTON; MOSES SMITH; ANTHONY TRIPP; ALLEN PORTER; ELIZUR HART; JARVIS M. SKINNER; NATHANIEL BRALEY; LUCIUS STREET; THOMAS W. ALLIS; JOSEPH BARKER; ENOS RICE; LUTHER PORTER; NEHEMIAH INGERSOLL; JUSTICE INGERSOLL; LORENZO BURROWS.; GEORGE E. MIX; "THINGS I CAN REMEMBER"; BY GEORGE E. MIX; MRS. LYDIA MIX; JOSEPH HART; ADEN FOSTER; ALEX WARD; THE LEE FAMILY; ABRAHAM CANTINE; CAROLINE P. ACHILLES

DEDICATION.

TO THE ORLEANS COUNTY PIONEER
ASSOCIATION, BY REQUEST OF MANY WHOSE
MEMBERS THIS WORK WAS UNDERTAKEN, BY
WHOM THE AUTHOR HAS BEEN GREATLY AIDED IN
PREPARING IT, AND TO WHOM HE FEELS UNDER
OBLIGATIONS FOR MANY PERSONAL FAVORS, THIS
BOOK IS RESPECTFULLY DEDICATED BY THE

AUTHOR.

THIS ADAPTED EDITION IS RESPECTFULLY
DEDICATED TO THE MEMORY OF MY GREAT-
GRANDMOTHER, GRACE EMILY HAMILTON-PIERCE,
A 4TH GENERATION DESCENDANT OF ARETAS
PIERCE, AN ORIGINAL ORLEANS COUNTY PIONEER.

A.BURRIS

FORWARD.

by A.Burris

Having grown up in a modern American single-parent household and separated from my grandparents by thousands of miles, I had only a vague understanding of my family's history. In 1989 I was a young adult, hungry to learn more. My mother gave me a stack of documents with details of our family's past. Among them was an old book with hundreds of stories written in a language from a bygone era. This book was an original copy of *Pioneer History of Orleans County, New York*, by Arad Thomas, which had been passed down through generations of my family.

Within its pages are over thirty chapters detailing the history of Western New York, the Holland Purchase, the county's settlement, biographies, and first-hand stories told in the pioneer's own words.

Despite my repeated attempts, I found it difficult to read more than a few pages at a time. Yet, I felt a strong connection to its content and the stories of my pioneer ancestors. For years, I have felt called to share these tales with a wider audience but lacked the resources to do so. Until now. Recently retired and with new advancements in technology, I finally had the time and means to turn this dream into reality.

My goal was to update the language of the original piece for a contemporary audience. While refreshing the language, I worked hard to maintain its elegance and preserve every detail. Highly detailed information, difficult to understand in this format, such as the description of civil divisions in chapters 2 through 4, has been added to an online repository along with a glossary, high-resolution maps, and other information that bring the material to life.

Arad Thomas's poignant 1851 speech to the Pioneer Association and the first-hand accounts of the Pioneers remain unchanged.

And so I'm delighted to present to you, dear reader, this annotated version of Arad Thomas's original work, completed just in time for the Orleans County Bicentennial Celebration in 2025.

If you, like me, feel disconnected from your family roots, I hope this book instills in you a sense of strength and pride in our shared heritage. For history enthusiasts, this book offers a detailed glimpse into the lives of early Americans during the birth of our nation—stories that have been lost in time but that deserve remembrance.

[Ague, Currier, Gill, Halcyon, The Creature]
19th Century American English Can Be a Bear!
View the glossary—you'll be glad you did.
Sample terms are highlighted
in ***italics*** within this text.

PREFACE.

by Arad Thomas

The origin of this book is briefly this: the Orleans County Pioneer Association had collected a volume, in manuscript, of the local history of many of its members, written by themselves, which they desired to publish.

Some difficulty existed in getting the work by the Association out, and many of his friends requested that the author write a book on his own account, which should contain the substance of the histories and such other material and matter connected with the Pioneer History of Orleans County as might be of general interest to readers.

The author used records from the association and histories of the Pioneers and extracted and condensed the parts that he believed would be of more general interest.

Many of the facts were collected from his own knowledge and the testimony of early settlers and others familiar with the matter.

The character of this book is local, many names of persons and events of private history have been introduced, of little interest perhaps out of the families and neighborhood of the parties; but with these, the author has endeavored to collect and preserve the memory of such events of a more public character, as marked by the progress of settlement in this portion of the Holland Purchase, and as many be worthy of remembrance.

For this purpose, *O'Reilly's Sketches of Rochester, Turner's History of Phelps and Gorham Purchase*, and of the Holland Purchase and French's *Gazetteer of New York* have been consulted, and such extracts and compilations made as could be found there.

It has been an object, kept in view, to collect as much personal reminiscence as possible, for the gratification of the older inhabitants of Orleans County for whom the book was more particularly designed.

Errors and dates, events, names and narratives, no doubt may be found in the work. Such errors are unavoidable in giving details of statements of aged people, often conflicting in their character, and the intelligent reader may sometimes regret that he finds no notice here of facts and incidents in the Pioneer History of this region of country, which he may deem of more importance than what the book contains.

Some such facts and incidents may not have come to the notice of the author, and he has been compelled to omit much matter of interest, lest his work should be too large, beyond the plan proposed.

Much as an apology may seem to be needed, the author has little to make, more than to say he is not a professional book maker, and has no hope of founding a literary reputation on this work. He has little fear therefore of critics, and will be happy, if by this labor he has pleased the old settlers of Orleans County and done his part to save from oblivion, good matter for history, fast passing away; for in the beautiful language of Whittier—

> *"Still from the hurrying train of life, fly backward far and fast,*
> *The milestones of the fathers—the landmarks of the past."*

—John Greenleaf Whittier

A MAP of the Western parts of the Colony of VIRGINIA.

INTRODUCTION.

After Columbus discovered America, the first European settlements on the Atlantic Coast were made by the English and Dutch on the South and by the French on the extreme north. Ascending the great river St. Lawrence, the French founded the cities of Quebec and Montreal; following the river and the lakes westward, they established the settlements at Pittsburgh and Detroit, many years before the English settled Western New York.

When the French arrived, the *Algonquins* and *Hurons* lived in Eastern Canada. They formed a strategic partnership with the French, as the Canadian Indians and the Iroquois in Western New York were at war. The French sided with their Indian allies in this conflict, which led to deep-rooted hostility from the Iroquois.

Many intense battles occurred between the French and these Native Americans with varying levels of success. Eventually, the Algonquins and Hurons were displaced or obliterated, and the Iroquois nearly wiped out the French settlements in Canada. They effectively prevented the French from establishing themselves in New York, even though the French claimed the entire territory. Only a few French missionaries were permitted to stay in Iroquois territory, except at the mouth of the Niagara River, where the French founded a trading post in 1678. The English, led by Sir William Johnson, captured the post in 1759 and held it until it was surrendered to the United States in 1796.

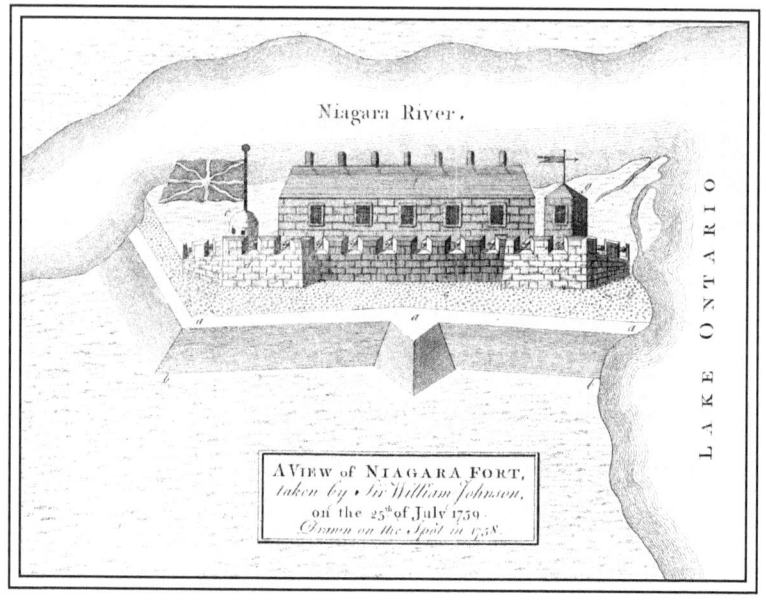

A VIEW OF NIAGARA FORT

Meanwhile, in 1722, the **colonial government** of New York built a trading house at Oswego, and in 1727, a Fort was added to strengthen it.

The French objected to this **encroachment** on the territory they claimed and sent military expeditions multiple times to drive out the English.

These English establishments at Oswego were captured by the French in 1756 and destroyed. The English reconstructed them in 1758 and held them until

1796 when they were handed over to the United States under Jay's treaty.

The French maintained communication through Lake Ontario to connect their western settlements with Quebec but did not establish any other locations within the bounds of New York due to the power of the Iroquois.

In 1760, General Amherst led a formidable army consisting of British, Indians, and Provincial Americans to Canada. In the end, the French surrendered Canada and all of their western possessions, including their claim to Western New York.

JOS. BRANT THAYENDANEGEA

The Iroquois, also known as the Six Nations, established friendly relations with the English early

ix

on. They remained loyal to their alliances even after the French were defeated in America, continuing this loyalty through to the time of the Revolution.

At the beginning of the Revolutionary War, American General Philip Schuyler met with the leaders of the Six Nations at *German Flats* in June 1776 and secured their agreement to remain neutral in the war.

SR. WILLIAM JOHNSON, BART. MAJOR GENERAL OF THE ENGLISH FORCES IN NORTH AMERICA.

But Sir John Johnson, Joseph Brant, Colonel John Butler, and other Tories persuaded the Indians to break their promise and encouraged them to fight alongside the British against the Americans. Throughout the war, all the Indians, except for the Tuscaroras and Oneidas, remained loyal to the British.

Many of the Tories came from a British settlement that had been established in the Mohawk Valley by Sir John Johnson and his father, Sir William Johnson, where they had been trading with the Mohawk. In fact, many of the white residents in the Mohawk Valley were Tories, and so they allied themselves with the hostile Indian groups led by Butler, Brant, and others. Together, they launched attacks against the Americans, causing death and destruction in the frontier settlements of the Colonies.

MAJ. GENERAL JOHN SULLIVAN

After their raids, they would retreat to the British strongholds at Niagara and Oswego, where they were safe from retaliation. This predatory warfare continued intermittently from 1775 to 1779, particularly along the Mohawk and Susquehanna rivers.

In 1779, American General Sullivan led an army of five thousand men sent by General Washington to punish the Indians and Tories of New York for their conduct in the Revolutionary War. He encountered them in force at a fortified camp near Elmira, where they were defeated with great loss. General Sullivan's army pursued the enemy to Canandaigua and then through their villages in Livingston County, destroying everything belonging to the Indians along their route.

Following the Battle of Elmira, only a few Indians were killed. However, the survivors were left feeling scared, weakened, and defeated. Instead of returning to their settlements east of the *Genesee River*, they resettled near Geneseo, Gardeau, Mount Morris, and other areas in the western part of the state after fleeing from Sullivan's forces. The Oneidas, who did not participate in the war, were able to remain in their homes undisturbed.

General Sullivan's expedition severely defeated and humbled the Indians, but they remained peaceful towards the whites thereafter.

CHAPTER 1.

THE INDIANS OF WESTERN NEW YORK

The history of the Indians who inhabited Western New York at the coming of the white men is comparatively unknown. Their own traditionary accounts go back little more than a century, but the numerous relics and ruins and the marks of ancient fortifications scattered over this region of the country, upon which no doubt human labor and skill have been employed, seem to prove conclusively that here men have lived for many centuries past.

All these traces of former habitations of men are found within the bounds of Orleans County. When they were made and by whom seems to be as inexplicable to the Indian of the present day as to his white brother. The commonly entertained opinion of those who have investigated the subject most is that this country has been inhabited by a people who have become long since extinct. A people of higher civilization and more skilled in the arts than those found here now, known as the Six Nations.

The most considerable of these ancient fortifications to be found in Orleans County is thus described in *Turner's History*:

"About one and one-half miles west of Shelby Center, in Orleans County, is an ancient work. A broad ditch encloses in a form nearly circular, about three acres of land. The ditch is, on this day, well-defined and several feet deep. Adjoining the spot on the south is a swamp, about a mile in width, by two in length. This swamp was once doubtless, if not a lake, an impassable morass. From the interior of the enclosure made by the ditch, there is what appears to have been a passageway on the side next to the swamp. No other breach occurs in the entire circuit of the embankment.

There are accumulated, within and near this fort, large piles of small stones of a size convenient to be thrown by hand or with a sling. Arrowheads of flint are found in or near the enclosure in great abundance, stones, axes, etc.

Trees that have grown for four hundred years stand upon the embankment. Underneath them are earthenware plates and dishes wrought with skill, presenting in relief ornaments of various patterns.

Some skeletons have almost entirely been exhumed. Many are giants, not less than seven or eight feet in length. The skulls are large and well-developed in the *anterior lobe*, broad between the ears, and flattened in the *coronal region*.

Half a mile west of the fort is a sand hill. Here, a large number of human skeletons have been exhumed in a perfect state. Great numbers appear to have been buried in the same grave. Many of the skulls appear to have been broken in with clubs or stones."

The Indians found occupying this part of the country when white men began to settle here were the Senecas, a tribe of the Six Nations. They had no village or permanent settlement within Orleans County, but they counted this as part of their territory, occupied it as their hunting and fishing grounds, and were accustomed to following these pursuits here.

Their places of residence were their villages in Genesee and Niagara Counties. These Indians were friendly to the whites, and the pioneer settlers of Orleans County never feared their hostility. In the War of 1812, with Great Britain, they took up arms on the side of the United States and made themselves useful to us in checking the invasions of the hostile Indians from Canada, who acted with the British.

SA-GO-YE-WAT-HA (SENECA CHIEF RED JACKET)

These Indians had formerly been favorably disposed to the British Government, and it was a source of alarm at the breaking out of the war lest they should be found with their old allies. Their great chief, Red Jacket, counseled them to maintain neutrality. This neutral state was construed unfavorably by the pioneers, and rumors of contemplated Indian atrocities were circulated from time to time until the Senecas had resolved to *take up the hatchet* with us.

The rapid settlement of the county by white men diminished the number of wild game animals that the Indians had been accustomed to hunting. Fishing in the Oak Orchard and Johnson's Creeks with seines and nets soon exterminated the salmon and drove away other kinds of fish that had formerly come up these streams from Lake Ontario in abundance. The Indians eventually found the occupation worthless and ceased to come here.

In the early days, parties of Indians came over from Canada and wintered in Carlton to hunt. In the spring, they would return to Canada. As game became scarce, they discontinued their visits.

Indians, in families or singly, frequently traveled about among the dwellings of the pioneers to beg or sell their small wares, or get whisky. They were generally harmless and made no trouble. Their claim to the land was long since settled by treaty transferring it to white men, except the reservations to which they retired.

CHAPTER 2.

PHELPS AND GORHAM'S PURCHASE

The King of England had granted, in a charter, to the colony of Massachusetts, all the land between its north and south boundaries, stretching from the Atlantic Ocean in the east to the Pacific Ocean in the west. The western boundary had not been explored, and the extent of the continent was unknown.

The King of England had also granted New York land that overlapped the Massachusetts charter, causing considerable confusion. After the close of the Revolutionary War, Massachusetts urged her claim. The difficulty was finally compromised by giving New York the sovereignty of all the disputed territory lying within her chartered limits and giving Massachusetts the property in the soil or the right to buy the soil from the Indians, who were then in possession.

Massachusetts then sold the property lying west of Sodus Bay, an estimated 6 million acres, to Phelps and Gorham for $1 million, subject to the Indians' then-existing title. The sale was to be paid for in a kind of scrip, or stock, issued by Massachusetts called Consolidated Securities.

Phelps and Gorham then made a treaty with the Six Nations of Indians, purchasing 2,250,000 acres from the Pre-emption Line to a line just west of the Genesee River.

With this sale and other causes, the market price of these Consolidated Securities rose so high that Phelps and Gorham could not buy the scrip necessary to fulfill their contract with Massachusetts, and so they were compelled to give back all the lands lying west of the Genessee River.

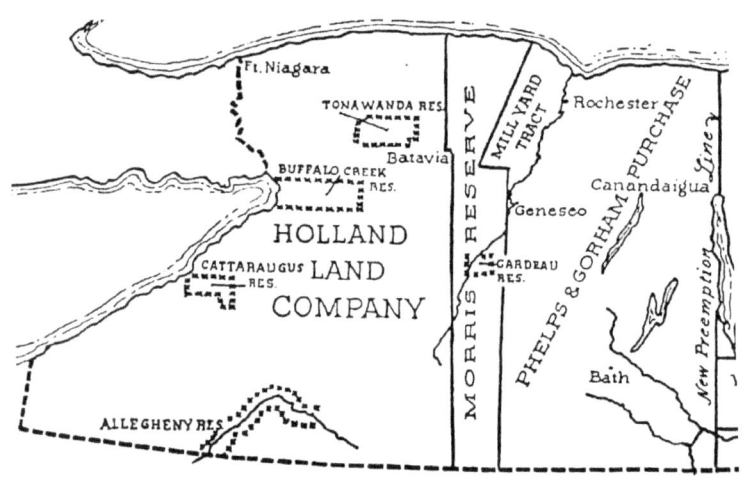

WESTERN NEW YORK LAND PURCHASES EARLY 1800S

The State of Massachusetts then sold the land to Robert Morris, who purchased the pre-emption right for $333,333.34. Morris was a signatory of the Declaration of Independence and a financier of the American Revolution, and at the time was the richest man in America. He, in turn, sold portions of the land to other speculators, including The Triangle Tract, containing 87,000 acres, The 100,000 Acre Tract, and The Holland Purchase, containing 3,600,000 acres. Morris retained a small strip of land on the easternmost boundary, for himself known as the Morris Reserve.

CHAPTER 3.

THE 100,000 ACRE TRACT

The 100,000 Acre Tract is bounded by Lake Ontario on the north and is situated between The Triangle and Morris Reserve on the east and the Holland Purchase on the west.

The Transit Line runs from Pennsylvania north to Lake Ontario along the eastern boundary of the Holland Purchase. It forms the eastern boundary of the towns of Carlton, Gaines, and Barre. It is called the Transit Line because it was run out first with the aid of a Transit instrument. The Land Company cut a track through the trees along this line to the width of about four rods (about 66 feet), thus affording a convenient landmark to the early settlers in locating their lands and serving as a guide in finding their way through the woods.

CHAPTER 4.

THE HOLLAND PURCHASE

I n 1792, approximately nine years after the close of the Revolutionary War, a group of thirteen Dutch investors from Amsterdam purchased the remaining parcels of land, containing 3,600,000 acres, from Robert Morris. This became known as the *Holland Purchase*.

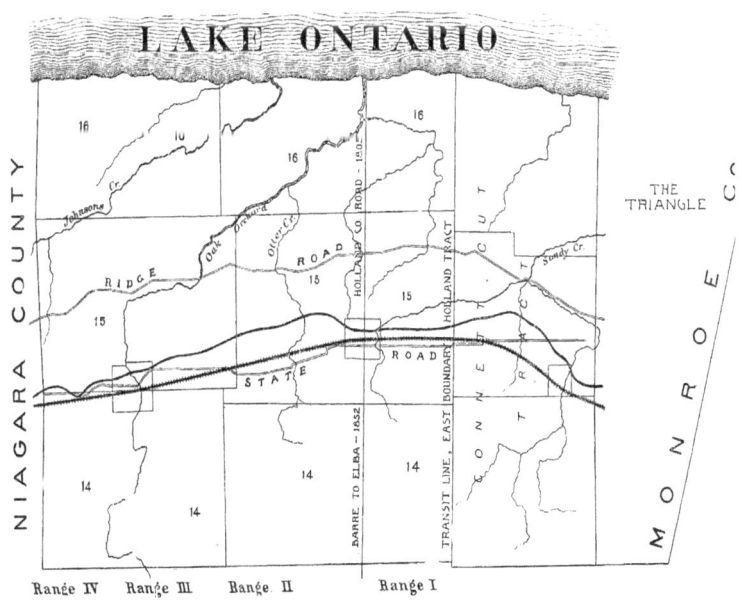

TOWNSHIPS AND RANGES IN HOLLAND PURCHASE

They then formed the **Holland Land Company** and opened a general land office in Philadelphia to oversee this and other purchases they had made in Pennsylvania.

The Holland Purchase encompassed all the land west of the Genesee River, excluding the Indian Reservations. At that time, this area was an unbroken wilderness, inhabited only by Native Americans to the west of the river and a few white settlements to the east. It was commonly referred to as the **Genesee Country**, named after the Genesee River, the region's most significant waterway.

Before Morris could give the Holland Land Company title to this land, it was still necessary to extinguish the Indians' title to it. This was achieved at the 1797 Treaty of Big Tree, where the Indians ceded most of their lands on the Holland Purchase to the white men, reserving tracts of the best land for their own occupation. The native Indians were to receive $100,000 for their rights to about 3.75 million acres, and they reserved about 200,000 acres for themselves.

It was at this time that Mr. Joseph Ellicott was engaged as the principal surveyor. In 1798, assisted by his brother Benjamin and others, he commenced surveying the lands embraced in the Holland Purchase by running and establishing the aforementioned *Transit Line* as the eastern boundary. These surveys continued for ten or twelve years until the whole tract was divided into townships, ranges, sections, and lots.

Joseph Ellicott was appointed as local agent and over twenty years, he had almost exclusive control of all the company's local business. This was all managed from the principal land office in *Batavia*, with smaller offices established in different parts of the Purchase for the convenience of the parties involved.

JOSEPH ELLICOTT

The company originally intended to quickly sell the land at a significant profit. However, they ended up having to invest more money over the course of many years to improve the land by surveying it, building roads, and digging canals in order to make it more appealing to potential settlers. The first sale was made in 1804.

It was usual for a person to select the parcel of land they desired to take, go to the Land Office at Batavia, and make a contract with the Company's agent there for the purchase. Very seldom indeed was payment in full made and a deed taken right away.

The common practice was for the purchaser to make a small payment down and receive from the Company a contract in writing, known as an **Article**. In the Article, the Company agreed to sell the parcel of land described, and the purchaser was to pay the price in installments for five to ten years, with interest, at which time they would receive a deed.

On receiving the Article, the settler took full possession of the land, cleared it up, and made improvements. All the while, they made payments on the purchase as they were able.

These land Articles were frequently transferred through assignments, often passing from one person to another multiple times before being returned to the Company. A settler wanting to sell their interest in the land would do so by *assigning* their Article. Or, if he desired to give security to a debt or obtain credit in his business, he would pledge his Article. Tradesmen and speculators of every class were accustomed to dealing largely in these Articles, and men, who had means to lend, often held numbers of these contracts transferred to them by absolute sale or in security for some obligations to be later redeemed by the owner.

The Holland Land Company sold its wild lands in Orleans County for from $2 to $5 per acre, depending on the quality and location of the land. In later years, the Company often provided a deed to the settler while taking a **bond and a mortgage** on the land to secure the remaining balance of the purchase money.

The Company generally treated its debtors very leniently, frequently renewing their Articles when they expired without payment, sometimes abating interest accrued and unpaid, or throwing off a part of the original sum when the bargain proved a hard one for any reason to the debtor.

Another form of relief for the settlers was the Company's agreement to accept cattle as payment for overdue land Articles. For some years before the Company ceased to exist, they would send agents to various locations on the Purchase to collect the cattle and credit their value towards the settlers' outstanding payments. The collected cattle were then driven to distant markets. While this arrangement helped the settlers, it resulted in significant losses for the Company.

An early School Act of New York State required that school districts secure schoolhouse sites either through *deeds* granting full ownership (deeds in fee) or through leases from the landowners.

Before 1828, there were times when suitable land for schoolhouses was unavailable. To address this, the Company introduced a policy to grant half-acre plots to school districts for free, provided the land was owned by the Company. If the desired site was under contract with another party, the school district had to get that party's agreement to give up their rights to the half-acre plot.

Another instance of the Holland Company's generosity, as shown in the conduct of their general agents, is recorded in the case of Mr. Busti, who for many years was their head agent in Philadelphia.

Mr. Turner, in his *History of the Holland Purchase*, says in a note (as paraphrased):

"In the fall of 1820, Mr. Busti was visiting the Land Office in Batavia. The Rev. Mr. R. of the Presbyterian sect called on Mr. Busti and insisted on a donation of land for each society of his persuasion, then formed on the Holland Purchase. Mr. Busti treated the Rev. gentleman with due courtesy but showed no disposition to grant his request.

Mr. R., encouraged by Mr. Busti's politeness, persevered in his solicitations day after day until Mr. Busti's patience was almost exhausted. That subject was finally brought to a crisis when Mr. R. followed Mr. Busti out of the office as he was leaving to take his tea at Mr. Ellicott's and made a fresh attack on him in the piazza.

Mr. Busti was evidently vexed and, in reply, said: 'Yes, Mr. R., I will give a tract of one hundred acres to a religious society in every town on the Purchase, and this is final.'

'But,' said Mr. R., 'You will give it all to the Presbyterians, will you not; if you do not expressly so decide, the sectarians will be claiming it, and we shall receive very little benefit from it.'

'Sectarians, no!' was Mr. Busti's hasty reply, 'I abhor sectarians. They ought not to have any of it. And to save contention, I will give it to the first religious society in every town.'

On which Mr. Busti hastened to his tea, and Mr. R. to his home (about sixteen miles distant) to start runners during the night and next morning to rally the Presbyterians in the several towns in his vicinity to apply first and thereby save the land to themselves.

The Land Office was soon flooded with petitions for land from Societies organized according to law and empowered to hold real estate and those who were not. Before he left, one of the petitions was presented to Mr. Busti, directed to 'General Poll Busti,' on which he insisted it could not be from a religious society, for all religious societies read their **bibles** and know that P-o-l-l does not spell Paul.

Amidst this chaos and the overwhelming number of applications, it was deemed unwise to hastily approve the land donations. And so the entire responsibility for managing this situation fell on Mr. Ellicott, who then had to fulfill the vague promise made by Mr. Busti.

As a result, the distribution of the **Gospel Land** deeds was delayed for a period, despite the persistent requests from petitioners seeking their land deeds. During this delay, the matter was carefully reviewed and organized to the best of their ability, given the circumstances.

Careful consideration was given to each application, and eventually, tracts of land not exceeding one hundred acres in total were granted, at no cost, to religious societies lawfully organized in each town within the Purchase where the Company still owned land. This included all organized towns except Bethany in **Genesee County** and Shelden in Wyoming County. Recipients were permitted to choose from unsold farming lands in their respective towns. In some towns, it was all given to one society; in others to two or three societies, separately; and in a few towns to four different societies of different sects, twenty-five acres to each.

In performing this thankless duty, where many applicants asserted an absolute right to the land, Mr. Ellicott's careful guidance ensured that amidst the inevitable clamor and disputes, there were no accusations of favoritism towards any specific religious group or undue influence on any individual. His leadership and that of his associates remained untarnished by complaints or claims of bias."

It is understood the Rev. Mr. R. referred to was Rev. Andrew Rawson of Barre and Mr. Busti was, by profession, a Roman Catholic.

THE BOUNTIFUL LAND

Some of the first settlers of this territory north of Tonawanda Swamp came from Canada in boats across Lake Ontario; others came from New England and the east by boats along the south shore of the lake. Those who came on foot or with teams usually crossed the Genesee River at Rochester and then took the Ridge Road west.

The Ridge in this locality had been used as a highway ever since the county had been traversed by white men, and it was a favorite trail of the Indians. Bridges had not been made over the streams by which it was intersected, and it was difficult crossing these with teams. Sir William John, going with a large body of soldiers to Fort Niagara, went along the Lakeshore from Genesee River and encamped for the night on the Creek in Carlton, west of Oak Orchard. He gave it the name of Johnson's Creek, which it has since retained.

The Oak Orchard Creek was named after the beautiful oak trees that grew along its banks, which were seen by the first discoverers.

Orleans County was originally densely forested. The dry, hard land was predominantly covered with beech, maple, white, red, and black oak, whitewood (tulip tree), basswood, elm, hickory, and hemlock. Swamps and low wetlands were filled with black ash, tamarack, white and yellow cedar, and soft maple. Large sycamore, or "cotton ball" trees, were common in low areas, while some pine grew along Oak Orchard Creek and in the swamps of Barre. A few chestnut trees grew along the Ridge in Ridgeway and other areas north of the Ridge. Early settlers estimated that each acre of land in the county averaged seventy-five to one hundred cords of wood (a hundred 28 cubic feet each).

The principal wild animals found here were the bear, deer, wolf, raccoon, hedgehog, woodchuck, skunk, fox, the black, red striped and flying squirrel, mink, and muskrat. Bear and deer were plenty, and hunting them furnished food and sport for the pioneers. For some years, the wolves were so destructive to the sheep and young cattle that it was difficult to keep them. The bears would kill pigs if they strayed into the woods. As the forests were cut down and settlers came in, these large animals were hunted out till not a bear, deer, or wolf had been seen wild in Orleans County for several years.

Fish were plenty in the streams, coming up from Lake Ontario in great numbers.

At the country's first settlement, white men and Indians caught an abundance of salmon. In high water, these fish would run up the Oak Orchard and Johnson's Creek and out into their tributaries, where they were often taken. Salmon were once caught in a small stream in the west part of the town of Gaines. It is related that at an early day, after a high freshet, Mr. John Hood caught several salmon on the bank of this stream where a tree had overturned, leaving a hole through which the water had flowed and where they were left when the water subsided.

A kind of sucker fish, called red sides, used to run up from the lake in plenty. They were taken in April and May, in seines, by wagon loads. The salmon disappeared years ago, and very few red sides run now.

Rattlesnakes were numerous along the banks of Oak Orchard Creek and the Niagara and Genesee Rivers when the country was new. They had several dens, to which they retired in winter and near which they were frequently seen in springtime. Lemuel Blandon relates that in 1820, he went with a party to fish near the mouth of Oak Orchard. They intended to stay all night and built a shelter of **boughs** on the lake shore, on the east side, near where the hotel now stands. They set fire to an old log that lay there. After the fire began to burn, two or three rattlesnakes came out from the log and induced the fishermen to fix their camp in another place.

Enos Stone, an early settler in Rochester, said, "The principal colony of the rattlesnakes was in the bank of the river, below the lower falls, at a place we used to call

Rattlesnake Point; and there was also a large colony at Allen's Creek, near the end of the Brighton Plank Road. I think they grew blind about the time of returning to their dens in August and September. I have killed them on their return, with film on their eyes."

Rattlesnake oil was held in great esteem by early settlers. Zebulon Norton of Norton's Mills was a kind of backwoods doctor, and he often came to this region for the oil and the gall of rattlesnakes. The oil was used for stiff joints and bruises, and the gall for fevers in the form of a pill made up with chalk. A rattlesnake's den, where they used to winter and out of which they would crawl in early spring to sun themselves, was situated on the west bank of Oak Orchard Creek, on the Shipman farm, in Carlton. No snakes have been seen there for many years.

Raccoons were plenty. Their fat was used to fry cakes, and their flesh was much esteemed for food by the inhabitants.

Hedgehogs were also common. They frequently came around the log cabins in the night in search of food. Dogs, who were unacquainted with the animal, sometimes charged upon him so rashly as to get their heads filled with quills, which were very difficult to extract because of their barbed points.

Before the settlement, there were no natural openings in the woods or prairie grounds adapted to the habits of the quail in this county. It was supposed that they came in with the emigrants. The quail soon became plentiful as the large wheat fields afforded them sustenance.

Quails, raccoons, and hedgehogs are now nearly exter-minated in Orleans County. A rattlesnake is very seldom seen.

The beavers were all destroyed by the first hunters who came here.

Those who assume to know, say, skunks and foxes are more numerous now than ever before, which, if true, may be due to the abundance of field mice they feed on.

Before the settlement of this county, streams of water were, on average, twice as large as they are now. And they were more durable, flowing year round, whereas now they are dry part of the year.

Large tracts of low land, now cultivated to grass and grain, originally were marshes too wet even to grow trees. The marshes were near the beaver dams, which flooded the land and destroyed the timber once growing there. As the beavers were hunted and destroyed, their dams were opened or worn away, and their ponds, in time, became cultivated fields.

Quite a number of these beaver dams existed in Orleans County. The largest in Barre perhaps was at the head of Otter Creek, on lot 15, from which a stream flowed north and near which, some years ago, E. P. Sill had a sawmill that did a large business. This beaver pond covered a hundred acres or more, which, after the beaver were gone but before the pond had been effectively drained, became a *cranberry marsh*.

Old people still recollect going there to get cranberries. Near the outlet of this pond or marsh was a favorite camping place of the Indians, who made this a kind of headquarters during their visits here to hunt and fish. As the water subsided in these marshes, different kinds of forest trees gradually came in.

Another beaver dam was erected on the headwaters of Sandy Creek, on the farm of William Cole. Another is on the farm of Amos Root, at the head of a small stream that flows into Tonawanda Swamp. Remains of beaver dams are seen in Ridgeway and other towns.

When white settlers first arrived in this county, the winters were much milder than they are today. According to old settlers, the ground in the woods rarely froze so hard that a stake couldn't be easily driven into it. Snowfall was not as deep as it sometimes is now. The thick canopies of tall trees reduced the strength of the winds, and the moderating influence of the Great Lakes, Erie and Ontario, helped prevent extreme temperatures. These extremes of heat and cold have become more common since the trees were cut down and the wetlands dried up.

Soon after *clearing*s began to be made in the forest, peach trees were planted. They grew luxuriantly and ripened the choicest fruit in great abundance. The peach crop was never a failure, and apricots and nectarines were also grown successfully.

The cultivation of apples received early attention, and some orchards, now in full health and bearing, are almost as old as the first settlement.

In the woods, the first pioneers occasionally found a wild plum tree bearing a tough, acrid plum of a red and yellow color and a small purple fox grape of no value.

For many years before and after the opening of the Erie Canal, wheat was the great object of cultivation among farmers. Between 1830 and 1840, the quantity of wheat raised and exported from Orleans County yearly was immense. Barley did not come into cultivation until much later than wheat, and no rye was sown for many years.

It was not until after the ravages of the weevil, or wheat midge, had begun to seriously interfere with wheat growing that the cultivation of beans attracted considerable attention.

THE TONAWANDA SWAMP

This swamp lies in the counties of Genesee and Orleans, covering parts of Byron, Elba, Oakfield, and Alabama in Genesee County and parts of Shelby, Barre, and Clarendon in Orleans County. Originally, it contained about twenty-five thousand acres, most of which were too wet to plow and covered with swamp timber, open marsh, flags, or swamp grass. Oak Orchard Creek drains this swamp.

Around 1820, the State built a feeder canal from Tonawanda Creek in Genesee County to direct its water into the Oak Orchard Creek, which then fed the Erie Canal.

The swamp's outlet was a ledge of rock too small to naturally drain it sufficiently. When the Tonawanda Creek was thus brought into this, the swamp's level was raised, and the State did nothing to facilitate the discharge, thus increasing the stagnant water.

In 1828, the Holland Company sold a considerable portion of these wetlands to an association, which expended about twelve thousand dollars in enlarging the capacity of the outlet to drain the swamp through Oak Orchard Creek.

The Canal Commissioners then appropriated the whole of the Creek for the canal, and further attempts at drainage were abandoned.

In April 1852, an Act was passed appointing Amos Root, John Dunning, Henry Monell, and David E. E. Mix as *Commissioners* to lay out and construct a highway across the Tonawanda Swamp on the line between ranges one and two of the *Holland Purchase*. A road was made and opened to travel under this Act at a cost of about $2,750.

As the surrounding country became settled, this swamp became an obstacle. Passing through it required a great expense to make and maintain highways. This large tract yielded but little return to the owners and paid but little tax to the public, so no further attempts to drain were made. The association sold their lands to different individuals, and nothing was done to reclaim this tract until April 16, 1855, when an Act of the Legislature appointed Amos Root, S. M. Burroughs, Ambrose Bowen, Robert Hill, John B. King, and Henry Monell, as Commissioners to drain the swamp.

The Act specified that the Commissioners should allocate the costs of their work to the landowners directly impacted by the drainage. The expenses would be distributed based on the benefits each landowner was expected to receive, with the total assessment not exceeding $20,000.

The Commissioners began their work and estimated and assessed the expense. This offended the parties assessed, who united almost unanimously the next year in a petition to the Legislature to repeal the law, and it was repealed.

In 1863, an Act was passed appropriating $16,306 again to improve Oak Orchard Creek and the Canal feeder. The Act provided that all persons who had claimed damages from the State on account of making the feeder from Tonawanda Creek and Oak Orchard release all such claims before the money was extended.

CHAPTER 5.

THE LOG HOUSE

The log house, constructed and used by the first settlers of Western New York, is now an institution belonging to a generation gone by. No new log houses are being built, and the few old ones that remain will soon be destroyed by the relentless tooth of time. Of those who were their builders and occupants, soon, no one will be left to tell their story.

The most primitive log house, to which we refer, was rather a rough-looking *edifice*, usually 12 or 15 feet by 15 or 20 feet square. It was made of logs of almost any kind of uniform-size timber nearest at hand. These were used with the bark on by rolling one log upon another horizontally, notching the corners to make them lie close together, and then built up to the height wanted for the outer walls of the house.

An opening in one side was left for a door, and commonly another for a window. Poles were laid across the walls for a bed chamber floor to rest on, to be reached by a moveable ladder. A ridge pole and rafters supported a roof, which was made of oak or hemlock splints or elm bark.

Bark for roofs was peeled in June in strips about four feet long and laid upon the rafters in courses, held to the rafters by heavy poles laid transversely and bound by strips of bark. An opening in the roof at one end was left for the escape of smoke from the fire, which was built upon the ground under the opening. The remainder of the ground enclosed was covered with a floor of basswood logs, split or *hewed* to a flat surface.

The crevices between the logs were filled, or *chinked*, as they called it, by putting in splints in large openings and plastering with clay inside and out.

When a sash, lighted with glass, could not be procured for use in the window, oiled paper was sometimes substituted for the glass. In extreme cases, the door was made of splints hewed flat and thin. But ordinarily, it was made of sawed boards, hung upon wooden hinges, and fastened with a wooden latch. The latch was raised by a string that was put through a hole to lift it from the outside. Hence, to say of a householder, "his latch string was always out," was equivalent to declaring his generous spirit in opening his house to whoever applied for hospitality.

Now, with the latch complete, the carpenter and joiner work on the house was done. Masons, painters, glaziers, and all other house builders had nothing to do here. The owner was his own architect, and commonly, the house was put up at a *bee*, a gathering of all settlers in the neighborhood, gratis.

We read that Solomon's Temple rose without the sound of a hammer. In that respect, the temple has no advantage over these early homes of the settlers of Orleans County. There was no hammering here, for there were no nails to be driven. Sturdy blows with the ax did the business, and everything was fastened with wooden pins or withees.

If time and means permitted, and the owner wished to indulge in the luxury of a chimney, he was gratified by building a portion of an end wall with stone. The stone portion of the wall was built several feet high and laid in clay mortar, and then the rest of the end wall was completed with logs in the usual way. A high cross beam, or mantel, was put in. On this, a superstructure of sticks was laid in a square. Layer upon layer of sticks was added until the structure was higher than the roof. Then, as with the walls of the house, the walls of the structure were filled in with clay and called a *stick chimney*. This chimney and all the woodwork exposed to the fire, being well plastered with the clay mud, rendered the whole tolerably safe from the danger of burning. But this gave little encouragement to insurance companies, whose agents never ventured to take risks on such property.

As wealth increased and a higher state of civilization and architectural development was introduced into the structure of log houses, stone chimneys were built from the ground up. About the time stone chimneys were first made, cellars under the log houses began to be constructed. These cellars were found to be exceedingly convenient as a depository safe from frost, adding much to the storage capacity of the house.

The introduction of **brick oven**s marks an era that may be called modern compared with the primitive log house. These ovens, sometimes made far from the house and standing on a frame, were called Scotch ovens.

When the family had become sufficiently affluent to afford it, sometimes a chamber floor of boards was laid upon the cross beams overhead. A hole was left in the flooring, through which a person from below could mount a moveable ladder into the chamber.

Sometimes, a wealthy settler who felt cribbed and confined too closely in a single room would build an addition to his log house. The new room was like the first, adjoined with a door between. The owner of such a **double log house** was looked upon with envy and admiration by all the neighboring housekeepers, who wondered what he could do with so much room. It would be a remarkable and exceptional case if the owner and his family did not put on some airs and go to **keeping tavern**.

It would be several years before the general class of log householders got a barn. Until then, straw and **fodder** would be stacked outside for the livestock. If a shelter for them was desired, **crotches of trees** would be cut and then set in the ground for posts. Poles were laid across on these, and then a pile of straw heaped on top. The result was a shed that was warm and dry.

The log house, in general form and structure, was copied from the wigwam of the Six Nations of Indians. The *bark roof* was similar in both cases, but the Indians built the walls of their wigwams of bark fastened to upright poles without a floor. Their fire was on the ground in the center, and the smoke rose without any chimney, finding its way through a hole left open in the center of the roof.

In the log houses of the white men, Fires were sometimes made by cutting a log eight or ten feet long from the largest tree they could find that would go through the door of the house without being split. This log was then run upon rollers endwise through the door and rolled to the back of the fireplace. A fire was built in the middle of the log in front, and fuel was applied to that spot until the fire consumed the center of the log. The ends would then be crowded together. This process continued until the whole log was burned. Sometimes, such a *backlog* would last a week or ten days, even in cold weather. The light from such a fire was commonly sufficient to illuminate the single apartment of the house at night. If more light was wanted, a *dipped tallow candle* was made by the mistress of the household. Or a taper made of a dish of fat or grease with a rag stuck in it for a wick would answer the purpose.

CHAPTER 6.

LOG HOUSE FURNITURE

All household furniture used in the farmers' log houses, at their first beginning in the woods on the Holland Purchase, was about as primitive in its character as their new dwellings. It was adapted to the wants and circumstances of its owner and such as he could readily procure.

For temporary use, a few *hemlock boughs* on the floor, covered with blankets, made a comfortable bed. If a better bed and bedstead were wanted, they were made by boring holes in a set of logs at the proper height and putting in rods fastened to upright posts. Upon this bedstead, they laid such a bed and bedding as the taste and ability of the party could furnish.

Kettles were suspended from a cross pole over the fireplace by wooden or iron hooks, often by an instrument called a trammel. The trammel was a flat iron bar filled with holes hanging from the pole, on which a kettle was suspended on a hook. The kettle might be raised or lowered at pleasure by moving the hook from one hole to another.

Their nearest approach to an oven was a *cast* iron *bake pan*, covered with a moveable lid, standing on legs, and lifted by a bail. The dough was placed inside the vessel, and coals were put on and under it when in use.

Another cooking utensil was a frying pan, with a handle long enough to be held in the hand of the cook while the meat was frying in the pan over the fire.

It was many years after the first settlement of Orleans County before a stove of any kind was seen here.

The table was a board or box cover laid on a barrel. Many of the first families took their meals quite happily for some time, off a *barrel head* or a *chest cover*. Their chairs were often blocks of logs or benches and homemade stools.

The pewter mugs, platters, and wooden trenchers that adorned the shelves and tables of our grandmothers, the early settlers of New England, were rarely found among the belongings of young couples starting their households in this part of the Holland Purchase. Here, spoons of tinned iron, or homemade spoons of pewter, and a slender stock of necessary crockery, including the veritable *blue-edged plates*, comprised the table furniture.

A black earthen teapot was used to prepare the family's tea, regardless of whether the ingredient was store-bought tea, sage, pennyroyal, or any other herb from the fields. These small black teapots, which held about a quart, were reputed by their owners to make better tea than any other material. They were used daily and remained popular even for some time after block tin teapots became fashionable, introduced by increasing wealth and pride.

To this day, one of these interesting relics of antiquity is occasionally seen. The **black earthenware teapot**, with its spout probably broken off, may adorn the upper back shelf of some kitchen pantry in the great new house, which has succeeded the log one. The kettle may have been carefully preserved and dusted each year by the loving hands of the venerable dame who once used it. Or it could have been maintained by her granddaughters, who, inheriting the family's long-standing frugality, found a practical use for everything, including using the old teapot to store garden seeds.

CHAPTER 7.

CLEARING LAND AND FIRST CROPS

Orleans County was originally covered with a heavy growth of trees. These had to be removed to open the soil to cultivation. This was commonly done by cutting the trees so as to leave a stump two or three feet high. The felled timber lay upon the ground until it was dry. Then fire was put in, and the whole field was burned over at once. The logs were then cut at the proper length to be hauled together in heaps by oxen and burned again. The ashes of the heaps were collected and leached to make *black salts* and *potash*.

The land being thus cleared of wood, the first crop was wheat, sown *broadcast*, and covered with earth by harrowing the ground with a triangular *harrow*, or *drag*. A field with the trees lying as they fell was called a *slashing*, and sometimes a *clearing* or a *fallow* as the work progressed.

Wheat was sown in the fall to be harvested the next season; no spring wheat was raised. Sometimes, *corn* and potatoes were planted among the logs during the first season by digging in the seed with a hoe.

On account of the stumps it was several years before the land could be plowed to much advantage after the trees were felled. But as these were chiefly hardwood, they soon rotted out.

For some years, the first settlers cut their wheat crop with a sickle, threshed the grain with *flail*s or trod it out with horses and cattle, and freed it from the chaff by shoveling it in the wind or fanning it with a hand fan.

The lack of barn floors and other conveniences made all these operations exceedingly laborious and slow compared with such work today. Before barns with threshing floors were made, some farmers made floors or platforms of split logs and laid them on the ground without any roof over them. They stacked their grain beside the logs and threshed it on these floors in fair weather or trod it out with oxen or horses.

NEW ENGLAND SETTLERS. FROM "ONE HUNDRED YEARS
OF PROGRESS OF THE UNITED STATES"

CHAPTER 8.

HARDSHIPS AND PRIVATIONS

The scarcity of bread and breadstuffs before the war, and even down to 1818, is to be numbered among the hardships and privations which beset the settlers. Even when they could get a bushel of wheat or corn, the difficulty in reducing the grain to flour or meal was truly formidable.

The nearest mill was 15 to 30 miles away; there was no road leading to it and probably no horse to draw or carry the *grist* if a road had been opened. But meal must be had and so the undaunted emigrant would hitch his oxen to his sled or wagon, pile on a bag for himself, take as many bags for his neighbors as the occasion required and start for some mill.

We will leave imagination to describe his journey. After three or four days' absence, it is announced in the settlement that Mr. A. has gotten back from the mill, and marvelously soon each family would be eating pudding or having a cake. But, what if the family had no neighbors? No horse or ox, to carry their grist? Still, the grist must go at once. And so, its owner would shoulder half a bushel or a bushel, according to his strength, and carry it to the mill, be the distance what it may, threading his way past marked trees to make it through the woods. Such journeys were not thought of lightly, and they were honestly performed.

Some of the settlers made and used a sort of domestic mill in which corn could be reduced to meal. They would make a mortar from a hollow in the top of a hardwood stump, rig a heavy pestle on a spring pole over the mortar, and thus pound the corn fine enough to be cooked.

But even if the newcomers had enough bread and enough to spare, they all had to pay a penalty to Nature in the acclimating process, which they all went through almost without exception. *Fever and ague* attacked the pioneer, his wife, his children, or all of them together whenever an opening was made in the forest or the earth was turned up for the first time to the hot rays of the summer sun.

Oh, the amount of *quinine* and *blue pill* consumed in those days! by those who could get a doctor to prescribe in their case! Meanwhile, those sick ones, who had no doctor because there was none to be had, wore out their ague and let it work itself off the natural way. They generally came out about as well as those who doctored and tried to break it, except they took more time to do it. The first professional doctors who came in were most intensely *allopathic* in their practice and dealt out quinine and blue pill in most heroic doses to their patients. Infinitesimal prescriptions and homeopathic practice had not then been thought of.

Another privation, if not a hardship, was the lack of post offices and mail facilities. Most of the pioneers came from New England, which they and their fathers regarded as a civilized country and where they had always had all the post office accommodations they wanted. It was rather hard to be shut out completely from the outer world. The first settlers in Orleans County got their letters from Batavia or Clarkson, and they did not take newspapers by mail.

The first winter was a hard time for the pioneer to keep his cattle on account of the scarcity of fodder. It took several years to clear the trees and get a crop of hay grown in their places. A year or two was required before *cornstalks* or straw could be produced.

If nobody in the neighborhood had fodder to sell, the new settler had to cut down trees for his cattle to *browse* or feed upon the boughs. This was a work of immense labor, especially in severe cold weather and deep snows. It was a sad time for the poor cattle, compelled to lie out exposed to all storms and feeding on such a diet.

Special care had to be taken to keep the fire from going out in their dwellings as it was so difficult to recover it again. An instance is given of such a loss in the house of Widow Gilbert, in Gaines, who, returning from the funeral of her husband, found the fire was out and no means at hand to kindle it.

Fire had to be procured from the nearest neighbors, who were several miles away. Tinder boxes and powder horns were the usual resorts in such cases, but these might be out as well as fires. Friction matches had not yet been invented.

And it was an inconvenience, at least, to be deprived of soft water. The bark roof of a log cabin was a poor contrivance for collecting it when there was no snow to melt. The hard water from the ground was prepared for washing clothes by cleansing, as they called it, by putting in wood ashes enough to form a weak *lye*.

The Holland Company commonly sold their lands for a small down payment and gave a contract, extending payments for the balance from five to ten years, with interest annually after about two years. This seemed to be a good bargain to the settler at first, for, although he was poor, he felt hopeful and strong. He went into the woods to begin his clearing, sanguine in the belief that he could meet his payments as they fell due from the produce of his land, besides paying the necessary expenses of his living and his improvements.

But after a year or two, a part of his family is taken sick, doctors and nurses must be paid, and stock, a team, tools, furniture, and provisions must be bought. He may have cleared a few acres, built a log cabin, and raised some crops, more than was needed for home consumption, but he could not sell the surplus. The road to market was impassible for teams, and if the roads had been opened, it was hard work at best to pay for land by raising wheat at the price of thirty cents a bushel.

Is it surprising that under circumstances like these, some of the earlier settlers of this county, after toiling several years and finding themselves constantly running behind, got discouraged and wanted to sell out and go away? Many would have sold their claims and left the country or gone anyway, whether they sold or not if the Land Company had enforced their legal rights on their Articles as they fell due.

But the Company was lenient. They gave off interest due them, and sometimes principal, in cases of great hardship to the settler. Many times, when he went to the Land Office to say he could not make his payments and must give it up, the agents of the company, finding him industrious and frugal, trying to do the best he could, would meet him with such words of kindness, generous encouragement and cheer, that he would go back to his home with fresh courage, to renew his battle with the mosquitos, the ague, and the bears; and wait a little longer for the good time coming.

Only a few were able to take deeds of their lands and pay for them until after the Erie Canal was navigable. They kept on clearing land and enlarging their fields, and between the years 1830 and 1836, good crops of wheat were raised and sold at the canal for about a dollar a bushel. The clouds of gloom began to lift from the face of the county. Prosperity had come. There were no more hardships, privations and sufferings after that, and more deeds of land were taken from the Holland

Company in this county in those years than were given in all others together.

Despite their many challenges, the pioneers never succumbed to present hardships or lost their great hope for the future. They had their joys as well as griefs, running along their pathway together. Social amusements, conviviality, fun, and good feeling! were intermingled with their sadder experiences.

They visited together, labored for and with each other. They exchanged work in chopping, logging, and in heavy toil on their lands, where several together could work at better advantage than alone. They were given to hospitality. They aided, assisted, and helped one another with a liberality and kindness that seems remarkable in contrast with the selfishness of older society.

If a family came in who had not built themselves a cabin for their residence in advance, they had no difficulty finding a stopping place with almost any settler who had a house until a log house could be built. And the best of it was that all the men in the neighborhood assembled at a *bee* and built a log house gratis for their new friends if it was necessary.

If a man fell sick in seed time or harvest and could not do his work, his neighbors would turn in and sow his seed or gather his crop for him. If a family was out of provisions, everybody who had a stock shared with the needy ones.

A happy feature of this primitive society was the absence of caste, which divided people into classes and made social distinctions. Everybody was considered just as good and no better than everybody else. All met and mingled in terms of social equality. At the dancing parties, quilting frolics, weddings, and other gatherings of the people for social enjoyment, everybody in the neighborhood was invited, whether they wore store clothes or common homespun, and commonly everyone attended!

People were generally acquainted with everybody near them. Old people who lived during that time say that for several years, they knew every family in town and often visited with them, walking miles through the woods by marked trees to meet together.

Clearing the forest and undertaking the heavy work of establishing settlements in the woods was the primary task of the pioneers. Through this experience, they learned to value the ability to excel in all aspects of their work. Hence, at their loggings, raisings, and other assemblings for work or play, friendly trials of strength or skill found favor. Contests in chopping, lifting, cutting wheat, and other tests of muscle were common and seldom did a number of young men meet on a festive occasion without forming a ring for wrestling.

The pioneers, at their first coming here, were generally young. They were resolute, intelligent, determined, and persistent, for no others would quit the comparative ease, safety, and comfort of older society to encounter the certain hardships, perils, and discouragements of frontier settlement in the woods in such a country as this.

The true grit of the emigrant was proved by the fact that he came here. Such men were not to be driven back by hardships, want, sickness, or misfortune. While the settler's hope and resolution could not protect him from sickness and calamity, they filled him with fortitude to endure them and gave him a keen relish for enjoying whatever in his way might afford a pleasure.

Looking at these pioneers from the standpoint of the present day, an observer might well conclude they were as happy then as their descendants are now on the same ground. Many who began here in poverty and want, who worked their way through every difficulty to wealth and abundance, have often said that in their old age, their happiest days in life were spent in their old log houses, away back among the stumps.

EARLY MERCHANTS – THEIR STORES AND GOODS

Soon after the settlement of this county, asheries were built. In these early days, the large quantities of wood ash produced in burning the log heaps, made while clearing land, were an easier source of money than crops of grain. The lye obtained was boiled down to a semi-solid state known as black salts, which were then sold to Mr. James Mather or another *ashery* owner. These facilities processed the black salts into potash and perlash, a refined type of potash that has since been replaced by saleratus.

These products of ashes brought some money and were taken by the merchants in exchange for their goods. Before the canal was made, merchants' goods were brought in by water, by way of Lake Ontario, or on wagons from Albany.

Robert Hunter and his brothers of Eagle Harbor were teamsters who traveled to and from Albany with large teams of horses hitched to wagons. They brought in most of the goods used here for several years until later, when they came by way of the canal.

A wagon load would go a great way in stocking a store. The substantial delivery of whisky included in the supplies was sufficient to meet home consumption needs.

Merchants did not then, as now, confine their trade to a single line of goods, such as hardware, drugs, or groceries. In the common language of their advertisements, their stock comprised all the articles usually called for at a county store, which meant everything the people wanted to buy at a store.

The wants of the settlers were few and simple in the line of such goods. They confined their purchases to articles of prime necessity, which they could not well do without, such as tools to work with, and building materials which did not grow upon their land; an occasional *calico* dress, and a few kinds of utensils, such as they could not make at home.

These goods were generally bought on credit, with a promise to pay when the merchant went to New York, a journey he undertook about twice a year. These debts were not all paid when due, and many of them were collected by legal process, and many of them were lost to their owners.

The **credit system** was bad for both parties in many cases. Before the canal was made, people found it very difficult to pay their store debts. Though they had a large and good farm, plenty of the finest wheat, and possibly a stock of cattle, hogs, and horses, they had no money and could not sell their possessions for money, as they could not get it to a market.

About the time the canal became navigable, timber was plentiful, and sawmills were built. Sawed lumber paid many store debts. Soon, wheat, pork, flour, and all kinds of produce that could go to market on the canal were found to be ready for sale at fair prices, and thus, debts could be paid.

DOMESTIC MANUFACTURERS

Most of the early settlers were New England Yankees of that class, who, if they wanted something, made it. With very few tools and those of the simplest kinds, they made almost everything required that could be produced from the materials on hand.

They brought a few clothes with them. When these were worn out, they supplied their wants with cloth made at home. The women made the common articles of clothing for their families. If the man needed a new coat or other garment his wife did not feel competent to make, the cloth was taken to someone properly skilled to be cut out, and a tailoress would come to his house and make it up.

These itinerant seamstresses did most of the needlework required by the family, and which they could not do themselves. The modern classification of needlewomen into milliners, manteau makers, dressmakers, etc., did not then prevail. The people got their leather made by neighboring tanners, and from such stock, a traveling shoemaker visited the houses of his customers and made and mended their shoes and boots. The boys and girls, and some of the older folks, commonly went barefoot in the summer and often likewise in the winter.

POST OFFICE AND MAIL

Mr. Merwin S. Hawley of Buffalo, son of Judge Elijah Hawley, who resided in Ridgeway in his boyhood, speaking from his recollections, says:

In 1815, the only mail to and through Ridgeway was carried on horseback twice a week between Canandaigua and Lewiston. On Oct. 22, 1816, a post office was established at Ridgeway Corners, named Oak Orchard, with Elijah Hawley, appointed as the postmaster. At that time, the mail was carried in two-horse carriages, three times a week each way, stopping overnight at Huff's tavern in East Gaines.

A year later, on Aug. 24, 1817, another post office was established at Oak Orchard Creek, on the Ridge, which was then growing to be a smart village! James Brown was appointed postmaster there. To make the names of the offices conform to their locations, the new post office was called Oak Orchard, and the name of the other was changed to Ridgeway, with Mr. Hawley holding the office of postmaster there until his death. During this year (1817), a daily line of mail stages, each way, between Rochester and Lewiston, on the Ridge Road, was commenced.

A post office was established at Gaines on July 1, 1816, with William. J. Babbitt appointed as postmaster. The next post office in Orleans County was located at Shelby Center and got its mail from Ridgeway. Other Post offices were located in other parts of the county from time to time, as the wants of increasing population required.

CHAPTER 9.
THE ERIE CANAL

Digging began with the middle section of the canal near Utica on July 4, 1817. Construction was slow as the workers blasted through mountainous terrain and dense rock. But by November 1823, the eastern part of the canal was sufficiently completed, allowing boats from Rochester to reach Albany simultaneously, with boats traveling from Lake Champlain through the *Champlain Canal*.

DEWITT CLINTON MINGLING THE WATERS
OF LAKE ERIE WITH THE ATLANTIC.

On October 26th, 1825, the Erie Canal was officially completed. Governor Dewitt Clinton led a fleet of boats from Buffalo to New York Harbor in just 8 days for the Grand Canal Celebration. At the harbor, Clinton ceremoniously poured Lake Erie water into New York Harbor, symbolically *"Wedding the Waters."* Despite being only four feet deep and 40 feet wide, the canal was a significant engineering achievement, spanning nearly 400 miles and featuring 83 locks to manage different water levels.

No part of New York State has benefited more from the Erie Canal than Orleans County.

Although the soil was fertile and productive and yielded abundant crops to reward the farmer's toil, its inland location and great difficulty of transporting produce to market rendered it of little value at home. Settlers who had located here, in many instances, had become discouraged. Others who desired to emigrate to the Genesee country were kept back by the gloomy accounts they got of life in the wilderness, with little prospect of easy communication with the old Eastern States to cheer the hope.

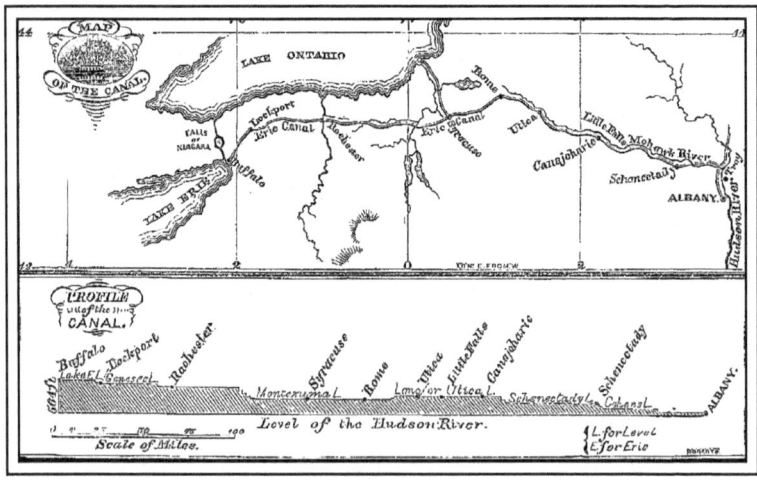

PATH AND ELEVATION OF ERIE CANAL

As soon as the Canal became navigable, Holley, Albion, Knowlesville, and Medina, villages on its banks, were built up. *Actual settlers* took up all the unoccupied lands and cleared them up. No more speculators were buying large tracts of land to leave them undeveloped, waiting for market prices to rise.

The lumber of the county now found a ready market and floated away. Wheat was worth four times as much as the price for which it had been previously selling. Prosperity came in on every hand; the mud dried up, and the mosquitoes, the ague, the fever, and the bears left the county.

Farmers paid for their lands, surrendered their articles, and took deeds from the Company. Good barns, *framed house*s, and houses of brick and stone began to be built as the common dwellings of inhabitants. "*The good time coming*," which the first settlers could not see but waited for, with a faint and dreamy but persistent hope, had come indeed.

The price of land rose rapidly, making many wealthy, who happened to locate farms in desirable places, from the rise in value of their lands. From this time forward, rich men from the Eastern States and older settlements began to come in and buy out the farms and improvements from those who had begun in the woods.

The original settlers now found themselves, like Cooper's Leather Socking, "*lost in the clearing*" and wished to move further out, closer to the borders of civilization, where the hunting and fishing were better and where the ruder institutions, manners, and customs of frontier life, to which they had become attached, were better enjoyed among like-minded individuals.

The removal of shade trees dried up the mud. The construction of substantial bridges over streams and the development of leveled and graveled highways, made possible by the growing population and their resources, created a demand for new types of carriages to transport these now self-sufficient farmers and their families.

People had been content to travel to the mill, attend meetings, visit socially, or participate in quilting frolics using an ox sled. However, as progress, pride, and ambition grew, horses and lumber wagons gradually replaced oxen and sleds as the common means of transportation.

A *buggy* was no more known or used than a balloon in those wagon days, and when the canal was first made navigable, there was probably not a one-horse buggy in Orleans County. Indeed, several years after boats began trips on the canal, merchants R. S. & L Burrows brought on six or eight one-horse wagons and put them on sale. They had been manufactured in Connecticut and had wooden springs under the seats. People were amazed and frequently commented on the luxury, comfort, and ease of riding in these small, rattling, jolting machines.

CHAPTER 10.

PUBLIC HIGHWAYS

Although Ridge Road had been used by the Indians from time immemorial, after the land was newly purchased from Morris, Judge Porter and others became interested in surveying and locating the large tract of land west of the Genesee River, known as The Triangle. The Indians informed them about a gravelly ridge extending from the Genesee River to the Niagara River. Consequently, in 1798, Porter and his associates hired a surveyor named Eli Granger. Granger, along with a few men, traced a road along this ridge from river to river, which became known as the Ridge Road, aligning closely with its current location.

Improvements were made by cutting out trees and making the crossings at the streams of water more passable. Yet many large trees still obstructed the carriageway, and bridges were wanted in many places. In April 1814, the Legislature of the State appropriated $5,000 and appointed commissioners to apply the sum on improvements to the road between Rochester and Lewiston, as the commissioners should think proper for the public benefit.

This appropriation, together with the labor of the few inhabitants then living on this route, made the Ridge Road a tolerably fair wagon road. The following year, the road was formally planned, surveyed, and established by Philetus Swift and Caleb Hopkins under an Act of the Legislature passed Feb. 10, 1815.

Thirty-seven years later, in 1852 a subsequent act provided for a re-survey of the Ridge Road from Rochester to Lewiston. John LeValley, Grosvenor Daniels, and William J. Babbitt were appointed commisioners to superintend the work through Orleans County. Darius W. Cole of Medina was the Surveyor, and the road was re-surveyed and established six rods wide. (approximately 100 feet)

The Oak Orchard Road was the first highway crossing Orleans County north and south that was opened and worked. Supposing, as everybody then did, that the trade from this part of the county must go by the lake and that Oak Orchard Harbor would be its place of *embarkation*, the Holland Company and the settlers, at an early day, opened this road for teams by making log *causeway*s through wet places and bridging the streams.

It was a rough road, but teams could get through with light loads as early as before the war. Andrew A. Ellicott built a mill on the Oak Orchard Creek at Shelby Center about the year 1813. To accommodate travel to this mill and promote the sale of the land, the Holland Company cut out a highway leading from the Oak Orchard Road, near the County Poor House, to Shelby Center. This highway followed the highest ridge of land, crooking about on places where it could be easiest constructed.

It is still used as a public highway and is traveled on or near the line originally followed. This was the first road cut out for teams, east and west, south of the ridge.

As the timber that grew in this County was generally hardwood and decayed soon, few fallen trees or logs lay in the woods to obstruct teams passing anywhere in the forest, where standing timber or swamps did not prevent. The course of travel was directed by marked trees, until enough inhabitants had come in to lay out and work roads.

Before the forest was cleared from this county, much of the land was wet, and in fitting a highway for travel, a large amount of log causeway had to be laid in places now dry hard land. Where the Oak Orchard Road crosses the canal in Albion and for many rods north and south of the canal, such a causeway was laid. Indeed, many farms in a wild state were not taken by settlers at first because they were so low and wet; now, by draining the water off and cutting away the trees, they are the best farming land in the neighborhood.

The Ridge Road was six rods wide, and the Oak Orchard Road was four rods wide. When selling lands bordering the Ridge Road or the Oak Orchard Road, the Holland Company bounded the tract they sold by the outer lines of the road. Which made the land, covered by the roads, public property.

In selling lands on all other roads, they deeded to the center of the highway. When no natural obstruction prevented it, highways were laid out on the lot lines according to the Company's survey. The owners of the lots on each side then gave up their half of the road.

Works were put up by the Holland Company for the manufacture of salt at the salt springs north of Medina as early as 1805 and opened for use by the settlers. To facilitate access to these works, the company cut out two roads at about the same time, one leading south from the works to the Old Buffalo Road and the other south-easterly to the Oak Orchard Road. These highways were known as the Salt Works Road. When the manufacture of salt there was discontinued, the Salt Works Road was abandoned.

Frequently, when a new road became a necessity, all the settlers would turn out with their teams, cut out the trees and clear them from the roadway, and build such sluiceways as were necessary. A highway could then be worked up when the roots had rotted out, and the people of the district were able to do so. And so, about the year 1824, the people along the Ridge Road turned out on the 4th day of July and celebrated the day by cutting out a highway from the Ridge north to Waterport, which is now the road leading from Eagle Harbor to Waterport.

On April 2, 1827, the Legislature passed an Act appointing John P. Patterson, Almon H. Millerd, and Otis Turner as commissioners to locate and lay out a public highway, four rods wide, from Rochester to Lockport, on or near the banks of the Erie Canal. These commissioners, with Jesse P. Haines of Lockport as the surveyor, established the highway. For most of its length, the road was laid out on the south side of the Canal. The records of the survey and highway were filed in the County Clerk's offices and in the towns it passed through on October 1, 1827.

The law required town commissioners of highways to open the road for travel where it served public convenience, which they did in most areas. However, many sections of the road were never opened, resulting in the public losing the right to use it due to non-use. This road was known as the State Road and is referred to as State Street in the village of Albion.

CHAPTER 11.
RAILROADS IN ORLEANS COUNTY

On May 5, 1834, an *Act of Legislature* was passed incorporating the *Medina and Darien Railroad Company* to construct a railroad. The road was built from Medina to Akron in Erie County, a distance of twelve or fourteen miles, and was fitted for cars to be drawn by horses. It went into operation in about 1836. However, after a short trial, it was found to be an unprofitable investment. The track was taken up, and the road was discontinued. This failed railroad had been the only one officially incorporated to be made in this county.

In 1836, the Legislature incorporated the *Medina and Ontario Railroad Company* to construct a railroad between Medina and Lake Ontario at the mouth of Oak Orchard Creek, though nothing further was done to open the road.

Finally, the *Rochester, Lockport, and Niagara Falls Railroad Company* was organized on December 10, 1850. The railroad passes through the county near the Erie Canal on the south side. This road has since been consolidated in the *New York Central Railroad*, by which name it is now known, its original corporate name being dropped. The construction of this railroad has proved to be of immense benefit to Orleans County.

CHAPTER 12.
STATE OF EDUCATION

Settlers on the Holland Purchase reverenced the institutions existing in New England, from which the majority of them came. And so endeavored to *engraft* them upon their social organization in their new homes in the woods. They believed the safety and performance of the free government of their country was found in the intelligence of the people. So among their first labors, after providing shelter and food for their children, was the building of schoolhouses and furnishing instruction there.

Before enough families had located in a neighborhood to erect even a log schoolhouse and supply it with scholars, it was not uncommon for a school to be opened in some log cabin where a family resided. All the children in the neighborhood came in through the pathless forest or were brought upon the backs of their fathers when the weather was bad to attend these schools. Schoolhouses were built and well patronized before school districts were organized, and parents did the best they could to give their children the elements of a common education, at least.

Orleans County was not behind any part of the country in its zeal for schools. The earlier schoolhouses were made of logs, much after the same pattern as the dwelling places of the people; such structures would now be considered extremely uncomfortable, inconvenient, and ill-adapted to the purpose for which they were made. They were badly lighted, badly ventilated, small, cold, cheerless, and dismal places. Every internal arrangement was uncomfortable compared with school houses now. But nobody complained. After a few years, this state of things improved. As the population increased and wealth began to accumulate, better accommodations were procured.

ALBION ACADEMY

The people of Gaines, living along their beautiful natural Ridge Road, believed that trade and business for the county should be centered there. Before the county buildings were located in Albion, the residents of Gaines began planning projects to develop a village that would maximize the benefits of their location. They established several stores and mechanic shops, set up a printing press, published the first newspaper in the county, and proposed founding an *Academy*.

The location of the Court House in Albion was a sad disappointment to them. However, they did not despair and went on to establish their Academy, which was incorporated in 1827 as the first incorporated literary institution in Orleans County. Through the joint efforts of the school district and the Academy's supporters, a three-story brick building was erected, which housed both schools for several years.

The Academy was well patronized while it was without a rival, but when Academies were erected in other towns in the neighborhood, Gaines Academy began to languish and finally ceased to exist as a school. The building was fitted up as a dwelling house and, as such, still remains.

Academies were established at Albion in 1837, at Millville in 1840, at Yates in 1842, at Medina in 1849, and at Holley in 1850. The Phipps Union Seminary was established at Albion in about 1833 and incorporated by the Regents of the University in 1840. This seminary is a boarding and day school for girls only. Its course of study includes all the solid and ornamental branches of education usually taught in the best schools for females in this country. It is one of the oldest institutions of its kind in this part of the state and has sustained a high reputation.

CHAPTER 13.

STATE OF RELIGION

The first settlers of Orleans County did not forget religion, and amid all their hardships and difficulties, they never omitted attending to the public worship of God. For some years, they had no church organizations, settled ministers of the gospel, or houses built expressly for places of public worship. They had religious meetings, however, in their log cabins, sometimes conducted by a preacher, sometimes with none. As soon as schoolhouses were built, they held their meetings in them.

Though many of the settlers were members of Baptist, Methodist, Presbyterian, or other *denomination*s in the old States from which they came, they maintained no denominational distinction here. If a religious meeting was to be held, everybody for miles around attended it, never stopping to inquire to what denomination the preacher belonged to. Many old people remember with deep emotion some of those solemn seasons of prayer and praise, enjoyed by them in company with all those who loved God and his worship, in their neighborhood, in some little log shanty in the woods.

As the first settlement of the county began on the lakeshore in Carlton and gradually extended along

Ridge Road, religious meetings were initially held in Carlton. Around 1809, Rev. Mr. Steele, a Methodist preacher from Canada, visited Carlton as a missionary, preaching to the settlers whenever he could gather a congregation. He is said to have been the first preacher of any denomination in the area. He was soon followed by Baptist *elder*s Irons, Dutcher, and Carpenter, as well as Puffer, Hall, Gregory, and others.

Before 1820, a Baptist church was established in Gaines, a Congregational church in Barre, and another in Ridgeway. From that time forward, people began forming church organizations that aligned with their individual views of religious truth and duty, moving away from the common meetings that had prevailed earlier.

In the year 1824, a company of citizens of Gaines united together and built the meeting house now standing in the west part of the village, "for the benefit of the Congregational and Baptist Societies in the town of Gaines, each society to use the same for one half of the time alternately. When not occupied by said societies, to be free for public worship for any other religious society."

The proprietors sold the slips in the house and, after paying for building the house, gave the purchase money to aid in building Gaines Academy. This was the first church edifice erected in Orleans County, and for several years, it was occupied according to the founders' intent. It has now been transferred to the Methodists.

CHAPTER 14.

BURYING GROUNDS

D uring the early settlement of Orleans County, burial places were established in convenient locations. One of the oldest cemeteries is in the village of Gaines, on Ridge Road. Mr. Oliver Booth, who owned the land, donated half an acre on the condition that the local residents would clear the trees from it, which they did.

According to the statute, many of these old rural burial places have been placed under the care of *Cemetery Association*s, which are duly incorporated under the general law. Others have been vested in the towns where they are located, according to an old law that stipulates burial grounds used by the public for a certain length of time should be vested in the town.

In the vicinity of the large villages, however, more extensive grounds have been devoted as burial places. The most considerable of these is MOUNT ALBION CEMETERY, situated two miles southeast of the village of Albion. This burying place, including about twenty-five acres, was purchased by the village of Albion in May 1843 for $1,000.

The land was then an unbroken forest. The natural advantages of this Cemetery, for the purpose designed, can scarcely be equaled by any similar grounds in the country. It was dedicated on Sept. 7, 1843.

Before Mount Albion was purchased, a *burying ground* was used on the south side of the canal, east of the creek, in Albion. The bodies have all been removed from that ground and burial there has been discontinued.

From its inception until 1862, Mount Albion Cemetery was managed by the Trustees of the village. An Act passed on March 26, 1862, transferred control of the cemetery to three commissioners appointed by the village Trustees. Dr. Lemuel C. Paine, Lorenzo Burrows, and Henry J. Sickels were appointed as commissioners and have continued to serve in that capacity since then.

Lots in this cemetery are available for purchase by anyone, not just residents of the village of Albion. As a result, lot owners come from every town in the county. The first person to die in Medina was buried wherever their friends could find a place. However, in the fall of 1830, Mr. David E. Evans, through his agent Mr. Gwynn, donated an acre of land for a burial ground on the east side of Gwynn Street, south of the railroad depot. The first person buried there was the wife of Edmund Fuller in 1830. These grounds have been used for burials ever since.

In 1860, Mr. John Parsons interested himself in getting the fences around these grounds repaired, with contributions furnished to him for the purpose. He wanted to suitably mark the spot with some fitting memorial, which at small expense would be likely to stand many years.

He procured and planted a fir tree as near as possible to the center of the grounds. Under the center of the tree, in a glass jar enclosed in lead, he deposited various articles as mementos of the times and people of Medina at present. This tree is now growing vigorously.

BOXWOOD CEMETERY lies a little north of Medina, on the east side of the gravel road leading to the Ridge, and contains about six acres. It is owned by the village of Medina. Messrs. S. M. Burroughs, Geo Northrop, Caleb Hill, and others bought this ground for a Cemetery in 1848 from Mr. Gwynn while it was still a forest.

They sold it to the village for $600. It was laid out in lots and formally opened for burial purposes in 1850. David Card was the first person buried here in 1849. Many bodies of the dead buried in the old ground in Medina have been removed to Boxwood Cemetery, and this is now the principal burying place for the village and vicinity.

HILLSIDE CEMETERY is the name of a burial place belonging to The Holley Cemtery Association, which was organized on Dec. 11, 1866. A month later, the association purchased about seven and three-fourths acres of land, lying about half a mile south of the business part of Holley Village and south of the corporation limits, at a cost of $1,100.

A large sum has since then been expended by the Association in improving these grounds, grading the street, and ornamenting and fitting up the premises. A large part of this burying place has been laid out in lots, carefully numbered, mapped, and the map filed in the County Clerk's office. These lots are sold by the Trustees and deeded to purchasers.

On August 17, 1867, this cemetery was formally dedicated with appropriate religious ceremonies. The affairs of the Cemetery Association are managed by nine Trustees, who serve staggered three-year terms. As of 1871, the current Trustees are John Berry, Sargent Ensign, Nelson Hatch, James Gibson, Samuel Spear, Humphrey Ruggles, Simon Harwood, Ely H. Cook, and Orange A. Eddy. John Berry serves as President, and Orange A. Eddy serves as Secretary.

Shade trees have been set around the grounds, and many trees and ornamental shrubs have been planted. The soil is well adapted to the purpose designed. The location is pleasant and commodious to the village of Holley and the surrounding country. The good taste and liberality displayed by the people of Holley and the vicinity in founding and fostering this Cemetery are creditable to their public spirit, refined feelings, and proper regard for their best interests.

CHAPTER 15.

THE TOWN OF BARRE

This town, named after Barre, MA by Judge John Lee, was separated from Gaines by an Act of the Legislature on March 6, 1818. When the town was first settled, the main road for travel to and from the old states was the Ridge Road. The Ridge was always dry and comfortable for travel when the streams that crossed it could be forded before the bridges were made. However, roads leaving the Ridge, especially when the ground was not frozen, were extremely muddy. Long stretches of low land had to be covered with logs laid transversely side by side to create a carriage track called *corduroy*. Since this was a labor-intensive task, the settlers had to wallow through the mud as best they could until they were able to build proper highways.

There were no sawmills. Even if there had been mills, lumber could not be moved to market upon such roads, and there was no market for lumber south of the Ridge before the canal was dug.

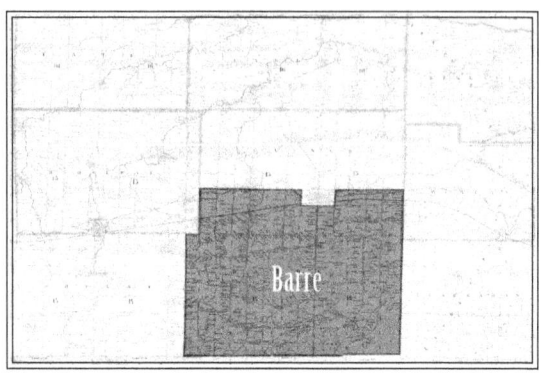

TOWN OF BARRE

The Indians had a trail, or Indians' road, from their settlements in Livingston County on the Genesee River to an Indian village in Niagara County. Another trail ran from the mouth of Oak Orchard Creek and intersected the Indians' road. This trail was used by white men and is known as the Oak Orchard Road. It passed through Barre from north to south. On this trail or road, the travel to Batavia was conducted. It was not passable for carriages, as the Indians had none, and so the settlers had to clear the brush and remove the fallen trees, which obstructed them before they could get their teams through. This was done by the Holland Company in an early day.

Several families came into Barre before the War of 1812, but the war nearly suspended *emigration* while it lasted.

Salt was made on the Oak Orchard Creek north of Medina before the canal was made. To accommodate the people and benefit themselves, the Holland Company opened a road from the Salt Works in a south-easterly direction to intersect Oak Orchard Road, about two miles south of Albion. This road was known as *Salt Works Road* and was discontinued many years ago.

The Holland Company offered a tract of land to the first religious society formed in each town. In line with this offer, the company deeded 100 acres of land to the Trustees of *The First Congregational Society* in the town of Barre on March 8, 1822. The land is located on the north part of lot nineteen, town fifteen, range two, which is part of the farm owned by Azariah Loveland.

The deed conveys this land to said "Trustees and their successors in office, for the benefit of the said Congregational order, and those who preach the doctrines contained in the *Assembly's Catechism*, and no other." So careful were our fathers in Barre to provide for keeping their religious faith pure and free from heresy, as they regarded it.

That religious society was the first organized in Barre. It still exists, now located at Barre Center. Its first board of Trustees was Orange Starr, Cyril Wilson, Ithamar Hibbard, John Bradner, Caleb C. Thurston, and Oliver Benton.

The church connected with this society was organized December 5, 1817.

The First Presbyterian Society of Albion was incorporated on March 20, 1826, and was the second religious society incorporated in the town of Barre and the first in the village of Albion. Its first Trustees were Harvey Goodrich, Joseph Hart, Ebenezer Rogers, William White, Hiram Sickels, and Milton W. Hopkins. Their first house of worship, the same now occupied by the Episcopalians, was erected in 1830. The number of communicants in this church at its organization was sixteen. Rev. William Johnson, their first pastor, commenced his labors here in 1824.

The first tavern in Barre was kept by Abram Mattison in 1815 on the west side of the Oak Orchard Road, about two miles south of Albion. The first tavern in Albion was kept by Mr. Churchill on the south corner of Main and Canal Streets. Mrs. Silas Benton taught the first school in the southern part of what is now the village of Albion.

The first store, for the sale of *dry goods* and groceries, is believed to have been kept by E. & A. Mix at Porter's Corners. In 1817, Mr. Abiathar Mix moved to that place and took an Article for a tract of land. Being a mason by trade and having no mason work to do, he went into the business of making potash and selling goods, his brother, Ebenezer Mix, of Batavia, furnishing a part of the capital.

In about 1819, Orris H. Gardner opened a store near Benton's Corners on Oak Orchard Road.

The Oak Orchard Road was the first public highway established in this town. In around 1803, the Holland Company commissioned a survey for this road from *The Five Corners* in Gaines, which is about a mile north of Albion, to the fork of the road south of Barre Center. The survey was meant to straighten the old trail, running due north and south. However, the highway was not opened and worked exactly as surveyed.

Many of the earliest land locations were made by settlers along this road. These locations, along with the Erie Canal, established the village of Albion.

Theophilus Capen was the first regular lawyer in this town. He came about the time work on the Canal was begun and kept an office for a while in Albion. William J. Moody came to Albion to practice law a short time before the county of Orleans was organized. He was followed by Alexis Ward, Henry R. Curtis, A. Hyde Cole, Geo W. Fleming, and several others.

Dr. Orson Nichoson was the first physician. He settled in Barre in 1819.

The first deed of land from the Holland Land Company in the town of Barre was given to Jacob Young on June 7, 1813. It conveyed one hundred acres of lot thirty-three, town fifteen, range one. This land is now owned by Stephen N. Whitney and lies about a mile and a half south of Albion on the east side of Oak Orchard Road.

On December 3, 1819, William Bradner took a deed from the Company for two hundred sixty-six acres in Albion, from the east side of Main Street to Bailey Street to the north bounds of Barre.

On October 11, 1825, Roswell Burrows acquired a deed for 161 acres on the west side of Main Street, bounded to the north by the town line of Gaines. This tract had originally been taken up by Jesse Bumpus in 1815.

The land so deeded to William Bradner was taken by Article from the Land Company, by William McCollister, about the year 1811. Mr. McCollister made the first clearing in the village of Albion, where the courthouse now stands.

The first dwelling house erected in Albion was a log cabin built by McCollister near where Phipps Union Seminary now stands. In that, he lived, and there his wife died, about the year 1812, being the first white woman who died in the town of Barre. No clergyman was then in town to conduct religious services on the occasion, and no boards could be obtained to make her coffin. Her sorrowing husband, assisted by two or three men, split and hewed some rough planks from trees and pinned them together with wooden pins to make a box in which the corpse was placed and buried. This little company, present at this first funeral, comprised almost the entire population of the town.

Nehemiah Ingersoll built the first warehouse in town on the canal, about fifteen rods east of Main Street, in Albion.

The first sawmill in town was built by Dr. William White on the creek southeast of Albion, about eighty rods south of the railroad, in 1816. William Bradner built a small *grist mill* on this creek farther down in 1819.

For several years after the Erie Canal was first opened, there was a brisk trade in white wood lumber, which was cut near the canal for easy transport. Good whitewood boards were sold on the canal bank for $5 per thousand feet, and other types of lumber were sold at similar prices. Whitewood was a common tree in this area, and the lumber was transported to Albany. As buildings began to be constructed, carpenters and joiners mainly used whitewood for floors and finishing.

The first regular "ball" in Barre took place at Mattison's tavern on July 4, 1819. To prepare for the party, they removed the split basswood floor and installed dance boards in the barroom to dance on.

After the town was organized, the initial town meetings were held at Mattison's tavern, and later at Benton's tavern.

On July 4th, 1821, the people of Barre celebrated Independence Day in a grove near where the round schoolhouse was later built on Lee Street. A committee was appointed to procure gunpowder, liquor, and sugar from Batavia. The tables were provisioned through voluntary contributions, and a picnic-style dinner was enjoyed by everyone. Dr. Orson Nichoson delivered an oration, and patriotic toasts were made with the sound of musketry as they did not have a cannon. In the evening, the leftover food and bottles were taken to a nearby log cabin and enjoyed by those who participated. The music, dancing, and festivities continued until the next morning by a group of both old and young. This was the first public celebration of National Independence in Barre.

Among the first settlers in Barre were William McCollister, Lansing Bailey, Joseph Hart, Joseph Stoddard, Elijah Darrow, Reuben Clark, and Silas Benton.

The first marriage in what is now the village of Albion took place under the following circumstances: Robert Anderson, a Justice of the Peace, presided over a trial in the village of Gaines to recover damages for a hog that the defendant had wrongfully killed. The plaintiff successfully recovered a judgment.

After the result was announced, the defendant took the judge aside and asked him to go immediately to a specific house and marry him. The defendant's reason for urgency was that a fine would soon be imposed on him as part of the verdict, which he was unable to pay, and he would be taken to jail in Batavia. If he remained unmarried, he was unsure when he would be released. However, if he were married, he could be released in thirty days.

The judge objected that it was already midnight, the house in question was three miles away, the night was dark, and most of the road passed through the woods. However, he eventually agreed to go after having supper. In the meantime, the prospective groom hurried to the house to wake up the family and the bride, and put a light in the window to guide the judge. The wedding proceeded as planned. The house was located on the west side of Main Street, about a quarter of a mile north of the canal.

BIOGRAPHIES OF EARLY SETTLERS

LANSING BAILEY

The following is Lansing Bailey's history, written by himself, for the Pioneer Association:

"I was born in the town of Stephentown, Rensselaer County, New York, Nov. 11, 1787. When I was seven years old, my father moved to Whitestown, Oneida County, New York.

In 1809, being then in my twenty-second year, I was married to Miss Loda Parmelee, and in Nov. 1811, I started, in company with two others, for the Genesee Country, on foot, with knapsacks and provisions on our backs.

On the evening of the fifth day, we arrived at Daniel Pratt's, an old acquaintance and relative, then residing on Ridge Road in the town of Gaines, a little west of Gaines Corners.

The best locations on the Ridge Road had been taken, and also the best lots on the Oak Orchard Road, for several miles south of the Ridge Road, but they were not settled south of '*Five Corners*,' in what is now Gaines.

Myself and brother took an Article from the Holland Land Company of two hundred and sixty acres, lying one mile west of where Albion now stands. Five days after making our location, we started for home by way of Batavia. We had but little money, consequently we bought but one meal on our outward and homeward trip, $3.50 being the entire amount of our expenses, which consisted in lodging and a little of **the creature** to wash down our dry meals.

In February 1812, putting all on board an ox sled covered with cloth, with two yoke of oxen attached, after bidding farewell to friends, with wife and child aboard, whip in hand, we set out for our wilderness home, my brother driving two cows, and three young cattle.

After a journey of nine days, we arrived at Daniel Pratt's, where we unloaded our goods. I soon started out to find some wheat, which I found in Riga, and got it ground in Churchville. Soon after my return, myself and my brother set out for our future home.

There was a track as far as the Five Corners. Thus far, we took a *grindstone* and six pail kettles, with some other articles, and were then about a mile and a half from our place, and no tract. The snow was about three feet deep, with a hard crust about two feet from the ground, sufficient to bear a man but not a beast.

We commenced breaking the crust in the direction of our place, and drove the cattle as far as we could break that day. We fell some trees for them to browse, and one across the path to keep them from returning, and we went back to the Five Corners for lodging.

In the morning, we took a straw bed and some other articles on our backs, and went and found the cattle all safe. That day we got through just before night, foddered our cattle on browse; fell a dry stub and made a good fire from it; shoveled away the snow, made us a *bush shanty* with some boughs to lay our bed on, took supper and went to bed.

Next morning the snow on our feet and limbs, which were a little too long for our shanty, was two or three inches deep. However, we had a good night's rest. We stayed there until some time in April, going to the Ridge every Saturday night and returning every Monday morning with a week's provisions.

On one occasion we found one of our cows cast. We divided the loaf with her, put a bell on her, and if we could not hear the tinkle of the bell in the night we got up and looked after her. Thus we carried our cattle all safe through the winter.

We went to the Five Corners to fetch our kettle while the snow crust was hard. On our return, our dog barked earnestly at a large hollow tree. On looking into the hollow, we saw two eyes, but could not tell what animal it was within. My brother went after an ax and gun, while I watched the hole. After filling the hollow with sticks, we cut several holes in the log, to ascertain the character of the animal. Soon however she passed one of the holes, and we knew it was a bear. We then moved the sticks, and put in the dog. The bear seized the dog, and my brother reached in his hand and pulled the dog out badly hurt. The bear presented her head at the hole, and I killed her with the ax.

On searching the log, we found a cub, which we took home with us. It could not bite, but would try.

A Mrs. Adams, who had recently lost a babe, took it and nursed it, until it got to be quite a bear, and rather harsh in its manners.

As soon as the snow settled, we made us a *hovel house*, such as we could lay up ourselves of logs, twelve by fourteen feet square, with split logs for floor and roof, the roof projecting over, to afford a shelter to put things under outside the house.

When the snow was mostly gone, three of us with axe in hand went through on a line as near as we could, cutting out the underbrush for a road, coming out a little west of where Gaines village now is, on the Ridge

Road, which is now called the *Gaines Basin road*. This we accomplished in less than a half a day.

In a few days we had the satisfaction of introducing Mrs. Bailey, my wife, into our new house and we were happy to get home.

Our next work was to clear a small patch and sow some apple seeds, carrying dirt in a tray to cover them; from those seeds originated many of the orchards in Orleans County.

In June following, we peeled basswood bark for our chamber floor and elm bark for a roof to our house.

Harvesting came, and we went to Mr. James Mather's in Gaines to reap wheat. He would not give us one bushel of wheat per day for our work, as he gave his other hands. But would give us seven bushels for cutting a certain piece, which we did in two days. On my return home at night I found Mrs. Bailey had left home. Where she had gone, I knew not till next morning. I learned she had been sent for to attend Mrs. Daniel Pratt, who was sick and died soon after.

We cleared fifteen acres the first season. It was a task, in time of logging, to get up our oxen in the morning. Especially on Mondays, as they would have Sundays to stray away into the woods.

On one occasion, I started after them and found their tracks near where Jonathan Whitney now lives, on the Oak Orchard road, a mile and a half south of Albion. I followed the tracks eastward all day, crossing the Transit Line several times. I could tell that line by the timber having been cut on it by the Holland Company.

After a hard day's toil and travel, making a good fire I camped by it for the night and had a good night's rest. In the morning I heard a dog bark and a bell tinkle. I followed in the direction of these sounds, carefully noting where I left the cattle tracks and came out on the Ridge Road, at Huff's tavern, in East Gaines and was right glad to get something to eat.

Mr. Rosier was there returning from the dangers of the war, driving some cattle and mine had got in with them.

I renewed my pursuit and found my oxen two miles south of the marsh, which lies south of the Ridge in East Gaines. I was glad to get them home again.

When it was time to sow our wheat, we went without bread for three days rather than leave our work to go to mill. I have been to Churchville, Johnson's Creek, Rochester and Salmon Creek, for milling, before there were mills built nearer.

In the fall, I built me a good, comfortable log house, without a board, nail, or pane of glass in it, using bark for roof and chamber floor, split stuff for gable ends, lower floor and doors and oiled paper for windows, being compelled to exercise strict economy and also to be quite independent in building my house. I found it, however, a good shelter and a comfortable home for several years.

Soon after I moved into my house, my brother left for the east, leaving me in the care of seven head of cattle through the winter, with no fodder except a few cornstalks. Winter set in early and by the time I had killed my winter's supply of venison, the corn stalks were all gone and I found all I could do to keep fires and fodder my cattle, Sundays not excepted.

Thus I labored, cutting trees for the cattle as best I could, until my brother's return, the latter part of winter. We should not have attempted to winter our cattle, had not persons here assured us our cattle would winter with little or no care.

In June, 1812, the town of Ridgeway was set off from Batavia, which before then comprised the whole present county of Orleans. In April, 1813, the first town meeting was held on the Ridge Road, west of Oak Orchard Creek. At that time, the flats along the creek were covered with water from bank to bank. In going to the town meeting, we, who lived east, crossed the creek as best we could, on rafts of *felled trees*.

At that election I was chosen one of the assessors for the east part of town. On the day appointed for holding the general election, I started for Mr. Brown's, on Johnson's Creek, where we were to open the polls. When I came to the Oak Orchard Creek, I took off my clothes and went through.

On opening the polls, the Board was challenged by Paul Brown as not being free-holders; true, we were not, but we did not regard it. We adjourned at noon to Mr. Elicott's, at Barnegat, in what is now the town of Shelby and next day to Ridgway Corners and from thence to Gaines Corners, where we closed.

The above journey was performed by the Board of Inspectors of the Election on foot. I do not think there was a horse in town at that time.

Thus far all had passed off pleasantly, soon after, however, I was taken sick with the fever and ague, which was so severe as to confine me to the house. Dr. Wm. White was called to attend me. He came, said he could give me something that would stop it, but would not advise me to take it. I replied I would take it on my own responsibility. He gave me *arsenic*. I took it. It stopped the ague, but I did not get well for a long time.

On the 3rd of May, 1813, my wife was confined. My brother went to Five Corners for assistance, and when he returned with one of the neighboring women, they found me on one bed, my wife and one babe on another bed, and another babe on a pillow, on a chair, all right and doing well.

I thought the woods was a fruitful place. I made a cradle from a hollow log, long enough to hold one baby in each end, and being round, it needed no rockers, and served our purpose nicely.

In July after, I called upon my neighbors, some of whom lived several miles from me, to help me put up a log barn. Some fifteen came. We found we could not get through in time for them to get home that day. Rather than come again, they finished it, though it got to be late before it was done. They all stayed overnight, on beds spread on the floor, pioneer fashion.

About this time, in 1813, one morning while we were at breakfast, a man came in from the Ridge and said the British had landed from the lake at the mouth of Oak Orchard Creek and would probably come up to the Ridge, if not repulsed. We were well armed. My brother took the rifle and started on quick time. I could not go as fast as they, but followed on as fast as my strength would admit. I soon reached the Ridge Road and was glad to learn there was no danger. The enemy only wanted to steal some of Mr. Brown's cattle, from near the Two Bridges, in Carlton.

After I left home on this military expedition, Mr. Farr and Mr. Holsenburgh came to chop for me. They had left their homes before the news of the British landing came.

We returned home from the Ridge about 4 o'clock in the afternoon the same day. Mr. Darrow had come with us to get a pig.

With some difficulty, the men chopping could see my cabin from where they were at work. My brother, as we came near, gave a loud whoop, like an Indian. I stopped him. He then blew a blast on a tin horn he had. I stopped him again, saying supper was not ready. I then threw my frock over my shoulders and went to the pen to catch the pig. Farr and Holsenburgh heard the whoop and the horn and saw me going to the pen and mistook my frock for the blanket of an Indian; and hearing the pig squeal soon after, they concluded the Indians had come and killed my family and were going to finish with a feast from the pigs; and they started for their homes to get their guns to fight the Indians.

Mr. Farr then lived at the Five Corners in Gaines and Mr. Holsenburgh lived on the place later owned by Ebenezer Rogers, a mile south of Albion. Mr. Farr hurried home, got his gun and was ready for a fight. Mr. Chaffee, on hearing the story, told Mr. Farr it could not be true, as there were no Indians landed and he had seen us when we started for home from the Ridge.

Holsenburgh went directly to Mr. Darrow's and before any of the party had got back, told what had happened at my house. He said Mrs. Darrow and Mrs. Hart and their families must hide in the woods, as the Indians would soon be there and he actually got them started. The men soon returned, however, in time to stop them.

While the above was being performed, we could hear no sound from the axes, and knew not the reason until near sunset, when Mr. Farr came and explained the whole transaction.

About the first of August, my brother had a fever and ague. Someone told him of a remedy. He tried it, and a violent fever ensued, which lasted but a few days, and he died August 8th. Before my brother was buried, my wife was taken sick with the same fever and died on the 13th of the same month. They were both in succession carried by friends to the burying grounds in Gaines and interred there. Some friends living on the Ridge took my children home with them while I returned to my desolate house to spend one of the loneliest nights I ever knew, as there was no one to accompany me home.

I informed my father of what had transpired. He soon came and took two of my children home with him. I hired a Mrs. Adams, a cousin of mine, to take care of the other.

I was now so lonely that as soon as I could secure my crops, I left home and went to my father's.

In the fall before leaving, Mr. Parmelee, a brother-in-law, came with a wagon to help secure my corn, which we had planted among the logs. I had done but little work that season, not logging one acre.

On going into my cornfield we found it badly torn down. We got a dog and, with a lantern in hand, went at night to the field. The dog started off furiously and soon treed some animal up a large hemlock. On looking up I could at times see eyes shine. We concluded it was a bear, and each one selected a small tree to climb. In case the bear should come down and attack us, I went to try my skill in shooting in the darkness. Soon as I fired there was a screeching up the tree, and the creature must have gone nearly to the top. Directly there was a cracking heard among the limbs, I scrambled up my tree, and the bear came down from hers.

No sooner had she struck the ground than the dog grappled in with her but soon cried out piteously. We thought the dog was being killed. I hastened down from my tree and called for the light to see to load my gun. We walked up to the combatants and found the dog biting instead of being bitten. Parmelee had some sport afterward, saying he had not climbed his tree and how he had saved my life by holding the lantern so that I could see and not climb off the top of mine.

Before my return to the east, Mr. Caleb C. Thurston came to view the country, said he would move into my house if I would drive my oxen down and help him up, as he did not wish to buy another yoke, and would hire me to clear five acres when he bought a Lot. To this, I consented.

In the winter of 1814, Mr. Thurston had moved on with oxen and wagon. While I was gone to my father's, Lewiston and Buffalo were burned, and Capt. McCary, with a part of the Company to which I belonged, went as far as Molyneaux tavern. There they surrounded the house, shooting one Indian through the window. Finding another helpless on the floor drunk, a Mr. Cass pinned him to the floor with his bayonet. The British soldiers ran up stairs and were taken prisoners. Mr. Molyneaux said he would find rails for as long as they would find Indians, and so they burned the bodies of the killed.

In the summer following, I took my oxen and wagon and seventeen bushels of wheat, along with Mrs. Thurston, on the road for a visit to Mr. Pratt's, and then to mill beyond Clarkson. I returned as far as Mr. Pratt's the next night about dark. I asked Mrs. Thurston if she would venture through the woods with me. She said she would and if we had to lay out, we would do the best we could. When we left the Ridge and turned into the woods, it was so dark I could not see my oxen, although I was sitting on the foreboard. We arrived safe at home, without accident.

I think it would be difficult in these days to find women of sufficient fortitude to endure such hardships and privations, as did these early pioneer women. At this time there was no clearing between my place and the Ridge Road. The war with Great Britain was now raging along our frontiers, in all its horrors. More settlers were then leaving the county than were coming in. There were then but five families in what was then called Freeman's settlement, west of Eagle Harbor. No road had been opened. We had to follow marked trees as our guide.

Mr. Thurston's eldest daughter, then about ten years old, went to stay with our friends there a few days. She was taken sick and not able to walk home. Her father and myself went after her and carried her back to her father's house, the most of the distance on our backs. It was a hard lift for us to get her up the bank of Otter Creek.

The first of September, our militia company was ordered to Buffalo. On the fifth we reached Batavia. Mr. Thurston, being infirm, was allowed to return to his family in their solitude. I was kept with the Company until the first of October, when I was discharged and returned home, having received seven dollars and fifty cents pay for services and two dollars for extra labor.

I lodged the first night on my return with the Tonawanda Indians. I have never since turned an Indian away, who desired to stay with me overnight.

Before I left home to go to Buffalo, as a soldier, I had baited some pigeons. After we were gone, Mrs. Thurston took the net and caught them and in this way herself and children were provided with a rich repast, even though so far off in the wilderness alone.

In the winter of 1815, with my pack on my back, I returned to Whitestown, and on the 8th day of February, was married to Miss Sylvia Pratt, who returned with me to share alike the toils and blessings of life, where, by the blessing of God, we still remain.

I have had twelve children; three died young, I had the pleasure of sitting down with all the others at my own table the present summer (1861) although some of them reside eight hundred miles away from me.

At the close of the war, settlers came in rapidly, and soon I was out of the woods, having it cleared and settled all around me.

In the early settlement of the county, it was difficult to raise pigs, as the bears would catch them in the summer. Consequently, pork was high priced, and scarce. With my rifle, I could take what venison I needed, and therefore fared well for meat. The oil of the raccoon was first rate for frying cakes. Thus we fared sumptuously.

At one time, I had a sow and pigs in the woods. One day I heard the sow squeal. Being nearer to them than to the house, I ran, supposing I could save her. As I came near and hallooed, the bruin dropped his prey and reared up on his hind legs. When he saw me he ran off, but he had killed the hog. I got my rifle and pursued, but saw no more of him.

In the summer of 1816, I heard a man's voice halooing in the woods south of my house. I went to see what was going on, saw several men there, and inquired what they were about. One of them said they were going to make us a canal. I laughed at them, and told them they would hardly make water run uphill between here and Albany. I added, it would be as long as I would ask to live, to be able to see such a canal as they talked of in operation. How little did I then know of what men could perform, aided by intellectual culture and public wealth, having up to that time spent most of my life in the woods. Before this we had to go to Batavia for our merchant's goods and to the Post Office.

The foregoing comprises what I think of now of my pioneer life.

I cannot look back upon the past of my life and contemplate what the good Lord has in his loving kindness done for me, without acknowledging his preserving care, and that too when the most of my days have been spent in rebellion against him, in not obeying his commands and in neglecting to acknowledge him under the sore affliction he has seen fit to bring upon me and to sustain me under them; and above all, that in after life, He by his good spirit should call after me, until I was brought to see and feel his goodness, in the forgiveness of my sins and to thank and praise him for all his mercies and to ask that I may be accepted by him through the merits of his Son, and have the pleasure of meeting in his kingdom above, with all the old pioneers, not of the woods only, but all those that are seeking a better and a heavenly country.

LANSING BAILEY."

Barre, August 1, 1861.

In December 1866, Mr. Lansing Bailey, the author of the preceding sketch, passed away at his residence in Barre at the age of 79. Prior to his passing, he had sold the land he had acquired from the Holland Company and purchased the northeastern part of lot 10, town 15, range 2, of the Holland Purchase. This land is now owned and inhabited by his son Timothy.

Lansing Bailey, known for his strong native good sense, was highly esteemed by all who knew him, particularly those who were closest to him. He often recounted that when he left his father's house, his father gave him a *hoe* and three sheep. He felt grateful for this gesture, as he not only received a hoe but also learned the skill of digging. Mr. Bailey was always diligent and frugal, which allowed him to amass a significant fortune through a life of thrift and prudence. He was known for his generosity and public-spirited nature, and typically held various public offices and trusts. For many years, he served as the Supervisor of the town of Barre, relinquishing the position only after he declined to stand for re-election, contrary to the wishes of a majority in his town.

GIDEON HARD

Hon. Gideon Hard was born in Arlington, Vermont, on April 29, 1797. His grandmother was the sister of Col. Seth Warner, who was known for his role in the Revolutionary War. In his youth, Gideon worked on a farm and later as a house joiner. Despite being poor and dependent on his own exertions, he managed to get a college education. He taught school during the winters and studied for the rest of the time until he graduated from Union College at Schenectady in July 1822. He then began studying law and was admitted to the Supreme Court in 1825.

In 1826, he started practicing law in Newport, now known as Albion. He also took on roles such as Commissioner of Schools for Barre and County Treasurer. Gideon was elected as a Representative in Congress in 1832 and was re-elected in 1834. During his time in Congress, he served on the committee on elections and had a notable achievement in the case of James Graham from North Carolina. In 1837, he left Congress and returned to Albion to continue his law practice.

In 1841, Gideon was elected as a Senator in the State Senate to represent the eighth district of New York. He became a member of the Court for the Correction of Errors and was known for his thorough examination of cases and his well-researched opinions. He was re-elected to the State Senate in 1845 and appointed as the Chairman of the Committee on Railroads.

In 1848, the new constitution of the State ended his position as a Senator, and he was appointed as a *Canal Appraiser* for two years. In 1850, he returned to practicing law until he was elected County Judge and Surrogate of Orleans County in the fall of 1856, a position he held for four years. In 1860, he faced ill health and spent most of his time attending to his sick wife. After his wife's passing, he lived with his children and wasn't actively involved in business.

Gideon married Adeline Burrell in August 1824, and they had two children, Samuel B. Hard, a lawyer and businessman in New York City, and Helen B. who married George H. Potts and also resided in New York. Mrs. Hard passed away in Albion on September 15, 1864.

EBENEZER ROGERS

Ebenezer Rogers was born in Norwich, Connecticut, October 3, 1769. He married Betsey Lyman of Lebanon and moved from New England to Onondaga County, N.Y., in 1812. In March, 1816, Rogers settled on the farm in the south part of the village of Albion. When he came, not more than twenty families had settled in Barre, and his house was a home for many of the young men who came here to select a farm for themselves or who, having a lot, were clearing it and building a cabin to occupy with their families.

As a professor of religion and someone who deeply valued the subject, he was one of the most dedicated individuals to push for the regular observance of public worship. Alongside his close neighbor Joseph Hart and others, he helped form the first Congregational Church and Society in Barre, which later became established at Barre Center. After Albion became a village, he played a prominent role in organizing the First Presbyterian Church and Society in Albion, an offshoot of the previously mentioned organization. Within the latter church, Mr. Rogers served as a long-time *deacon* and a ruling *elder*.

He was by trade a tanner and shoemaker, but never followed that business.

Mr. Rogers, who had a strong physical constitution, lived long enough to see his children settled comfortably around him, enjoying the abundance of this good land. He and his worthy companions had put in a lot of effort to reclaim it from the wilderness of nature. Mr. Rogers passed away on January 28, 1865, at the age of ninety-six years, three months, and twenty-five days.

ASA SANFORD

The following is Asa Sanford's history, written by himself, for the Pioneer Association:

"I was born in the town of Farmington, Hartford County, Connecticut, June 2, 1797. My parents were members of the Presbyterian Church and gave their children a strictly religious, as well as a *common school education*, as was the custom in New England.

In February 1806, my father moved with his family, then consisting of a wife, four sons, and two daughters, to Candor, Tioga County, N.Y., a journey of about three hundred miles. My father, oldest brother, and myself, performed this journey, with a pair of oxen and one horse, attached to a sled, being twelve days on the road. A hired man brought my mother and her other children in a sleigh.

That country was then wild, with but few settlers scattered along the Susquehanna and Chemung rivers, with dense forests stretching back thirty miles without a human being, inhabited by bears, wolves, panthers, deer and smaller animals.

A road had been opened between Owego and Ithaca, on which a few settlers had located.

In the fall of 1806, I went to Ithaca with my father, with oxen and wagon, after a load of salt.

I think Ithaca was then the most loathsome and desolate place I had ever seen. It stood on low, black soil, surrounded north and west by a quagmire swamp. It rained hard, and the black mud was so deep, it was difficult for our oxen to draw two barrels of salt home.

My father and another man built the first schoolhouse in the town of Candor, and opened the first school there. The school house stood three miles from my father's dwelling and I went there to school through the woods, with no other shoes than such as my mother made from woolen cloth from day to day.

In June, 1806, my father, his hired man, my brothers and myself, were hoeing corn, between ten and eleven o'clock in the forenoon, when we noticed a singular appearance in the atmosphere; the sky looked somber, the birds retired to the woods, the hens to their roosts and we went to the house. The sun was all darkened, but a rim around the edge; the gloom and chill of evening settled on all the earth around. This lasted but a short time, when the sun came out from its dark pall; everything assumed its wonted activity and light and the *Great Eclipse* passed off.

I continued most of the time working with and for my father, occasionally working for others, till one day as I was chopping in the woods, a young man came along and said to me, he was not going to live longer in that hilly, sterile place; that he had been to the Genesee and found a country far preferable to that for beauty and farming purposes.

I heard his story and determined that at some time I would see that famous *Genesee Country*.

In the spring of 1816, I bought my time from my father, for $100. I was nineteen years old. I hired out to work for $14 per month and in less than a year earned enough to pay my father for my time, and had money left. I continued working where I could make it most profitable, got plenty of work and good pay, until in the summer of 1819, feeling as if I had worked for others long enough, having then ten acres of land and several head of cattle, I felt a desire to get a good wheat farm for myself.

I started with two young men, on foot, knapsacks on our back, Aug. 27, 1819, to go to the Genesee country. We went through Ithaca, and took the road to Geneva, traveling as far as Ovid the first day, forty miles. Next day through Geneva and Canandaigua, we reached West Bloomfield. Next day through Lima and Avon, we arrived at Batavia and went to the office of the Holland Company to see about land.

In the office the agent appeared rather sour, little disposed to be sociable. We asked him if he had land to sell. He said he had. He was asked where it lay and replied 'everywhere, all over, you cannot go amiss.' I asked him if it was wild, or improved farms? He answered, 'go and look, when you run your head into a great improvement you will know it, won't you?' I turned indignantly and walked out of the office, saying 'I had a mind to boot that fellow.'

The agent followed us out to close the blinds and hearing our conversation, said rather pleasantly, 'boys keep a stiff upper lip.'

We stayed that night at the old Pioneer tavern. The landlord tried hard to convince me that the agent was a New England gentleman, one that I would be pleased to do business with.

We were informed of the rapid growth of a new town north from Batavia, called Barre, lying between the Tonawanda Swamp and the Ridge road. Towards this new town we set out the next morning.

After examining various parts of Barre and Gaines, we selected our locations in Barre, and returned to the Land office to secure our Articles for our land; but finding we lacked a few dollars required to pay the first payment, the agent kindly offered to *book* the lots to us, until we got the money.

We made no further complaint against the agent, who booked the land to us and we returned to make preparations for felling the timber on our new farms. Never before did we complain of the rapid flight of time, but here, while laboring for ourselves, we thought these the shortest days we had ever seen.

On the 12th of October, 1819, having obtained the money, we went to the office and took out our Articles for our land, went back to our work and after chopping five or six acres apiece, we returned to our friends in Tioga County.

During the next winter, we fitted out with teams, tools, clothing and a quantity of pork, and in March,

1820, set out for our new homes and after a tedious journey of twelve days, through snow, water and mud, we arrived home April 1st.

Having no hay for our cattle, we cut browse to feed them, giving a few ears of corn procured from our neighbors, till vegetation grew so that they could live in the woods.

We hired our board, cooked at a neighbors, and cleared off what we had chopped the previous season and planted the land with corn. The season being propitious, we had good crops of corn, with oats, potatoes, beans and other vegetables and melons in abundance. We also cleared off and sowed several acres with wheat.

In the autumn the bears were very troublesome in our cornfields, committing their nightly depredations, till it became necessary to put our veto upon them; this we did in various ways by trapping, shooting, night watching, etc., until we had captured four of them and thus saved our corn.

After securing our crops and preparing for winter, we sold our teams and returned to our parent's homes.

During the next season we experienced much inconvenience in getting our board dressed for us. The woman who did it became quite tired of doing the work for the old bachelors, and I began to realize the truth of the Divine declaration that 'it is not good for man to be alone.'

After visiting among friends in Tayoga County for a few days, I hired out for three months. March 1, 1821, I was married. About the middle of the month, putting all on board a covered wagon with two yoke of oxen attached, and in company with the two young men previously referred to, we set out again for our new wilderness home in the Genesee country.

After two weeks hard labor, we arrived at our home to the great joy of our neighbors, especially the women. We moved into a small house with one of our neighbors, until we could build us a house, which we built in a few weeks after.

While the early pioneers of a new country are necessarily subject to many hardships and privations, unknown to settlers of older countries, still there are many enjoyments and pleasing reminiscences for these pioneers, which they never forget. Aristocracy is unknown in a new country. The people are all friendly and kindly disposed toward each other. If any are sick, they are at once cared for. If a farmer was attacked with ague, that dread disease, so common among the pioneers of this county, before he could get his spring crops into the ground, his neighbors would turn out and put them in for him and if necessary, they would keep his work along until he was able to do it himself. If there is any state of society where men fulfill the *Divine Injunction* 'love thy neighbor as thyself,' it is found among the pioneers of a new country.

If any one got lost in the woods, and did not return at night, search was at once made by everybody and no sleep was had until the lost one was found.

After we moved into our new house, I started out to buy me a cow, bought one and we now commenced housekeeping under circumstances quite favorable, at least our neighbors thought so. My wife had a few necessary articles of furniture, so that we were about as well off as any of our neighbors.

There were no pianos or melodeons in those days. The little wheel for spinning flax and the great wheel for spinning tow, furnished the music. A few years later we had other house music.

I plodded on for eight years, adding field to field of my cleared, improved land and then found myself unable to pay even the interest due on my Article to the Land Company.

I raised about $70, and with this went to Batavia to see the agent. I determined this time to walk into the office with my head up and meet any insult I might receive with manly independence.

I found the agent alone in the office, went up to him and laid down my Article and all the money I had, saying my Article has expired and here is all the money I have. I want to renew my contract, as I have no idea of giving up my premises yet.

The agent walked up, took my Article, unfolded it and said 'you have not assigned it I see.' Then taking up the money he said pleasantly, 'walk into the other room.' I did so and in less time than I have been writing this, my new Article was made out, my payment endorsed and I was ready to start for home. But on returning to the contractor's room, the agent said to me he had relinquished all the back interest and $1 per acre of the principal, making an entirely new sale, with eight years' payday, as at first, and asked me if I was satisfied. My gratitude had by this time become almost unbounded and I left the office, thanking the old agent for his kindness and thinking after all, beneath a rough exterior he had a generous heart.

I mention this incident to show the kind and generous treatment extended towards the poor industrious settlers upon the lands of the Holland Company. Many incidents of a like character might be recorded to the credit of the Company.

I came home inspired with new energy and determination to struggle on and overcome every hardship and difficulty in my way.

We had but little sickness compared with our neighbors as yet. In the spring of 1823, I had severe inflammation of the lungs, and in the spring of 1828, I was taken with fever and ague, which held me through the season.

The next spring my wife was sick with fever and ague and thrush, which kept her ill till the October following.

Our children, then four in number, had their full shares of fever and ague. It was painful to see the little ones draw up to the fire while suffering their chill, then see them retire to their beds, tormented with the raging thirst and fever following the chills, while their mother could do little for them except to supply their frequent calls for water.

In the fall of 1824 or 1825 two men living near Barre Center, named Selah Belden, and Nathan Angel, started on Saturday morning to hunt deer west from the Center. They parted in the afternoon, each after a separate game. At night Mr. Belden returned, but Mr. Angel did not. Next morning Belden, with some of his neighbors went out and spent the day looking for Angel, but not finding him, the next morning a general rally of all the men in town was made and the woods thoroughly searched and the dead body of Mr. Angel found, having apparently fallen and died from exhaustion. The body was carried to Benton's Corners, then the center of the settlement. A jury was called by Ithamar Hibbard, *Esquire*, one of the first coroners, and it is believed this was the first coroner's inquest in Orleans County. As the county was cleared up and the lowlands drained of their surface water, the people suffered less from ague.

The canal being now opened, farmers found a ready market and better prices for their produce. Home manufacturers were protected from foreign competition and the price of domestic goods greatly reduced. It was then the farmers began to thrive and soon to pay up for their lands. The price of real estate advanced and some even predicted the time would come when the best farms would be worth one hundred dollars per acre, hardly expecting to live to see their predictions fulfilled as they have done.

The attention of the early pioneers was called to the subject of common schools for their children, and the next building to go up after a log cabin for a dwelling was a log schoolhouse.

One of our statesmen, while a member of the Legislature being asked where he graduated, replied: 'In a log school house up in Orleans County.' I have often carried my eldest son to and from school on my back through the deep snows of winter.

More than forty years ago I united with the Methodist Episcopal Church at West Barre and in 1843 withdrew from that church and united with the Wesleyan Methodists.

Many years ago, convinced of the sin of intemperance, I resolved to use no more intoxicating liquor as a beverage, a resolution to which I have strictly adhered ever since.

Asa SANFORD."

January 28th, 1862.

ANDREW H. GREEN

Andrew H. Green, of Byron, Genesee County, N.Y. writes for the Orleans County Pioneer Association records, his local history as follows:

"I was born in Johnstown, Montgomery County, N.Y., Oct. 16th, 1797, and in June, 1809, came to Genesee County from Rome, Oneida County, N.Y.

In 1792, my father and Judge Tryon of New Lebanon came to Irondequoit, near Rochester, and built a storehouse. In 1808, my father came to what is now Bergen and Sweden, and purchased a farm. He started from the north bounds of what is now the Methodist campground in Bergen, running north to the road that runs east to Sweden Centre. He bought twenty-five lots containing three thousand acres at twenty-two shillings per acre.

It was a hard country to settle. There were but few inhabitants and the roads were very bad. As soon as they began to erect mill-dams there was a great deal of sickness.

We went to Handford's Landing, at the mouth of the Genesee River, to trade and sell potash. I found but two houses between our house and Clarkson Corners and but two from there to Genesee River. For several years I was as familiar with every family from my father's to Genesee River as I am now with my near neighbors.

The first time I passed through Rochester was in the summer of 1809. The next thing I remember about it was the bad roads and that I was very much frightened crossing the Genesee River. The water was deep and ran very swiftly. I expected to go down stream and over the falls.

I think there was one mill and two or three shanties to be seen there then. There was a small clearing where the Eagle tavern formerly stood, but I had as much as I could do to get my load through the mud. I thought little then that *black ash swamp* was ever to be the place it now is. Late in the fall of 1809 my father sent me to Sangersfield Huddle after a load of merchandise. East of Canandaigua was a new turnpike where I got stuck in the mud and had to wait until the next teamster came along to help me out. I was then fourteen years old.

My father had fifteen workmen and the first summer cleared one hundred acres. The *latch-string* was always out and none ever went away hungry as we had plenty of pork and wild game to season it.

Deer, bears, and wolves were plenty. I never heard of but one panther. The surveyors had their tent near where the steam saw mill now stands in Clarendon. Their cook came in on Wednesday night for bread. One evening he had got to where Col. Shubael Lewis later lived when he heard someone halloo. He soon found it was a panther on his track. It followed him to the clearing. The man was much exhausted when he came in. He was an old hunter and said he knew it was a panther.

The men all came on Saturday afternoon. The Sabbath was as well kept in 1809 as in 1863. We were seldom without Evangelical preaching. We had one close communion Baptist Elder, some Methodists and some Presbyterians. All could sing the good old tunes and sing them with a will.

The year 1809 was productive and healthy. In 1810, about July 20th, we had a frost that killed most of the wheat and corn. The fall of 1811 was very sickly. There were several families settled at Sandy Creek Village. They were all sick. We made up a load of some six or seven and went down to help them. I never saw so happy a company. We carried two loads of necessaries and stayed two nights, and when some of them got so they could take care of the others, we left for home.

I used to have many hard and lonesome rides through the woods on horseback. One very dark night I had been to Dr. Ward's after medicine. Coming home I lost my road and also my hat. Before I found my hat the wolves began to howl. I took off my shoes so that I might find the road, and by the time I had mounted my horse to go on, the wolves were within speaking distance and before I had gone far they struck my barefoot tracks; then they made a terrific roaring. I thought I was a goner sure enough, but I presume if the wolves had seen me then on the old white horse they would have been as frightened as I was.

Our men had all kinds of musical instruments and any time when the drum was beat the wolves were almost sure to respond.

About the beginning of winter my father started me off with an ox team and load of grain to find Judge Farewell's grist mill. After a tedious day's travel I came in sight of water pouring over rocks. It was no small stream. I thought it must be Niagara Falls. I was glad to find I could get my grist ground, so I chained my oxen to a tree and found a comfortable night's lodging among the bags in the mill. I got home the next day with my grist. Our folks thought I had done well and I thought so too.

The first winter I walked seven miles to school every day and back again.

A. H. GREEN."

Byron, Genesee Co. N.Y., June 16, 1863.

In a letter written by the above named A. H. Green to the Secretary of the Orleans County Pioneer Association, dated June 14, 1866, he says: "I was quite interested the other day, while hunting up the old road records of our town, Byron, in 1809. It was then the town of Murray, but now contains eight or nine town entire."

LINUS JONES PECK

Mr. Peck furnished his local history for the Orleans County Pioneer Association Records as follows:

"I was born October 27th, 1816, in a very cheap log house on Onondaga Hill, in Onondaga Co., N.Y., about a mile and a half from the old Court House. Up to eleven years of age I was engaged principally in endeavoring to get something to eat, not always however with much success, and in going to school barefoot both summer and winter.

I never had anything made of leather to wear on my feet until the spring of 1828.

My amusements consisted in listening to the howling of the wolves and in gymnastic exercises with the mosquitoes.

In May, 1828, I had a pair of shoes and was sent to Pike, Allegany County, to live with my brother Luther. I stayed there until May 1833, when I returned to my parents with whom I lived until 1836, when I went to Wyoming to attend the Middlebury Academy.

In the spring of 1838 I returned to Pike to read law in my brother's office. In 1841 he moved to Nunda, now in Livingston County and I stayed with him in his office till 1848. In July of that year I commenced jobbing on the canals and continued in that business until the summer of 1861, since which time I have done little business of any kind. I was never married.

I left the town where I was born in 1817 and arrived in Clarendon, or what is now Clarendon, Orleans County, just forty years ago today (March 20, 1864.) I came to Holley first in the spring of 1856 and stayed until December. I then returned to Pendleton in Niagara County and completed a large job I had on the Erie Canal through the Mountain Ridge and went back to Holley in the spring of 1857, since which time Holley has been my residence.

My mother died March 4, 1848, aged 71 years. My father died June 2, 1852, aged 82 years. I am the youngest of my brothers, all of whom are living.

There are, or were, no incidents in my early history or that of my brothers, not common to all the early settlers in this vicinity, except I thought we managed to be a little poorer than anybody else. My father had the misfortune of having two trades, that of a farmer and carpenter and joiner. He worked his hands altogether too much and his brains altogether too little, and dividing the time between the two, necessarily resulted in doing neither well. Consequently neither prospered. This, his sons turned all about in 1825, when my brothers became old enough to take charge of affairs. Since which time there has been an improvement.

LINUS JONES PECK."

Holley, March 20, 1864.

HARVEY GOODRICH

Harvey Goodrich was born in Herkimer County, N.Y., in November 1791. His father, Zenas Goodrich, moved to that place from Berkshire, Mass. When he was a young man, Harvey Goodrich moved to Auburn, N.Y., and worked for some time in the hat-making business. He also served as a *constable* for several years. With his success in accumulating property, he and his brother-in-law, George W. Standart, took on a job working on the construction of the Erie Canal. After completing his work on the canal, he settled permanently in Albion in 1824, where he and George W. Standart engaged in selling dry goods and groceries.

Following Mr. Standart's passing, Mr. Goodrich discontinued selling dry goods and focused on the business of manufacturing and selling hats, dealing in furs, and buying produce. He also held the position of postmaster in Albion for several years. Being an active and energetic individual, and having the education and inclination to participate in public affairs, he became one of the prominent figures in the community, often holding official positions and being active in public events.

Mr. Goodrich was a faithful and loyal democrat in his political views. Additionally, his ardent and earnest character was most prominent in his dedication to religion. He made a public profession of religion and joined the First Presbyterian Church in Auburn around 1817, under the guidance of Rev. Dr. Lansing.

Upon arriving in Albion, one of his earliest undertakings was establishing a Presbyterian church. With his help and that of other Presbyterians in the area, the Presbyterian Church in Albion was organized in February 1824, aided by Rev. William Johnson from Auburn Theological Seminary and led by Rev. Andrew Rawson, a missionary in the region. Mr. Goodrich was one of the sixteen founding members. On July 29, 1824, along with Messrs. Hart and Phelps, he was elected as a ruling elder in the Presbyterian Church, a position he held until his passing.

Mr. Goodrich was known for his outstanding care for the sick and his involvement in funeral ceremonies in his neighborhood. He would provide assistance to those in need according to their requirements and often took charge of funeral ceremonies.

For over forty years, Mr. Goodrich was a valuable and prominent member of the church and the community, actively contributing to the business and growth of Albion. He was known for his support of the poor and was esteemed by the county's residents. Two years before his death, he suffered a stroke, which left him disabled. He passed away on August 4, 1863, at the age of 71, after lingering and languishing from the effects of the stroke.

ORSON NICHOSON

Dr. Orson Nichoson was born in Galway, Saratoga County, New York, on March 2, 1795. He was educated as a physician. In 1822, he moved to the village of Albion, which was just beginning to be settled. He enthusiastically participated in various public endeavors and organizational activities.

He was elected as the first County Clerk of Orleans County and served two terms, holding the office for six years.

ORSON NICHOSON

In August 1819, Dr. Nichoson settled about two miles south of Albion. In 1822, he moved to Albion and established a successful medical practice that lasted for many years. Due to declining health, he entered into business with Dr. L. C. Paine and began trading in drugs, medicines, and books, which he continued until a few years before his passing.

Dr. Nichoson was the first regular physician to settle in Barre, and also the first to do so in Albion. In 1820, Dr. Nichoson married Lucy Morris, and they had three children: Adeline E., Caroline A., and Helen J. Adeline E. married Jonathan S. Steward, and Helen J. married Charles A. Stanton. She passed away on May 12, 1862. Mrs. Lucy Nichoson passed away on October 8, 1864, and Dr. Orson Nichoson passed away on May 7, 1870.

TIMOTHY C. STRONG

Timothy C. Strong was born in Southampton, Massachusetts, on March 15, 1790. At the age of sixteen, he became an apprentice to J. D. Huntington to learn the art of printing in Middlebury, Vermont. He married Aurelia Goodsell, daughter of Dr. Pensfield Goodsell of Litchfield, Connecticut, on April 14, 1811. He started his own business in Middlebury, publishing the **Vermont Mirror** newspaper, a magazine edited by Samuel Swift, and a literary work called the **Philosophical Repository** edited by Professor Hall of Middlebury College.

In September 1817, he moved to Palmyra, New York, where he published a newspaper. In the fall of 1823, he moved to Ann Arbor, Michigan, and in February 1825, he moved to Newport, now Albion, Orleans County, New York, where he purchased a newspaper establishment called **The Newport Patriot** from Franklin Cowdry, who started it on February 9th, 1824. Mr. Strong changed the name of this paper to **The Orleans Advocate**. In February 1828, amidst the excitement following the abduction of Morgan, he changed it to **The Orleans Advocate** and **Anti-Masonic Telegraph**, and soon after to **The American Standard**. It was published under this name for two years by Mr. J. Kempshall, before it returned to the hands of Mr. Strong, who changed it to the **Orleans American** and continued to publish it until April 1844, when he sold it along with his printing establishment to J. & J. H. Denio. They continued the paper until 1853 when they sold it, and it passed through several hands before being bought in January 1861 by H.A. Bruner, its current proprietor.

In November 1834, Mr. Strong was elected County Clerk of Orleans County, a position he held for nine years through re-election. He made a profession of religion in early life and joined the Presbyterian Church. He passed away from cancer in Albion on August 6th, 1844, at the age of fifty-three, leaving behind his wife and twelve surviving children.

NATHAN WHITNEY

Nathan Whitney was born in Conway, Massachusetts, on January 22, 1791. In February 1814, he moved to Orleans County and settled in what is now Barre. He participated in the taking of *Fort Erie* in September 1814. When the town of Barre was organized, he was elected Justice of the Peace, a position he held for several years. When Orleans County was established, he was elected Supervisor of Barre and served in the year 1826. He enjoyed military exercises and held various military offices from Lieutenant to Lieutenant Colonel. His fellow citizens regarded him as a capable, honest, and efficient man, often electing him to official positions. He moved from Barre to Elba, Genesee County, in 1827, and later relocated to Lee County, Illinois, where he was living in the fall of 1869.

AVERY M. STARKWEATHER

Avery M. Starkweather was born in Preston, Connecticut, on October 3rd, 1790. He lived in Palmyra, N.Y. for a while before moving to the town of Barre, where he acquired a farm in April 1816. After the Erie Canal opened, for thirteen years he was responsible for the first State repairing scow boat on this section. He held the position of Superintendent of Canal Repairs for a year, overseeing maintenance from Holley to Lockport. During the navigation season, he was required to personally inspect his section at least once a week, which he faithfully did.

In addition to his canal work, Starkweather served as an assessor for the town of Barre for thirteen years and was the town's Supervisor in 1842 and 1843. He was known as an active, thorough business man, respected for his honesty and conscientiousness. Avery M. Starkweather passed away on October 3, 1865.

AMOS ROOT

Amos Root was born in Sand Lake, Rensselaer County, N.Y., on July 12, 1803. He was apprenticed to learn the trade of **blacksmith** and moved to Allegany County, N.Y., in 1818. After completing his *apprenticeship*, he worked as a blacksmith for nearly thirty years before becoming a farmer.

In 1836, he moved from Allegany County to Michigan, and then returned to the town of Barre in 1838, where he lived since. He married Rhoda Ann Bennett on July 11, 1824. In his youth, he was known for his strength and was particularly noted for his skill as a wood chopper. While living in Allegany County, he participated in a group that was cutting out a new road. A bet of fifty dollars was made among the group to test his chopping power, and he won the bet by out-chopping his opponent. Unfortunately, his opponent overworked himself and died a week later from the exertion.

Amos's father, Mr. Israel Root, a Revolutionary War soldier, moved from Allegany to Orleans County in 1825 and settled on the farm now owned by Amos in Barre. Mr. Israel Root arrived in a wagon with his family, while Amos brought the goods on two canoes made of large pine logs lashed together. He launched these canoes on the Genesee River at Gardeau, paddled down to Rochester, and then placed them in the canal to reach Gaines Basin, which was a popular landing place for emigrants settling in the area.

OZIAS S. CHURCH

Ozias S. Church was born in Windham, Connecticut, on January 31, 1785. He worked as a farmer, but also helped his father with blacksmithing when he was young. He married Parmelia Palmer on October 13, 1809. She was born in Windham on October 3, 1786. They moved to Otsego County, N.Y., in 1812, and then to Henrietta, Monroe County, N.Y., in 1817, and finally to the town of Barre in 1834.

Mr. Church was involved in politics as a democrat and was active in his party. He served as the United States Marshal and took the census of Monroe County in 1830 and Orleans County in 1840. He also held the position of Postmaster at South Barre for twenty years.

Mrs. Church passed away on December 7, 1861, and Mr. Church on December 10, 1863. They had two sons, John P. Church, who passed away in December 1858 while serving as County Clerk of Orleans County, and Hon. Sanford E. Church, who is currently the Chief Judge of the Court of Appeals of the State of New York.

WILLIAM BRADNER

William Bradner moved to the town of Gaines from Palmyra, N.Y. Soon after, he purchased lot thirty-five on the east side of Main Street in Albion from Mr. McCollister, and received a deed from the Holland Company for 266 1/2 acres on December 3, 1819. His brother, Joel Bradner, also received a deed from the Company for ninety-two acres located on the southwest corner of lot thirty-five. Subsequently, William Bradner sold one hundred acres from the northwest part of his tract to Ingersoll, Smith & Buckley on April 22, 1822.

A. HYDE COLE

Hon. Almeron Hyde Cole was born in Lavanna, Cayuga County, N.Y., on April 20, 1798. His parents relocated to Auburn in 1807, where he prepared for college and joined the sophomore class at Union College in 1815. Some of his classmates included George W. Doane, the late Bishop of New Jersey, Alonzo Potter, the late Bishop of Pennsylvania, Dr. Hickok, the late President of Union College, and William H. Seward, the late Governor of New York and Senator. He spent two years in college and then left without completing his college course due to his mother's passing and other family changes.

In the fall of 1817, he began studying law at the office of Judge Joseph L. Richardson, who was the first Judge of Cayuga County at the time. He was admitted as an attorney in the Supreme Court when he was twenty-one years old and then formed a partnership with Judge Richardson to practice law. After a few months, he ended the partnership with Judge Richardson and joined Mr. George W. Fleming to practice law. After some time in Seneca Falls, they moved to Albion in the spring of 1825, where they continued to practice law together until 1832. Following the dissolution of his partnership with Mr. Fleming, Mr. Cole practiced law with his brother, Hon. Dan H. Cole, for several years.

Mr. Cole served seventeen years as a Justice of the Peace of the town of Barre, and transacted an immense amount of official business.

In November 1847, he was elected as a member of the State Senate of New York, where he served a single two-year term and chose not to seek re-election. After leaving the Senate, he resumed his law practice in Albion. However, due to a significant amount of business as the executor of an estate in Cayuga County, he decided to close his law practice and focus solely on his duties as executor and managing a large farm he owned in the town of Gaines.

Although a good advocate and a strong and logical reasoner at the bar, Mr. Cole was not so fluent and polished a speaker as his partner Mr. Fleming. In their earlier years of practice together, Mr. Cole furnished his quota of brains to the firm, while Mr. Fleming furnished the tongue.

Mr. Cole was highly regarded as a knowledgeable and competent lawyer whose opinions on legal matters were often sought and trusted. His counsel and advice were held in high esteem by the public, and he quickly gained a reputation as the "*counselor*" or "*counselor Cole*," by which title he was always known and respected.

HON. ALMERON HYDE COLE

In temperament, he was ardent, impulsive, and sensitive, feeling quick and sharply the irritation of the moment. But nothing like hatred ever had a place in his bosom.

From the peculiarity of his character he sometimes appeared brusque and rough to those who approached him, but no man had a kinder heart. The sternness or apparent harshness of manner which he possessed was more than balanced in his case by the keen regret he felt when he knew he had caused pain to any and the hearty sympathy and generosity he ever manifested to those in distress.

Mr. Cole was never married. Coming to Orleans County when it was first organized, among the first lawyers who settled here, he was a prominent man in public affairs and well known to the people of the County.

He died Oct. 14, 1859.

"I was born in the town of New Baltimore, Greene County, N.Y., March 12th, 1807. The death of my mother, which occurred when I was twelve years of age, threw me upon the family of my grandparents where I remained until I was fourteen years old. My father, a blacksmith by trade resided in the county of Chenango. He married a second time, closed up his business in Chenango, then started for the State of Ohio with a view of commencing business there as a farmer. This was in the fall of 1821. When he arrived in the town of Clarence, Erie County, a snow storm set in and prevented his further progress that fall, and having with him some tools and a small stock of iron he rented a shop and began work as a blacksmith at Ransom's Grove, as it is now called, at Clarence Hollow. He soon after purchased one hundred and sixty acres of land at the Great Rapids on the Tonawanda Creek, six miles south of Lockport.

In the summer of 1822, having obtained a scanty common school education, and being large enough to help my father in his shop and on his farm, he wrote to me giving a glowing account of the county, of his farm, of the fine fish in the creek and the fine sport in taking them, and desiring me to come and help him.

I accordingly went to Albany and put my baggage on board a seven horse wagon, then about to sail for Buffalo, loaded with specie for the United States Bank at Erie, Pennsylvania. Thus equipped I started for the Holland Purchase in July, 1822, in care of Mr. Hockins, the owner of the establishment. We traveled slowly, not making over fifteen miles a day, sleeping in our wagon nights and watching our treasure. Getting tired of this slow mode of traveling, when we arrived at Canandaigua I took the stage and came on to Clarence, and arrived at my father's on July 22nd, 1822. In a few days I went with my father to explore his new farm. He, carrying a bag of provisions and I, a compass and chain with other articles for our journey. My half-brother William, then thirteen years old, accompanied us.

It was here, in July, 1822, in what was then called *the north woods* that I commenced my pioneer life, and for the next three years, and until October, 1825, I shared in the hardships, labors and privations of the early settlers. During that time I assisted in chopping and partly clearing forty acres of heavily timbered land and erecting a comfortable log building. Being possessed of a strong, athletic frame, and a good robust constitution, and never having been sick a day in my life, I endured the hardships and labors of the wilderness with cheerfulness and pleasure, and I often look back to those days and reckon them among the happiest of my life. And I would not omit to record here with grateful heart the kind care of my Heavenly Father in preserving my life amid the dangers and accidents through which I passed in my youthful days.

Not possessing at my father's the advantages for mental improvement which I desire, I concluded in the fall of 1825 to abandon my pioneer life, return to the east, obtain an education and study a profession. Accordingly October 2nd, 1825, I left my axe and *handspike* and went to Lockport, got on board the canal boat De Witt Clinton and sailed for the east. Stopping in Albion for the boat to take on loading I took an excursion through that low, muddy, and as I thought unsightly young village. I little thought then that Newport, as it was called, was destined to be my future home. I then pronounced Newport a queer place on which to build a town.

I returned to the boat and passed on through Holley, Brockport, Adams' and Spencer's Basins, all little straggling hamlets, as I thought them, arriving in Rochester in the night. Here I expected to meet a gentleman from Tompkins County by appointment, with whom I was intending to travel to visit my relatives in this vicinity and then go by boat with some relatives to Albany. But the gentleman did not come as I expected. My little stock of money was exhausted on Tuesday night in paying for my supper. I was now a stranger in a strange land. I knew not what to do or how I should be provided for. I wandered about Rochester until Saturday morning, eating nothing except a few apples which I picked up in an orchard in the town of Brighton. I slept nights on the piazza of the Exchange Hotel, on the corner at the intersection of the canal with the *basin*, where the packet boats used to lay up. Every morning when a fire was made up in the old bakery at the west end of the *aqueduct*, I went into the front room and warmed myself, tantalized by the smell of the bread which was piled up on the counter, steaming hot, and for which I was starving. I was too proud to beg, and I thank God for it, too honest to steal.

Thus the week passed until Saturday morning when I had a pressing invitation to join a circus company then performing there. I was then young, active and strong, but my good Quaker training, and above all the hand of Providence shaping my ways, kept my youthful feet from that path.

On Saturday morning I met a man who asked me if I would work, and I gladly hired to him for a part of the day. He led the way to the barn back of the canal, between Fizhugh and Sophia Streets, where the ground was literally strewn with heavy cannon, and I worked until the middle of the afternoon assisting to put them on a scow boat for distribution along the canal, to be used in firing a grand salute at the meeting of the water of Lake Erie with the Hudson River, November 2nd, 1825, a day never to be forgotten in Western New York. I received half a dollar for my work and went to a humble tavern for supper and had lodging in a bed. A better meal or sweeter sleep I never enjoyed. The next morning I went out on the street and almost the first man I met was the friend for whom I was waiting.

After writing to my relatives in Tompkins County I left for Albany and entered the City with the fleet of canal boats in the canal celebration November 2nd 1825, amid the roar of artillery and the sound of martial music.

The Erie and Champlain Canals were now finished. Navigation between the ocean and lake was now opened, and a new era of unparalleled prosperity had commenced, and the exultant people were duly celebrating the auspicious event. Peace hath her victories.

After mingling with the throng that crowded the streets a few hours. I started on foot for the home of my childhood, where loved ones I had not seen for more than three years were daily expecting me. It was nightfall when I ascended the last hill and the well known trees were standing like sentinels around the old **homestead** in the fading twilight. My truant feet once more passed the threshold. The old watchdog knew my step. With a fluttering heart I looked in at the window, and for a moment surveyed the group as they sat around the cheerful fireside. God in his goodness had kept them all and the wandering child had got home.

I was past eighteen years of age when I returned from Western New York. I had seen something of the world and had some experience in pioneer life. My education was not such as the district schools of the day afford. My mind had been somewhat improved by reading in a desultory and aimless manner. I taught a winter school in my native town, and in the spring of 1826 hired out as farm laborer at nine dollars per month in the county of Albany.

I taught school in the same county the winter of 1826-27, and in the spring entered the Greenville Academy, in Green County, where I remained, until the coming fall, and by this time I had succeeded in preparing myself to enter the sophomore class at Union College; my friends however preferred that I should follow a mercantile life, and procured me a situation in a wholesale dry goods house in the city of New York, where I remained until the termination of fall business. I then returned to my native town intending to go back to New York the following spring.

I taught school at Marbletown, Ulster County, N.Y., the winter of 1827-28, with great success, forming many pleasant acquaintances that have been cherished through subsequent life.

Early in the spring I was attacked with Pleurisy, and lay at the point of death for a number of days. On recovering the spring had so far advanced I did not go to New York as I intended, but continued my school until the spring of 1829, when laying down the ferule, I commenced business on my own account in the village of West Troy, Albany County, being nearly twenty-two years old.

April 11, 1830, I was married to Deborah, daughter of Rev. Simeon Dickinson, of East Haddam, Conn. She was at that time a teacher in Mrs. Willard's Female Seminary at Troy.

I continued my business at West Troy, until the fall of that year, when I sold out and moved with my wife to the city of Mobile, Alabama, where she opened the Mobile Female Seminary, under the most favorable auspices.

I was clerk in the United States Bank in that city. In the month of Dec. 1831 my wife died suddenly, and I was left alone in a strange city without a relative nearer than the State of New York.

I transferred the Seminary to other hands, resigned my clerkship in the Bank, closed up my business matters, and in March 1832 returned to my old home.

I spent that summer and the following winter in traveling for recreation, and in the spring of 1833, being twenty-six years old, I entered upon the study of the law with Amasa Mattison Esq., then a promising lawyer of Cairo, in the county of Greene, where I remained until fall, when I entered the office of Judge Hiram Gardner of Lockport and remained with him until April 1835, when I came to Albion where I have ever since resided.

June 18, 1835, I was married to Caroline G., daughter of Samuel Baker of Coeymans, in the county of Albany and in August following purchased the property on which I have since resided.

I am now (1862) nearly fifty-four years of age, and must soon, in all human probability, lay aside the active duties of my profession, and yield my place to those younger and better fitted for the responsibilities of the station.

In reviewing the pathway of my life I behold it plentifully strewn with incidents, always overshadowed by the watchful care of my Heavenly Father, who unnumbered mercies I am called upon to record.

When fourteen years of age I met with the reformed Dutch Church in Greene County, upon a confession of my faith, and in 1842 I united with the Presbyterian Church in Albion, my wife coming with me to the same altar.

B. L. BESSAC."

Albion, January 8, 1862.

HENRY R. CURTIS

Hon. Henry R. Curtis was born in Hoosick, Rensselaer County, New York, in the year 1800. He spent his youth working on a farm and received a basic education through his own efforts and his widowed mother's limited means. He began studying law with Daniel

Kellogg in Skaneateles and later with Hon. Hiram Mather in Elbridge, New York.

In the fall of 1824, he settled in Albion, Orleans County, before being admitted to the Bar. He formed a partnership with Alexis Ward, who was already established in Albion and had been admitted to the Supreme Court.

In 1831, he was appointed District Attorney for Orleans County, a position he held through subsequent appointments, except for the year 1832, until June 1847. He was then elected County Judge and Surrogate, becoming the first County Judge chosen under the constitution of 1846. He was re-elected to the same office in November 1850 but passed away before the end of his second term.

Before becoming a judge, he held various civil offices in town and village, including Examiner and Master in Chancery. He was a dedicated student of the law, devoting himself to the duties of his profession with unwavering dedication and avoiding other business ventures.

For twenty-five years, he served as a ruling Elder in the Presbyterian Church and was a faithful teacher in the Sunday School at his church for much of that time. Known for his honesty and sincerity, he was a persuasive and composed advocate, often winning favor with the courts and juries.

As a counselor, he was a peacemaker, known for his judicious, cautious, and sensible advice, never encouraging litigation when it could be avoided. He was a man with few enemies and many friends, renowned for his integrity as a lawyer and as a good person. He passed away on September 20, 1855.

ZENAS F. HIBBARD

"I was born in Schroon, Essex County, New York, April 4, 1804. My Ancestors were of Scotch descent, and were among those who fled to this country from the oppressions of the old world, to enjoy civil and religious liberty in the new world.

My father afterwards moved from Schroon to Brandon, Vermont, and from Brandon he moved in the summer of 1816, to what is now Barre, New York, July 12, 1816, on lot 10, township 15, range 2, of the Holland Purchase, one mile west of Albion where he lived sixteen years. He then moved to Barre Center where he resided until his death, which occurred February 5, 1853.

I attended the first school taught in Barre, in a log school house, which stood on the west side of Oak Orchard Road, in what is now the Village of Albion. I also attended the first town meeting in Barre after the town was organized, at the house of Abraham Mattison, about two miles south of Albion. I also attended the great celebration of the opening of the Erie Canal, when the waters of Lake Erie mingled with those of the Hudson River. I was also present when the site for the county buildings was located at Albion, which was the most exciting time, perhaps, ever known in this county.

I was present when the first Congregational church in the town of Barre was formed, at the house of Joseph Hart. This church then consisted of the following named persons: Joseph Hart and wife, Ebenezer Rogers and wife, Ithamar Hibbard and wife, Artemas Thayer and wife, Artemas Houghton and Thankful Thurston.

I was married to Amanda Wrisley, in Barre, June 19, 1828. She was born in Gill, Mass., Nov. 18, 1809.

Z. F. HIBBARD."

Dated--Barre Center, April 4th, 1865.

WILLIAM TANNER

Letter from William Tanner, formerly of Orleans County, N.Y., written to the Pioneer Association:

"To the officers and members of the Orleans County Pioneer Association:

Gentleman: As fond memory often sharpens old ears to catch some word of the old home of our youth, so now at three score years and one I have heard of your society. What you do or what you say, I do not know, but I do know if you are the real pioneers I should be glad indeed to meet with you at your annual gathering.

Tell me, dear sirs, are you together to speak of the days when Albion was a mud hole, and Jesse Bumpus and Dea. Hart and a few others owned the whole of it? And when the old log school house half a mile north of Albion was built, where Francis Tanner first declared martial law among the little folks; and when Mr. Jakeway so well adapted to the business by his six feet four inches of body and legs, used to break the road through four feet of snow, with three yoke of oxen, from the Ridge Road to father Crandall's near one Angel's, not Gabriel, but 'Cabin Angel,' as he was called by way of distinction.

And there was Dea. Daniels, and Esq. Babbitt a little east, the workings of whose face denoted wisdom as he sat in judgment to decide weighty matters between neighbors.

Never shall I forget envying that man his high office as justice of the peace when I was a small boy.

Then there was John Proctor and his tall and amiable wife and large farm.

Then again at Gaines Corners, the corpulent landlord Booth, together with Dr. Anderson, with his mild and pleasant way of telling people it wouldn't hurt much to pull teeth, and then almost taking their heads off with his strong arm.

Later, there was good Jeptha Wood, who first taught me that hot and cold iron would not weld together.

But I must not name others lest I have not have room to say a word to the old Pioneers.

How simple was I in my boyhood days to envy the honored Esq. Babbitt, or the rich farmer Proctor of those early times. I have since been Esquire myself. I have been rich also; but neither the honor of the one nor the gold of the other, brings happiness while here on this mundane sphere. When I turn my thoughts to the spot of all others most dear to me, Samuel N. Tanners old farm, and the *city of the dead*, Mount Albion, opposite to his once earthly habitation, where I once chased the deer, and see the monumental slabs erected over heads many of whom were my friends in youth. I am ready to exclaim, 'Where are the pioneers I once knew?'

But sirs, some of you still live, and allow me to speak of what you have done. You are among the greatest men of the nation. You have leveled the sturdy forest, planted fruitful fields, orchards and gardens, built railroads and canals, set up talking wires by which we carry our freight and travel cheaply over three hundred miles a day and converse with lightning speed with far distant friends.

I imagine I see De Witt Clinton standing in his beautiful garden in the city of New York, listening, as it were, to hear the sound of the axes of Dea. Hart, Bumpus, Proctor, Babbitt, and a long list of names I have no room to refer to. And I see him turn to give the Commissions to the Chief Engineer and Surveyor; and what do I hear him say? 'The pioneers are there at work. You can accomplish your work now.'

Teach it to your children and grandchildren, that they are indebted to you for all the vast improvements made in the great west, as the result of hard toil and labor. Labor, which always precedes the development of everything great and good; labor, the God ordained, sanctioned and approved; labor that is so conducive to health and comfort and that brings its sure reward. I love labor, even in deepest old age. I would obey God and benefit myself by laboring when able, seeing it Is the only sure road leading to individual and national wealth and greatness, as well as to personal happiness and comfort.

Had our statesmen spent money without stint and built your railroads and canals, unless preceded and accompanied by the pioneers, it would have availed but little.

Education is a priceless acquisition; give it to the young by all means, but do not forget to teach them the great value and benefit of intelligent and well directed labor.

And now, gentlemen, I ask your patience in deciphering my trembling writing, and excuse bad spelling, for I see much of it. I have labored too long and hard to be able now to write elegantly.

Respectfully, your obedient servant,

WILLIAM TANNER."

East Liberty, Allen Co., Ind., March 13, 1865.

ROSWELL S. BURROWS

Roswell S. Burrows was born in Groton, Conn., on February 22, 1798. He attended Bacon Academy in Connecticut and entered the Sophomore Class at Yale College in 1819. Due to prolonged illness, he took a leave of absence in the fall of 1820 and never returned to college. However, in 1867, he was awarded an *honorary A.M. degree* by Yale College.

After receiving an inheritance from his grandfather, he used the capital to buy a cotton factory in Rhode Island. However, the factory did not yield the expected profit and he eventually sold it, incurring a loss due to fraudulent activity by another party.

ROSWELL BURROWS

In July 1824, he moved to Albion in Orleans County and with financial support from his father and father-in-law, he started a business as a merchant with a stock of goods. His younger brother, Lorenzo Burrows, later joined him as a clerk, and in 1826, they formed the firm R. S. & L. Burrows, engaging in business as dry goods merchants, produce dealers, and in warehousing and forwarding on the Erie Canal for over a decade.

When Burrows settled in Albion, the Erie Canal had been made navigable up to Lockport, and he was promised the appointment of *Collector of Canal revenue* by Canal Commissioner Wm. C. Bouck. He held this position from 1825 until 1832.

In 1827, Burrows built a warehouse on the canal in Albion. After selling their entire stock of goods, the Burrows brothers continued their warehouse business and also dealt in produce. When the general banking law went into operation, they established the Bank of

Albion in 1839, which operated for about twenty-seven years before being closed under the new National Banks policy. Burrows also organized the First National Bank of Albion in 1863.

ROSWELL S. BURROWS BLOCK DOWNTOWN ALBION

Over the years, Burrows held director and trustee positions in various corporations, railroad companies, telegraph companies, the Niagara Falls Suspension Bridge company, and a mining company. He was also a trustee of religious, benevolent, and literary institutions.

After the extensive and very valuable library of Professor Neander, of Germany, was offered for sale, Mr. Burrows acquired and donated the library to the Rochester Theological Seminary. This library consisted of several thousand volumes of rare and valuable books collected through many years by one of the best scholars of his time in Europe. It was valued between fifteen and twenty thousand dollars. He also offered a substantial gift of one hundred thousand dollars to the Theological Seminary, although it was never formally acted upon. As a businessman, Burrows is known for his shrewdness, clear-headedness and was never disturbed by panics or deceived by false appearances. His

139

prudent investment strategies, led to his considerable success in accumulating wealth through hard work and perseverance.

WILLIAM PENNIMAN

Judge Penniman was born in Peterborough, Hillsborough County, N.H., on August 5, 1793. After receiving a good education in his home state, he moved to Ontario County, New York, in September 1816, and then to Shelby, Orleans County, in October 1820. He acquired land in Shelby and lived there for about eight years before moving to Albion for over two years, and finally settling on a farm near Eagle Harbor in Barre, where he has resided ever since.

In 1825, Mr. Penniman was appointed as a Judge of the *Court of Common Pleas* for the newly organized Orleans County. He served in this capacity for five years. In 1831, he was elected Justice of the Peace for Barre and held this position until his move to Eagle Harbor, at which point he resigned.

In 1846, he represented Orleans County as a member of the Convention to revise the Constitution of the State of New York.

Judge Penniman was also a well-regarded school teacher for many years in Orleans County, teaching for fourteen winters and seven summers. He actively supported common schools, serving as Commissioner of schools and town inspector during his time in Shelby for eight years, and as town superintendent of schools in Barre for three years. He was known for being a popular and hardworking Justice of the Peace, even once issuing 108 summonses in one day, all of which were for Dr. William White. As a Judge, he was known for being firm, upright, and impartial, always aiming to support the right in his decisions. In all his official and social relations, he was known for his sound judgment, honesty, faithfulness, sagacity, and truthfulness. In his old age and retirement, he is respected by all who know him.

JESSE MASON

Jesse Mason was born in Cheshire, Massachusetts, on July 24, 1779. He worked as a farmer and moved to Phelps, Ontario County, New York around 1810 where he lived for six years before relocating to Barre, Orleans County, and settling on lot 17, in township 15, range 2, which is now owned by Wm. H. Pendry. In 1837, he sold his property in Barre and moved to Ohio, where he lived until his death in November 1854. During the War of 1812, Mr. Mason served one campaign and was among the last American soldiers to leave Buffalo when it was burned by the British. Described as a man of strong convictions in his political, moral, and religious beliefs, Jesse Mason was energetic, enterprising, and generous when it came to public affairs in his community. He took on more than his share of the work, expenses, and challenges involved in building roads, establishing schools and churches, and organizing society in the new area. He considered these tasks as labors of love, in which he found delight. Hannah Mason, Jesse Mason's wife, was the daughter of Rev. John Leland, a Baptist minister from Orange County, Virginia. She was born on December 18, 1778. Mr. Leland originally hailed from Massachusetts. While living in Virginia, he became close friends with President Jefferson, and it is said that Mr. Jefferson gained his first clear understanding of true democracy from observing the principle in action at a church where Mr. Leland was the pastor. Miss Leland married Mr. Mason in Cheshire around 1800, relocated with him to the west, and proved to be a supportive partner throughout his long and active life, sharing in his toils, hardships, and anxieties. She passed away on January 21, 1867.

STEPHEN B. THURSTON

"I was born in Westmoreland, Oneida Co., N.Y., January 3, 1808, and moved with my father, Caleb C. Thurston, to Barre to reside in the spring of 1814. My father being a farmer, brought me up to labor in that honorable calling. I resided with my father, attending school occasionally in winters, until I was twenty-two years old, when I bought seventy-six acres of land, part of lot 19, township 15, range 2, in Barre, on which I resided until April 1865, when I moved into the Village of Albion, where I now reside.

I was married to Miss Julianna Williams, daughter of Samuel Williams, of Barre, January 11, 1832. She was born in Burlington, Otsego Co., N.Y., April 5, 1812.

S. B. THURSTON."

Albion, July, 1867.

RUFUS HALLOCK

Rufus Hallock was born in Richmond, Chittenden County, Vermont, on November 7, 1802. His father was a farmer, and Rufus worked on the farm during the summers and attended school in the winters.

In February 1815, Rufus and his family moved to Murray, Orleans County, New York. In 1823, they moved to Louisville, St. Lawrence County for two years before settling in Barre, Orleans County. They lived on lot 43, township 14, range 2 of the Holland Purchase until Rufus's death in 1870. He married Susan Tucker from Shelby on July 3, 1826. Susan was born in New Hampshire on May 9, 1804, and passed away in Barre on May 18, 1868, at the age of 64.

Rufus Hallock accumulated a considerable amount of property through his hard work and thrift. He was a Baptist in his religious beliefs and was known as a respected Christian man.

He had a resolute and prompt character, and he overcame or moved many obstacles and adversities in his life. He also shared a story about his father, reflecting the courage and perseverance that were passed down to him and his descendants.

Traveling alone through the woods one day after he came to this county, he saw a bear and two cubs asleep under the roots of a fallen tree. Resolving to capture a cub, Mr. Hallock stealthily crept up to the spot where they lay and seized a cub by its hind legs and backed away dragging his prize and keeping his eyes fixed on the mother bear who followed after him growling and gnashing her teeth. He kept on in this way several rods until he backed and fell over a fallen tree, when the old bear, attracted by the cries of the cub left behind, returned to that and came after him no more. Mr. Hallock carried the cub home, tamed and raised it. He died Jan. 16, 1871.

"I was born in Londonderry, Rockingham County, New Hampshire, July 3rd, 1790. My father died when I was quite young. I lived with my grandfather John Clark until I was fifteen years of age; I then went to live with my Uncle, John Clark, Jr., in Salem, Massachusetts, where I remained until I was twenty-one years of age.

March, 1812, I went aboard the schooner Talbot, with Capt. George Burchmore, headed for the East Indies, with a miscellaneous cargo in the capacity of a common seaman.

Nothing worthy of note happened to us until we reached the equinoctial line, when the Captain said 'Old Neptune must come aboard that afternoon and the green ones must be shaved and sworn.' The oath which we were required to take in connection with the other raw hands, was as follows:

'I promise to never eat brown bread when I can get white; never to leave the pump until I call for a spell; and never to kiss the maid when I can kiss the mistress.'

The shaving process consisted, in brief, in placing the subject on the windlass, brushing his face with filth and scraping it off with an iron hoop, as a substitute razor, the subject in the meantime being in great danger of having the unsavory lather thrust into his mouth while taking the oath. Luckily for me I passed the ordeal more happily than my comrades, having, in advance, circulated a bottle of sailors 'O be joyful.'

Crossing the line is a great occasion for jokes and fun in general among sailors.

In due time, and without harm, we reached the vicinity of the capes, when we encountered heavy weather.

We ran twenty-three days under close reefed topsails, shipped a heavy sea on our starboard quarter which washed the whole length of the deck and carried away our bulwarks. We doubled the Cape at Good Hope and reached the Isle of France one hundred and thirteen days out from Salem. We lay there two months, discharged cargo, took in ballast and sailed for the Island of Sumatra. We were running into Lemonarger when we were met by an armed boat commanded by a man claiming to be King of Archeen, who demanded of us a duty on the pepper we might purchase. We regarded him and his crew as savages and pirates, and declining to trade with them, put to sea again. We ran to Soo-Soo and saw a sail approaching. That excited our apprehension of danger.

The Captain inquired if we would fight should the occasion demand it. Our unanimous response was 'we will.'

We were then stationed where we could do the best execution in self defense.

My station was on the side of the ship with an ax to cut off their hands should they attempt to board us. All the men were armed with deadly weapons, and we had a six pounder ready for any emergency.

The strange vessel sent a boat to us with a letter written in English, requesting us to trade with the king of Archeen, or in case of our refusal he would seize us and our vessel.

The night following being very dark we weighed anchor and put to sea, bidding his suspicious majesty good-bye.

We then sailed to an English port, Topanooley, where we took in a cargo of pepper and sailed for home.

We were to touch the Brazils to receive the orders of the owners. Here we were hailed by what we regarded as a hostile vessel and chased and fired at astern; and when forced to yield, to our great joy we found the strange vessel to be a man-of-war from our own Salem, named *The Grand Turk*, a privateer sent out to re-take our ship, which the owners supposed to be in the hands of the British.

The mutual congratulations between the crews of the *Talbot* and *The Grand Turk* were very pleasant to us all. Here we first learned of the war between the United States and Great Britain, which had then been doing its work of destruction ten months.

We entered the port of Pernambuco, March 18th, 1813, having been absent just one year. The cargo was put in Portuguese bottoms and sent to Europe. The second mate and myself remained to take care of the ship until November, 1815, when I left for Gibraltar on board the Rebecca, with a cargo of hides and sugar. We stopped at Gibraltar a few days, then ran down to Naples and discharged cargo and took in a miscellaneous loading and returned homewards, landing in New York where I was discharged, and started for Salem where I arrived January 1, 1816.

I give the names of the places in the East Indies as I heard them pronounced. I may have spelled them wrong. Thus ends my seafaring life.

July 5th, 1816, I left Boston for Western New York. I traveled through Albany, taking the Great Western Turnpike, walking on foot all the way, until near Auburn when a traveler kindly permitted me to ride with him, saying he would take me to where I could find good land.

We passed through Rochester, and taking the Ridge Road came to Sheldon's Corners, now West Gaines. We then turned south, and traveling about a mile reached a school house just as the school was out for noon. A little sunny-faced girl ran up to us and said to the man who had so kindly assisted me: 'Well dad, we are glad you have come for we are about half starved out.'

That man was Gideon Freeman and the little girl was Sally Freeman.

I looked around a little and finally bought the farm on which I have ever since resided, part of lot fifty, in township fifteen, range two, of the Holland Purchase, lying in the north-western part of Barre, then Gaines, near the south end of what is now known as *The Long Bridge* over the Erie Canal. My land cost me five dollars per acre. I took an article for it and was able to pay in full in about eight years.

I underbrushed five acres, built a log house and went back to Salem.

I was married November 25, 1816, to Abigail Simonds, who was born in Salem Massachusetts, July 6th, 1790.

While I was preparing to start on our journey west I was accosted by an old sailor friend who inquired where I was going? I said 'to the Holland Purchase.' Said he, 'where can that be, I never heard of that place before.' I told him 'It was a fine country in Western New York;' that 'I had bought a farm there, built a log house and was going to live there.' Said he, 'I would not give the gold I could scrape from a card of gingerbread for the entire Holland Purchase.' But he did not know everything.

My wife and I left Salem for our new western home with a span of horses and a wagon. We were twenty-one days on the road. We arrived at my place and began house-keeping January 1st, 1817, without a table, a chair or a bedstead, all of which I soon made in true Genesee pioneer style.

For many years in the settlement I was called 'Sailor Clark' to distinguish me from another Clark who was, I am happy to say, a very decent man.

Money being very hard to get, we made black salts, which became practically a legal tender or substitute for money.

I and my neighbor, Mr. Benjamin Foot, worked together in the manufacture, but after a time he sold to a Mr. Elijah Shaw, who conducted the business with me until that necessary calling was played out.

Mr. Shaw and myself are the only persons living in this school district who came in as early as 1816.

My wife having been reared in the city knew nothing of spinning wheels, though she was a good housekeeper, but under the influence of her neighbor's example, she urged me to raise flax and purchase her a Pioneer Piano, which I did, bringing home one of the largest size on my shoulder from a distance of several miles; and before long she could discourse as melodious music as any in the settlement.

In the early part of my pioneer life, like others, I had to cut browse for my cow. One evening I went out and felled a tree, thinking it would certainly fall west, but alas for my sagacity, it fell east striking our house, breaking down about half the roof and alarming me greatly for the safety of my family. However no one was hurt except by being badly frightened. The roof was easily repaired, but a fine mirror, a very elegant one for a new country, which my wife's father, who was a seaman, had brought from Hamburg, in Europe, was broken into fragments, and could not be repaired.

During the cold seasons many of the settlers suffered for the necessaries of life, but happily for me and mine we did not suffer. I went east with my team far enough to find all the provisions we needed and brought home a full supply for all our necessities.

The fall of 1824 was a sad period to me. My wife died October 20th of this year.

I desire here to record my grateful sense of the kindness of our neighbors during her sickness. Their attentions were timely, cordial and continued. All those kind women then living in the district are dead except Mrs. Benjamin Foot.

I married my present wife, Elizabeth Stephens, in Gaines, March 20th, 1825. She was born in Middletown, Rutland County, Vt., June 20th 1806.

We left our pioneer log house and moved into our present dwelling in 1825. About this time the boats were seen passing along in 'Gov. Clinton's big ditch,' the Erie Canal, on the north border of my farm, connecting the great commercial and agricultural interests of our country. And I trust that our natural and artificial channels of trade may remain open, and the love of freedom among our people continue to aid, with the blessing of God, to preserve and perpetuate our nationality, restore the Union of these States and the free institutions of our country.

In 1825 I experienced religion, and about 1829 my wife and myself connected ourselves with the Methodist Episcopal Church, in whose communion we still remain.

JONATHAN CLARK."

Barre, April 7th, 1864.

OLIVER BENTON

Oliver Benton was born in Ashfield, Massachusetts, on April 10th, 1791. He moved to Barre in 1812 and married Elvira Starr on May 15th, 1817. Mr. Benton acquired a large piece of land two miles south of Albion where he lived. After the town of Barre was established, the first post office in the area was created around 1818 or 1819 and was named Barre. Mr. Benton was appointed as the postmaster, a position he held for many years. He was also well-known as a tavern keeper on the Oak Orchard Road, and his spacious house was often used for town meetings, balls, and other social gatherings.

Following the death of William Lewis, the first Sheriff, Mr. Benton was elected as the Sheriff of Orleans

County in November 1825 and served for three years. He passed away on February 12th, 1848.

MOSES SMITH

Moses Smith was born in Newburg, New York, February 6th, 1785. He married Chloe Dickinson, of Phelps, New York, April 11th, 1811, and moved to Barre, Orleans County, Nov. 16th, 1824, and took a deed from the Holland Company of a part of lot two, township fifteen, range one, on which he continued to reside until his death May 16th, 1869. He had fourteen children, eight of whom survived him. He was a carpenter and joiner by trade, but the main occupation of his life was farming.

He was of Scotch descent. His grandmother emigrated from Scotland and settled on what is known in history as the Hasbrouck place, in the South part of the city of Newburgh, on two hundred and fifty acres. On this farm Mr. Moses Smith was born, and on this farm stands the celebrated building known as *Washington's Headquarters*.

ANTHONY TRIPP

Anthony Tripp was born in Providence, Rhode Island. He moved with his father's family to Columbia County, N.Y., during his childhood and grew up there. He later got married and settled in Delaware County. In 1811, he came to Barre and acquired one hundred acres of land, which was claimed to be the first land issued by the Holland Company in Barre. Due to the outbreak of war the following year, Anthony Tripp didn't settle on his property at that time. In 1817, his eldest son Samuel began clearing the land and built a log house, where the family moved in 1824. Anthony Tripp lived there until his passing. His children were Samuel, Talitha (who married Sylvester Patterson), Stephen R. (who married Ruth Mott), Anthony, Alvah (who married Jane H. Blakely and unfortunately passed away in 1866 due to a tragic accident), Mary (who married Psalter S. Mason), and Almeron (who married Sylvia Burns).

ALLEN PORTER

Allen Porter was born in Franklin County, Mass., on August 24, 1795. He married Electa Scott on December 22, 1819.

When Mr. Porter was a child, his family relocated to Seneca County, N.Y. During the War of 1812, he was drafted while still a minor and stationed on the frontier. He volunteered in Buffalo to reinforce troops in Fort Erie, and participated in the sortie from that fort in September 1814.

In the fall of 1815, he acquired a farm in the town of Barre and relocated there in March 1816. He started clearing the land by felling trees and has lived there ever since. When Mr. Porter arrived, there were only about fifteen families settled in Barre.

Prior to his arrival, the Holland Company had cut a road from the Oak Orchard Road to Shelby Center, which now passes the County Poor House. Some lots had been taken, but no dwellings had been built along the road in Barre, and there were no settlements in this town south of the Poor House Road and west of the Oak Orchard Road. Mr. Porter recalls transporting wheat from his farm to Rochester and selling it there for thirty-one cents per bushel. He also remembers buying salt for five dollars per barrel, nails for seventeen cents per pound, and other goods at similarly high prices.

Mr. Porter has served in various civil and military offices and is a well-known and highly respected citizen.

ELIZUR HART

Elizur Hart was born in Durham, Greene County, N.Y., on May 23rd, 1803. His father, Dea. Joseph Hart, moved to Seneca County, N.Y., in 1806, and then to Barre, Orleans County, in October, 1812. It took several years after he arrived in Barre before there was a school in his father's neighborhood, and so Elizer didn't receive much formal education. While living with his father, he mainly worked on clearing land and farming, growing up like other boys in the new county, with little exposure to books, business, or the world outside his community. Around 1827, he was elected constable, a position he held for two years. His work then required him to spend a lot of time in Albion.

He had about five hundred dollars, and his brother William entrusted him with a similar sum for their joint benefit. Elizur used the money to buy small promissory notes and lend small amounts to customers, sometimes helping debtors whose assets were being collected. At this time, his father deeded one hundred acres of his land to his sons William and Elizur for five hundred dollars. They were joint owners for some years until William gave Elizur the five hundred dollars and all its profits for the entire one hundred acres, which is situated in the village of Albion and is still owned and

153

occupied by William. This land's increased value has made William a wealthy man.

As Mr. Hart's means increased, he began investing in bonds and mortgages, as well as land issues by the Holland Company. He rarely incurred losses and generally profited from his trades, continuing this business for many years. In 1852, he became an assignee, and soon after, a receiver of the property of the Orleans Insurance Company. When the old Bank of Orleans failed, he was appointed its receiver.

ELIZER HART

On February 10th, 1860, in partnership with Mr. Joseph M. Cornell, he established The Orleans County Bank in Albion, with a capital of $100,000. He served as President of this bank for its entire existence. When all State Banks were superseded by National Banks, he transformed his institution and established The Orleans County National Bank in its place on Aug. 9th, 1865, of which he was President for the rest of his life.

Mr. Hart was not a speculative businessman, risking money in uncertain ventures. His investments were based on careful calculations and usually yielded anticipated profits. Diligent and exemplary in all his habits, he started with little, without any help or influence from wealthy connections, and became one of the affluent country bankers in the state, amassing a fortune amounting to hundreds of thousands of dollars at his death.

In his will, he bequeathed fifty thousand dollars to the Presbyterian Church in Albion, of which he was a member, for the construction of a house of worship, and an endowment of five thousand dollars for the church's Sunday school. Mr. Hart married Miss Loraine Field in May, 1835, who died on Feb. 11th, 1847. He then married Miss Cornelia King on Oct. 16th, 1849.

He is survived by his children Frances E., who married Oliver C. Day and lives in Adrian, Michigan; Jennie K.; and E. Kirk, who married Louisa Sanderson, resides in Albion, and is the Cashier and principal owner of the Orleans County National Bank.

Elizur Hart passed away on August 13th, 1870.

JARVIS M. SKINNER

"I was born in Providence, Saratoga Co. N.Y., June 3, 1799. I married Mary Delano, Feb. 14, 1822. She was born in Providence, Dec. 25, 1800.

I labored on a farm, of which my father had a lease, in the summer season, and with my father in the winter, a part of the time, in his shop, making saddles and harnesses, he being a saddler by trade.

When I became of age, I hired out to work on a farm for Earl Stimson, then a large farmer in Galway, first eight months, at $11 a month, then a year for $110. My wages for this work, deducting my clothing bills, constituted all my capital.

On the 18th day of March, 1822, I started for the Holland Purchase, and came alone to Durfee Delano's a little west of Eagle Harbor, in Gaines.

I bought fifty-five acres of land of Winsor Paine, for which I agreed to give him $250. $100 down, my horse, saddle and bridle, for $80, and $70 worth of saddles, to be delivered in a year.

I worked in my place until the next fall; Mrs. Paine did my washing and cooking and I furnished a portion of the provisions. I chopped and cleared and sowed with wheat six acres; raised one acre of spring wheat, and one hundred bushels of corn. I returned to Saratoga in the fall, made the saddles in the winter, to pay for my farm, and in January 1823, moved my wife to our new home in Barre, where we have since resided, on lot 33, township 15, range 2.

JARVIS M. SKINNER."

Dated, Dec 1, 1863.

NATHANIEL BRALEY

Nathaniel was born in Savoy, Berkshire County, Massachusetts, on December 14, 1796, and has always been a farmer. He moved to Palmyra in 1801, then settled in Gaines, Orleans County, New York, in 1819. He married Sarah Wickham in 1821; she was born in Chatham, Columbia County, on July 15, 1799, and moved to Gaines in 1816. Mr. Braley moved to Barre, where he currently resides, in 1838.

LUCIUS STREET

"I was born in West Springfield, Massachusetts, Dec. 19, 1795. My father gave me a good common school education for those times and brought me up in his occupation, as a farmer. I followed the business of teaching school for several winters, when I was a young man.

May 5, 1818, my brother Chapin and myself started from my father's house in Hinsdale, Mass., on foot, with knapsacks on our backs, for the Genesee Country.

After going to Batavia and looking over the towns of Orangeville and China, we came to Barre and settled on lot 3, township 14, range 2, of the Holland Purchase, about two miles south of Barre Center where we still reside. (1864.)

We took our article for our land, May 18, 1818, and immediately began chopping, boarding with a family named Cuthbert.

I taught a district school, in all, seven winters, and singing school two terms.

One of our neighbors, Henry Edgerton, a strong, athletic man, carried a bushel and a half of wheat on his back, to Farwell's mill, in Clarendon, eight miles, got it ground and brought it home.

In the fall of 1820, my brother and myself, having partially recovered from fever and ague, from which we had suffered, and getting somewhat homesick, went on foot back to Mass., being quite discouraged at the prospect of ever paying for our land, as the price of produce was so low. We wanted to sell out.

Finding no opportunity to sell our articles, we worked out for farmers in Massachusetts the next season, at $8 a month, then the common wages, and returned to Barre, in the fall of 1821, to sell our improvements, but found no buyers.

We had agreed to give six dollars an acre for our land, on ten years' time, the first two years without interest. At this time, wheat was worth in Rochester from thirty-one to thirty-seven cents a bushel.

While I was teaching school in Springfield, Mass., in 1821, I saw Esq. Brewster of Riga, Monroe Co., N.Y., who, with one of his neighbors, had come to Springfield from Riga, with two large loads of flour, drawn by four yoke of oxen. The flour sold for $5 a barrel. They sold their oxen and Genesee sleds, bought a span of horses and an old sleigh and returned to Riga.

In the summer of 1822, I boarded with Mr. Edgerton, and worked two days of every nine for him, to pay my board. That season I cleared, fenced and sowed ten acres with wheat, from which next season I harvested 255 bushels of good wheat. The canal being then navigable west as far as Brockport, I could sell my wheat there for $1 a bushel.

My brother and myself divided our land, giving me 109 acres. I then abandoned the intention of selling, and Nov. 16, 1823, was married to Miss Martha M. Buckland, daughter of John A. Buckland, of South Barre.

In those days we were required by law to train as soldiers, two days in each year: on the first Monday in June and September, company training, and one day for a *general muster*, which was often held at Oak Orchard Creek. We were often called to meet at Oak Orchard and made the journey, 16 miles, on foot, carrying our gun and equipment and paying our own expenses. We would drill until near night, then on being dismissed, return home the same day, if indeed we were able to reach home before the next morning.

In the early times in this county, inspectors of Common Schools were allowed no compensation for their services, the honor of the office being deemed sufficient remuneration. After serving the town in that office several years gratis, Dr. J. K. Brown and I agreed and declared to the electors, that if appointed to that office again we would pay our fines of $10 and thus relieve ourselves of the service, whereupon the town voted to give us seventy-five cents each per day, for the time we might be on duty.

Under circumstances like those, not as many were seeking the small town offices then as now.

Bears, wolves, wild cats, deer, raccoons, hedgehogs and other wild animals, were plenty here then.

In the summer of 1818, my brother and I being at work chopping on our farm, heard a hog squeal, and saw a bear walking off very deliberately carrying a hog in its paws. We gave chase and as we came near, the bear dropped his prey and ran off, he had killed the hog. We then made *a dead fall*, as it was called, in which to entrap the bear, which was a pen made by driving stakes into the ground, and interweaving them with brush horizontally, in which the hog was placed. Into this pen we expected the bear would come and spring a trap, which would let a weight fall upon him. It proved a success, for in the morning we found the bear in the pen; he had sprung the trap, and a spike of the dead fall through his leg held him fast.

Religious meetings were early established and maintained at South Barre and Barre Center. Deacon Orange Starr was among the foremost in these meetings.

Many pleasant reminiscences of pioneer life might be mentioned, for though we endured many hardships and privations, we had plenty of sport mingled with them, giving us a pleasant variety of mirthful enjoyment. Major Daniel Bigelow, being a good horseman, and having no horse, broke one of his oxen to the saddle, and was accustomed to ride him through the settlement.

Riding out one day, his ox being very thirsty and coming near a large puddle of water, started forward to the drink on double-quick time, and plunging into the water, stopped so suddenly as to throw his good natured rider over his head, sprawling into the mud, much to the amusement of those looking on.

I am a descendant, on my mother's side, of the seventh generation, from Samuel Chapin, an early pioneer of Springfield, Mass., who settled there when only three families were in place. At a gathering of his descendants at Springfield, on Sept. 17, 1862, fifteen hundred such descendants were present. Dr. J. G. Holland, known as Timothy Titcomb, delivered a poem on the occasion, which he said he was requested to do because he had married into the Chapin family.

I am also descended in the sixth generation on my father's side, from Rev. Nicholas Street, who came from England and was ordained pastor over the first church in New Haven, in 1659.

LUCIUS STREET."

Dated, Barre, Feb 25, 1864.

THOMAS W. ALLIS

Extracts from the local history of Thomas W. Allis, written by himself for the Pioneer Association.

"I was born in Gorham, Ontario Co., N.Y., Nov. 1, 1798 . My father died in the year 1805, and I was brought up from that time until I attained my majority, in the family of an uncle, in Hampshire, Mass.

In March 1820, in company with a younger brother, I moved to Murray, in Orleans County, to what is now the town of Kendall.

We brought with us four barrels of flour, one barrel of pork, one barrel of whiskey and a bed.

We located three and one-fourth miles north of the Ridge Road, and one mile east of the Transit Line.

In going from the Ridge to our place, we passed but one family and they lived in a log house, in the woods, with no plastering between the logs, with only part of the ground covered by a floor, a bark roof, and no chimney.

We hired our provisions, cooked, and lived with a family nearby, in a log cabin similar to the one above described.

We bought a contract for one hundred acres of land, by the terms of which we agreed to pay $300 for the improvements, and $600 for the soil.

We kept *bachelor's hall* there most of the time for four years.

I soon bought fifty acres more land, with six acres improvement on it, for which I agreed to pay $450. But few families were then north of the Ridge, in that section of country.

I worked at clearing land and raising crops. Wheat was worth only three shillings per bushel, delivered in Rochester.

The first plow in our settlement, I bought in company with two neighbors. We walked to Gaines village, bought one of Wood's patent plows and carried it on our backs from the Ridge Road three and one-fourth miles to our home.

I was married Nov. 18, 1824, to Miss Elizabeth Clements, of Queensbury, Warren Co. N.Y.

On the 9th of January, 1826, my house was burned with all my furniture and clothing and one year's provision. Our neighbors turned out and drew logs and rolled up part of a house, but a snow storm came on and stopped the work before it was finished. My brother and myself afterwards built a log house, commencing on Thursday at noon, built a stone chimney, finished, and moved into it the next Saturday. Size of the house was sixteen by thirteen feet. We lived in this small house about two years and then I finished the house which had been begun by my neighbors soon after the fire.

I resided in the house last built about fourteen years.

I paid interest on the purchase money, for the first hundred acres I bought, to about the amount of the principal before I took a deed.

I afterwards bought fifty-three acres for $450, for which I paid with the avails of one crop of wheat.

In 1837, I bought a timber lot of 48 acres.

In 1840 I built a frame house, thirty by seventy feet, which cost me $2,000.

In March, 1860, I sold my farm in Kendall, part of which I had held for forty years, and bought a house and fifteen acres of land in Albion, on which I now reside.

THOMAS W. ALLIS."

Albion, January, 1863.

Mr. T W Allis, above referred to, was for many years one of the solid men of the town of Kendall, honored and respected by all who knew him. He was a Justice of the Peace and held various other town offices. Having acquired a competency, by many years steady toil and economy, he retired from hard labor on a farm, to a village residence, where he is now (1871) spending a quiet old age, in the enjoyment of the fruits of his labors.

JOSEPH BARKER

Extracts from the local history of Col. Joseph Barker, written by himself.

"I was born in Todmorden, Lancashire, England, September 21st, 1802, and emigrated with my father's family to America in the spring of 1816. I arrived in the town of Seneca, Ontario County, in July of that year, and resided there until I bought the farm in Barre, in November, 1825, on which I now reside. I was married in October, 1822, to Miss Submit Cowles, who was born in Heath, Franklin County, Massachusetts, by whom I had nine children. My wife died February 15th, 1851. I lived a widower two and a half years, and then married Widow Elizabeth Guernsey, who was born in Middleburgh, Schoharie Co., N.Y., March 19th, 1810.

In the fall of 1819, I started with another man from Seneca, N.Y., to go to Lundy's Lane, in Canada. We traveled on foot with knapsacks on our backs. Passing through Rochester, then a small town and very muddy, we took the Ridge Road, then thinly settled. Before we arrived at Harland Corners our provisions gave out; we tried to buy some bread; could get none; then tried begging, with no better success. We went on to Buck's tavern in the Eleven Mile Woods. It was very dark when we got there and rained very hard. We had not a dry thread in our clothes, and our shoes and stockings were full of mud and water. Buck's tavern was a log house with a *Dutch fireplace*, and had a good rousing fire. After taking some rum and supper, we hung our other garments up to dry and went to bed. The next morning we started early, and after getting through the woods, I went into a house and bought six pence worth of bread which lasted us through to Lundy's Lane. We stayed there three weeks and returned home.

In September, 1823, I set out to look me up a farm; came by way of Batavia, and through the Indian Reservation to a place now called Alabama Center, and took up sixty acres of land lying about three fourths of a mile north of that place. I chopped the trees on about one acre, when finding half of my lot was swamp I felt sick of it and left for home, where I stayed, working out until the fall of 1825, then started again and bought the place on which I have ever since resided in Barre, lot fifty-four, township fourteen, range two.

I moved to my place in January, 1826. There was a shanty on my land with a shingled roof. I got ready to begin work about February 1st, and measured off ten acres of woods for my next year's work to chop, clear, fence and sow with wheat; all of which I did, sowing the last of my wheat in October. The reason of my being so late sowing wheat was, my wife was taken sick soon after harvest. I could get no girl to work and I was obliged to take care of my sick wife and do all my work indoors and out of doors. I had to milk, churn, work butter, wash and iron clothes, mix and bake bread, and in fact do all there was to be done. I worked on my fallow days and nights whenever I could leave my sick wife. At last I hired a girl, but she stayed with us only four or five days, and I then had to do housework again. My wife recovered so as to be up and about the forepart of October.

I worked out some the next winter to get potatoes to eat and to plant and to pay my doctor's bill. I bought four small pigs in the summer, and beachnuts being plenty they grew finely and when killed weighed about one hundred and twenty pounds apiece. The pork was rather soft but tasted good.

The second winter I chopped about seven acres. The weather was fine, but on the night of April 13th, the wind blowing a fearful gale while we were snugly in bed, took the roof off our shanty leaving us in bed, but with neither a roof or chamber floor in our house. I got up and put out the fire; we put on our clothes and, taking our little girl, went to Mr. Russells, our nearest neighbor, about forty rods, where we stayed until, with the help of our kind neighbors, we got up the body of another log house. In two or three weeks we had our house so far made that we moved into it and lived in it all summer without a chimney. In the fall I built a Dutch fireplace and a stick chimney.

It was about two years after I moved on my lot before the highway was chopped out either way north and south from me. The logs and underbrush were cut so that we could drive a team through. I was poor when I came here and I live according to my means. One-fourth pound of tea lasted us over seven months. I bought a barrel of pork and half a barrel of beef, when I got the tea, and they were all gone in about the same time together.

We had plenty of flour and some potatoes. My cow was not used to the woods, and sometimes I could find her again and sometimes I could not, so we were obliged to eat only our bread and potatoes for a meal. I thought it rather dry living to work hard on, but we lived through it, always hoping for 'the better time coming.'

The next year I fatted three fine hogs and put them all down for home use. The third summer I had over 20 acres cleared and had got to living pretty comfortably. In July of this year I was elected Second Sergeant in Capt. Gates Infantry Company rather against my wishes. I however accepted.

In August following I was taken sick with fever and ague which lasted me three months. I could hire no men to work for me for love or money. Almost everybody was sick this year. The neighbors turned out however, late in the fall and sowed about six acres with wheat for me, and I hired a boy a month to husk corn and dig potatoes. About the time the boy got through work the ague left me and I was pretty well all the next winter.

The next spring I had three fits of ague, then sores came all over my face. I had no more ague shakes for the next three or four years.

About this time my wife was taken sick with inflammation in the bowels just at the commencement of the wheat harvest. I had fourteen acres to harvest and no one to help me. I got a physician to attend to my wife, and my little girl and myself nursed her as well as we could; and when I could spare I went to my harvest field and worked, whether by day or night. Thus I harvested my fourteen acres and took care of my wife. Just before I finished cutting my wheat however, I was again taken with chills and began to shake, and kept on shaking about an hour. I did not stop cradling, but when the fever came on, I had to quit and steer for the house and had a hard time getting there. I had two more fits, when my face broke out in sores as formerly and I had no more fever and ague.

My wife getting no better, I went to find a girl to take care of her, feeling I was not able to take proper care of myself, much less her. I traveled all day, found plenty of girls that wanted to go out to spin, but would not do housework. I went a second and third day with like results, and came home sick both in body and mind, and found my wife some better. I finally succeeded in getting a woman to help until my wife was able to be about.

I kept chopping and clearing my land as fast as I could alone, for I was not able to hire. I changed work occasionally with my neighbors, and sometimes hired a day's work. My crops were sometimes good, sometimes poor; but I got along and made money.

In July, 1833, I was elected Captain over the Company in which I had served as Sergeant over four years and I was afterward elected Colonel. This military office, as everybody knows, was not a money making business in those days; but I had got into it and determined to carry it through to the best of my ability. It cost me much time and money, for which I received nothing back. I had the honor of commanding as good a regiment as there was in the county, and felt proud of it.

I did military duty nineteen years; eleven years as an officer, serving as a Captain before I was naturalized, or a voter in town or State. I resigned all military office April 20th, 1839.

I have labored steadily as a farmer, enjoying good health, except having the ague, as I have stated, and had a good degree of prosperity attending my labors.

JOSEPH BARKER."

March 9th, 1863.

ENOS RICE

Enos Rice was born in Conway, Hampshire County, Massachusetts, in 1790. In 1804, he moved with his father's family to Madison County, N.Y. In June 1816, carrying a pack on his back, he arrived in Barre, Orleans County and settled on lot eighteen, in township fifteen, range two, where he cleared about twenty acres. After living in Shelby for a few years, he purchased a farm near Porter's Corners in 1831, where he has resided ever since. Mr. Rice started with little wealth, but through hard work and thrift, he accumulated enough property to ensure a comfortable old age.

LUTHER PORTER

"My father, Stephen Porter, was born in Lebanon, Connecticut. About the year 1812 or '13 he started with his wife and five children on an ox sled, with one yoke of small oxen to come to 'York State.' He had but few articles of furniture and but $65 in money. After a journey of twenty-two days, with extraordinary good luck, he landed in Smyrna, Chenango County, N.Y., with cash reduced to $18. Here he hired an old log house in which he resided one year. Then he hitched his oxen to the old sled, and with his traps and family aboard, started for Ontario County. After traveling seven days, he arrived at his place of destination and hired a house and twenty-five acres of land.

In the fall of 1815, he took an article from the Holland Land Company, of the west hundred acres of lot 40, township 14, range 2, in Barre, the same on which I now reside, about three fourths of a mile west of Porter's Corners. In March following, in company with Allen Porter, Samuel Porter and Joseph Rockwood, he started with provisions for five weeks, to make a beginning on their lands. They established their depot of provisions at the house of Dea. Ebenezer Rogers, in the south part of what is now the village of Albion.

They took what provisions they wanted for a week on their backs, with their axes, and started through the woods to their lands, about five miles away, the snow being about knee deep.

The first thing in order was to select a place to build their cabin. The site was fixed on the farm now owned by J. W. Stocking, about twenty rods east of where Stocking's house stands. They cut such poles as they could carry and built their first cabin ten by twelve feet square, covered it with split basswood troughs, got it tenable, and the colony moved in and took possession the same day. They cut hemlock boughs and spread them on the ground, covering them with blankets, which made a good bed. The room not occupied by the bed served for culinary and dining purposes. After thus preparing their house they commenced chopping in earnest, working through the week until Saturday afternoon, when they all returned to Mr. Rogers' to spend the Sabbath and get another weeks' provisions. In this way they worked until they had chopped about five acres each, when they all returned to Ontario Co., to spend the summer.

In January, 1820, my father moved his family to his new home in Barre, where he made a comfortable residence the remainder of his life, and died in the fall of 1831, aged 53 years.

My father paid little more than the interest on the purchase money for his land, while he lived. It was paid for by his sons and has been a home for the family ever since.

In the spring of 1816 there was no house occupied by a family in Barre, west of the Oak Orchard Road, on the line on which my father located, although several were in process of erection. My mother died on the homestead, August 1857, aged 77 years. I was my father's second son, and now own and reside on the old premises, to which I have made additions by purchase.

I was born in Ashfield, Mass., in 1805, and came to this county with my father, in 1820, being then about fifteen years old.

I have had abundant experience in pioneer life. I have chopped and logged and cleared land. I boiled black salts three or four years, a part of the time barefoot, because my father was too poor to furnish me shoes, with little other damage than the occasional loss of a toe nail, or a small wound in the foot from sharp stubs.

I have lived through it all, and by dint of economy and industry have advanced from poverty to competence.

I have held various offices in the gift of my fellow citizens. I was Supervisor of the town of Barre from 1857 to 1862, five successive years.

There was no school in my neighborhood for several years after 1820. The first district school house built there was erected at Sheldon's Corners. The district was afterwards divided and a log school house built about a mile north of Ferguson's Corners. Again the district was divided and now stands as district No. 12, with a good school house.

I married my first wife, Lydia Scoot, daughter of Capt. Justin Scoot, of Ontario County, Oct. 20, 1830. She died Dec. 3, 1842. I married for my second wife, Caroline Culver, daughter of Orange Culver of South Barre, June 27, 1844, with whom I am still living.

LUTHUR PORTER."

Barre, May 27, 1863.

NEHEMIAH INGERSOLL

Nehemiah Ingersoll was born in Stanford, Dutchess Co., N.Y., in 1786. In 1816, he moved to Batavia for a year or two before buying a farm in Elba, five miles north of Batavia. He ran a public house there for several years. In April 1822, along with James P. Smith and Chillian F. Buckley, he purchased one hundred acres of land in Albion from William Bradner for $4,000. Mr. Ingersoll later acquired all of Smith and Buckley's interest in this land.

After buying the land, Mr. Ingersoll had part of it surveyed and laid out into village lots, anticipating the growth of a town. While he didn't immediately move to Albion, he began to develop his property there. He and his partners constructed a large warehouse on the canal at the foot of Platt Street and a framed building for a store on the corner of Main and Canal Streets, where the Empire block now stands. Ingersoll & Wells (Dudley Wells) operated a store at this location, while business was conducted in the warehouse by Ingersoll and Lewis P. Buckley.

NEHEMIAH INGERSOLL

Mr. Ingersoll played a significant role in securing the location of the County buildings in Albion. When competing with the Village of Gaines, he offered the grounds on which the Court House now stands as a free gift to the commissioners appointed to locate the Court House. This offer was eventually accepted, and the location was secured in Albion.

In early 1826, he relocated to Albion and became prominently involved in organizing Orleans County from Genesee County and establishing the necessary institutions for a new county to function.

In 1835, having sold or arranged the sale of most of his land in Albion, Mr. Ingersoll moved to Detroit and pursued significant business ventures, which unfortunately led to substantial losses. In 1845, he relocated to Lee, Oneida County, N.Y., where he lived until his death.

He married Miss Polly Halsey in his youth, but she passed away in 1831. His second wife, Miss Elizabeth C. Brown of Lee, outlived him. Mr. Ingersoll passed away on February 21, 1868, at the age of eighty-two. He was buried beside his first wife in Mount Albion Cemetery after his remains were brought to Albion, as per his request.

His second wife, Mrs. Elizabeth C. Ingersoll, died on August 17, 1869. After her marriage, she lived in Albion for several years and shared her husband's attachment to the place and its people. This was demonstrated in a generous gift of ten thousand dollars, which she bequeathed to the Protestant Episcopal Church in Albion, as both Mr. Ingersoll and his wife were members of that congregation.

JUSTICE INGERSOLL

Hon. Justice Ingersoll was born in Stanford, Dutchess County, N.Y., in 1794. He learned the trade of tanner.

When the war broke out with Great Britain in 1812, he joined the United States army as an *ensign* in the twenty-third regiment of infantry. He fought on the northern frontier in several battles and was part of the famous charge on Queenstown Heights. Due to his meritorious service, he was promoted to the rank of Captain.

In one of the battles in Canada while serving as Captain of Infantry, he was wounded in the foot. Despite his injury, he refused to leave his company and, unable to walk, he continued with his men by mounting a horse. In another engagement, he was shot through the body, but he decided not to have the bullet removed as doing so would require cutting away a portion of his rib, which would likely cause him to stoop for the rest of his life.

He was well-liked by his company and highly esteemed by Gen. Scott, under whom he served.

In 1818, he moved to Elba, Genesee County, N.Y., and later settled at Shelby Center in Orleans County. There, he ran a tanning and shoe-making business and also served as Justice of the Peace.

When the canal became navigable and Medina began to be settled as a village, he relocated there, built a large tannery, and transferred his business to that location. He was appointed Indian Agent and postmaster at Medina by President Jackson, and he also served as a Judge of Orleans County Courts.

After his tannery accidentally burned down and his business faced other setbacks, he moved to Detroit with his brother Nehemiah in 1835 to pursue the leather business on a large scale, but they were ultimately not successful.

Mr. Ingersoll was known for his firm and persistent character, as well as for being active and enterprising. He was admired among his acquaintances for the uprightness of his conduct and his polite manners. He passed away in 1845.

LORENZO BURROWS.

Lorenzo Burrows was born in Groton, Connecticut, on March 15, 1805. In his youth, he attended the Academy at Plainfield, Connecticut, and Westerly, Rhode Island. In November 1824, he came to Albion, New York, to assist his brother, Roswell S. Burrows, as his clerk. He continued in that role until 1826 when he became a business partner with his brother under the firm name of R. S. & L. Burrows.

He played a key role in establishing the Bank of Albion in 1839 and subsequently served as its Cashier, focusing on bank operations and also undertook the responsibilities of Receiver of the Farmer's Bank of Orleans. In November 1848, he was elected a Member of the House of Representatives in Congress for the district that included Niagara and Orleans Counties. He was re-elected to Congress in November 1850 and served for a total of four years.

After his tenure in Congress, he ceased active involvement in the bank's operations. He was elected as the *Comptroller of the State of New York* in November 1855, serving one term of two years. In February 1858, he was appointed as a Regent of the University of the State of New York, a position he has held ever since.

In addition to these roles, he previously served as the County Treasurer of Orleans County in 1840, and as the Supervisor of the town of Barre in 1845. He also held the position of *Assignee in Bankruptcy* for the county of Orleans under the law of 1841. In 1862, he was appointed as one of the Commissioners of Mount Albion Cemetery, a position that involves significant labor but no salary. The beautiful terraces, trees, paths, and other improvements in the cemetery are a testament to his dedication and skill in this role.

Since leaving Congress, Mr. Burrows has mainly focused on managing the offices mentioned above, looking after his considerable real estate holdings in Albion and elsewhere, and enjoying his leisure time with family and friends, all made possible by the ample fortune he secured earlier in life.

GEORGE E. MIX

"I was born in Greenfield, Saratoga County, N.Y. My father's name was Abiathar Mix. In May, 1817, when I was less than one year old, my father moved with his family to what is now Barre, Orleans County, N.Y. There I had my bringing up and I have ever since resided. My Genesee cradle was a sap trough. Genesee school rooms were log houses, log barns and other accommodations.

I stayed at home and worked on the farm summers, and went to school winters when I could, until I was eighteen years of age. My father then gave me my time, saying he had nothing else he could give me then, but that I could make his house my home.

After that I worked by the day and month summers, and attended school winters, went several terms to an Academy.

At the age of twenty-three I commenced teaching district school and taught five winters in succession. During those five years I traveled considerably in the western and southern states, and became quite a radical reformer in sentiment.

I was nominated County Clerk by the Liberty Party but was not elected.

I married Miss Ellen De Bow, of Batavia, N.Y., in 1852.

I have always made a living, and got it honestly I think, and have laid by a little every year for myself and others I have to care for. I never sued a person and never was sued. I never lost a debt of any great amount, for if a person who owed me could not pay it, I forgave the debt.

I made a public profession of religion when I was eleven years old, and several years afterwards united with the Free Congregational Church in Gaines and remained a member of that Church as long as it was in being.

I never held any civil office of profit. My political principles were not formerly popular with the majority of the people.

I held military office in the 214th regiment N.Y. State militia, from 1837 to 1844, and served as ensign, lieutenant and captain.

I have lived to see slavery abolished in this country. The landless can now have land if they will. Now, let us drive liquor and tobacco from the country.

GEORGE E. MIX."

Barre, February 1869.

"THINGS I CAN REMEMBER"

BY GEORGE E. MIX

"I can remember the dark and heavy forest that once covered this land, with only now and then a little clearing that made a little hole to let in the sunshine; the large creeks that seemed to flow and flood the whole county during a freshet; the large swamps and marshes, in almost every valley; the wild deer that roamed the woods almost undisturbed by men; the bear that plodded his way through the swamps and the wolf that made night hideous with his howling.

I remember when the roads ran crooking around on the high grounds, and when roads on the low lands were mostly causeways of logs. When almost all the houses were made of logs, and almost all the chimneys were made of sticks and mud, and the fireplaces were of Dutch pattern.

But the sound of the axman was heard at his toil through the forest, hurling the old trees headlong. The woods and the heavens were lit up with the lurid glare of fire by night, and the heavy forest soon melted away. Those little holes in the old woods soon became enlarged to broad fields of waving grain that glistened in the sunlight.

The foaming creeks soon became rivulets, or dried up. The swamps disappeared and nothing remains to show where many of the great marshes of the old time were. The deer, bear and wolf have departed. The crooked roads have been straightened, and the log causeways have been buried out of sight. The log houses, stick chimneys, and Dutch fireplaces, are reckoned among the things that were and are not now.

I can remember when my mother spun flax on a little wheel and carded wool and tow by hand and spun them on a great wheel; when she colored her yarn with the bark and leaves of trees and had a loom, and wove cloth and made it up into clothing for her family.

I can remember when my father plowed with a wooden plow with an iron share and reaped his grain with a sickle and threshed it with a *flail*; when he mowed his grass with a scythe and raked it with a hand rake. I remember when no fruit grew here but wild fruit, but we soon had peaches in profusion, bushels of them rotting under the trees.

At the first settlement of this county, fruits, such as grapes, strawberries, cranberries, blackberries, gooseberries, raspberries and mandrakes, were to be found growing wild. We had nuts from the trees, such as butternuts, chestnuts, beachnuts and walnuts.

Pumpkins, squashes and melons were largely raised and of great value to people. Pumpkins were cut in strips and dried on poles in the log cabins and kept for use the year round. Maple trees furnished us nearly all our sugar. At our fall parties and our husking and logging bees we had pumpkin pies. At our winter parties we had nuts and popped corn and in the summer, berries and cream.

I can remember when the common vehicle for traveling about was an ox sled with wooden shoes and the only wheel carriages were lumber wagons and they were few, when the Ridge Road was the main thoroughfare by which to reach the old settlements and stagecoaches were the fastest means of conveyance.

It was considered an impossibility to make the Erie Canal. People said possibly water might be made to run uphill, but canal boats never.

Some said they would be willing to die, having lived long enough when boats in a canal should float through their farms; but afterwards when they saw the boats passing by, they wanted to live more than ever to see what would be done next.

Next after the canal came the railroad. I heard the cars were running at Batavia and I went out there to see the great wonder of the age, and saw them. We were next told of the telegraph. Knowing ones said that was a humbug, sure. I remember even some members of Congress ridiculed Professor Morse and his telegraph as a delusion. But in spite of ridicule, and doubt, and incredulity, the telegraph became a success, and by it the ends of the earth have been brought together. These things I have seen and remembered while living here in Orleans County.

GEORGE E. MIX."

MRS. LYDIA MIX

"I was born in Brantford, Connecticut, in 1783. At the age of eighteen I married Abiathar Mix, and moved to Dutchess County, N.Y., where my husband owned a farm, on which we lived, working it chiefly by hired men. My husband being a mason by trade, labored at that business in the summer and winters he made nails and buttons.

We resided there until May, 1817, when we sold our farm and moved to Barre, Orleans Co., and located on lot 32, township 14, range 2. Very little land was then cleared in that neighborhood, and even that was covered with stumps of trees. Mr. Mix had been here the year before and engaged a man to build a log house for him. When we came on we found our house with walls up and roof on. My husband split some basswood logs and hewed them to planks, with which he laid a floor, and we began housekeeping in our new house.

My husband had ten or fifteen hundred dollars in money when he moved here. He took an article for a large tract of land and went to making potash and selling goods and merchandise, in company with his brother, Ebenezer Mix, who was then a clerk in the land office of the Holland Company, at Batavia.

The settlers, building their houses of logs and their chimneys of sticks and mud, my husband found nothing to do at his trade, until they began making bricks and making their chimneys of stone, with brick ovens.

He then closed out his mercantile business and went to work at his trade and being something of a lawyer, he used to do that kind of business considerably for the settlers.

We had pretty hard times occasionally but managed to get along with what we had and raised our seven children to be men and women.

My husband died in 1856. Three of my children have died. I shall be 86 years old in a few days, if I live.

LYDIA MIX."

Barre, February, 1869.

JOSEPH HART

Joseph Hart was born in Berlin, Hartford County, Connecticut, in November 1755. He passed away in Barre, Orleans County, New York, in July 1855.

Mr. Hart moved to Seneca, Ontario County, New York, in 1806. In the fall of 1811, he came to Barre and took an article from the Holland Land Company of lot 34, township 15, range 1, containing 360 acres, with the principal part still owned by his sons, William and Joseph.

In April 1812, along with Elijah Darrow, Frederick Holsenburgh, and Silas Benton, he built a log house on his lot and moved his family into it in October of the same year.

Elijah Darrow initially held the land next to Mr. Hart's, worked on it for about two years, and then sold it to Mr. Hart, who, in turn, sold it to Ebenezer Rogers around 1816.

Silas Benton, who took an article of part of a lot lying next north of Darrow's, made a clearing on his land, built a log house, and later his wife, Mrs. Silas Benton, taught a school in the same building. Frederick Holsenburgh held the land next north of Benton's and it is now the location of the N.Y. Central Railroad depot in the village of Albion.

Joseph Hart married Lucy Kirtland, who was born in Saybrook, Connecticut. She passed away in Adrian, Michigan, in January 1868, at the age of 89.

Mr. Hart was actively involved in the war of 1812, participating in military service several times. He played a significant role in the organization of society in the new country, helping to establish the Presbyterian Church in Albion, where he served as a ruling elder and was known as Dea. Hart.

He also held various town offices and for many years was the overseer of the poor of the town of Barre, a position the kindness of his nature well qualified him to fill. His fortunate location near the thriving village of Albion, which expanded over a part of his farm, made him a wealthy man. Throughout his long life, he was known for his integrity and sound judgment, and he passed away, widely respected by all who knew him.

ADEN FOSTER

Aden Foster was born in Sudbury, Vermont on July 20, 1791. He married Sarah Hall of Brandon, Vermont on January 23, 1817. In the winter of 1817, he moved to Barre and settled on lot 36, township 14, range 1, half a mile south of Barre Center. He cleared up his farm and lived there until he passed away on February 18, 1838.

Mr. Foster was an active businessman and a prominent figure among the early settlers of the area. He served as the Captain of a militia company for several years and was also a Justice of the Peace for some time.

ALEX WARD

Alexis Ward was born in Addison, Vermont on May 18, 1802. When he was young, his family moved to Cayuga County, New York. He studied law with Judge Wilson of Auburn and became a lawyer in 1823. In 1824, he moved to Albion, where he was appointed as a Justice of the Peace.

After Judge Foot retired, Alexis Ward was appointed as the First Judge of Orleans County on February 10, 1830. He served in this position until January 27, 1840, after being re-appointed. In 1834-1835, he played a major role in obtaining the charter for the Bank of Orleans, the first bank incorporated in Orleans County. He was elected as its President in 1836 and served until his passing.

Alexis Ward was involved in establishing the Phipps Union Seminary and the Albion Academy, and he was known for supporting public schools. He was instrumental in the construction of the Rochester, Lockport, and Niagara Falls Railroad, and was a driving force behind the development of the Suspension Bridge across the Niagara River.

He also initiated the construction of plank roads from the Ridge through Albion to Barre Center and made significant investments in them. Additionally, he, along with Roswell and Freeman Clarke, built a large stone *flouring mill* in Albion and several residential properties.

Known for his philanthropy and dedication to the betterment of Albion, Alexis Ward was described as fair, honorable, and generous in his business dealings. He was recognized for his energy, perseverance, and commitment to completing projects.

In his personal interactions, he was kind, affable, and generous, despite appearing reserved to those who did not know him well. As a devout member of the Presbyterian Church of Albion, he made substantial financial contributions to support the church and its ministers. He passed away on November 28, 1854, before assuming his position as Member of Assembly for Orleans County, to which he was elected in November 1854. He married Miss Laura Goodrich in 1826.

THE LEE FAMILY

Judge John Lee, the ancestor of this family and the man after whom the Lee Settlement in Barre was named, was born in Barre, Massachusetts, on June 25, 1763. He moved to Madison County, New York, at a young age and lived there for fourteen years. In 1816, he settled in Barre, Orleans County, and acquired a piece of land. Although he returned home, his sons Charles and Ora, who were young at the time, stayed behind and cleared several acres of their father's land. They then built a log house, where Judge John Lee and his family moved in February 1817.

Mr. Lee was an intelligent, energetic man, benevolent and patriotic in his character, always among the first to engage in any work tending to promote the good of his neighbors or the prosperity of the country. With the hospitality common to all the pioneers, he kept open house to all comers and frequently half a dozen men looking after land or waiting till their log houses could be put up, would be quartered with him though his own family was large.

He was always conspicuous in aiding to lay out and open roads, build school houses and induce settlers to come in and stay. He was appointed a Judge of the Court of Common Pleas of Genesee County and his opinions and counsel in all matters of local interest were much sought by his neighbors. He died in October 1823.

His children were Dencey, wife of Benjamin Godard, who died in Barre in 1831. Submit, wife of Judge Eldridge Farwell, who is still living. Charles, Ora and Asa. And Sally, wife of Andrew Stevens. She taught the first school kept in the settlement in a log school house in which the family of a Mr. Pierce then resided, in 1818-19. She died at Knowlesville in 1828. Esther, wife of Gen. Wm. C. Tanner, died in 1835. John B. who died in September 1860. Clarissa, wife of John Proctor, who died in 1832. Cynthia married William Mudgett of Yates, in 1837, she is now living, the widow of John Proctor. Charles has always resided on a part of the land originally taken up by his father. He has always been a prominent man in public affairs in town and county, and was for a number of years a Justice of the Peace.

Ora Lee also lived on a piece of land that was originally owned by his father. It is said that he cut down the first tree between the village of Millville in Shelby and the Oak Orchard Road in Barre. General John B. Lee moved to Albion around 1832 and started a warehousing and forwarding business on the canal. Soon after, he bought a large number of contracts from the Holland Company that were made with settlers buying land in the northern part of the county. He then transferred these lands to the buyers as they completed their payments.

A few years afterwards he engaged in selling dry goods in Albion. In a short time he left this and devoted himself mainly to buying and selling flour and grain and in manufacturing flour during the remainder of his life. He took delight in military affairs, held various offices in the State militia, rising gradually to the rank of *Brigadier-General*.

Abraham Cantine was born in Marbletown, Ulster County. He volunteered as a soldier in the United States Army during the war with Great Britain in 1812 and served as a Captain in the stirring scenes of that war on the Canadian frontier. He was wounded in the sortie at the *battle of Fort Erie*.

After the war, he was discharged from the army and returned to Ulster County, where he was appointed Sheriff by the old Council of Appointment in February 1819. Soon after finishing his term as Sheriff, he moved to the town of Murray in Orleans County. In 1829, he was tasked with re-surveying a portion of the 100,000 acre tract in Murray, which belonged to the Pulteney estate. This area was part of township number three, and he executed the task carefully and faithfully.

In 1827, he represented Orleans County in the State Legislature. He also served as an Associate Judge of the Court of Common Pleas of Orleans County for five years. In 1835, he worked as the Collector of Tolls on the Erie Canal at Albion.

Several years before his death, he relocated to Albion and passed away there around August 1, 1840, at the age of fifty. Judge Cantine was described as a clear-headed man, possessing sound judgment, well-informed, and always maintaining a high reputation for his abilities. He was a close personal and political friend of President VanBuren.

CAROLINE P. ACHILLES

The daughter of Mr. Joseph Phipps was born in Rome, New York. She was one of several daughters and received a well-supervised education at home from her father. Additionally, she attended top private schools and nearby district schools.

When she was quite young, her father settled in Barre. At an early age, she was allowed to fulfill her ambition of becoming a teacher, by taking a small district school job at a salary of one dollar per week, with board around, as was customary in such schools at the time.

The salary, however, was no concern to her. She wished to teach at a school, not to make money. After teaching at this school for two or three terms, she attended the Gaines Academy, which was then at the height of its prosperity. After spending some time there, she was sent to a *finishing* ladies' school run by Mrs. and Miss Nicholas in Whitesboro, N.Y.

On leaving Whitesboro, she decided to pursue teaching as a permanent career and accepted a position as an assistant instructor in a classical school that had been established by two women in Albion.

Finally, an arrangement was reached between the two principals and their assistant. They transferred their lease of the premises and all their interests in the school to Miss Phipps.

Then associated with an elder sister, the two began their work as teachers in a building that was located on the site of the current Phipps Union Seminary, in April 1833.

She believed it was better to teach boys and girls in separate schools. As a result, she divided her students accordingly. After a while, she refused to admit boys as pupils and focused all her efforts on her school for young ladies.

It was a success. So many students had enrolled that in August of her first year, she was joined by a younger sister as a teacher, along with a music teacher, and all found themselves fully employed.

Convinced that a Female Seminary could be supported in Albion and that she was capable of superintending it, she became determined to establish such an institution of learning. Encouraged by the counsel and influence of some of the best citizens of the village, she issued a public circular announcing the founding of the seminary.

After a year-long trial, it was clear that the new Seminary needed additional buildings to accommodate the large school. Miss Phipps invited some of the most wealthy and influential men of Albion to meet and hear her proposition to erect a new Seminary Building. Her proposal was that they should loan her four thousand dollars. With these funds, along with others she could procure, she would erect a building and repay the loan to the subscribers in installments, thus permanently establishing the proposed Seminary.

The required amount was successfully subscribed with the condition that Miss Phipps would repay the loan, and the avails of the loan would be used for an academy for boys in Albion. Eventually, in 1836, a brick building was constructed for the academy, which later became known as Phipps Union Seminary after its incorporation in 1840.

PHIPPS UNION SEMINARY

Thus, Miss Phipps played a key role in establishing two incorporated schools in Albion, both of which have been of great public benefit.

Miss Phipps married Col. H. L. Achilles of Rochester, N.Y., in February 1839. Soon after, she resigned from the Seminary and moved to Boston, Mass., where she lived for the next ten years. Her younger sister took over the Seminary but later married, and the responsibility for the Seminary was transferred to others who were less competent. As a result, the Seminary lost a large patronage and was nearly ruined.

This compelled Mr. and Mrs. Achilles to return to Albion in 1849 and resume charge of the Seminary or lose a large pecuniary interest they had invested there.

Tired and worn down by the burdensome responsibilities, anxieties, and work of overseeing such a large establishment and school for many years, in 1866 Mrs. Achilles reluctantly agreed to once again transfer her beloved Seminary to new owners.

After three years of trial, it was decided that Mrs. Achilles should once again take charge of Phipps Union Seminary. She brought with her the skills, experience, and practical ability that have led to her success as a teacher.

Mrs. Achilles has dedicated the prime years of her life to the advancement of female education. She has worked tirelessly in her chosen field with the zeal and enthusiasm of a genius. Her reward lies in the knowledge of the good she has accomplished and the success her work has achieved.

CHAPTER 16.

THE VILLAGE OF ALBION

O ak Orchard Road intersects this village and now forms Main Street, running north and south through the center of the area. The village was established due to the presence of this road and the Erie Canal. Initially, Albion was used as farmland, but as the canal became navigable, a significant town developed.

In 1812 William McCollister cleared the land where the CourtHouse and Female Seminary now stand and built his log house on what is now the Seminary lot. He then obtained lot thirty-five, township fifteen, range one, on the east side of Main Street by article from the Holland Company. He sold this lot to William Bradner, who received a deed from the company for two hundred and sixty-six and a half acres of the north part.

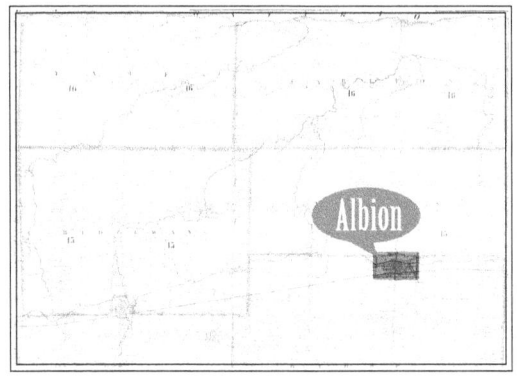

William's brother Joel also obtained a deed for ninety-two acres on the south part, on the west side of Main Street.

Jesse Bumpus took up, by article from the company, the land from the town line of Gaines on the north, to near State Street on the south. John Holtzbarger, or Holsenburgh, as he was sometimes called, took up the next land south of Bumpus, and Elijah Darrow took the next.

Before the canal was made, Mr. William Bradner sold one hundred acres of the northwest part of his tract to Nehemiah Ingersoll and others. Mr. Ingersoll employed Orange Risden to lay out his land bordering on the Oak Orchard Road and canal into village lots and to make a plat of the same. Mr. Ingersoll bought out his partners, then sold the lots and opened the streets.

The Bumpus tract, located on the west side of Main Street, was owned by Mr. Roswell Burrows, who was the father of R. S. & L. Burrows. Instead of laying out his land into village lots using a general survey and plan, he would divide the land into lots and open streets as needed. The land along Main Street in the village was purchased from the original owners around the time the canal became navigable and was mostly occupied.

By this time, the County Seat was located in Albion. There was a lot of activity related to building county buildings, setting up courts and public offices, and organizing the affairs of the new county, town, and village. This led to a sudden influx of inhabitants, representing various occupations pursued by those who settled in villages along the canal.

The south side of the canal, the north being the towing path, was soon occupied by buildings put up for the canal trade, such as warehouses and grocery stores. The large number of passengers who filled the canal boats made the grocery stores, from which they and the boatmen procured their supplies, places of lively trade, by night and day. Variety stores, each filled with goods of every name, class, and description demanded by the customers, were numerous, though small.

Among the first merchants were Goodrich & Standart, John Tucker, O. H. Gardner, R. S. & L. Burrows, Alderman Butts, and Freeman Clark, of late years a prominent banker in Rochester, N.Y.

When the commissioners were appointed to choose a site for the Courthouse, they had to decide between Gaines and Albion. Gaines had the advantage of being the largest village on the Ridge Road, with plenty of mechanics and merchants, along with well-established community institutions. On the other hand, Albion was closest to the geographical center of the county and was intersected by the Erie Canal and Oak Orchard Road. The west branch of Sandy Creek ran through the eastern part of the village. Although it provided enough water for machinery after the snow melted in spring and after rains, it almost dried up in summer. There were two sawmills on this stream, one in the village and the other to the south of it.

The Commissioners arrived to assess the claims of the competing villages at the beginning of the dry season. Mr. Nehemiah Ingersoll, Philetus Bumpus, Henry Henderson, and a few other Albion residents decided to employ a bit of strategy to support Albion. Anticipating that the creek would be too low to operate the sawmills when the Commissioners arrived and recognizing the advantage of having a good mill stream, they patched up the two dams and flumes and closed the gates to store water several days before the Commissioners' visit. Additionally, they sent teams to transport logs and lumber around the sawmill and mill yard in the village to mark the ground and create the appearance of activity.

"When the Commissioners visited Albion, they were treated well and then taken on a carriage ride to see the area. During the ride, they passed by the creek and saw the sawmill in full operation, with workers and teams handling the lumber and utilizing water from the ponds. The Commissioners were impressed by the water power and decided to give the county buildings to Albion before the ponds dried up."

Mr. Ingersoll donated to the county the grounds now occupied by the courthouse, jail and public park.

The first courthouse, built in 1827, was brick, with the County Clerk's office in the lower story. Gilbert Howell, Calvin Smith, and Elihu Mather were the building committee.

This Courthouse was pulled down, and a new one was erected in its place in 1857–58 at a cost of $20,000. W.V.N. Barlow was the architect, and Lyman Bates, Henry A. King, and Charles Baker were the building committee.

The present jail was built in 1838, and the clerk's office in 1836.

The first hotel was kept on the southwest corner of Main and Canal Street by Mr. Churchill. The next hotel, Albion Hotel, was built by Philetus Bumpus about twenty rods south of the canal on the west side of Main Street and kept for several years by Bumpus & Howland, succeeded by Hiram Sickles. Mr. Bumpus then built the Mansion House, a hotel on the north side of the canal on Main Street, which he kept for several years.

Mr. Philetus Bumpus and his father, Jesse Bumpus, built the first framed dwelling house in Albion on the lot where Mr. L. Burrows now resides.

The first warehouse was built by Nehemiah Ingersoll on the canal about twenty rods east of Main Street. The next was by Cary & Tilden on the west side of Main Street on the canal.

The first sawmill in the corporation of Albion was built in 1819, by William Bradner.

Mr. William Bradner built the first grist mill, the mill stones for which he cut in person from a rock in Palmyra. One of these stones is now used for a corner stone on the corner of State and Clarendon streets. These mills were cheap structures and were taken away after a few years.

The stone flouring mill on the canal was built by Ward & Clarks in 1833.

The first lawyer in Albion was Theophilus Capen. He remained here for only a short time. The next lawyers were William J. Moody, Alexis Ward, Henry R. Curtis,

Gideon Hard, William W. Ruggles, and others who came about the time the county was organized.

Dr. Orson Nichoson was the first physician. Originally located two miles south of the village in 1819 he moved to Albion in about 1822. Dr. William White, who had been in practice at Oak Orchard in Ridgway, came here about the time the county was organized. He opened a drug store and partnered with Dr. Nichoson in the practice of medicine.

Dr. Stephen M. Potter was one of the early physicians who settled in Albion. He was born in Westport, Mass., moved to Cazenovia, N.Y., and from then to Albion. About the year 1837 he moved to Cazenovia again. He represented Madison county in the State Legislature in 1846.

The first tanyard was located on the south side of the canal, on the lot now occupied by the gas works. It was established by Jacob Ingersoll around 1825 and tanning operations continued until the gas works were built in 1858.

The first blacksmiths were John Moe, Rodney A. Torrey, and Phineas Phillips.

Albion was originally known as Newport for several years. However, due to mail confusion and the presence of another post office in the state with the same name, the residents gathered to incorporate the village. At a meeting chaired by Gideon Hard, the name was changed to Albion in the first Act of incorporation passed on April 21, 1828. The first firemen's company was organized in 1831.

John Henderson settled in Albion in September 1825 and established the first shop for making carriages. He kept the first livery stable in 1834 and started the first horse and cart for public accommodation in 1837. Henderson has been an active man, an ingenious mechanic, and has built ten or twelve dwelling houses and numerous shops, barns, and other buildings here.

CHAPTER 17.

TOWN OF CARLTON

C arlton was set off from Gaines and Ridgeway on April 13, 1822, by the name of Oak Orchard. The name was changed to Carlton in 1825.

In early times, the region lying north of Ridge Road in this vicinity was called the north woods. It was heavily timbered land, containing large numbers of immense whitewood trees and white and red oaks of the largest kind. Some pine grew near the Oak Orchard Creek. Hemlock was abundant in some localities, and basswood, elm, beech, and some maple comprised the principal kinds of trees.

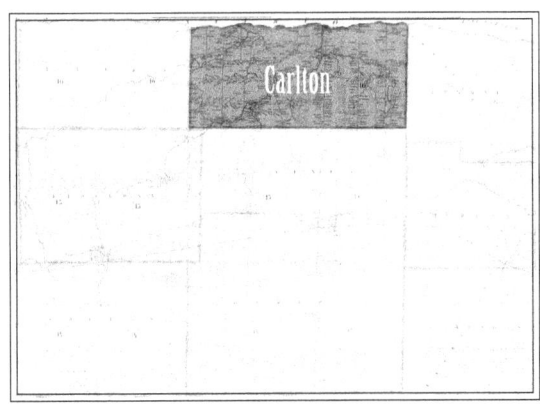

TOWN OF CARLTON

The settlers, in their haste to clear their lands, generally burned up all of this fine timber that they did not want for fencing in the first few years of their settlement. After sawmills were built, white wood was sawed, and the boards hauled to the canal for sale. Large quantities of oak trees were squared to the top and sent down the Lake to Europe for ship timber. The prices obtained were barely sufficient to pay the expense of the labor required to move the lumber, but the destructive work was kept up till most of the timber trees of every kind had been cut down through this town.

The first settlement of white men in Orleans County was made in this town in the year 1803 by William and James Walsworth, who came from Canada. James settled near the mouth of Oak Orchard Creek, and William near the mouth of Johnson's Creek.

James Walsworth was the pioneer settler of this county. He came across from Canada in May 1803 in an open boat with his family and built a log cabin for his residence. At that time, it was the only house near the shore of Lake Ontario, between Fort Niagara and Braddock's Bay. His nearest neighbor, at first, resided near Lockport, Niagara County. Mr. Walsworth was very poor then. The only provisions they had when they landed were a few potatoes; these and fish from Oak Orchard Creek, in which there was then an abundance, supplied their sustenance, except an occasional barter with boatmen, who, coasting along the south shore of the lake, would put into the mouth of the Oak Orchard for shelter.

Walsworth hunted and fished mainly for a living, and when he collected any store of peltries, he took them east along the shore of the lake to a market. After two or three years, he moved to what used to be called The Lewiston Road, between Lockport and Batavia, where he was afterwards well known as a tavern keeper. The Walsworths and the few other settlers who came in and stopped along the Lake Shore in Carlton comprised all the settlers in Orleans County before the year 1809, with one or two exceptions.

In 1803, Joseph Ellicott concluded that a village would eventually grow up at the mouth of Oak Orchard Creek. In anticipation of that event, he made a plat for a town there and called it Manilla, a name which is now found on some maps for the place more commonly known as Oak Orchard Harbor.

It was supposed, in those days, that most of the trade to and from the Holland Purchase would take the lake route and that Manilla would be the depot. At that time, the sand bar at the mouth of Oak Orchard Creek was less than in later years, and the small schooners then on the lake could come over it without difficulty. It was in furtherance of this, though, that the Holland Company did what they did toward opening the Oak Orchard Road to travel. The Erie Canal, however, effectually stifled this project and turned trade and commerce in another direction.

John G. Brown took up two and one-half acres of land from the Company on the west side of Oak Orchard Creek near the mouth and held it on speculation for a time, but nothing was done in the way of founding a village. This land was deeded to him by the Holland Company on Dec. 2, 1806, and was described in the deed as lot No. 15 on a plan of the village of Manilla. This was the first deed of land in the town of Carlton given by the Company. Brown conveyed the land to Silas Joy on Nov. 28, 1815. Matthew Dunham and his sons Matthew, James and Charles, came from Berkshire County, Mass., to Wayne County, New York, about 1795. They moved to Carlton in 1804. They were chair makers and began working at their trade as soon as they could get settled.

Henry Lovewell from New Hampshire and Moses Root and his family from Cooperstown, N.Y., came to Carlton with Mr. Dunham and his family.

Matthew Dunham, Jr. married Rachel Lovewell, daughter of Henry Lovewell, in 1814. Mr. Dunham died in 1854, but Mrs. Rachel Dunham was still living in 1871, aged about eighty-six years.

In the summer of 1804, Matthew Dunham and his sons built a dam across Johnson's Creek, where the dam now stands at Kuckville, and erected a small building on it with machinery for turning wood. The Dunham family carried on the business of turning, in a small way, in this building for several years. They did not find many sales for their goods near home, but they sold some chairs and wooden bowls to the new settlers. Most of their work was taken across the lake and disposed of in Canada. They continued this commerce until the *embargo* was declared in 1808, and after that, they smuggled their chair stuff over, to a considerable extent, on a sailboat that they owned.

It is related by some of the first settlers that in this turning shop, the Dunhams fixed an apparatus for pounding corn by making a tub or box in which the corn was placed, and a heavy pestle was made to fall at each turn of the water wheel. Into this box, they would put about a bushel of corn, occasionally stirring it up to bring it under the pestle and thus pound it until it was reduced to meal. It took considerable time to turn a bushel of corn into meal by this process, and aid could be afforded to but few families in this way.

Several families came to settle in the neighborhood, and the need for a sawmill and a gristmill was greatly felt. Three or four years after the Dunhams built their turning shop, the Holland Land company offered to furnish the irons for a sawmill and the irons and a pair of millstones for a gristmill if they would erect such mills on their dam. A sawmill and a gristmill were built accordingly.

These were the first saw and grist mills built in Carlton. They were small, coarse affairs, but they were very useful to those living near them. The Dunhams owned them until about 1816 when George Kuck purchased them and rebuilt them on a much larger pattern.

Mr. Reuben Root owned a small sailboat, weighing a few tons, which he used to sail across the lake. Pine lumber was transported from Canada on this boat before sawmills were built here. It served as the primary means of transporting passengers and goods across the lake for several years.

Mr. Moses Root built a framed barn before Dunham's sawmill was erected, bringing the boards from Canada. This is supposed to have been the first frame barn built in Orleans County.

Reuben Fuller and John Fuller came from Bradford County, in Pennsylvania, and settled near Kuckville in 1811.

THE UNION COMPANY

In December 1810, eight young men in Stockbridge, Massachusetts, formed a company, which they named The Union Company, and agreed each to contribute an equal share of stock and go together and form a settlement on the Holland Purchase, where each partner should buy for himself a farm with his own means, and the company would help him clear a certain portion of land and build a house and barn. The buildings were to be alike on each man's farm.

They limited the company to two years, during which they would all live and work together and share the avails of their labor equally.

Before leaving Stockbridge, they drew up and signed their agreement in writing.

Thus organized, they came to Carlton and took up land west of Oak Orchard Creek, each a farm, which was worked according to the contract.

Fitch Chamberlain was married but left his wife at home until he could get a home for her made ready.

They brought no women with them and kept bachelor's hall the first year when Giles Slater, Jr., went back to Stockbridge and married a wife and brought her to his new home, and soon after, his example was followed by the remainder of the company.

The company made judicious selections of land; its affairs were well-managed and successful. All the partners were fortunate in accumulating property, the sure reward of honest, persevering industry. Their families have ever been among the most respected and influential in town.

Fitch Chamberlain was a physician and practiced medicine in the later years of his life. The members of the company are all dead except Anthony Miles, now aged 84 years, in 1871.

The Union Company consisted of Minoris Day, Fitch Chamberlain, Charles Webster, Anthony Miles, Selah Bardslee, Moses Barnum, Jr., Russell Smith, and Giles Slater, Jr.

The first death among the settlers was Elijah Brown. The first birth was a pair of twins, children of James Walsworth, in 1806. At their birth, no physician or person of her own sex was present with the mother. The first marriage was that of William Carter and Amy Hunt in 1804. Peleg Helms taught the first school in 1810-11. And George Kuck kept the first store in 1816.

The first public religious services in Carlton were held about the year 1810 and were conducted by Rev. Mr. Steele, a Methodist preacher who came from Canada.

Elder Simeon Dutcher, of the Baptist denomination, settled in Carlton in 1817. He was the only preacher residing in town for several years.

Among the first settlers were Elijah Hunt, Moses Root, Henry Lovewell, Paul Brown, Elijah Brown, Job Shipman, and Matthew Dunham.

Dr. Richard W. Gates was the first regular physician to settle into the practice of his profession in Carlton. After a few years, he moved to Barre and thence to Yates. He represented Orleans County in the State Legislature in 1841 and was Supervisor of Carlton in 1826.

BIOGRAPHIES OF EARLY SETTLERS

GEORGE KUCK

Rev. George Kuck was born in the city of London, England, on December 23, 1791, and was educated at King's College, London. He moved to New York City in 1806 and then to Toronto, *Canada West*, in 1807. During the war between England and the United States in 1812, he served as a Lieutenant in the Canadian militia. After the war, from 1812 to 1815, he worked as a clerk for the Canadian Government in Toronto. In October 1815, he moved to Carlton and purchased a farm, which became known as Kuckville.

He built a frame gristmill on the site of a log mill previously built by Mr. Dunham on Johnson's Creek. In 1816, he opened a store near his residence, which was the only store north of the Ridge in that area at the time. He carried a large stock of goods and conducted a flourishing trade. He later constructed a warehouse at the mouth of Johnson's Creek. At one point, he managed a store, gristmill, sawmill, ashery, warehouse, and farm, all under his direct supervision and all operating successfully. His investments were prudent, and his business affairs were managed with skill and economy, which led to his wealth.

On March 25th, 1819, he married Miss Electa Fuller. In March 1821, he joined the Methodist Episcopal Church, where he became a prominent member. He played a role in forming the first religious class in his church in the town of Carlton and served as its leader. In 1825, he organized and taught the first Sunday School in the county north of the Ridge. He was licensed to exhort in April 1829, licensed to preach in 1833, ordained Deacon by Bishop Hedding in 1837, and ordained Elder by Bishop Morris in 1849 at Albion.

He was the Postmaster at West Carlton since Kuckville, and he held that position for about 30 years. Rev. George Kuck was a well-educated man with fine natural abilities, and his life was marked by usefulness. He was actively involved in matters of reform and progress, particularly in the causes of temperance, morality, and religion. He held a leading role in church matters and died on March 16, 1868, at the age of 76.

DANIEL GATES

Daniel Gates was born in Rutland County, Vermont, on March 11th, 1786. He married Ann Anderson on March 12th, 1808.

About November 1811, he moved to Orleans County and bought an article of part of lot twenty-nine, township fifteen, range two, on the south side of the Ridge. A former owner had cleared a small spot and built a log house there. On this farm, Mr. Gates resided for several years. He afterward bought a farm in Carlton, where he resided at the time of his death, January 31st, 1858.

Mrs. Ann Gates died January 1st, 1866. They were the parents of John and Nehemiah F. Gates of Carlton, Lewis W. Gates, residing in Michigan, and Matthew A. Gates of Yates.

Mr. Gates moved his family in with a yoke of oxen and wagon. No bridge had been built across Genesee River, and he forded the stream at Rochester, a man riding a horse hitched before the oxen to guide them through the river.

Few settlers along the Ridge Road came in advance of Mr. Gates or braved the hardships and difficulties of pioneer life with better courage. They had very few of the conveniences and comforts of civilized life and sometimes were in want of food. Once, about the last year of the war, a scarcity prevailed among the four families that comprised all the inhabitants in the vicinity of Mr. Gates. But one pan full of flour remained among them all, and that they kept to feed the children, the older folk expecting to substitute boiled green wheat in place of bread. Mr. Gates cut a few bundles of his wheat and then put them in milk and dried them in the sun. They rubbed the soft grain out of the straw and boiled it. This was eaten with milk and relished very much by the family, and it supplied them until wheat ripened and dried fit to grind.

For several years, no settlers were located between Mr. Gates's place on the Ridge and Shelby. Along the line of the canal was then a solid forest. Mr. Gates' cattle were suffered to range the woods to browse in summer. They usually returned to the clearing at night. Once, his oxen, one of which wore a bell, with his cow, failed to come in at night. Mr. Gates armed himself with a bayonet on the end of a staff to repel a bear or wolf if he chanced to be attacked and went out to hunt for them, his old English musket being too heavy to carry. After several days of hunting, he found his cattle where Knowlesville now stands, attracted by some wild grass growing along the brook.

ELIJAH HUNT

Elijah Hunt was born in Pennsylvania. He served as a soldier in the Revolutionary War. While on a scouting mission in Pennsylvania, he and his party were captured by the Indians. They were forced to run the gauntlet from one fixed point to another along with the other prisoners.

The Indian men, women, and children posted themselves on each side of the track and assaulted the prisoners as they passed with clubs, hatchets, knives, stones, etc. If the prisoners were fortunate enough, they might get through and live, or they might be severely wounded or even killed by the way.

Mr. Hunt emerged from the ordeal without serious harm. Upon arriving at their village on the Genesee River, the Native Americans decided to subject Mr. Hunt to their traditional form of sacrifice. He was stripped and painted black in preparation for his ordeal, but before they could begin torturing him, an elderly woman, whose son had been killed in the same fight where Hunt was captured, stepped forward. She asserted her right, according to Indian custom, to adopt him as her son in place of the one she had lost. Mr. Hunt was then released to her and adopted as she had proposed. He stayed with the Native Americans near the Genesee River in Livingston County for about three years. When the war ended, he was allowed to return to his family and friends in Pennsylvania.

He was always treated kindly after his *adoption by the Indians*, especially by his new mother. Many years after his settlement in Carlton, the Indians sought him out and visited him with many demonstrations of their friendship.

He came to Carlton in the summer of 1804 and took up a farm about a mile west of the mouth of Johnson's Creek on the Lake Shore. After a year or two, he went back to Pennsylvania with his family and remained until October 1806, when he returned and settled permanently on his farm.

In the midst of winter, following the harsh summer of 1816 and fearing that he might not have enough to support his family due to the crop loss that year, two Native Americans arrived at Carlton to visit Mr. Hunt. One of them claimed to be his brother, as he was the son of the woman who had adopted Mr. Hunt. They came to offer assistance if it was needed.

Mr. Hunt passed in 1830, aged seventy-nine years, on his farm in Carlton.

The prolonged stay of Mr. Hunt among the Native Americans equipped him to be a trailblazer in this new community and prepared him to withstand the hardships and challenges he had to face.

Mr. Hunt's daughter, Amy Hunt, married in that town, and it was probably the first marriage in Orleans County.

RAY MARSH

Ray Marsh was born in Connecticut. Around the year 1800, he moved to Canada West where he worked as a schoolteacher. In 1803, he married Martha Shaw, who was born in Nova Scotia. That same year, he left Canada at Queenstown in a small boat and traveled along the south shore of Lake Ontario to Oak Orchard Creek in Carlton. There, he took an article for land near the lake.

In 1805, due to an outbreak of illness near his home in Carlton, he moved to Cambria in Niagara County, settling on the Ridge about five miles from Lewiston. During the war with England, he was forced to leave when Lewiston was attacked by the British and Indians, losing nearly everything he owned, except for the lives of himself and his family. They fled to Ontario County, but returned the following year and settled in nearby Ridgeway Corners. He had a large family to provide for, and to support them, he had to sell his farm in Cambria. During the harsh winters of 1816–17, they struggled to obtain necessary food, and like many families, they suffered from the prevalent illnesses of the time, worsened by their poverty and lack of resources for relief.

Mr. Marsh passed away around 1852. His widow, who is now 86 years old (in 1870), is still alive. She had seven grandsons who served as soldiers in the Union Army during the **Great Rebellion**. Throughout the war, she dedicated a significant amount of her time to knitting stockings for the soldiers. Women like her deserve to be called "Revolutionary Mothers" and bring honor to the American name.

JOBE SHIPMAN

Job Shipman was born in Saybrook, Connecticut, on June 2, 1772. After reaching adulthood, he lived in Greene County, N.Y. for a while before joining the family of Mr. Elijah Brown and moving to Wayne County. In the summer of 1804, they traveled via Lake Ontario to the town of Carlton.

While coming up the lake, Mr. Elijah Brown died, and his body was brought to Carlton and buried there. His sons were James, John Gardner, Paul, Elijah Jr., and Robert.

Mr. Shipman took an article from lot twelve, section two, range two. His son Israel later obtained a deed for the land on which he still resides.

Job married widow Ann Tomblin in May 1815. Israel Shipman was his only child.

Job Shipman died on January 12th, 1833. His wife died on February 8th, 1858.

The first town meetings in Carlton for two or three years were held at his dwelling because it was one of the best log houses in town. It had a shingled roof and board floor and stood near the middle of the town, but it was so small that few of the voters assembled could get in the house at once. They compromised the matter by allowing the Inspectors to sit in the house while the voters handed in their ballots to them through the window from outside.

Since it was cold outside, the generous amount of whisky they drank wasn't enough to keep them warm, so they built a large *bonfire* near the house, and it did the trick.

LYMAN FULLER

Lyman Fuller was born in Pennsylvania on August 16th, 1808. In February 1811, his father, Reuben Fuller, moved with this family to near the lake shore in West Carlton. In the fall of 1811, Capt. John Fuller, a brother of Reuben, settled in Carlton.

Mr. Reuben Fuller died July 4th, 1837. Mr. Lyman Fuller succeeded in the possession of his father's homestead, on which he resided and where he died on March 22nd, 1866. He was a much-respected man among all who knew him.

CHAPTER 18.

TOWN OF CLARENDON

C larendon comprises a portion of the 100,000 Acre Tract and was formed from Sweden on February 23rd, 1821.

Due in part to the challenge of obtaining clear land titles, settlers arrived slowly at first.

The land was divided between the State of Connecticut and the Pulteney Estate in 1811, but the lots that fell to the Pulteney Estate were not surveyed and put in the market for sale until about the year 1821. Settlers were allowed to take possession of land and make improvements with the expectation that when the lands came on the market, they would retain what they had so taken and then get a title.

Some settlers located on these lands under these circumstances and cleared them up and built houses. When they finally came into the market, the settlers were charged $8 or $10 per acre, a much higher price than was expected and a higher price than the Holland Company charged for their lands of like quality, but they were compelled to pay it or leave and lose their labor.

Among the first settlers in Clarendon were Eldridge Farwell, John Cone, Bradstreet Spafford, Elisha Huntley, David Church, and Chauncey Robinson. Eldridge Farwell erected the first sawmill on Sandy Creek in 1811 and the first gristmill at the same place in 1813. A village grew up in the vicinity of these mills, which, in honor of Mr. Farwell, was called and known as Farwell's Mills. Situated a little northwest of the center of the town, it has been the principal place of trade and business.

Judge Eldridge Farwell was the pioneer settler. The next settler was Alanson Dudley in 1812.

The first store was kept at Farwell's Mills by Frisbie & Pierpont, in 1821.

Mrs. Amanda Bills taught the first school. The first schoolhouse, built in 1813, stood a little south of Farwell's Mills, or Clarendon, as the place is now being called. It was fourteen by eighteen feet square and made of logs.

Frisbie & Pierpont traded in the little red store building in which, after they left, David Sturges sold goods for many years.

In addition to his business as a merchant with Mr. Frisbie, William Pierpont kept a tavern. After two or three years, he moved away, and Mr. Hiram Frisbie, his partner, succeeded to the store and tavern to which had been added an ashery, all three of which Mr. Frisbie carried on two or three years, until he moved to Holley about the year 1828.

In 1815, Joseph Sturges built a *distillery* at Farwell's Mills, which he operated with his brother David for eight or ten years. When Mr. Frisbie moved away and Joseph Sturges passed away in March 1828, David Sturges started selling dry goods and groceries at the location. He was a shrewd businessman and conducted a thriving trade. He was the second merchant in town after Pierpont & Frisbie. David Sturges passed away in September 1848.

Judge Eldridge Farwell was the first postmaster in town, and Dr. Bussy was the first physician.

On the 4th of February, 1823, a Presbyterian Church was organized in Clarendon. For several years it maintained a feeble existence until, in 1831, it united with the Presbyterian Church in Holley and became extinct as an organization in Clarendon.

The first town meeting held in and for the town of Clarendon was at the schoolhouse at Farwell's Mills on April 4th, 1821.

Eldridge Farwell was a candidate for Supervisor on the Clinton ticket, and William Lewis on the Tompkins ticket. The Meeting was opened with prayer by Elder Stedman. The election of the Supervisor was concluded to be first in order. No chairman had been formally appointed, but at somebody's suggestion, the entire meeting went out of doors in front of the schoolhouse. Someone held his hat, and half a dozen voters stood by to see that nobody voted twice or cast more than one ballot, and ballots for Supervisor were thrown into the hat by all the voters present. Eldridge Farwell was elected the first Supervisor, and Joseph M. Hamilton, Town Clerk.

Jonas Davis manufactured spinning wheels, and Alanson Dudley engaged in tanning and shoemaking at Farwell's Mills in the early days.

BIOGRAPHIES OF EARLY SETTLERS

HORACE PECK

"I was born in Farmington, Hartford Co., Conn., April 15, 1802. In the spring of 1817, I hired out to drive cattle, sheep and hogs to Buffalo, and went on with a drove. The mud was deep and I had a hard time wading through it after my drove. I went through however, and come back to Farwell's Mills in Clarendon, expecting to meet my father and his family there, as they had made arrangements to move when I left them.

On my journey back from Buffalo, all I had to eat was six crackers, and I drank one glass of cider.

I found my father had not come on. I was alone, but fourteen years of age, had but four dollars in money, my pay for driving the drove, and had no acquaintances there. This was the next spring after the *cold season*. It was difficult for me to find a place to stay for the reason no one had anything to eat or to spare. I found friends, however, in Mr. and Mrs. Leonard Foster. They said I might stay with them till my folks came on. After that I fared well. They divided their best fare with me, which consisted of *hoe cake* and maple molasses, and we had to be sparing of that.

I stayed with my **benefactors** three weeks, when my parents and their family arrived. My father had prepared a small log cabin shingled with bark the summer before. We moved into it. All the provision we had on hand to eat was half a barrel of very lean pork.

My father had no money left, owned no living creature except his family. We had no table and only two chairs. We had an acre of cleared land on our lot sown with wheat. These were gloomy times to me. The first thing was to procure something to eat. I paid my four dollars to David Church for two bushels of Wheat. The next thing was to get some straw to sleep on. This we got of our neighbor, Chauncey Robinson, for two cents a bundle.

We had hard fare until the next harvest. We ate **bran bread** and had not enough of that. After harvest we had enough to eat, and I thought at this time, could I be sure of enough to eat hereafter I should be content.

The next year my father bought a two year old cow, which helped us very much.

In the winter of 1818–19, my eldest brother, Luther C. Peck taught a district school near where Holley now stands, for three months, for which he was to have thirty bushels of wheat after the next harvest. When father received the wheat the price had fallen. Father drew the wheat to Rochester and received, after deducting expenses, thirty-one cents per bushel.

In 1820 we bought a yoke of Oxen. We then considered ourselves well off. Previous to this I went to school winters. I went one winter to Farwell's Mills, three miles from my fathers. I worked summers chopping and logging with my father, working out for others when I could get an opportunity.

In the winter of 1819-20, I taught school on the fourth section road for ten dollars per month. I followed that business for ten winters, and had higher wages as I advanced in experience. During this time and up to my majority I began to consider myself a man, used to attend parties, would yoke the oxen and hitch them to a sled, go after the young ladies and wait on them very politely. And I enjoyed it as well and even better than in after times riding in a fashionable carriage.

I once thought it quite smart to visit a young lady who resided in LeRoy. On one occasion I had been to see her, had a very pleasant visit, time passed very agreeably, and before I was aware it was getting rather late. Sometime before daylight, however, I started for home on foot through the woods near three miles. When I came about the middle of the woods, a wolf appeared in the road before me. I hallooed right lustily, the wolf left the road rather leisurely, and I passed on rapidly. Soon a howling commenced, which was answered by other wolves at a distance, and before I got through the woods, a pack of these animals was on my track, and near to me judging by their cries. They made all sorts of noises but pleasant ones to me. I saved myself from them by the energetic use of my locomotive powers. I came readily to the conclusion that this business of being out so late nights, 'would not pay.'

I married Miss Anna White January 22, 1829. She was born June 19, 1802, and died January 15, 1834. I married Miss Adaline Nichols January 31, 1836. She was born February 6, 1809.

HORACE PECK."

Clarendon, 1871.

BENJAMIN G. PETTINGILL

"I was born in Lewiston, Lincoln County, in the state of Maine. In 1817, I started for the Genesee country with my pack on my back and walked to Portland, thirty-five miles, where I went on board a vessel and sailed to Boston. I left Boston on foot with my pack on my back for the place of my destination. My pack was not very heavy, but I had in it, among other things, forty silver dollars. After a hard journey I arrived at Ogden, Monroe County, on the first day of April. I stopped there a while with an uncle of mine, was very homesick, and wished myself back in Maine many times.

I worked out that summer by the month, and in the fall bought some land in what is now Clarendon, Orleans County, then a part of Sweden.

I settled on my land, cleared it up, and in due time raised excellent crops, and in a few years found myself out of debt and considered myself rather *forehanded*.

I labored hard in the commencement, had considerable sickness in my family, but a good Providence had been mindful of me and mine, and in all my lawful

223

undertakings I have been blest, for which I feel truly grateful.

BENJAMIN G. PETTINGILL."

Clarendon, 1864.

BRADSTREET SPAFFORD

Mrs. Harriet S. Merrill, a daughter of Mr. Spafford, gives the following account of him:

"My father came from Connecticut about the year 1811, and purchased a farm about a mile south of Holley, on which he resided until his death in 1828. He was twice married. My mother, Mrs. Eunice Darrow, was his second wife. My father had but one child by his first wife, a daughter named Hester, who in after years became Mrs. Daniels, and is now Mrs. Blonden.

When this sister was four years old, her mother died of consumption. At that time my father's house was the only one between Holley and Farwell's Mills. In other directions it was a mile to the nearest neighbors. During her last illness my father was her principal physician and nurse. He used frequently to say to his friends he feared she would die suddenly while alone with him.

It was arranged between my father and his nearest neighbors, that if anything more alarming occurred in her case, he should blow the horn as a signal for them to come.

Not long after, at midnight of a dark winter night, death knocked at his door; he took the tin horn and blew the warning notes; but the winds were adverse, and nobody heard. Again and again he blew, longer and louder, but no one heard or came. His wife soon expired. My father closed her eyes, placed a napkin about her head and covered her lifeless form more closely, fearing it would become rigid before he could obtain assistance to habit it in the winding sheet preparatory for the tomb, for such were the habiliments used in those days.

He dressed his little daughter, placed her in her little chair by the fire, gave her her kitten to play with, and told her to sit there until he came back. He then went a mile to his nearest neighbors and roused them to come to his aid, and returned finding his little daughter as he had left her, along with her dead mother.

I was one of the first children born in the town of Clarendon, being now 46 years of age.

HARRIET S. MERRILL."

Clarendon, June 1863.

NICHOLAS F. DARROW

"I was born in the town of Chatham, Columbia County, N.Y., April 1st, 1808; and have been a farmer by occupation. My father, John Darrow, came to Wheatland, Monroe County, N.Y., in 1811, and worked there two seasons, then returned to Columbia County, sold his farm and was nearly ready to move his family to the Genesee country when he was taken sick and died March 22nd, 1813.

In June, 1815, my father's family moved to the farm he had bought two years previous. My mother, then a widow, married Mr. Bradstreet Spafford, who had settled in Clarendon, about the year 1811 or 12. I grew up among the hardships of the new country, and on December 30th, 1830, was married to Sarah A. Sweet, daughter of Noah Sweet, who came to Clarendon from Saratoga County, in 1815. My wife was born in Saratoga County in 1812.

My father was a blacksmith by trade, but owned and worked a farm. He was one of the leading mechanics who made the great chain which was put across the Hudson River to prevent the British fleet from coming up in the Revolutionary War, links of which are now in the State Library at Albany.

I have resided most of the time since 1815, in Clarendon; and for the last twenty-four years on the same farm. I lived a short time in Murray and a short time in Ohio.

I attended school in the first schoolhouse built in Clarendon. It stood a little south of Clarendon village, and was built in 1813, of logs, and in size was about fourteen by eighteen feet square, with slab floor and benches. The writing desks were made by boring holes in the logs in the wall, driving in pins and putting boards on these.

We have ten children, nine of whom are living. My second son is now serving in the Army of the Potomac in the War of the Great Rebellion.

I should have said in connection with my father's history, that himself and three of his brothers served in the Revolutionary War.

NICHOLAS E. DARROW."

Clarendon, April 1864.

ELDRIDGE FARWELL

Eldridge Farwell, born in Vermont in 1770, settled near Clarkson village on Ridge Road prior to 1811. In that year, he moved to the town of Clarendon, which was then an unbroken wilderness. He constructed the first sawmill in the town on Sandy Creek, producing the first boards in the region. In 1813, he established a grist mill on the same stream, which was the first of its kind in the town. When Orleans County was formed in 1825, Mr. Farwell was appointed as one of the Judges of the Court of Common Pleas, a position he held for five years. The village, at times referred to as Farwell's Mills, was named in his honor due to his status as the area's first settler. He married the daughter of Judge John Lee of Barre and passed away on October 15, 1843.

WILLIAM LEWIS

William Lewis served as a Deputy Sheriff of Genesee County and was the first Sheriff of Orleans County. He had previously held the offices of Supervisor and Justice of the Peace in Clarendon. Known for his prompt and efficient service, he was a highly regarded and worthy man. He passed away on July 23rd, 1824, at the age of around 43 years.

MARTIN EVARTS

Martin Evarts was born in Riga, Monroe County, N.Y., July 21st, 1812. He moved with his father's family to Clarendon in 1817. Until within a few years he resided on the farm originally taken up by his father. Mr. Evarts was Supervisor of Clarendon in 1863. He married

Charlotte Burnham, August 19th, 1835. She died June 20th, 1862.

LEMUEL COOK

Lemuel Cook was born in New Haven County, Connecticut, on September 10, 1763. His father passed away when Lemuel was a child, leaving his widow and children in dire circumstances.

In the Revolutionary War, he, with his two brothers, entered the army, Lemuel enlisting on November 1st, 1779, being then in his 17th year. He was honorably discharged June 11th, 1783. After leaving the army, his poll tax was remitted to him by the Selectmen of his town on account of wounds he had received in battle while serving the armies of his country. In 1792, he settled in Pompey, Onondaga County. In 1838, he moved to Bergen, Genesee County, and from thence to Clarendon, where he died May 20th, 1866, of old age, being 102 years, 8 months, and 10 days old. He was probably the oldest man that has lived in Orleans County. He was a Revolutionary War pensioner.

ISAAC CADY

Isaac Cady was born in Alstead, New Hampshire, July 26, 1793. He married Betsey Pierce, October 26th, 1816. He came to Clarendon in 1815, on foot, from Kingston, VT., and located the land on which he afterwards settled and has since resided.

CHAPTER 19.

TOWN OF GAINES

Gaines was formed from Ridgeway on February 14th, 1816. It included the town of Barre and the principal part of Carlton within its original limits. William J. Babbitt was prominently active in getting this town organized, and on his suggestion, it was named Gaines in honor of Gen. E. P. Gaines of the U. S. Army.

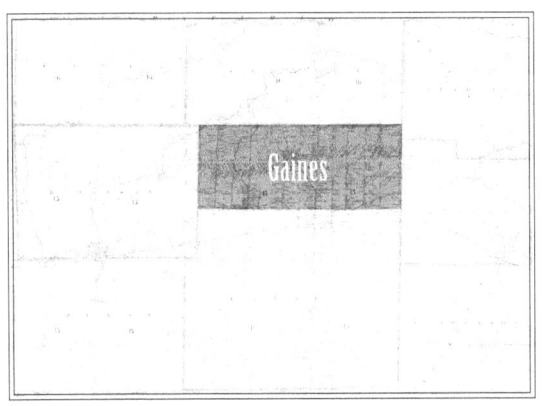

TOWN OF GAINES

A number of families had located along the Ridge Road before the war with England in 1812. One of the first settlers, if not the first, within the present bounds of the town of Gaines, was a Mr. Gilbert, who was living about two miles east of Gaines village, in 1809. He died in or about that year and was buried in Murray. A man who accompanied the widow and her niece home from the funeral, they, being all the family, found their fire had gone out, and they had no means to kindle it until this man, on his way home, called and notified Mr. Elijah Downer, and he sent his son several miles to carry them fire, they being the nearest neighbors.

The records of the Holland Land Company show that articles for land in the town of Gaines, parts of township fifteen, range two, were taken in the year 1809 by the following named persons: Andrew Jacox, Whitfield Rathbun, William Sibley, Cotton M. Leach, Noah Burgess, James Mather, and Henry Luce.

Turner's *History of the Holland Purchase* says: "Whitfield Rathbun was the pioneer upon all that part of the Ridge Road, in Orleans County, embraced in the Holland Purchase."

Noah Burgess came from Canada in a boat with his family and effects and landed at the head of Stillwater, in Carlton. He located on the south side of the Ridge, on the farm now occupied by Hon. Robert Anderson and his son Nahum.

Mr. Burgess was sick and unable to work when he first arrived, and the widow Gilbert, above referred to, took her oxen and moved the family and effects of Mr. Burgess from Stillwater to his place on the Ridge, a distance of about four miles. Mrs. Burgess, who was a strong, athletic woman, then chopped down trees and cut logs for a log house, and Mrs. Gilbert drew them to the spot with her oxen, and the walls of the house were rolled up from these logs by men who came along to look for land. The house so built was occupied for a time by Mr. Burgess and stood where the Ridge Road is now laid, in front of the dwelling house of Nahum Anderson. Mrs. Burgess set out a small orchard of apple trees near her house, which is supposed to be the first orchard set in Gaines.

Mr. Burgess sold his land to William Bradner and located a mile farther east, where he died some twenty years ago, and Mrs. Burgess, referred to, died in the summer of 1869.

The widow Gilbert was a hardy pioneer. The next winter after the death of her husband, aided by her niece, Amy Scott, she cut down trees to furnish browse for a yoke of oxen and some other cattle through the winter. She moved to Canandaigua in 1811.

Rowley, Wilcox, Leach, Adams, Rosier, Sprague, and Daniel Pratt were some of the settlers along the Ridge in 1810.

Daniel Gates came in 1811 and bought an article of a farm about two miles west of the village of Gaines, on the south side of the Ridge, since known as the Palmer farm.

A former proprietor had chopped down the trees on a small spot and built a cabin of logs, twelve feet square, with a single roof.

The Holland Company agreed with their settlers that if they would make a clearing and build a log house, they might have the land for two years without paying interest on the purchase money.

This cabin was built to save such interest and acquired additional notoriety from the fact that in this building, Orrin Gleason taught the first school in Gaines in the winter of 1813.

Henry Drake came to Gaines in 1811. In 1812 he built a dam and sawmill on Otter Creek, a few rods north of the Ridge, the first sawmill in this town.

When war was declared against Great Britain in 1812, the settlers in this area were concerned about potential danger from being near the frontier. They gathered together and chose Eleazer McCarty as their captain to lead them in defense if the settlement was attacked by the enemy.

In December 1813, the British burned Lewiston, and news was brought to Capt. McCarty by the fleeing inhabitants, that British and Indians were coming east on the Ridge. He sent a messenger in the night to John Proctor, the only man who had a horse in the settlement, to carry the news to Murray and call the men together to resist them. The next morning the company was en route towards the foe. The next night, they came in sight of Molyneaux tavern, ten or 12 miles east of Lewiston, and saw a light in the house. Captain McCarty halted his men and advanced himself to reconnoiter. Approaching the place, he saw British and Indians in the house, their guns standing in a corner. He returned to his men and brought them cautiously forward, selected a few to follow him into the house, and ordered the remainder to surround it and prevent the enemy from escaping. McCarty and his party rushed in at the door, sprang between the men and their guns, and ordered them to surrender.

The British soldiers and the Indians had been helping themselves to liquor in the tavern, and some were drunk and asleep on the floor. The surprise was complete. Most of the party surrendered; a few Indians showed fight with their knives and hatchets and tried to recover their guns, and several of them were killed in the melee. One soldier made a dash to get his gun and was killed by McCarty at a blow. The remainder surrendered and were put upon their march toward Lewiston, near which our army had then arrived. One prisoner would not walk. The soldiers dragged him forward on the ground awhile, and getting tired of that, Henry Luce, one of McCarty's men, declared with an Oath that he would kill him and was preparing for the act when McCarty interfered and saved his life.

McCarty encamped a few miles east of Lewiston. While there, he went out with a number of his men and captured a scouting party of British soldiers returning to Fort Niagara laden with plunder they had taken from the neighboring inhabitants. McCarty compelled them to carry the plunder back to its owners and then sent them prisoners of war to Batavia.

After fifteen or twenty days of service, McCarty's company was discharged and returned home. Most of his men resided in Gaines and comprised nearly all the men in town.

The first regular practicing physician in Gaines was Dr. Jesse Beach.

The first licensed attorney was Orange Butler, who settled here before it was determined whether the county seat would be Gaines or Albion. Judge Elijah Foot and W. W. Ruggles followed soon after.

The first marriage in Gaines was that of Andrew Jacobs to Sally Wing in the fall of 1810 or 11.

The first child born in Gaines was Samuel Crippen, Jr., in 1809.

The first printing press in Orleans County was located in Gaines by Seymour Tracy, who published the first newspaper there. Tracy was succeeded by John Fisk.

The publication of this paper commenced in about 1824 and continued for about four years.

The first grist mill was built on Otter Creek, about the year 1822, by Jonathan Gates.

The first tavern was kept by William Sibley in 1811. The first store was kept by William Perry in 1815.

Among the early merchants were E. & E. D. Nichols, V. R. Hawkins, and J. J. Walbridge.

James Mather, though he never kept a store of goods, was an active trader in black salts, potash, and staves, which he purchased from the settlers and took to the mouth of Oak Orchard Creek, or Genesee River and shipped to Montreal, for which he was paid in iron, salt fish, leather, and some kinds of coarse goods most needed, and some money.

Money to pay taxes, and to meet the pressing wants of the pioneers in this vicinity, was for some time mainly derived from this source.

The merchants of Gaines constructed a warehouse at Gaines Basin, on the canal, shortly after it became navigable. This is where goods for Gaines and other northern towns were mainly unloaded from boats, and where produce from the same region was primarily shipped.

A brisk trade was conducted here for several years until improvements in the highways and competition from neighboring villages redirected the business elsewhere. The warehouse was moved.

About the time the canal was completed, the village of Gaines was a place of more trade and business than any other in the county.

E. & E. D. Nichols, V. R. Hawkins, Bushnell & Guernsey, and John J. Walbridge were thriving merchants doing a lively business in the dry goods trade.

A full line of mechanic shops was established. The only academy, meeting house, and printing press in Orleans County were located here.

Two hotels were popular, stagecoaches were abundant on the famous Ridge Road. Considering all this, the people of Gaines, and most of the county in fact, excluding Newport (now named Albion), were convinced that the courthouse would surely be built in Gaines. They subsequently raised the price of village lots, while the people of Newport (referred to as Mudport by Gaines residents) offered to give away lots and make other generous offers if the Courthouse was located there.

But the courthouse went to Albion, and the stream of travel that once went on the Ridge took to the boats on the canal, and the post coaches were hauled off. Villages grew up along the canal, and trade went there.

The resolute businessmen of Gaines tried hard to retain their high position. They got their academy, village, and bank (The Farmer's Bank of Orleans) incorporated by the Legislature and lowered the price of building lots. But their glory had departed; their academy stopped, village franchises were lost by non-use, and their bank went bad. But their fine farms, choice garden spots, and unrivaled Ridge Road remained as good as ever.

BIOGRAPHIES OF EARLY SETTLERS

RICHARD TREADWELL

"I was born in Weston, Fairfield County, Connecticut, May 15th, 1783. In the winter of 1796, my father, in company with a neighbor, set out to move his family to the Genesee country. He had a covered sled drawn by a yoke of Oxen and a span of horses. I well recollect as we were about to start, our friends around us thought my parents very cruel to take their children away to the Genesee to be murdered by the Indians.

My father and all his children had the measles while on the journey. My father never fully recovered and died the next August. My mother was then left a widow with seven children, of whom I was the eldest, being then thirteen years old.

When I was about fifteen years old I revisited my native town and took along some bear skins and other skins, to exhibit as trophies of my skills as a hunter.

I attended school some and worked out the remainder of the time till fall, then returned to my mother on foot, and then went to work to help her support her family.

After my father's death, my mother sold her oxen for one hundred dollars and took a note in payment. The maker of the note failed and mother never received five dollars on the debt. One of her horses died, and the other was so ugly she gave him away, and thus lost her team, and the bears killed all her hogs.

When I was eighteen or twenty years old I resolved to build a log house for mother on the land my father took up. It was usual then to raise such buildings at a *bee*, and that could not be done without whisky.

I went to a distillery in Bloomfield on horseback, with two wooden bottles in a bag to get the liquor. Following the Indian trail through the woods on my way back, I saw a cub climbing a tree and the mother bear coming toward me with hair erect and about two rods off. I put whip and spur to my horse and did not stop to look back until I was out of her reach.

I had a small flock of sheep about that time. Neglecting to yard them one night, the wolves killed nearly all of them.

A year or two after I first came into the county, a man hired me to take a horse to the Genesee River, where Rochester now stands. There was but one house on that road then. I forded the river with my horse.

I was married January 17th, 1809, to Miss Temperance Smith, of Palmyra. She died in May following.

For several years after I came into the county, the Indians were numerous here, hundreds of Indians to one white man. They were very friendly. I used to go to their wigwams and have sport with them wrestling and pulling stick, at which I was an expert, frequently throwing their smartest young men at back hold, or what we called Indian hug.

Bears, wolves, and raccoons were plenty, and I caught them frequently.

In March, 1810, I married Frances Bennett, and commenced housekeeping again, and went to work clearing my land. I think I have chopped and logged off as much as one hundred and fifty acres in my day.

I have had the fever and ague several times, but generally let it work itself off. I used to work hard all day in my fallow, and frequently worked evenings there when it was good weather.

My wife would often come out when I was at work and sometimes help me pile brush.

During the war with England I was several times called out to do military duty.

I moved into the town of Shelby in 1827, and after a few years sold out and moved to Gaines, on the farm on which I now reside.

RICHARD TREADWELL."

Gaines, 1863.

Mr. Treadwell died June 9th, 1866 aged 83 years.

"I was born in Pittsford, Vermont, September 10, 1788. I married Polly Harwood in Pittsford in 1809. In August 1810, I bought the farm I now own, in the town of Gaines, of the Land Company, for $2.50 per acre, part of lot five, town fifteen, range two, on the Oak Orchard Road, about a mile south of the Ridge.

In February, 1811, I moved my wife from Vermont to Gaines, and in April of that year we moved into a log cabin, in which James Mather was then keeping bachelor's hall, and lived with him. In June afterwards I put up a log house 18 by 20 feet square and covered it with bark, with split basswood logs for a floor sufficient to set a bed on, and then we moved in. Our nearest neighbors south following the Oak Orchard Road, were south of the Tonawanda Swamp.

In August following, my wife was taken sick. I could get no one to help about the house, for such help was not in the county, and I was compelled to leave my work and attend to my wife for six weeks, during which time I did not take off my clothes except to change them.

I was poor and had to work out for all I had. I came very near being homesick then, but I stood it through. The next winter I chopped two or three acres on my land, and in the spring burned the brush and planted it with corn among the logs, but squirrels and birds got the greater part of it, so we got but little corn that year.

In the spring of 1812, some families located south of where Albion now is. Of those families I had stopping at my house at one time, while they were building their cabins, William McCollister, Joseph Hart, Silas Benton, Elijah Darrow, Frederick Holsenburgh, and John Holsenburgh, and the families of some of them.

The war of 1812 put a stop to the settlement for a while. We were troublesome with British deserters.

Up to 1813, our provisions were mainly fish, potatoes, and turnips, this is among the poorer class of settlers like myself. Sometimes we would have hulled wheat and *hulled corn*. Sometimes I went to Parma or Rochester to mill, and when I got back my grist would not pay my expenses.

After the war and the cold seasons, the county filled up with settlers very fast. Roads and improvements were made, and the land cleared up and cultivated, and the conveniences and comforts of life procured, thus relieving the wants of the people and supplying their needs.

WALTER FAIRFIELD."

Gaines, 1863.

Mr. Walter Fairfield died January 9th, 1865.

JOHN PROCTOR

"I was born in the town of Dunstable, Middlesex County, Massachusetts, January 22nd, 1787. In March, 1810, I arrived in Batavia, since changed to Gaines on the Holland Purchase, and purchased a lot of land near the Transit Line. I chopped over five acres of land and built a log cabin in what was then called the Nine Mile Woods. My cabin was situated seven miles from any cabin going east, and two miles west. There were no inhabitants going south nearer than Batavia village. Here I kept bachelor's hall, sleeping in the open air on hemlock boughs until I had completed the roof of my cabin, which I covered with bark. I had to travel seven miles to get bread baked.

I went to Massachusetts in the summer and returned to my cabin in January. In the spring of 1811, I cleared off and planted three acres to corn, and in the fall sowed five acres to wheat.

In December I went back to Massachusetts on foot. February 11th, 1812, I was married to Miss Polly Cummings, of Dunstable, and started on the 12th with my wife for my home in the woods, in a sleigh drawn by two horses.

When we arrived at our new home, at what has since been called Fair Haven, in the town of Gaines, there were but three families in Gaines: Elijah Downer, Amy Gibert, and Mr. Elliott.

The nearest grist mill was at Black Creek, twenty miles distant, and on account of bad roads it was as easy for us to go to Rochester, a distance of thirty miles.

In the fall of 1812, I harvested a good crop of wheat and corn.

In the winter of 1813-14, the British and Indians came over from Canada and massacred several of the inhabitants on the frontier, and many of the settlers fled out of the country for safety. The people throughout this region were in great consternation. The news of the approach of the savages spread rapidly.

William Burlingame, who resided about four miles west of my place on the Ridge, called me out of bed and requested me to go immediately and arouse the people east. I immediately mounted my horse, the only horse then owned in the vicinity, and before next day light visited all the inhabitants as far east as Clarkson.

The effect of the notice was almost electric, for quite a regiment of men in number were on the move early the next morning, to check the advance of the enemy. We marched west to a place called *Hardscrabble*, near Lewiston, and there performed a sort of garrison duty for two weeks, when I with some others returned, for, having been elected *collector of taxes*, it became necessary for me to attend to the duties of my office.

Again in September, while the war was in progress at and near Fort Erie, in Canada, news came to us that the British were about to attack the Fort and our troops there must be reinforced. In company with several others I volunteered to go to their relief. On arriving at the Fort, via. Buffalo, we made several attacks on the enemy near the Fort, and in the woods opposite Black Rock.

A sortie was made from the Fort September 17th, in which we routed the enemy. In these actions several bullets passed through my clothes, and one grazed my finger.

A man of our company named Howard was killed, another named Sheldon was wounded in the shoulder, and Moses Bacon was taken prisoner and carried to *Halifax*.

In that sortie General Davis, of LeRoy, was killed, and Gen. Peter B. Porter was taken prisoner, and rescued again the same day. We came home after an absence of twenty-four days.

About February 1st, 1815, I was notified to attend the sitting of the court in Batavia as constable. Owing to the situation of my family I could not be long absent from home; and in order to get released from court, it was necessary for me to appear before the judge; so taking a rather early start I reached Batavia before the court had opened in the morning. After the court had organized for business I presented my excuse and was discharged.

After that I collected over one hundred dollars taxes, made my returns as town collector, on half a sheet of paper, took a deed of one hundred acres of land of the Holland Company, and an article for another hundred acres and started for home, where I arrived in the evening of the same day, having traveled a distance of not less than forty-four miles.

In December, 1818, I made arrangements to visit my friends in Massachusetts, on horseback. Several of my neighbors were in to see me off. As I was about to mount my horse a deer came down the creek from the south. I ran into the house and got my gun and some cartridges I brought from the war, loaded my gun as I ran out, and as the deer was passing leveled my gun and snapped it, but it missed fire. I took up a stone and struck the flint, and snapped the gun again before the deer got out of range. This time it discharged, killing the deer instantly. I remained now and helped dress the deer and divided it with our neighbors, and then went on my journey. I rode to Vermont, there exchanged my horse, and drove to my destination, near Boston. After an absence of about sixty days I returned home in time to dine off a piece of the venison I killed just before starting, which had been kept by my wife.

Our associations in our wilderness home undergoing fatigue and hardships together, sharing alike in gratitude for every success, and in sympathy for every adversity, bound the early settlers together as a band of brothers.

For many years our religious worship was held in common together, with no denominational distinctions.

JOHN PROCTOR."

Gaines, June 1863.

Mr. John Proctor died in 1868.

SAMUEL HILL.

"I was born in Barrington, Rockingham County, N.H., November 18th, 1793. I was married February 28th, 1815, to Miss Olive Knight.

In the winter of 1823 we moved to Gaines, with means little more than enough to defray the expense of the journey, and settled on part of the farm on which I now reside. We began by building a log house, the crevices between the logs serving for windows. The children would sit on the *fire sill* in front of where was to be a chimney. Thus we lived from May 10th, to fall, when we made our house comfortable for winter.

My father was a practical farmer, and my first recollections of work were of helping clear land. He with the help of his boys, of whom I was eldest but one, cleared one hundred and fifty acres.

Beginning with little, we have by hard labor, strict economy and the blessing of God, succeeded in securing a comfortable home and a *competence of this world's goods*.

SAMUEL HILL."

Gaines, March 1864.

SAMUEL SALSBURY

"I was born in Newport, Herkimer County, N.Y., July 24, 1804. In January, 1817, I moved with my brother Stephen to the Holland Purchase and settled in Ridgeway. The country with few exceptions was a wilderness. Provisions were scarce and dear, wheat worth three dollars a bushel, corn two dollars, potatoes one dollar, and other things in proportion. Before harvest nearly every family was destitute of bread. Their resort for a substitute was the growing wheat, which was boiled and eaten with milk; or by adding a little cream and maple sugar together, to make a kind of dessert after a meal of potatoes and butter, and possibly a little deer, squirrel and raccoon meat.

Our milk was strongly flavored with leeks occasionally, with which our native pastures abounded, but we used to correct this by eating a fresh leak before eating the milk. We had plenty of maple sugar.

Schoolhouses were scarce, and of churches, there were none. I attended school in a log house two miles from home, south of what is now Lyndonville, and this school house was for many years used as a place for worship. Here I used to hear Elder Irons and Elder Dutcher, Baptists, and Elders Paddock, Boardman, Hall, and Puffer, Methodists.

Among my early school teachers were Gen. W. C. Tanner and Mrs. Mastin.

Chopping, clearing and fencing land was the principal business in those days.

My last feat in chopping was in 1832, when I walked three miles morning and evening, and chopped over three acres, leaving it fitted for logging in ten and a half days.

In February, 1825, I crossed Niagara river on the ice which had wedged in near the mouth of the river. It was a warm day, the water was on the ice, and large openings were frequent. In one place a seam of open water three feet across was passed on a board, which served as a bridge. I crossed in safety.

In the winter of 1826–27, I united with the Methodist Episcopal Church. I had never, to this time, heard a temperance lecture or known anything of temperance societies, but from that time I believed it wicked to use intoxicating drinks as a beverage, and I have never used them since.

I was married to Miss Electa Beal, February 23, 1829.

I was licensed to preach the gospel in July, 1832, by the Conference sitting in Penn Yan. Till then I had been a farmer and school teacher. From that time till 1844, I labored in that vicinity in the Methodist Episcopal

Church. In May, 1843, I withdrew from that church and joined in organizing the Wesleyan Methodist *Connexion* of America, and from then since, I have labored as a minister in that Connexion.

SAMUEL SALISBURY."

Eagle Harbor, March 1864.

PERRY DAVIS

Perry Davis was born in Westport, Massachusetts, January 1st, 1773.

In 1793, he married Rebecca Potter. She died May 12, 1825.

After his marriage, he resided about thirteen years in Galway, Saratoga County. He then resided about eighteen years in Palmyra, N.Y.; and in 1823, moved to Gaines, and took up land near the mouth of Otter Creek; and in 1825, moved to the village of Gaines and bought the farm next north of the Ridge, and west of the Oak Orchard Road. He was an active business man, being engaged at different times as a merchant, farmer, school teacher, and manufacturer; and while residing in Gaines, superintending at the same time three farms, a sawmill, a gristmill, and a small iron *foundry*, all in operation. He was a deacon, and a prominent member of the Baptist Church in Gaines.

He had eight daughters: Barbara, who died in childhood; Rowena married William Hayden; Cynthia married Daniel Ball; Cinderilla married Samuel Parker; Mary married Richard Workman; Ann married William W. Ruggles; Eliza married Elonzo G. Hewitt; and Laura married Dr. Alfred Babcock. In 1827, he married Sarah

Toby, of Stockton, N.Y. She died November 4th, 1856. Mr. Davis died April 3, 1841.

LEVI ATWELL

Levi Atwell was born in Canaan, Columbia County, N.Y.

He married Mabel Stoddard, and moved from Cayuga County to Gaines in February, 1812, and took an article of part of lot forty-four, township fifteen, range two, and resided on the same land until he died, February, 1847.

He took up his land in April, 1811, and in June after he came on, chopped down the trees on a few acres, and that season put up a log house, into which he moved his family when they came.

His brothers-in-law, Gideon Freeman and Joseph Stoddard, came on and took up land at the same time. He remained on his land during the war with England.

The house into which he moved had no door, or window or floor except the earth, and not a board about it. The logs had been merely rolled up for the walls, without stopping the crevices between them. The roof was covered with shakes split from oak trees like stave bolts, about three feet long, laid on in courses like shingles, without nails, and held on by poles laid on transversely, with no chimney, but a large hole in the roof left for the smoke, and which admitted the light.

The snow was about three feet deep. A huge fire was kept up in one end of the cabin; this heated the roof and melted the snow, which dripped most uncomfortably upon everything in the house. A blanket was hung at the doorway. Chips driven into the crevices between the logs stopped them in part till spring, when stones were laid for a hearth, and a stick chimney put in.

Mr. Atwell had a yoke of oxen and several other cattle that arrived a few days after he brought his family. He brought several bushels of ears of corn when he moved in, which he dealt out sparingly to his stock. They had no other food except the trees he cut down for them to browse, until they could get their living in the woods in the spring.

His family consisted of himself, wife and four children, the youngest about two years old. His children's names were Ira, Abbey, Roxy, Joseph and Martin.

In the fall of 1812, a man by the name of Crofoot died in the neighborhood. No boards to make his coffin could be found, not in use in the settlement. When Mr. Atwell moved in with his family, he brought a board for a side-board, on his sled. This he had put up for a shelf in his house for dishes, etc., and this shelf, and a board from some other house were taken for the coffin, in which the corpse was buried.

SAMUEL C. LEWIS

Samuel C. Lewis was born in Poultney, Vermont on June 8, 1796. When he was seventeen, he enlisted in the United States Army as a soldier in the War of 1812. He served in a company commanded by Captain Miller, who later founded the sect known as the Millerites or Second Adventists. Samuel participated in the battles of Plattsburgh and French Mills during his two years of service in the army.

In February 1816, Samual Lewis accompanied his brother Gideon, Jacob Clift, his brothers Roswell, Amos, Elias Clift, and their sister Esther (who later married Guy C. Merrill) on a journey from Poultney, Vermont, to Gaines. They arrived in Gaines on March 19th, 1816, after being on the road for twenty-five days, using a lumber wagon drawn by two yoke of oxen.

Arba Chubb, who was married to a sister of the Lewises, arrived in Gaines with his wife and child a day before Mr. Lewis and his company. They moved into the log house built by Mrs. Burgess, near where Judge Anderson currently resides. The house had been unoccupied for some time and was not in good condition to live in. However, it was the best option available, so the three Lewis brothers stayed there with Mr. Chubb. They had cleared away the snow and gathered a good supply of fuel to keep them warm because the weather was stormy and cold, and the house had large crevices open between the logs.

Mr. Chubb and his family had a bed in a corner of the room, while the three young men lay on the floor with their feet to the fire. During the night, the intense heat from the fire thawed the old chimney, causing it to collapse forward into the room. Fortunately, no one was injured. The following morning, they arranged the stones back in place and reconstructed a chimney that served its purpose.

Mr. Lewis and his brother purchased 125 acres of land from Lansing Bailey. The land is located at Gaines Basin and includes a log house that was built by Mr. Bailey. Interestingly, the log house is constructed without the use of nails or shingles, with all pieces fastened together using wooden pins.

They worked hard on this piece of land, clearing it the following summer and moving into their new house. They did their cooking and washing at Mr. Bailey's family's place on a nearby lot, in exchange for working for Mr. Bailey every seventh day that season to pay him back.

Samuel C. Lewis married Anna Frisbie, in March 1819. She died the next year.

January 30th, 1824, he married Anna Warner, of Cornwall, Vt. She died April 10th, 1841.

Mr. Lewis retains and resides on the lot of land on which he first settled.

He has walked and carried his knapsack on his back, twelve times the whole distance between Gaines and Poultney Vt. Once he performed the journey in October, in six days, walking on an average nearly fifty miles a day.

In the year 1819, he had a tax to pay and wanted a dollar to make the sum required. To raise the money, he cut four cords of **body maple** wood and drew it a mile and sold it to Oliver Booth for twenty-five cents a cord, and so paid his tax.

GIDEON S. LEWIS

Gideon S. Lewis was born in Poultney, Vermont, September, 1792. He married Betsey Mason, daughter of the late Jesse Mason, of Barre, N.Y., in the fall of 1820. She died in September, 1842. He then married Betsey Shelley, of Gaines. He had four children, Lestina, who married Henry Cox; Homer, who studied medicine, and died some years ago; Augustus and Augusta, twins. Augustus is dead. Augusta married Alonzo Morgan. Gideon S. Lewis died October 6th, 1865.

Roswell Lewis, brother of Samuel and Gideon, resided in Gaines about three years, then returned to Vermont.

NATHAN SHELLEY

Nathan Shelley was born in Hartford, Washington County, NY, on March 17, 1798. In May 1812, he moved with his father's family to Gaines, where his father settled on the Ridge Road, two miles west of the village of Gaines.

Shortly after his arrival, war was declared against Great Britain. Following the Americans' defeat at Queenstown in October 1812, many residents on the frontier moved eastward. Mr. Shelley relocated with his family but later returned in December.

Nathan Shelley married Dorcas Tallman, May 21st, 1820. She was born in Washington County N.Y., August 4th, 1795.

In 1821, he took up and settled part of lot forty-five, township fifteen, range two, on which he has ever since resided.

His first log house had but one room, only four lights of glass, and a bedquilt for an outside door, when he moved into it to reside in the the winter of 1821-22.

Beginning poor, by a life of steady industry and prudence he became a wealthy farmer.

THE BULLARD FAMILY

The Bullard family in Gaines is descended from David Bullard, born in Dedham, Massachusetts, in 1761. He later moved to Vermont and in September 1814, he relocated to Gaines, N.Y. with some of his children. Initially, he settled on lot twenty-three, just west of the village of Gaines, north of the Ridge, on land that had been claimed by his son William. After a year or two, he moved south of the Ridge to lot twenty-one, a farm now owned by his son Brigadier, where he lived until he passed away in June 1831.

David Bullard was married to Elizabeth Hadley. Their children were William, Polly, Judith, Olive, Betsey, Nancy, Sally, David, Brigadier, and Ransom.

William married Nellie Loveland, Polly married William Woolman, Judith married John Witherell, Olive married James Bartlett, Betsey married Frederick Holsenburgh, Nancy married Samuel Scovill, Sally married Alba Chubb, David married Elvira Murwin, Brigadier married Lovina Parker, and Ransom married Lydia Buck.

William, Judith, and Brigadier settled in Gaines in February 1812. William Bullard passed away in September 1861.

THE BILLINGS FAMILY

Joseph Billings, Sr., the ancestor of this family, was born in Somers, Connecticut and settled in Chenango County, New York, where he lived until his death. He bought a large amount of land in Gaines from Isaac Bennett, who had acquired it from the Land Company via an article. In 1822, he divided the land among his sons, Joseph, Timothy, and Lauren.

Joseph Billings married Charlotte Drake. His children are: J. Drake Billings, who married Melinda Shaw; Myron, who married Phebe Bement; Clinton, who married Esther Murdock; Harlow, who married Adeline King; William H., who married Sarah Everett; Clarissa, who married Elijah B. Lattin; and Helen, who married John Lattin.

Timothy Billings married Betsey Bidwell. His children were Newton and Sanford, who died in early manhood, and Pomeroy, who died in childhood.

Lauren Billings married Roxana C. Rexford. His children are: Karthalo R., who married Catharine Murdock; Pomeroy O., who married Harriet Thompson; Loverna C., who married Norman A. Beecher; L. Dwight; Simeon R., who married Carrie E. Gray; and Joseph F., who married Josephine Eldridge.

Joseph, Timothy, and Lauren Billings occupied neighboring farms, which they cleared and improved. Joseph and Lauren were each Justices of the Peace in Gaines for several years. Lauren was a Colonel in the State Militia, while Joseph was Supervisor of Gaines from 1837 to 1841, inclusive. Joseph Billings died on December 10, 1866, and Timothy Billings passed away on May 10th, 1837.

ARBA CHUBB

Arba Chubb was born in Poultney, Vt., September 18th, 1791.

He married Emily Frisbie on October 17, 1813. On February 20, 1816, they began their move to Gaines, N.Y. in a wagon and arrived after twenty days on the road.

He purchased a farm located between the Ridge and Gaines Basin and lived there until 1832. Then, he relocated to Gaines Basin, where he purchased a warehouse and conducted business as a produce dealer and goods retailer until 1840. In 1840, he moved to Gaines village and later, in 1856, he moved to Michigan.

His first wife passed away in 1829. He then married Sally, the daughter of David Bullard of Gaines.

In 1821, Mr. Chubb was appointed as a Justice of the Peace by the *Council*. Later, he was elected as a Justice of the Peace by the people of Gaines. He served in this role for thirty-three years, with only a one-year break during that time.

After moving to Michigan he was elected Justice of the Peace from time to time, until in the whole he served in that office 47 years. No man has held the office of Justice of the Peace in Orleans County as long as Esquire Chubb. He also held every other town office but constable, and every office in the militia, from Corporal to Major, inclusive. He was for some time postmaster in Gaines, and Member of Assembly from Orleans County, for the year 1848.

Esquire Chubb recounted a lawsuit tried before him shortly after he became a Justice, which caused him significant trouble at the time.

"Orange Butler was on one side, and a young lawyer named Capen, from Albion, on the other. I think they planned to give me a sweat. The plaintiff put in his declaration. The defendant demurred. The plaintiff put in a rejoinder. The defendant a surrejoinder. The plaintiff was a rebutter. The defendant was a surrebutter.

About all this special pleading I knew nothing. I supposed, however, they would ask me to make a special decision, but what the decision should be, I knew no more than the biggest fool alive. There I sat, the sweat rolling down my face, inwardly cursing the day I was appointed Justice and my folly in accepting an office I knew nothing about.

I think the lawyers saw my trouble, had pity on me and helped me out as well as they could, and went on and tried the case."

Esquire Chubb resides at Ionia, Michigan, and is now (1871) serving in his old office of Justice of the Peace.

THE ANDERSON FAMILY

The ancestors of this family originally emigrated from Scotland to Ireland, and thence to Londonderry, New Hampshire, at an early day.

John Anderson, the ancestor of most of the families of his name in Gaines, was born in Londonderry, Aug. 31, 1757. He was a soldier in the Revolution, fought at *Bunker Hill*, and was at the taking of Ticonderoga under Ethan Allen. He married Jane Archibald in Londonderry, Feb. 7, 1782, and settled in Ira, Rutland County Vermont, in the same year. He represented this town in the State Legislature eight or ten years in succession.

His children were: Ann, Jane, John, Robert, Matthew, Betsey, Thomas A., Margaret, Nancy, Eli B. and Samuel F., all of whom were early settlers in Gaines, except Betsey, who died in Malone, N.Y. January 11, 1813.

John Anderson, senior, moved with his family to Gaines in 1821, and located on lot twenty-nine, township fifteen, range two, on the north side of the Ridge road, where he died October 22, 1827. He was a man of very great physical strength, of good intellect, energetic and persistent in his character. One of his rules of action was: Do what duty required, and Conscience approves as right, without fear.

Indeed he never showed fear of anything. Many instances are recollected of his cool and determined courage in cases of danger. In several conflicts he had with bears, he performed exploits as hazardous and full of daring, as Gen. Putnam's battle with the wolf.

One evening while he lived in Ira, dogs treed a bear not far from his residence. A number of men were present, but they had no guns. Mr. Anderson told them to build a fire around the tree and keep the bear up it until morning, and then he would go up and drive him down. The fire was made. Next morning Anderson armed with a club, climbed the tree to the bear thirty feet from the ground, and crept out on the limb on which he had retreated.

Disregarding the growls and bristling of the ferocious creature, Mr. Anderson went within reach and aimed a blow at its head with his club which the bear warded off and knocked the club to the ground. Nothing daunted, Mr. Anderson descended, got two clubs, and again went up the tree to the bear. Taking a club in each hand, he made motions to strike with his left hand, and when the bears attention was attracted to these, he struck him a terrible blow on the head with the other club, which knocked the body of the beast off the limb, leaving him hanging by his fore paws. A blow or two on his claws loosened their hold, and the bear was killed by the men below when he struck the ground.

Another time while he lived in Vermont, being in the woods, he saw a bear coming towards him. Concealing himself in bushes on a steep place, he lay in ambush, and the bear passed him so near that with a spring he rushed upon him, and armed only with a stone, pounded his head until he killed him.

Ann Anderson married Daniel Gates of Rutland, Vermont, moved to Gaines in 1811, and settled on lot twenty-nine, township fifteen, range two. After a few years he sold this farm and moved to a farm in Carlton, where he died January 31, 1858. Mrs. Ann Gates died January 1, 1866. Two of her sons, John and N. F. Gates, now reside in Carlton, and another Matthew A. Gates, resides in Yates.

Jane Anderson married Phineas Rowley, of Rutland, Vermont, moved to Gaines in 1817, and settled on lot thirty, township fifteen, range one. They both died several years since. Two of their sons, John and Andrew J. Rowley, are yet living in Gaines.

Margaret Anderson married John Farnham Jan. 22, 1818. They moved to Gaines, Oct., 1824, and settled on lot forty, township fifteen, range two. John Farnham was born in Poultney, Vt., February 26, 1795, and died November 3, 1841. Margaret Farnham died in May, 1868.

Nancy Anderson married Solomon Kingsley in Vermont and moved to Orleans County about 1819. They moved to Michigan in 1835 and died there.

John Anderson, Jr., was born in Ira, Vermont, September 12, 1785. He settled in Gaines on lot twenty-two, township fifteen, range two, in 1810.

At the first town meeting held in Ridgway, April 6, 1813, he was elected overseer of the Poor. He was a man of positive character, a great lover of truth, withdrawing his confidence from the man who failed to keep his promises.

A neighbor owed him twelve shillings, which he promised to pay in a few days. John Anderson replied that he hoped the neighbor would pay because it was worth a shilling to remind a man about the debt at any time. In a few days, the neighbor met him, spoke of his debt, and renewed his promise to pay.

As they occasionally met afterward, the debtor would remind Anderson about the debt but paid nothing until, one day he repeated his acknowledgment and promise. John took out a shilling and handed it to him, saying, "Here is a shilling for you, we are now even. I have given you credit on account one shilling each time you have reminded yourself for me and broken your promise. Your credits balance your debt and one shilling over, which I have paid you. It is settled, don't speak to me about it again."

Eli B. Anderson got married in Poultney, Vermont, then moved to Gaines with his father. He lived with his father until his death and stayed at the same place six or eight years after his father's passing, after which he moved to Michigan.

Samuel F. Anderson moved to Gaines with his father, being then about eighteen years old. In 1836 he married Miss Mahala Phipps of Albion, and moved to Cassopolis, Michigan where he still resides. He has represented his county several years in the State Legislature and been Judge of County Courts.

Matthew Anderson moved to Gaines in 1816 and took an article of part of lot twenty-seven, township fifteen, range two, since known as the Hunter Farm a little north of Eagle Harbor, now owned by C. A. Danolds and S. W. Kneeland. He cleared some land and built a log house on his farm. He died September 30, 1816. In 1814 or 1815, he represented the town of Ira in the Vermont Legislature. He was Captain of a company of militia, which under his command volunteered and went to meet the British at Plattsburgh in the war of 1812.

Hon. Robert Anderson was born in the town of Ira, Vermont, April 21, 1787.

In June, 1807, he was elected Lieutenant in the militia. In October 1812 he was appointed Justice of the Peace in Rutland. He went with a company of volunteers to fight the British at Plattsburgh in the war of 1812.

In November 1812, he came to Gaines and bought an article for 150 acres, part of lot 22, township fifteen, range two, to which he moved his family in 1816, and where he has ever since resided. Two younger brothers,

Matthew and Dr. Thomas A. Anderson and their families came on at the same time from Vermont. The Dr. drove a two horse lumber wagon, which carried the women and children of the party, the other two men drove each a team of two yoke of oxen drawing a wagon laden with their goods with a cow led behind each team.

They arrived in Gaines March 25th, having been twenty-five days on the road.

Upon arriving in Gaines, Robert Anderson moved into the log house on the property. Mrs. Noah Burgess had purchased the logs for the house in 1809. The house was roofed with elm boards and had a floor made of split basswood in the traditional pioneer style. The following year, he constructed a small framed house and lived in that.

In the summer of 1821, David Whipple and wife, parents of Mrs. Robert Anderson, came to Gaines from Vermont to visit their children. They rode in a one-horse wagon with bolsters and box lumber style, covered with cloth over hoops. The seat was a chair, wide as the box, splint bottomed, the posts standing on the steel springs of a wolf trap. This was probably the first wheel carriage rigged with steel springs that ran in Orleans County, and was much admired for its novelty and convenience.

Robert and his wife started with her parents on their return to Vermont, to visit friends on the way. They went as far as Brighton, where she was taken sick and died. The death of his wife and the sickness prevailing in the country, with which he was attacked, so disheartened him he offered his farm for sale, and would have sold at almost any price, but no purchaser appearing and his health having improved, he concluded to stay.

In August 1822, he married his second wife, Miss Roxana Lamb, of Bridgewater, Vermont, who died March 27, 1837.

In 1840, he rented his farm to his eldest son and only surviving child, Nahum Anderson. He later sold it to Nahum but reserved the right to live in the family home during his life.

In 1817, Robert had been elected Lieutenant of a militia company in Gaines, later resigning. He also served as a Justice of the Peace until 1822 and was appointed as Judge of the Court of Common Pleas of Genesee County for over two years. In 1818, he was elected Supervisor of the town of Gaines and re-elected annually. In 1826, he became the first Supervisor from that town to serve in the new county of Orleans and was appointed Chairman. Additionally, he served as a member of the State Legislature in 1822.

Judge Anderson was never ambitious to hold public offices, generally taking office only when it was offered him without his asking, and resigning the first proper opportunity. He was regarded as a man of sound judgment, honest and faithful, and shared largely in the confidence of all who knew him.

For some years past, he has lived quietly, retired from the cares of business, possessing a competence of property acquired by his own exertions, happy in the society of his many friends, enjoying a pleasant home.

Dr. Thomas A. Anderson, son of John Anderson, senior, was born in Ira, Vt., May 14th, 1792. He married Sarah Whipple of Malone, N.Y., and moved to Gaines, as above stated, in 1816, and located at Fair Haven, or Proctor's Corners, in the town of Gaines, where he practiced his profession for some time in company with Dr. Truman S. Shaw.

Dr. Anderson had practiced medicine for several years in Rutland, Vermont before coming to Gaines. He was esteemed as a skillful physician and had as much business as he could handle. He was constitutionally feeble, never enjoyed good health, and passed away on September 2, 1829, leaving behind only one child, a daughter who is now the wife of S. Dewey Walbridge of Rochester N.Y. His wife Sarah had died a few months earlier on April 22, 1829.

MOSES BACON

Moses Bacon was born April 5, 1787, in Burlington, Hartford, County, Conn. He was a farmer.

In about the year 1809, he arrived in Gaines and obtained a piece of land from the Holland Land Company, comprising two hundred acres on the southern part of lot thirty-seven, township fifteen, range one. During that year, he worked for the Land Company, helping to open the Oak Orchard Road, as part of his effort to pay for the land. He then returned to Connecticut in the fall. The following spring, he came back and began working on his land as a permanent settler.

In December 1813, he joined Captain McCarty's company to defend the frontier. During the charge upon the British and Indians at Molyneaux Tavern in Cambria, Mr. Bacon was present and performed effectively.

In January, 1814, he married Miss Sarah Downer. In September of that year he was called out with the men on this frontier generally, to aid in repelling the British and Indians in the war with Great Britain. He was in the battle of Fort Erie, in which he was shot through the neck and taken prisoner by the British, who carried him to Halifax, where he suffered greatly under the cruel treatment of the officers who had the American prisoners under their charge. The next year he was discharged, the war having closed, and returned home broken in constitution from the hardships of his wound and imprisonment, and with a cough contracted in Halifax from which he never recovered, and for which he drew a pension from the United States ever afterwards.

Mr. Bacon sold the east part of his farm to his brother Hosea, and the north part to his brother Elias, reserving one hundred acres for himself. Upon this place he lived until his death, which occurred June 28th, 1848.

SAMUEL BIDELMAN

Samuel Bidelman was born in Manheim, Herkimer County, N.Y., June 29th, 1806. His grandparents both came to America from Germany, before the revolutionary war, and settled on the Mohawk river. In that war his grandfather's buildings were burned by the Indians, and his family narrowly escaped massacre by fleeing to the **block house fort** for protection.

His father, Henry, came to Shelby in 1816, and bought an article for one hundred acres of land of John

Timmerman. In January, 1817, he came to Shelby with a part of his children, leaving his wife and other children in Herkimer County until he could prepare a place for them. He was eleven days on the journey.

In July 1817, John Garlock, the brother-in-law of Henry Bidelman, brought Mrs. Bidelman and her remaining children along with three bags of flour. This was the year after the *cold season*, and the community was experiencing a lack of flour. Some residents hadn't even had wheat bread for weeks, and had been surviving on bran bread and sea biscuit (hardtack) obtained from the Arsenal at Batavia, which had been stored there to feed soldiers during the War of 1812.

When a new family arrived, it was customary for all the settlers from miles around to come together and greet them with a surprise party. This happened to the Bidelmans. After the party, Mr. Bidelman found that he only had a part of one bag of flour left out of the three brought by Garlock, as each visiting family took some flour home. Having only a part of one bag of flour for a family of twelve hungry people seemed like the end was near.

These sea biscuits furnished material for much talk, as well as food for the people. Mr. Joseph Snell, who had a good sense of humor, shared a story about a Mr. Simons, who lived south of Mr. Bidelman. It was reported that Mr. Simons had eaten a large amount of the sea biscuits, which had caused his stomach to swell and burst. According to the story, his companions tried to contain the swelling by tying handkerchiefs and straps around him, but were unsuccessful, and he ultimately passed away. Several people went to attend the funeral before they understood the hoax.

The first year after he came to Shelby, Henry Bidelman took some land of D. Timmerman which lay about a mile from his house, to plant with corn on shares. In hoeing time, in the long days in June, he would get his boys together, Samuel being then about twelve years old, get them a breakfast of bran bread and milk and say to them, "now boys you can go and hoe corn, and when you get so tired and hungry you can't stand it any longer, come home and we will try and get you something to eat again." This was the way they fared before uncle Garlock came with flour.

During the *cold season* of 1816, the crops were severely affected, leading to a scarcity of food. Flour was priced at fifteen dollars per barrel in Rochester, and wheat was selling at three dollars per bushel with no money to purchase it. However, the situation improved in 1817 with good crops, and by 1820 and 1821, the price of wheat plummeted to twenty-five cents per bushel due to difficulties in getting it to the market. Articles of clothing were enormously dear as as cotton cloth was then priced at fifty cents a yard.

In 1818, Henry chopped and cleared off six acres of land for A. A. Ellicott, for which he obtained flour for his family for that season. He cleared five acres for Elijah Bent, a little south of Medina village, for which he received in payment one-third of the pork of a hog that weighed three hundred pounds in all; that is, about one hundred pounds of pork cost twenty dollars, paid for in such hard work. So they managed to live as best they could until they were able to raise something of their own to live on.

About this time young Samuel, being then twelve or thirteen years old, and his brother William two years older, got disgusted with Western New York and agreed to run away back to the Mohawk country, fearing they would starve to death if they remained here. They did not go, however.

In the year 1820, May 20th, barefoot, with an old straw hat, a pair of tow cloth pantaloons and a second hand coat on, Samuel Bidelman started on foot and alone for Ridgeway Corners, to learn the trade of tanning and currying leather, and shoemaking, of Isaac A. Bullard, who carried on that business there.

Before that time, he had lived in Dutch settlements and could only imperfectly speak or understand the English language.

Mr. Bullard's tanning then amounted to about fifty hides a year, but gradually increased to about one hundred hides a year while Samuel lived with him. When he had been about three and a half years with Mr. Bullard, they had some difficulty and Samuel left him and went to his father. The difficulty was settled and Samuel was bound as apprentice, to stay with Mr. Bullard until he was of age, and he went back and remained.

Bullard was addicted to strong drink, which made him rather a hard master to his apprentice. He died April 9th, 1827.

After Mr. Bullard passed away, his wife took over the business he had left behind. Samuel worked for her on a monthly basis for six months, and then he bought the tanyard and dwelling house and started running the business by himself.

On May 17th, 1829, he married Eliza Prussia. She was born in Lancaster County, Pennsylvania, of German parentage.

At Ridgeway, Samuel tanned about seventy-five hides a year. He kept two journeymen, made leather and carried on shoemaking. Stoga boots were worth four dollars a pair, coarse shoes two dollars. Boots were not so generally worn as now. Tanner's bark, hemlock, was worth one dollar and fifty cents a cord.

In the spring of 1835, Mr. Bidelman sold his place in Ridgeway, retaining possession until the next October, intending to move to Michigan. He was then worth about fifteen hundred dollars and was twenty-nine years old.

He finally bought a tanyard at Gaines village of James Mather, and moved there Oct. 2, 1835. Gaines was then quite a place of business. It had in active operation: one academy, five dry goods stores, three groceries, one steam grist mill and *furnace*, three taverns, two churches, two tanneries, one cabinet shop, one large wagon factory, three law offices, three blacksmith shops, one millinery shop, one ashery, besides harness, shoe, and tailor shops, etc.

At Gaines Mr. Bidelman employed four or five men in his tannery, and five or six men in his shoe shop generally.

In 1838, the Patriot War, as it was called, in Canada ended. This part of the country had been in a high state of excitement for two years, and the people desired to aid the Canadian rebels. *Hunter's lodges*, as they were called, were formed along the frontier for this purpose.

Such a lodge used to meet in the upper room in Mr. Bidelman's Tannery, which was formerly occupied by the *Freemasons*. Mr. Bidelman took great interest in this movement and gave an old cast iron bark mill to be cast into cannon balls. He gave the last gun he ever owned and a pair of boots, to fit out a soldier who went to Canada to join the insurgents.

A cannon, which had belonged to an artillery company in Yates, in which Mr. Bidelman had held a *commission* as Lieutenant, was sent to the Patriots. *General Winfield Scott* passed through on the Ridge Road with some United States troops to maintain peace on our borders, and in a short time order was again restored.

The Ridge Road was then a great traveled thoroughfare; six to eight stage coaches passed through Gaines each way daily.

In 1841, Mr. Robert Ranney and Mr. Bidelman started a tanning business in Gaines for a term of five years. They put in a large amount of stock and worked hard, but the business was not profitable for them. They faced difficulties in settling their partnership matters, and overall, these five years were the most unpleasant and unprosperous in business for Mr. Bidelman. After parting ways with Mr. Ranney, he went on to work with his sons in business. Additionally, he served as the Supervisor of Gaines in the years 1842, '45, '46, '53, '54, and '57.

JOHN HENRY BEECH

The following extracts are taken from a memoir by Dr. John H. Beech, of Coldwater, Michigan, of himself and his father, Dr. Jesse Beech, who was the pioneer physician of the town of Gaines:

"Dr. Jesse Beech was born March 20th, 1787, at Ames, Montgomery County, New York. He studied medicine with Dr. Lathrop, of Charleston, and with Dr. Sheldon, of Florida, N.Y. In those days medical colleges were not accessible to students of ordinary means. There was a public prejudice against dissections, and the students of the two doctors named, occupied a room in a steeple on a church in Charleston, where they dissected bodies. One of the class would stay in the steeple all day Sundays with their cadavers to keep the hatch fastened down to exclude intruding boys.

Dr. Jesse Beech commenced practice at Esperance, N.Y., in the year 1813, and in February of that year married Susannah, a daughter of John Brown, of that place.

In the fall of 1815 he came to Gaines, where he met James Mather, with whom he was acquainted, and was persuaded to stop there, accepting a theory then believed in by settlers in that region, which was this:

'Batavia must be the *Gotham* of the Holland Purchase. Oak Orchard Harbor must be the commercial port. The great commercial highway of the country would be from the head of navigation on Oak Orchard Creek to Batavia. The country north of the Ridge was too flat and poor to be of any account, and the town second to Batavia must be on the Ridge where the road from Batavia to the lake crossed it. A kind of half shire town for Genesee county was then at Oak Orchard Creek on the Ridge. Genesee County would be divided at Tonawanda Swamp, and the new county seat would be Gaines.' Philetus Bumpus was then hunting bears where Albion now is, and the future greatness of Gaines was not dimmed by prospects of Clinton's Erie Canal.

Such was the theory. The canal made dough of the whole of that cake, and caused the whole country about here to change front.

James Mather, and Oliver Booth, the tavern keeper, were active men in Gaines, when my father came in, both being very attentive to newcomers, and Esq. Arba Chubb came in soon after. He was the best wit and storyteller of the times, full of talk and repartee, a most social and agreeable man.

My father bought some land near the Corners, and brought my mother there the next spring. She found the house only half floored and not all chinked. The fire was built against the logs on the side which had no floor, over which the roof was open for the escape of smoke.

She was told that the rule of the settlement was that newcomers must burn out three logs in the house walls before they could be allowed to build a stone back for a chimney; and they must have had at least three shakes of ague before they could be admitted to citizenship.

The records are silent as to when she burned out her three logs, but it is said that she soon attained the rank of full citizenship, having her first shake of ague on the fourth day after arriving in town.

My father must have found the people much in need of a doctor, for I find on page seventy-one of his day book, previous pages being lost, a large amount of business charged for so small a population.

The prices charged would now be deemed quite moderate: Leonard Frisbie is charged 'To visit and setting leg for self $2.50.' Subsequent visits and dressings from thirty-seven and a half to seventy-five cents each, and so in other cases.

In 1817, '18, and '19, it took him three or four days to make a circular visit to his patients. They resided in Murray, east of Sandy Creek, at Farwell's Mills, in Clarendon, in different parts of Ridgeway, Barre, etc.

On these circuits the kind people treated him to their best, which was often corn cake and whiskey, or Evans root coffee, with sorrel pie for dessert for the doctor, and basswood browse for his horse.

I found a bill rendered in pounds, shillings and pence to my father by George Kuck, for general merchandise had at his store in West Carlton, in 1818. Ira Webb was at the same time in trade at Oak Orchard Creek, on the Ridge, but the principal merchants were located at Gaines.

In the spring of 1816, my father had about half an acre of corn *dug in* among the logs near his house. When it was a few inches high a frost blighted the tops so that every leaf was held in a tight dead envelope. My mother cut off the tops with her scissors and a fair crop was harvested.

In order to save the pig from the bears, its pen was made close to the house. A piece of chinking was left out to haloo (shoo) through.

One day mother's attention was attracted by an unusual hackling of the pig. Looking through the crevice she saw a large rattlesnake coiled up in the hog trough, with head erect, buzzing like a nest of bees. Fearing to attack the old fellow, she ran to the neighbors for help and when she returned the snake had gone.

In 1816 they had a patch of oats near the house from which the deer had to be driven frequently.

Their first child, and only daughter, Elizabeth, was born Jun 22, 1817. She married Ezbon G. Guller, and settled at Coldwater, Michigan, where she died in 1853.

Their only son, your humble servant, was born September 24th, 1819. I think I must have been one of the first *draymen* in the county. I remember when I was a very small boy seizing the reins and backing my father's horse and cart loaded with merchandise, part of which was a demijohn of *aquafortis*, down a cellar gangway. Some smoke and some hurrying were among the consequences.

A few years later a young clerk and myself sent a hogshead of molasses from a wagon down the same gangway at one pop. The pop carried away the heads of the cask and poured the sweet out to the rats.

At the age of fourteen I tried clerking in a dry goods store for Fanning & Orton, in Albion. After six months probation I felt no further inspiration or aspiration in that line and resigned, I presume with the hearty consent of my employers, though they flattered me by expressing their regret, which I thought was proof of their politeness rather than my ability. I then attended Gaines Academy until I was eighteen years old, when I commenced studying medicine with Drs. Nichoson & Paine, in Albion; afterwards with Dr. Pinkney, at Esperance, and graduating at the Albany Medical College in 1841.

In January, 1842, I married Mary Jane Perry, of Clarkson, N.Y.

I practiced my profession from the old homestead until 1850, then moved to Coldwater, Michigan, where I have been engaged in the same business since, except during the rebellion. In the greater part of it, I served in the army as a surgeon, first of Battery D First Michigan Artillery. Afterward, I served the Twenty-Fourth Michigan Volunteers, in the Army of the Potomac. The greater part of the time, besides performing my regimental duties, I acted as Surgeon-in-Chief of the First Brigade, First Division, First Army Corps.

We have mentioned the expectations of the residents to secure the site for the county buildings in Gaines. The brick building standing on the hill south of the village, was built by contributions started with the intent to donate it to the county for a courthouse. It was originally three stories high, about forty by seventy feet on the ground. These anticipations of the contributors being blasted, they converted their building into an academy.

At the organization of Orleans County, the village of Gaines contained three stores, three asheries, three tanneries, two taverns, one chair factory, one carriage factory, one cabinet shop, three blacksmith shops, one distillery, one cloth-dressing and wool-carding establishment, two brick yards, one printing office where a newspaper was published, one hat factory, and one saddle and harness shop. Works requiring motive power were driven by horses.

The first chapter of Royal Arch Masons in County Number 82 was organized at Gaines. Dr. Jesse Beech was H. P. in 1826.

Previous to 1825, Col. Boardman's Calvary was a marvel in the eyes of us youngsters. Dr. Jesse Beech was its surgeon.

I find by an old receipt among my father's papers, that Gaines Basin, in the canal, was excavated by a subscription fund, subscribed mainly by Guernsey, Bushnell & Company, E. & E. D. Nichols, and James Mather.

Dr. Jesse Beech was a temperance man even to total abstinence, enforcing his principles by banishing decanters and wine glasses from his sideboard, a proceeding rather unusual in those times.

He was a fine horseman and occasionally officiated as marshal on public occasions. He was always exceedingly particular in his dress and personal appearance, and always wore an elaborate ruffle shirt. His dress never was allowed to interfere with business requiring his attention, and sometimes, when off professional duty, he would go into his field where his men were clearing land, and though he was small in stature, he would show by his agility and energy in working with his men that he was a match for their stoutest.

A few of the last years of my father's life, he kept a store of drugs and medicines on sale in connection with his practice as a physician and surgeon.

In February or March, 1826, he was hurt by a vicious horse from which he suffered greatly as long as he lived. He died March 4th, 1829. His widow afterwards married Captain Elihu Mather, and moved to Coldwater, Michigan, where she died March 16th, 1869.

J. H. BEECH."

OLIVER BOOTH

Oliver Booth was a well known tavern keeper on the Ridge Road in Gaines. He came here from Wayne County in the spring of 1811, and settled on the farm north of the Ridge and east of the Oak Orchard Road in the village of Gaines. He cleared his farm and built a double log house, with a huge chimney in the middle. Here he kept tavern a number of years.

His house was always full of company. Travelers on the Ridge Road stopped here because it was a tavern and there was no other. Here he dispensed a vast amount of whisky (for everybody was thirsty in those days) and some victuals to such strangers as were not acquainted with the proverbial filthiness of the kitchen.

After Gaines had become a village, and laid claims to the county seat, and people had come in who wanted more style, and whose stomachs could not stand such fare as Booth's tavern supplied, another tavern was opened and Booth sold out and moved away. He finally settled in Michigan where he died.

No description of Booth or his tavern would be complete without including Sam Wooster. Sam's father lived in the neighborhood, and he (Sam) then a great lazy boy, strayed up to Booth's tavern where by hanging about he occasionally got a taste of Booth's whisky in consideration of bringing in wood for the fire and doing a few other chores. For these services and the pleasure of his company, Booth gave him what he ate and drank, with a place to sleep on the barroom floor.

His clothes did not cost much. He never wore a hat of any sort, seldom had on stockings or shoes. Nobody can remember that he wore a shirt, and his coats and pants were such as came to him, nobody could tell how or from whence. Sam never washed his face and hands, or combed his head, and his general appearance to one who did know him might benefit a crazy prisoner just escaped from Bedlam. He was shirtless and shoeless, with his great black, frowsy head bare, his pants ragged and torn, and his coat, if he had any, was minus one sleeve, or half the skirt.

Yet Sam was not a fool or crazy. His wit was keen and ready, and his jokes timely and sharp. He would not work, or do anything which required much effort anyway. He was a good fisher, however, and with his old friend Booth, he would sit patiently by the hour and angle in the Oak Orchard, or any other stream that had fish, perfectly content, if he had an occasional nibble at his hook.

One year while he lived in Gaines, some wag, for the fun of the thing, nominated him for overseer of highways in the Gaines village district, and he was elected. He told the people they had elected him thinking he was too lazy to attend to the business, and would let them satisfy their assessments by mere nominal labor on the road; but they would find themselves much mistaken, and they did. Sam warned them to work as the law directed. He superintended everything vigorously, and every man and team and tool on the highway within his beat had to do its whole duty promptly that year at least.

Although Sam loved whisky and drank it whenever it was given to him, for he never had money to buy anything, he never got drunk. He never quarreled or stole or did any other mischief. Bad as he looked, and lazy and dirty as he was, he was harmless. When Mr. Booth sold out and moved to Michigan, Sam went with him and lived in his family afterwards.

A few months after landlord Booth got his double log tavern going, a man rode up to the west front door (each half of the house had a front door) and asked Mrs. Booth if he could get dinner and feed his horse there. She sent her daughter, then ten years old, to show the man where he could get feed for his horse in the stable, and she went to work getting his dinner.

Having taken care of his horse, the stranger came and took a seat by the front door of the room where Mrs. Booth was getting dinner and commenced talk by saying:

"Well, Mrs. Booth, how do you like the Holland Purchase?"

"O, pretty well," she replied, "I think it will be a good country when it is cleared up."

"What place did you come from Mrs. Booth?"

"We came from down in the Jerseys. Is the country settling about here very fast?"

"Yes, quite a good many settlers have come in," answered the stranger.

"How is it about the mouth of Oak Orchard? Are they settling there much?" inquired Mrs. Booth.

"No they are not, that cussed old Joe Ellicott has reserved all the land there and won't sell it," replied the stranger.

Just then Mr. James Mather passed by, and seeing the stranger sitting in the door, whom he recognized as Mr. Joseph Ellicott, the agent of the Holland Land Company, he turned to speak to him. As he came up, Ellicott motioned him to be silent, fearing he would pronounce his name within hearing of Mrs. Booth and end the fun. After a salutation to Mr. Mather, Mr. Ellicott said to Mrs. Booth:

"Has old Joe Ellicott then really reserved the land 'round the mouth of the creek?"

"Yes, the devilish old scamp has reserved one or two thousand acres there as a harbor for bears and wolves

279

to kill the sheep and hogs of the settlers," said Mrs. Booth.

Ellicott asked, "What can induce Uncle Joe to reserve that land?"

She replied, "Oh, the old scamp thinks he will make his Jack out of it. He thinks some day there will be a city there, and he will survey the land into city lots and sell them. Ah, he is a long-headed old chap."

Ellicott walked into the road and talked with Mr. Mather a few minutes till being called to his dinner. He said to Mather: "Don't tell Mrs. Booth who I am until I am out of sight."

After Ellicott was gone, Mr. Mather went over and Mrs. Booth asked him "Who was that old fellow who got dinner here?"

He replied, "It was Mr. Joseph Ellicott from Batavia."

"Good," says she, "didn't I give it to him? Glad of it! Glad of it!"

Mr. Booth was unable to read or write, and he was accustomed to keeping his tavern accounts in chalk marks on the walls. Thus, for an account of sixpence, he made a mark of a certain length; for a shilling, a mark longer; two shillings, longer still, and so on. He distinguished drinks, dinners, horse fees, etc, by peculiar *hieroglyphics* of his own invention.

Booth, the tavern keeper, must not be confounded with Oliver Booth II, better known to the old pioneers as Esq. Booth, who owned and resided on the next farm west, which lay on the west side of Oak Orchard Road, and north of the Ridge. Esquire Booth was among the very first settlers of Gaines village. He was not related to the tavern keeper. He was born in Granby, Connecticut, in 1779, and settled in Gaines, in 1810.

He moved to Michigan in 1833 and died there.

Esq. Booth was the first Supervisor elected north of Tonawanda swamp to represent the town of Ridgeway, then the whole of Orleans County, in 1813. He served several years as a Justice of the Peace. He was an odd man in appearance and manners, but upright and honest.

JAMES MATHER

James Mather was born in Marlborough, Vt., July 23, 1784. His family are said to be descendants from Rev. Increase Mather, President of Harvard University, who received the first degree of Doctor of Divinity that was conferred by that college.

JAMES MATHER

Mr. Mather came to Gaines in the summer or fall of 1810, to look for a place for his settlement. There was then some travel on the Ridge Road, with a prospect of more when the country was settled. The Holland Company had established their land office at Batavia, and it seemed to him sure that in time a village or city would grow up at the mouth of Oak Orchard Creek.

The Oak Orchard trail was then marked from Batavia to the lake, and Mr. Mather shrewdly predicting a village would be founded where that trail crossed the Ridge, took up some four hundred acres of land lying on each side of the Oak Orchard Road and south of the Ridge, on which he afterward settled and resided while he lived.

Before moving to Gaines, Mr. Mather had resided for some time in the town of Russia, Herkimer County, where he manufactured potash, which he sent to the Canadian market by way of Ogdensburg. He was in this business when the embargo declaring non intercourse with Great Britain was proclaimed. He continued his trade however, and by the skillful distribution of a few dollars among the government officials, his ashes were allowed to pass the lines and his profits were large.

In the winter of 1811, he broke up his establishment in Herkimer County and moved to his land in Gaines. A younger brother, Rufus, assisted by driving a team of two yoke of oxen before a sled, which was loaded, among other things, with three potash kettles. There was no bridge over Genesee River, at Rochester, and Rufus attempted to cross on the ice near where the canal now is. In the middle of the river the ice broke and let the loaded sled into the water. Rufus succeeded with great difficulty in getting out without loss, and followed the Ridge to his destination, and stopped at the house of Cotton Leach, west of the present village of Gaines.

Rufus stayed and worked for James the following summer. James had cleared some trees on a small area south of the Ridge, on the Oak Orchard Road, close to where his son George now lives. However, no clearing had been done within the village bounds on the Ridge at that time. Rufus claims that he cut down the first tree in the village of Gaines. This tree was located on Ridge Road, on the west side of Oak Orchard Road. A piece of land was soon cleared, and James Mather built his log house on that corner in the spring of 1811.

He married Fanny Bryant February 15th, 1813. She was born in Marlborough, Vermont, October 28th, 1788.

In the winter of 1813, they commenced housekeeping in the log house Mr. Mather had built on his lot, and remained there during the war, when so many went away.

Mr. Mather always kept open house, according to the custom of the country there, though he never professed to keep tavern; entertaining everyone who applied to him for accommodation as well as he could, and his house was generally full of newly arriving emigrants who were waiting till their own cabins could be built, or of such casual strangers as came along.

Oliver Booth, afterwards the tavern keeper, stopped with Mr. Mather when he first came in, until he got his own house built and fitted up.

Soon after Mr. Mather settled in Gaines, he set the potash kettles he brought with him. He then commenced buying salts of lye, or black salts, of the settlers as soon as settlers came in and made them. These salts he boiled down into potash and took them to the mouth of Genesee River, or the mouth of Oak Orchard Creek, and sent them to Montreal to a market.

He paid for these salts in salt fish, iron, leather, coarse hardware, and a few axes, chains, and such tools as farmers must-have, which he obtained in exchange for his potash, and took care to sell at a fair profit, and with these things, he paid some money. He was in fact almost the only source from which those who did not bring money with them got any to supply their wants.

Early in the spring of 1811, Mr. Mather, finding his provisions getting low, went to the Oak Orchard Creek, at the head of Stillwater, from the lake, with two men and a seine and caught three barrels of fish in a few hours. These he drew to the Ridge with his oxen and took them to Black Creek Mill, a few miles south of Rochester, and with these fish and money, he bought wheat and pork, got his wheat ground and took it home, and so he was well supplied the first year with these provisions. About the time Orleans County was organized, he built a large brick building for a tannery, in which with his brothers and others he carried on tanning a number of years, though he never worked at that business himself. He dealt considerably in land, at one time owning a large farm where Eagle Harbor village and flouring mills are now built, and several large farms in other places. From the rise of value in these lands, and the profits of his speculations, he became wealthy. He died August 29th, 1854.

Mr. Mather had seven children. Louisa, who married Wheeler M. Dewey. She died many years since. Dwight, who died in youth. Adeline married Paul H. Stewart. Eunice married Daniel F. Walbridge. George married Mary Ann Crane. He resides on his paternal homestead. Ellen married Hon. Noah Davis, of Albion, later a Justice of the Supreme Court. Mary married Howard Abeel, a merchant of Albion.

ELIHU MATHER

Elihu Mather was born in Marlborough, Vt., July 26th, 1782. He was a tanner by trade. He came to Gaines to reside in 1825, and went into business with his brother James in his tannery and working his farm.

In the great anti masonic excitement arising from the abduction of William Morgan, Mr. Elihu Mather was indicted as an *accessory* to the crime, and tried at Albion and acquitted. The trial occupied ten days. Mr. Mather continued to reside in Gaines until 1851, when he moved to Coldwater, in Michigan, where he died January 29th, 1866.

HENRY DRAKE

Henry Drake was born in New Jersey, April 6th, 1770. He settled in Gaines in March, 1811. In 1812, he built a dam on Otter Creek, a few rods north of the Ridge, in Gaines, on which he erected a sawmill, which was the first sawmill built within the present town of Gaines.

Mr. Drake learned the *clothier*'s trade in his youth, but followed farming as his business in life. He married

Betsey Parks, in New Jersey. She died April 16th, 1843. Mr. Drake died December 25th, 1863, at the age of almost 94 years.

SIMEON DUTCHER

Simeon Dutcher was born in Dover, Dutchess Co., N.Y., April 21st, 1772. For fifteen years after arriving at manhood he labored as a millwright, a trade he assumed without serving any regular apprenticeship. He then commenced preaching and was ordained an Elder in the Baptist denomination. In the year 1817, Elder Dutcher moved with his family to Carlton, New York, and in 1820 he moved to the town of Gaines, where he resided until he died. The primary object he had in coming to the Holland Purchase was to preach and serve as a missionary among the people, the Baptists having no church organization in Orleans County.

The people were few, poor and scattered, and Elder Dutcher never received much pay for his ministerial labors, but supported his family mostly by working a farm. He used to preach in several neighboring towns in the log cabins of settlers, or in the school houses after such were erected. And for several years he officiated at nearly all the marriages and funerals in this part of the country.

The first framed meeting house erected in Orleans County was built in the village of Gaines by a stock company, who sold the slips to whom they could, on the condition that the house should be used by different denominations, and it was so used.

A Baptist church was organized at Gaines in 1816, under the pastoral care of Elder Dutcher, to whom he preached until 1827, when the *anti-masonic excitement* prevailed in his church. Elder Dutcher, who was a Free Mason, was required to renounce Freemasonry. He declined to do so and was excommunicated and dismissed from his church.

In the later years of his life Elder Dutcher professed to be a universalist in religious sentiment. He was always regarded as a good man and was much beloved by the early settlers. He died January 22, 1860.

HONORABLE WILLIAM J. BABBITT

William J. Babbitt was born in Providence, Rhode Island, September 1786. He learned the blacksmiths trade of his father and worked at that business mainly until he came to reside in Gaines, where he had a small shop and occasionally worked at his trade for several years. In the year 1812, he took up the farm on which he ever afterwards resided, part of lot thirty, township fifteen, range one, and moved his family there in 1813.

For many years after Mr. Babbitt settled in Gaines no professional lawyer had come into what is now Orleans County. The people however would indulge occasionally in a lawsuit, and Mr. Babbitt being a good talker, and a man of more than common shrewdness, they frequently employed him to try their cases in their justices' courts. He improved under his practice until he became the most noted pettifogger north of the Tonawanda Swamp, and whichever of the litigants secured the services of Esq. Babbitt was quite sure to win his case. He was active in getting the town of

Gaines set off from Ridgeway in the winter of 1816, and July 1st of the same year, on his application a post office was established in Gaines and he was appointed postmaster, which office he held five years. This was the first post office and he was the first postmaster in Gaines.

In 1831-32, he represented Orleans County in the Assembly of the State. He was appointed a Justice of the Peace by the Council of Appointment in 1815 and reappointed from time to time until the elections to that office were given to the people under the constitution. He was then elected by the people, holding the office of Justice of the Peace in Gaines for all 23 years.

He was several times Supervisor of his town, and held various other town offices from time to time. He took pleasure in serving in official and fiduciary positions, and was largely gratified, in particular, by his fellow citizens.

He was known for his punctuality in attending legal proceedings. He acquired a character for uncompromising fidelity in business matters, and by a life of industry and economy laid up a large property.

He died July 20th, 1863. He married Eunice Losey, June 27th 1810. She died April 4th, 1867.

GIDEON FREEMAN

Gideon Freeman was born in Stillwater, Saratoga County, January 11th 1787. About 1799, he moved with his father to Ledyard, Cayuga County, and in March 1821, he settled northwest of what is called Long Bridge, and took up the southwest section of land now in the town of Gaines. He was the first settler in this area south of the Ridge and founder of what was for many years known as *Freeman Settlement*.

He cleared up a large farm and carried on a large business as a farmer. His son, Chester Freeman, now of Barre, related that in the *cold season* of 1816, his father planted forty acres to corn, which was a total failure. He had a large stock of hogs that year which he expected to fatten on his corn, from the loss of which, having nothing to feed them, many of them starved to death in the next fall and winter. He had a large stock of cattle at that time and but little food for them.

Mr. Freeman chopped over nearly fifty acres of woods to browse his cattle in the winter of 1816–17, cutting down all trees suitable for that purpose, and losing only about six of his cattle from starvation. Mr. Freeman owned a part of the section lying next east of his home farm. On that land one year he sowed forty acres to wheat, which grew very large. At harvest time he measured off one acre of his field and cut and cleaned the wheat on it, getting fifty-five bushels of wheat on that acre.

Mr. Freeman was a liberal, generous man, and labored hard to induce settlers to come in and to open the country to inhabitants. He sustained some large losses in his business and became insolvent, finally losing all his land. He moved to Ypsilanti, Michigan, where he died in 1832.

Mr. Levi Atwell, Joseph Stoddard and Reuben Clark were among those who moved into the Freeman settlement soon after it was commenced.

CHESTER FREEMAN

Chester Freeman, the son of Gideon Freeman, was born in Scipio, Cayuga County, on August 18th, 1807. He moved to Orleans County with his father in 1812. In 1835, he married Eliza Chidester, who passed away in March 1848. On October 30th, 1849, he married Amanda Morris. Since 1842, he has lived on lot thirty-one, in township fourteen range two, in Barre.

DANIEL PRATT

Daniel Pratt was born in Westmoreland, Oneida County, N.Y., March 25th, 1788. He married Polly Bailey, August, 1809, and moved to Gaines and settled on the Ridge in the spring of 1810. His wife, Polly, died August 30th, 1812. He married Caroline Smith, January 8th, 1815.

He went east during the War of 1812 and remained there for two years, then returned to his farm, on which he labored until his death, October 7th, 1845. Mrs. Caroline Pratt died September 18th, 1831.

The first wheat sold by Mr. Pratt was taken on an ox sled by him to Rochester, and sold for twenty-five cents a bushel.

Mr. Pratt was a man of quiet habits, trusty and faithful. He was much respected by his acquaintances.

He was Town Clerk of Gaines for many years and held the office of Overseer of the Poor for a long time.

DANIEL BROWN

Daniel Brown was born in Columbia County, N.Y., on June 15th, 1787. In 1800, he moved with his father's family to Upper Canada. He married Mary Willsea, in Canada, in the year 1807 and resided in Canada during the War of 1812. His refusal to bear arms in that war against his native country caused him much trouble. He was indicted and tried for treason and acquitted.

In January 1816, he moved to the town of Gaines and settled one mile northeast of Albion where he has established an enviable character for integrity among his acquaintances, and has been honored and respected. He was Supervisor of the town of Gaines in 1844 and has held various other town offices.

Mr. Brown is still living.

WILLIAM W. RUGGLES

Wm. W. Ruggles was born in Hardwick, Massachusetts, January 1st, 1800. His father, Seth Ruggles, moved with his family in 1804 to Poultney, Vermont, where Wm. W. labored on a farm until he was eighteen years old. He then entered the office of Judge Williams, at Salem, N.Y., as a student at law. Here he studied law eight months of the year, teaching school winters. He closed his preparatory law study with Chief Justice Savage, at Albany. Having been admitted to the bar, he came to Albion and formed a partnership with Judge Moody, which was soon dissolved.

He moved to Gaines in 1824, and began the practice of his profession there.

In the contest between Gaines and Albion for the county buildings, he took an active part for his village.

He aided in founding Gaines Academy and the *Farmers Bank of Orleans*, at Gaines.

He exerted himself to have the New York Central Railroad located along the Ridge, and used his influence in favor of the building of Niagara Suspension Bridge, and was a stockholder in that company.

In his profession as a lawyer he was diligent and successful. He held the offices of Master in Chancery, Supreme Court Commissioner, Judge of the Court of Common Pleas, and Justice of the Peace and various other town offices. He was several times the candidate of the Democratic party for the State Legislature, but failed an election as his party was largely in the minority.

Judge Ruggles had a cultivated mind, enriched by studious habits of life. He was particularly fond of Astronomy, on which he left some lectures in manuscript, written by him.

He spent a year surveying government land in Michigan, when General Cass was Governor, where he contracted fever and ague, from which he suffered ever afterwards.

He married Miss Ann Davis, daughter of Dea. Perry Davis, of Gaines, in 1827. She died Aug. 20th, 1846.

In the autumn of 1849 he went to Chicago, intending to reside and practice law there, but having taken a cold while on his voyage around the lake, he was compelled to return to Gaines sick, and never recovered, dying at Gaines, April 22, 1850.

He left three children, William Oakley, now a broker in New York; Henry C., a Civil Engineer in Cincinnati, Ohio; and Helen, who married Mr. Fred Boott and resides in Gaines.

Eagle Harbor, a thriving village on the Erie Canal, in the town of Gaines, is said to have been so named because a large bird's nest was found in a tree growing there about the time the canal was surveyed, supposed to have been built by an eagle.

The land on which the village is built was for a number of years at first held under articles from the Holland Company.

Harvey Smith took a deed of eighty acres on the south-east corner of lot thirty-six, November 1, 1819. Stephen N. Chubb took a deed of fifty-three acres next north, September 6th, 1834, and Macy Pratt, of one hundred and thirty-eight acres north of Chubb, November 29th, 1819.

On the East side, Asahel Fitch took a deed of one hundred twenty-five acres, part of lot twenty-six, February 20th, 1821. James Mather took a deed of two hundred acres next north of Fitch, November 27th, 1829; and Robert Hunter, one hundred and seventy-six acres next north of Mather, January 31st, 1828.

On the south side of the Canal, fifty acres of lot thirty-five were deeded to Amos S. Samson on December 22, 1836.

Stephen Abbott took up the land afterwards deeded to Harvey Smith, commenced cutting down timber on it in the winter of 1812. This was probably the first clearing done in Eagle Harbor.

Little improvement was made until work was begun on the canal. The high *embankment* over Otter Creek was constructed by a man named Richardson. He opened a store here to accommodate his workmen, which was the first store. Hicks and Sherman bought Richardson's store and continued it after him.

Hicks also built the old red warehouse, the first in the village, south side of the canal. This was later owned and occupied by Amos Samson. In 1832, this warehouse was sold to Willis P. Collins, who opened a dry goods store in it and continued it for about six years. He then built a store and warehouse on the east side of the street and moved there.

David Smith constructed the first sawmill about 40 rods north of the canal, on Otter Creek. In 1825, James Mather built another sawmill on the south side of the canal. In the same year, Mr. Pratt, Mr. Delano, and Mr. Northrop built the lower dam and another sawmill there.

James Leaton bought the Hunter farm, and he, in company with W.P. Collins, built the north flouring mill in 1837. This mill was burned in the fall of 1839 and rebuilt immediately. General E.S. Beach built another large flouring mill on the south side of the canal in 1847, which has since burned down.

The brick church was built in 1827 by the united means of Presbyterians, Methodists, and Baptists. Methodists owned half of it, and the other denominations each owned one-fourth.

The first meeting house was demolished and reconstructed in 1845, with the same parties building and owning the new house as they did the old one.

Eagle Harbor post office was established about the year 1837, with W.P. Collins first postmaster.

The first schoolhouse was built in 1822 on the west side of the street.

The second schoolhouse was built on the lot now owned by the district in 1841, and the third schoolhouse in 1846.

Col. Jonathon Delano was the first carpenter and joiner.

Samuel Robinson was the first shoemaker, and David Smith the first tavern keeper.

Col. Delono and Sam Robinson were the first grocers, Mr. Hurd the first blacksmith, and Dr. James Brown the first physician.

The growth of Eagle Harbor has been greatly promoted by the large capital employed there by Gen. Beach in erecting mills and manufacturing flour and by the active business energy of Mr Willis P Collins, for many years a resident in the village, and the foremost man in every enterprise, tending to add wealth and importance to the place.

CHAPTER 20.

TOWN OF KENDALL

Kendall was named in honor of Amos Kendall, who was the Postmaster General at the time when it was formed from Murray on April 7th, 1837. Due to its location, away from the main travel routes, and because the land was not surveyed into lots and officially put on the market for settlers as soon as other lands on the Holland Purchase, settlements were not established as early or as frequently as in towns on the Purchase. These lands were jointly owned by the State of Connecticut and the Pulteney Estate, and for a significant period, they remained undivided.

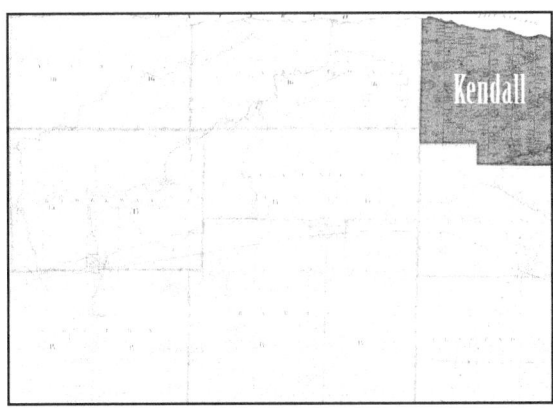

TOWN OF KENDALL

In July 1810, Dr. Levi Ward became an agent for the State of Connecticut to sell its lands on the 100,000 acre tract, of which Kendall forms a part. In 1811, a formal partition of land between the State of Connecticut and the Pulteney Estate was made, and Mr. Joseph Fellows was appointed agent of the Pulteney Estate.

These agents opened land offices, and settlers were invited to take lands. However, few came to Kendall until after the *cold season* of 1816, and for some time after that, they had difficulty acquiring a good title to farms bought from the Pulteney Estate.

Samuel Bates, from Vermont, is said to have been the first white man to settle in this town. He located on lot 111, in East Kendall, in 1812. He cleared some land and sowed wheat, but his family did not move in until 1814.

Soon after, David Jones, Adin Manley, Amos Randall, John Farnsworth, Zebulon Rice, Benjamin Morse, and Nathaniel Brown settled in 1815.

These were followed by Felix Augur, Rev. Stephen Randall, Ansel Balcom, George Balcom, Stephen Bliss, and James Wee in 1816.

And then, Ethan Graham, William Clark, and his son Robert Clark came in 1817.

The first marriage in town was that of James Aiken to Esther A. Bates, March 2, 1817.

The first birth was that of Bartlett B. Morse in November 1815.

The first death was that of a son of George Balcom, in 1816.

Hiram Thompson kept the first store in 1823 and the first inn was kept by Lyman Spicer in the same year.

In 1819, the first sawmill was built by Augur and Boyden and Gurdon Balcom taught the first school.

The first gristmill was built by Ose Webster on the site on Sandy Creek, now occupied by the mills of his son Ebenezer. This mill formed a nucleus for the settlement now known as Webster's Mills. Prior to the erection of this gristmill, the people of Kendall took their grain to Rochester or to Farwell's mill in Clarendon to be ground.

Farewell's mill was much nearer, but the road to it was almost impassable with a load, and the little mill had no capacity to do all the work in that part of the country.

The first religious service in Kendall was conducted by Elder Stephen Randall, a Methodist preacher.

The first physician who practiced in town was Dr. Theophilus Randall, though Dr. Rowell, of Clarkson, was frequently called.

When Mr. Bates settled in Kendall, there was no public highway in town. Settlers and others coming there usually left the Ridge a little east of Kendall, traveling on a road that had been opened into what is now Hamlin. From there they turned west.

The first highway leading south from Kendall to the Ridge was located and cut out by the early inhabitants without any public authority. It ran from Kendall Mills, following up the west side of Sandy Creek to Ridge

Road. This first highway is still traveled a part of the way.

The first settlers of Kendall were chiefly from Vermont, bred among the Green Mountains, and the change of climate, air, water, food, and occupation they experienced in this new and comparatively level country was attended with the usual consequences. They were almost all sick at times. The utmost kindness prevailed, and everyone did all they could to help themselves and others to alleviate suffering. Yet so few were well. Their little rude huts were furnished with only a scanty stock of conveniences, short of provisions, and no place near where the common necessaries for the sick could be obtained; some of these people suffered great misery.

If they sometimes felt discouraged and wished themselves away, when they were sick, they could not go, and when they got better, they would not go, for they came here to make their homes. And with the stubborn resolution of their race, they persisted in the work they had begun till their fondest hopes were more than realized in the beautiful country their toils and sacrifices made out of the wilderness.

The principal settlement in town for several years was originally located in the eastern part, near the center. The Randalls, Bates, Clarks, Manley, and other leading men there were intelligent and wanted the lights of civilization to shine into their settlement, even if it was away in the woods. Accordingly, they met together about the year 1820 and formed a Public Library Association. Among the names or prominent actors in this movement were H. W. Bates, Adin Manley,

Dr. Theophilus Randall, Amos Randall, David Jones, Calvin Freeman, Orrin Doty, James M. Clark, Benjamin Morse, Nathaniel Brown, Caleb Clark, and Noah Priest.

They pooled their resources and collected approximately seventy-five volumes of books through various means. They formed a society, elected their leaders, and maintained their organization for around ten years. Mr. Amos Randall served as the librarian, and the books were widely read in the neighborhood. The culture of thinking and studying that was established at that time has led to the development of numerous intelligent and influential individuals in the area.

They were too poor to afford individual newspapers, and the nearest post office was in Clarkson. So, several men pooled their resources to purchase a single paper. Whenever it arrived at the post office, the first person from the group to get there would pick it up, and then the neighbors would gather to listen to it being read aloud. This included even those who didn't contribute to the cost. Afterward, the paper would be passed to another family and read repeatedly until it was too worn out to use.

Saltwater was discovered early in Kendall, and salt was made there to supply the people.

In 1821, Mr. H. W. Bates and Caleb Clark dug a well and planked it up to obtain *brine* on Mr. Bates' farm. They made about one thousand bushels of salt there. They later sold their kettles to a Mr. Owen, who continued to produce salt in the southwest part of the town. Salt production in Kendall stopped when the Erie Canal opened.

In about the year 1825, a group of fifty-two Norwegians settled on the lake shore in the northeast part of the town. They came from Norway together and acquired land as a group. They were hardworking, prudent, and respectable people who were well-regarded by the local community.

After some years, they left to reunite with their fellow Norwegians who had settled in Illinois and only a few people from that original group still remain in Kendall today.

They thought it very important that every family should have land and a home of their own. A neighbor once asked a little Norwegian boy whose father happened to be too poor to own land, "Where does your father live?" He answered, "O, we don't live nowhere. We ain't got no land."

BIOGRAPHIES OF EARLY SETTLERS

AIDIN MANLEY

"I was born in Taunton, Mass., March 19, 1793. I was brought up among the boys of New England, never having belonged to the upper ten. I roughed with the hardy sporting ones, always ready for athletic games, and could commonly act well, my part.

When about twenty-four years old, I was taken with the western fever, and having laid up two or three hundred dollars, in time saved while sowing my wild oats, I bought a horse and wagon and started with three others for the Genesee country. Not knowing or thinking of any trouble ahead, we dashed away. One of my traveling companions was Stephen Randall, Jr., son of Rev. Stephen Randall, who had previously gone west and then resided at Avon. The son now resides in the town of Union, Monroe County, and has got to be an old man and wealthy.

We arrived in Avon in September 1815. From thence, we made our way into Murray and to what is now Kendall by way of Rochester. At Rochester we were glad to get into the barn with the horses for a night's lodging, there being about thirty men. And how many horses I could not tell. It would be difficult to tell which made the most noise; one thing I do know is that the men swore the most and drank the most whisky. That was an awful company. It seemed as if they were the filth and off scouring of the whole country.

In the morning, I proposed to sell my horse, for I was short of funds and had no further use for him. A gentlemanly appearing man by the name of Gilvreed offered to buy him.

He said he had good notes against a responsible man, but the notes amounted to more than the price of the horse, and I might give my note for the balance, and as to the value of the notes, I might enquire of gentlemen who knew, at the same time referring to some standing by, who said they were good and no mistake. So, the exchange was made in due form, and both parties were highly gratified.

But the result was that the maker of the notes was not worth a straw, and the man, Gilvreed, was worse. This was my first financial operation in the West. What added to my humiliation was that I thought I had such a vast knowledge of men and things as to be immune to being outwitted by anybody and that I knew more than old folks. I wonder if boys think so of themselves nowadays.

I then made my way west along the Ridge Road to Murray Corners, now Clarkson, where Dr. Baldwin had located and kept a tavern, which at that time was a very lucrative business, as people were flocking from the east rapidly.

From Murray Corners, we struck off north-west, what was then called **Black North**, a region where the probability was that if the mosquitoes did not eat you up, the fever and ague would kill. On we went, nothing fearing, until we came to what was called Yanty Creek, where we found three families located, who I believe were the only white inhabitants in what is now the town of Kendall. They were H. W. Bates, Amos Randall, and Benjamin Morse and their families. I concluded to make a pitch here. I now learn the customs and employments of the people among whom I was going to reside, which consisted mainly of chopping, rolling logs, raising log houses, drinking whisky to keep off the fever and ague, hunting deer, bear, raccoons, bees and catching fish.

After working hard at a log raising and taking cold after it, I was awakened in the night by an awful shaking and could not tell what it meant, but I found out sure enough afterward.

In the spring of 1816, I went to work in good earnest to clear a patch of land on which to raise a little of the needful, and behold, in June, there came a frost and spoiled all our labor and made our cornfields in the wilderness, instead of "blossoming like the rose," look as though the fire had run through them.

The next fall I was taken down with the ague proper, and in attempting to break it up I made it worse, until it became awful. I then made up my mind to make my way back to Massachusetts. But how was I to do it? I was so weak I could not walk a mile. Finally, I found some men going to Vermont and agreed with them to take me along with them and let me ride part of the time. If I could remember their names, I would record them with gratitude for their kindness.

I found my unconquerable will had a wonderful effect upon my body. I had no more ague on my journey, though I had it every day before I set out. I went to Massachusetts and remained till I got well recruited, and nothing daunted by what I had suffered.

I determined to return again to the west, and January 17th, 1817, I was married to Miss Miriam Deming. In February following, with my wife, my brother, and his wife and one child, Eri Twitchell and wife, and Nathaniel Brown, we started with three yoke of oxen hitched to a huge covered wagon.

The perils of that journey were neither few nor small. We passed over mountains covered with snow and ice, sidling roads with yawning gulfs below, crossing streams on ice, and floundering through snow drifts, with a constant headwind blowing in our faces for twenty-two days together.

When we arrived in the neighborhood of our new home, our neighbors hailed our coming with joy and wanted a little flour just to make a cake. I suppose they gathered some sticks and had baked their last meal.

We moved into a small log hut with only one room, the fireplace against the logs at one end, with a stick chimney, bark roof, and floor. Taking it altogether we thought it a terrible place to live in.

We had three yoke of oxen and nothing for them to eat; this was the worst of all. We turned them into the woods and cut browse for them, but the poor cattle suffered much.

In the next spring, we had to pay one dollar a bushel for potatoes and a like price for oats, and no money to buy with at that. We got some potatoes to plant, and they came up twice, once by natural growth and once rooted up by the hogs. We set them out again, my wife helping me, for she was a true yoke-fellow.

So we plodded on through the summer, with wheat costing $2.50 a bushel and pork twenty-five cents a pound. Our first child was born on September 24th of this year. It was very feeble and remained so for a long time, its mother having the fever and ague every day for nearly seven months and taking care of her child most of the time. At six months old, the child weighed only four pounds!

Thus, we toiled on for three years. The third year we raised wheat and other crops enough for our comfort, and had built a framed addition to our house. Our prospects now seemed favorable for going ahead, but in March following, our house took fire and was consumed, together with all our provisions, and nearly all our household furniture.

Under the circumstances, this was a sore trial for us. We then had three children and nowhere to lay our heads. We had nothing to eat except what came from charity. Our neighbors were poor but exceedingly good.

After a while, we got another house and toiled on, getting together some of this world's goods. We had ten children, all of whom lived to grow up to be men and women. We have sent nine of them to school at once.

My wife died July 30, 1857, aged 64 years. I have never experienced any calamity in my life that afflicted me like her death with such severity.

For several years after I came into this country, I spent considerable time going far and near to assist in raising log buildings, sometimes going several miles and carrying my dinner in my hand.

Mr. H. W. Bates and myself were accustomed to labor much together, changing works. In the winter of 1816, we went a mile into the woods to chop; there, by accident, a tree fell on him, crushing him badly. Had he been alone, he would have perished.

On another occasion, Mr. Bates and another man with myself went two miles into the woods one day in June and felled the timber on two acres. I think the like was never done in that neighborhood before or since.

In the early settlement of the Genesee country, intemperance prevailed to an alarming extent. Almost everybody drank whisky free as water when they could get it, and I am surprised so many escaped total and eternal ruin. Many years ago, I saw the evil and totally abandoned the use of everything that intoxicates as a beverage and labored faithfully as I could to save others.

For my zeal and persistence in opposing the traffic in liquor, I have suffered much from rum sellers. At an early day, I have seen Justices Courts in session with a bottle of whisky on the table before them, thus polluting the fountains of justice with the vile abomination, and if the Honorable Court happened to become too much absorbed with the creature, they would adjourn over to cool off.

I have had a large experience in hunting bears, deer, raccoons, and wolves, and camping out in the woods in cold and storm, without fire or food, working out in the dead of winter, eating frozen dinners in the woods, sharing fully my part in all sorts of hardships which fell to the lot of the first settlers here. I have endured it all and lived to a good old age, thankful to that good Providence which had carried me through so far and so safely.

AIDIN MANLEY."

Albion, February 26th, 1861.

Mr. Manley died in Albion, on July 29th, 1867, aged 74 years.

ROBERT CLARK

"I was born in Lisbon, Connecticut, October 25th, 1801. My ancestors came to America from England some time in the sixteenth century. My father moved to Columbus, Chenango County, N.Y., in 1805. In 1810, he moved to Utica, and in 1817, he settled with his family on what was then called the Triangle Tract, near the county line and between the towns of Kendall and Hamlin, about three miles from Lake Ontario. The place was then called Clark's settlement because three brothers of the name Clark settled there.

My uncles, Caleb and James, settled there one year before my father, whose name was William Clark, came on, which was quite a help to us, for they had a little wheat sown and some corn and potatoes planted.

When my father arrived, there was not a pound of pork or flour in the settlement, except what he brought with him, and the next day, the port, flour, and whisky were divided among the neighbors.

One reason for the entire destitution among the settlers was the anticipation of my father's arrival, for they all knew he could bring a supply for a time and so neglected to provide for themselves otherwise.

The names of the families then in the settlement were Bates, Priest, Randall, Balcom, Ross, Clark, and two by name of Manley.

The settlers, in anticipation of our coming, had peeled elm bark in the month of June previous, enough to form a roof to a house, and on our arrival, they commenced cutting logs for a house and to clear a spot of ground large enough to set it on, and in a few days, it was raised and covered with bark, in true pioneer style. They also split basswood and hewed slabs for a floor, which covered about two-thirds of the surface of the room, the remainder being left for the fireplace and hearth.

We now moved into our new house and commenced our pioneer labors.

The door of our house was a bed blanket, and windows were hardly necessary, for our house was not chinked, and sufficient light came in through crevices between the logs, and a large space was left open in the roof for the smoke to pass through. Our fireplace was the entire end of the house, and our hearth the solid earth.

My father soon obtained some boards and made a door and temporary windows. The next thing to be done was to chink the cracks between the logs. This being done, we dug up the soil and wet it, and made mud with which we plastered the outside over the chinks, which made our house quite warm and comfortable.

About this time, our stock of provisions began to get short, and the entire settlement was getting hard up for something to eat, but as potatoes were about ripe, we had plenty of them, and as we had a cow, we lived quite well until we could get wheat ground, which at that time was very difficult. Before our wheat was hard enough to grind, our mother hulled and boiled it, and we ate it with milk, and we thought it very good eating.

This state of things did not last long, for my brother James had a great propensity for hunting, my father having bought him a gun; he very soon supplied us with venison, which proved a luxury in the way of meat.

At length, our wheat crop having matured, a grist for each neighbor was prepared, and I started with an ox team and about twelve bushels of wheat, which, with fodder for the oxen, by the way, was about as much as the team could draw.

I stayed at Murray Corners, now Clarkson, the first night, and the next day, a little before night, I got to the mill at Rochester, chained the oxen to the wagon, and fed them for the night. I slept that night on the bags in the mill until my grist was ground, which was completed about daylight. After feeding my team and eating my venison, I started for home and got there about sundown the third day out. The next morning, I guess, all the neighbors had short cake for breakfast!

I will now give a description of what was called an Indian Mill which was used to some extent by the early settlers. We selected a solid stump of a tree in a suitable place near the house, cut a hole in the top with an ax as deep as we could, and then built a fire in the hole, burning it and putting in hot stones until it was sufficiently deep for a mortar. We then made a pestle of hardwood, took a strip of elm bark tied one end to the pestle and the other to the top of a limber sapling tree that would bend directly over the mortar, making a spring pole, which completed the machine.

Put a quart of corn into this mortar, and a man could soon convert it into samp, a coarse meal, which, when well boiled, made very good eating in milk. The Indians used it almost exclusively for bread.

I had never chopped down a tree or cut off a log when I first came into the forest. The next morning, after arriving in the woods, I took an ax and went to where my father was preparing to build a house and commenced chopping down a tree perhaps six inches through. I chopped all around the tree till it fell. When the tree started to fall, I started to run, and if the tree had not lodged on another, I know not, but I should have been killed, for I ran in the same direction the tree was falling. I was so scared at this, my first attempt at felling timber, that I picked up my ax, which I had thrown away in my fright, and made tracks for the house, concluding to chop no more until I had learned how to do it.

The first school in the settlement was taught by Gurdon Balcom, the next by Wesley Randall. The first minister of the gospel who preached in this settlement was Elder Randall, a Methodist, and a very good man. Dr. Theophilus Randall was the first physician.

In the fall of 1818, I went to Oneida County and learned the art of distilling whisky, which at this time was a very popular business. My mother died while I was there, which nearly broke up our home circle and which was, to me particularly, a cause of great sorrow.

I returned home in June following and found my father's family, as I expected, in a very lonely condition. I went to work with my father and brothers, clearing land and securing our crops. When that was done, I went back to Verona and worked in a distillery another winter. Next spring I returned and worked in Whitney's distillery in Rochester, and the fall after I went to Toronto, in Canada, and erected the first steam distillery ever erected in Canada, which at that time was one of the curiosities of the age.

I worked thousands of bushels of the finest wheat I ever saw into whisky. The wheat was bought for two and sixpence per bushel.

The next June I returned home, my father in the meantime had married again and moved to LeRoy, having let out his farm in Murray. I worked in LeRoy and Clarendon. I became 21 years old October 25th, 1822. I took a job clearing land in LeRoy, for which I received $600. My father's family and myself then moved back to Murray, and I paid up the balance for his farm.

I married Anna Augur, daughter of Felix Augur of Murray, now Kendall, Feb. 18, 1824. Mr. Augur had come in from Vermont the year previous and bought his land from the State of Connecticut for $3.00 an acre. Dr. Levi Ward was the land agent. Mr. Augur was a soldier in the Revolutionary War. Gen C. C. Augur, now of the United States Army, is his grandson.

The next spring after I was married, I bought a piece of land in Clark's settlement, which had some work done on it, and went to keeping house there.

I chopped over twenty acres with my own hands, all but four days with no help of a man. I then sold out my chance on this lot and bought fifty acres in another place, which is a part of my present farm. It was then entirely wild, so I commenced again in the woods.

I bought it second-hand and agreed to pay eight dollars per acre. I worked some on my land and worked out some by the day and by the job, but as grain brought but a small price, I concluded that was a pretty hard way to get a living and built a distillery near my farm.

At this time settlers had come in in numbers. Grain was raised in plenty, with no cash market for it. Money was scarce, and the little we had was what we received for ashes. We cut and burned our timber and made black salts from the ashes, which brought cash. I have carried ashes on my back to market until my shoulders were blistered to get a little money to buy necessaries for my family. I built my distillery because grain was plenty and cheap. I could distill it, take it to market at Rochester, and sell it for cash, at a good profit to me and to the settler, who sold me his grain, which he could not take to another market and make as much from it; and he could raise grain easier than he could make and market black salts.

I sold my distillery in 1830 and determined to make farming the business of my life after that.

The year 1828 is well remembered and distinguished as being the sickly season throughout this country. The sickness began in July. And in August, there were not well persons enough in town to take care of the sick. And in this neighborhood, there was but one well man, Ammon Augur, and not one well woman that could get out of the house.

Many families suffered much for lack of help. My family was all sick. One day Dr. Robert Nichoson was the only person who entered my house. He called, prepared our medicine, left it at the head of our beds, and went on to other scenes of suffering.

That was the most gloomy day I ever saw. My wife crept from her bed to mine, holding up by the door post, to see if I was alive, and then got back to her bed, where lay our little daughter, equally helpless. We all spent a dreary night. My hired man was down sick at the same time. The next day, we got help.

The years 1826 and 1827 were also sickly years. I could give many cases of suffering in those times, but amid it all, we had our pleasures, for we were all brethren and loved one another.

ROBERT CLARK."

Kendall, March, 1864

SAMUEL BATES

Samuel was the first white man who settled in what is now Kendall. He was born in Haddam, Conn., Aug 9, 1760. He was a soldier in the Revolutionary War during the last three and a half years of its continuance, serving in a New Hampshire regiment.

He wintered with Gen. Washington at Valley Forge and participated in several important battles. He served under Gen. Sullivan in his memorable expedition against the Indians in Western New York.

He had a fondness for military life and service, a trait of character transmitted to his descendants and honorably exemplified in his grandson, Lieutenant Col. Willard W. Bates, who was killed while leading his regiment, the 8th Heavy Artillery N.Y. Volunteers, in a bloody battle before Petersburg, Virginia, in the war of the Rebellion.

After accompanying General Sullivan, Mr. Bates developed a strong desire to settle in the Genesee region, a wish he later fulfilled. Following his military service,

Mr. Bates moved to Vermont, living in Randolph for several years before moving to Burlington.

Leaving his family in Burlington, he moved to Kendall and acquired lot 111, town 4, of the 100,000 acre tract. This was done by having the land booked to him, meaning that the State of Conn. agent noted in his books that he had taken possession of the land, with the intention of securing his right to it when it became available for sale. He eventually obtained the title to the land, which is now owned by his son, Captain H. W. Bates.

The first year he was in Kendall, he cleared several acres of land in the summer of 1813, sowed two acres of wheat, built a log cabin, returned to Burlington after his family, and brought them to Kendall in June 1814. His eldest son, Capt. H. W. Bates, then about twenty-one years old, accompanied him.

On arriving at his new log house, he found his wheat field in full head, looking fine. The crop so raised, furnished bread for the family the next year.

Mr. Bates and his family, coming as they did from the Green Mountain of Vermont, suffered severely from fever and ague some of the first years after they came to Kendall. They were all sick, Mr. Bates himself never fully recovering from his *acclimating fever*. He died August 21, 1822.

AMOS RANDALL

Amos Randall was born in Ashburnham, Mass. January 3, 1788. He married Fanny Tabor in 1814. She was born in Shelburne, Vt., Feb. 11, 1793.

In 1814, they relocated to Avon and in the spring of 1815, they established themselves in Kendall on the farm currently occupied by his son, Hon. Gideon Randall.

Mr. Randall was a public-spirited man who entered zealously into every undertaking for the benefit of his neighborhood. He frequently acted as counselor and arbitrator among the settlers to aid in arranging business matters in which his neighbors needed such help.

The first schoolhouse was erected on his land where the stone schoolhouse now stands.

The first cemetery in town was located on his farm, and the first burials of the dead were there.

He was a Supervisor of the town of Murray before the county of Orleans was organized, or Murray had been divided into the several towns included in its original territory.

Amos passed away on August 28, 1830. He left six children: Charles T.; Gideon who resides on his paternal homestead; Dr. James W., now a practicing physician in Albion; Fanny E., wife of O. M. Green; George W., and Amos S. Randall.

DAVID JONES

David Jones was born in Pembrokeshire, Wales, on July 17, 1792. He moved to America with his father's family in 1801. His father settled in New Jersey, and his son David remained with him until he was eighteen years old. He then came to Ontario County, New York, where he resided for four years and settled in Kendall in 1815.

He married Miss Catharine Whitney February 24, 1824. Their children are Claudius, who married Harriet Weed and resides in Illinois; Thomas, unmarried; Almiretta S. J., married C. G. Root; Seth, married Sylvia Shelly; Cynthia Ann, married James R. Whitney; and David, who married Lucy A. Chase, all of whom reside in Kendall.

DAVID JONES

Mr. Jones was poor when he settled in Kendall and bought his land on credit. He was a large strong man able and willing to labor. He cleared and improved a large farm and became a wealthy man.

Sickness in his family and the want of a market for farm produce made it very difficult for him to obtain means to pay for his land improvements for some years. He said he agreed to pay four hundred dollars for his first hundred acres, and it was fifteen years before it was all paid.

He was a man of strong native intellect and of sound judgment in matters that come within his observation or experience, but he never had the benefit of much instruction in school.

He died January 26, 1869.

CHAPTER 21.

TOWN OF MURRAY

A large part of the western portion of Monroe County was incorporated by the Legislature in March 1802 as Northampton. The town of Murray was formed from Northampton in June 1812. It received its name in honor of John Murray, a large proprietor and merchant of the city of New York.

Murray, at its formation, included what now comprises the towns of Murray, Kendall, Clarendon, Union or Hamlin, Clarkson, and Sweden.

Sweden, which included Clarendon, was formed from Murray in 1813, and Clarkson, which included Hamlin, in 1819.

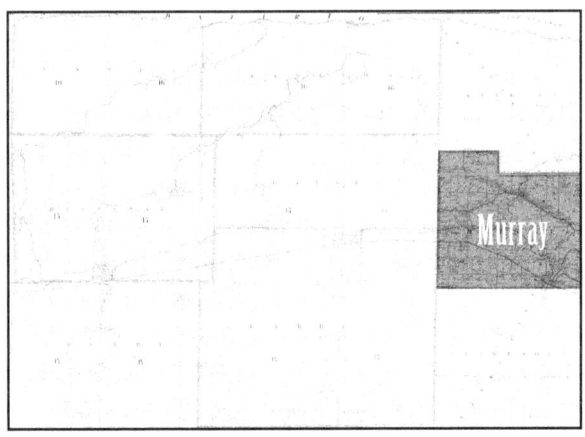

Kendall was set off in 1837, leaving the town of Murray in its present dimensions.

The first inn was kept in 1809 by Epaphras Mattison.

Messrs. Wait, Wright, Sisson, Farnsworth, and Rockwood were among the earliest settlers.

The first marriage was that of Solomon C. Wright and Tryphena Farnsworth.

The first birth was that of Betsey Mattison.

The first store was at Sandy Creek, by Isaac Leach, in 1815.

The first grist mill was built by Perry and Luce in 1817.

The first school was kept by Fanny Ferguson in 1814.

The first town meeting in the old town of Murray, before it was divided, was held in the barn of Johnson Bedell, about four miles south of Brockport.

The first church formed in this town was the Congregational by Rev. John E. Bliss, January 5th, 1819.

The first settlements in what is now included in the town of Murray were made on the Ridge at and near Sandy Creek.

Epaphras Mattison first settled here in 1809. In the year 1817, some fifteen or twenty families had located at Sandy Creek. In that year, Henry McCall and Robert Perry built mills on the creek, their dam raising the water so as to overflow eighteen or twenty acres then covered with heavy trees, which were left standing. The water killed the timber, and a terrible sickness followed among the inhabitants, about one-quarter of whom died in one season. The well persons were not numerous enough to take care of the sick and bury the dead, and settlers from other neighborhoods came there and helped the needy ones. The mill dam was taken down, and the sickness disappeared.

Mr. Andrew H. Green, of Byron, Genesee County, relates that several families were settled at Sandy Creek in 1811. In the fall of that year, settlers in Byron heard that these people at Sandy Creek were nearly all sick and in great suffering. They made up a company of six or eight and went over to help them, carrying a load of necessaries. Mr. Green says: "I never saw so helpless a company." Sandy Creek was regarded as an unhealthy location for some years after its first settlement, occasioned in great part by building mills there in the woods.

The first settlements in what is now Murray were made along the Ridge Road. Mills having been built in early times on Sandy Creek, near where that stream crosses the Ridge, mechanics and businessmen located there. At the time the Erie Canal was first navigable, here was a lively village known as Sandy Creek, a name by which it has ever since been distinguished.

The first post office in town was established here, called Murray.

Though the people suffered terribly from sickness about the time mill dams were first built in the Creek here, and while neighboring lands were being opened to cultivation, yet Sandy Creek was the principal place of business in the town until Holley and Hulberton, on the canal, were settled and gradually drew away most of the trade and business to these new villages.

BIOGRAPHIES OF EARLY SETTLERS

HARLEY N. BUSHNELL

Harley N. Bushnell was born in Starksborough, Vt., the youngest of thirteen children in his father's family, Feb. 18th, 1796.

At the age of fifteen, he traveled to Connecticut to apprentice as a clothier under his brother for five years. Despite receiving only thirty days of schooling during this time, he gained valuable experience in the trade. In February 1817, he moved to Batavia, Genesee County, and began working as a clothier. However, in August of the same year, his employer absconded, leaving him owed one hundred dollars. When the Sheriff seized all of his employer's property, Mr. Bushnell was forced out of business. He eventually purchased the establishment and operated it with a partner, but the venture proved to be unsuccessful. After abandoning the clothier trade, he was elected constable, but did not manage to save money through this occupation and ultimately found himself in a *break-even financial situation*.

He did some business as a justice, and labored some at his trade until February, 1823, when he moved to Holley, north of where the canal now is. The land was then covered with felled timber, not cleared off. He bought two acres of ground and leased two acres more for a mill pond. He got out the timber for a house eighteen by twenty-four feet square, hewing and framing it at the stump. There was considerable snow on the ground, and on the snow-cured mornings, he drew all the timber for his house to the spot with a rope over his shoulder. After getting his family settled in his new house, he cleared off part of his land, and with the help of his neighbors at one or two *bees*, he built a log dam, got out timber to build a sawmill, and began sawing about May 1st, 1824. In 1825, in company with Samuel Clark, he built works for wool carding and cloth dressing at Holley.

In October 1826, his house burned with all its contents. In two weeks, he had another house up. In June 1828, he bought the interest of his partner in the wool carding and cloth dressing works, which he carried on alone until 1833 when he sold out and bought a farm. After a few years, he sold his farm, moved to Holley, and ever after did business as an insurance agent.

For many years, he was Superintendent of the Presbyterian Sunday School in Holley.

He was one of the founders of the Orleans County Pioneer Association, and many years its President. He was a kind hearted, genial man, benevolent and philanthropic, earnest and zealous in support of every good cause, and died lamented by all who knew him, October 28th, 1968.

ARETAS PIERCE

Aretas Pierce was born in St. Johnsbury, Vermont March 27th, 1799. He came with his father's family to settle in Clarendon, where he arrived April 7th, 1815.

The family moved into a house built for a schoolhouse until they could build a house for themselves.

They built a house and moved into it April 24th, 1815. The first year, they lived on provisions they brought in with them. The next year, being the **cold season**, they bought rye at one dollar and twenty-five cents a bushel and pork at twenty-five dollars a barrel in Palmyra. The next year, they were out of bread stuff before harvest and ate green wheat boiled in milk as a substitute, and what is strange is that none of the family had *dyspepsia*!

He married Matilda Stedman May 8th, 1823, and has always resided on the lot originally taken by his father.

When his father came in, it was an unbroken wilderness on the west. From his place to the Oak Orchard Road, eight miles; north to Sandy Creek, four miles; east two miles; south to Farwell's Mills. Eldridge Farwell, A. Dudley, John Cone, Wm. Austin and Mr. West had settled in Clarendon, and other settlers towards Sandy Creek came in the same year with Mr. Pierce. A few came before them.

In the years 1817–18, the inhabitants in this settlement suffered for want of food.

Samuel Miller worked for Artemas Daggett, chopping wood for one dollar a day and board for himself. All he had to eat, most of the time, was cornmeal and water, but he did not complain or tell of it then.

Ebenezer Fox settled a mile and a half east of Murray Depot, and all they had to eat for a number of weeks was what they could pick up in the woods. The best they could find was the inner bark of the beech tree.

Mrs. Fox had a young babe, and her next oldest child was in feeble health, and she had to nurse them both to keep them from starving.

Almost all the money the settlers had was obtained by leaching ashes and boiling the lye to black salts, taking these to Gaines or Clarkson, and selling them for about three dollars a hundred pounds. After 1818, the country filled up rapidly with settlers, and more produce began to be raised than was wanted for home consumption. The price of wheat fell to twenty-five cents a bushel and only thirty-one cents after hauling to Rochester, and so it remained until the Erie Canal was opened.

Mr. Pierce settled on lands owned by the Pulteney estate. These did not come into market for sale until 1821, though settlers were allowed to locate themselves with the expectation of buying their land when it came into market. The price of his lot was fixed at eight dollars per acre, but having expended so much in building and clearing, he was compelled to pay the price or suffer loss by abandoning all he had done.

The company's reason for not bringing their lands to market was that they had "so much business on hand they could not attend to it," but the settlers thought they were waiting to have the canal located before establishing their price.

HUBBARD RICE

Hubbard Rice was born in Pompey, Onondaga County, on July 28th, 1795. In May 1812, he moved with his father to the town of Murray and settled on a lot adjoining the village of Holley. His father, Mr. William

Rice, continued to reside there until about 1830, when he went to Ohio to live with his children and died there.

Hubbard Rice lived with his father until 1825, when he moved to the south part of Clarendon. There, he remained until 1864, when he moved to Holley, where he still resides in 1871.

After Lewiston was burned in the late war with England, Mr. Hubbard Rice, then eighteen years old, volunteered as a soldier and served a *campaign on the Niagara Frontier*.

Coming to Holley as a boy, he grew up to manhood there, seeing and sharing in all the toils, dangers, hardships, and privations that the settlers endured.

He has been spared to a ripe old age to witness the founding, growth, and development of a beautiful village on a spot he had seen when it was a native forest covered with mighty hemlocks, through which now by canal, railroad, and telegraph, the commerce and intelligence of the world are flowing.

CHAUNCEY ROBINSON

Chauncey Robinson was born in Durham, Connecticut, January 5th, 1792. When he was two years old, he was carried with his father's family to Sauquoit, Oneida County, N.Y., where, to use his own words, "I was educated in a district school, and graduated, at twelve years of age, between the plow handles."

He relocated to Clarendon, Orleans County, and established himself approximately two miles south of Farewell's Mills in July 1813. He cleared a farm and managed it until May 1851, when he moved to Holley, where he lived until his passing on May 8th, 1866.

In the war with England in 1814, he was called out with the other inhabitants of the frontier generally to aid in repelling the British, who were then besieging Fort Erie.

He was several months in this service; was in the battle, a sortie at Fort Erie, September 17th, 1814, which was the last battle of the war fought on this frontier.

Very few families had located in Clarendon when Mr. Robinson went there. He began in the woods, built a log house, and all its fixtures, furniture and surroundings were in the primitive style of those times.

He was a man of *ardent temperament*, a fluent and earnest talker in private conversation or public debate. He was noted for his intense hatred of slavery and oppression, his love of freedom and free government, and his zeal for the cause of temperance. On these and other related topics, he frequently wrote articles for the newspapers.

He was an active man in organizing the town of Clarendon, laying out and opening highways, and locating school districts, frequently holding public office as the gift of his fellow townsmen. He was Supervisor of Clarendon four years in succession. He was an original and *free thinker* on those subjects of public policy which excited his attention, enforcing his doctrines with a zeal which some of his opponents thought fanatical.

In his personal habits, he was industrious, frugal, and temperate. When he was an old man, he said: "I have never used one pound of tea, coffee, or tobacco, and comparatively little liquor; none for the last thirty years; not even cider. My constant drink at home and abroad is cold water."

HIRAM FRISBIE

Hiram Frisbie was born in Granville, N.Y. in August 1791. He initially came to Orleans County with the intention of working on building the embankment for the Erie Canal in Holley. When this plan fell through, he, along with his brother-in-law William Pierpont, established a store at Farewell's Mills in the town of Clarendon in 1821. They sold goods and also produced pot and pearl ash. After Pierpont sold the entire business to Mr. Frisbie, he managed it alone for several years until the insolvency of some leading merchants in Holley created an opportunity for him to relocate his business there. Consequently, he closed out his operations in Clarendon and moved to Holley around the year 1828 or 1829.

In connection with Mr. James Seymour of Clarkson, he bought all the unsold land in Holley of a one hundred-acre tract, which had been taken up originally by Mr. Areovester Hamlin.

At Holley, he sold goods as a merchant, built houses, sold village lots, bought produce, opened streets, and became wealthy from the rise in the price of his lands and the profits of his trade.

He was appointed postmaster soon after he came to Holley, an office he held fifteen years.

Some years ago, he was thrown from his carriage while driving some **high-spirited horses**, several of his bones broken, and was so badly injured as to render him incapable of active bodily labor as before. He still resides in Holley, one of the few old men yet remaining who settled here before the canal was made, enjoying in quiet the avails of a long life of busy industry and sagacious investment.

JACOB HINDS

Jacob Hinds was born in the town of Arlington, Bennington County, Vt. He settled in the town of Murray in 1829, and bought a farm which had been taken up by article from the State of Connecticut by Jared Luttenton.

The Erie Canal passes through this farm. Boating on the canal was then brisk, and no station between Albion and Hulberton was established at which boatmen could get their supplies.

Mr. Hinds constructed a grocery store and started his own business.

It was a good location from which to ship wheat, which began to be produced in considerable quantities, and Mr. Hinds built a warehouse in 1830. About this time, his brothers Joel, Darius, and Franklin came on and joined him in business, and being active, energetic businessmen, a little settlement sprang up around them, which was named Hindsburgh.

Jacob Hinds had been engaged in boating on the canal and became acquainted with the canal and its boatmen and men engaged in traffic through it; in 1839, he was appointed Superintendent of Repairs on the western section, an office he held for three years.

After an interval of ten years, in 1849, he was elected one of the State Canal Commissioners and served three years in that capacity.

Since retiring from these offices, Mr. Hinds has followed farming as his principal occupation.

AUSTIN DAY

Austin Day was born in Winhall, Vermont, April 10th, 1789.

He married Polly Chapman, July 23, 1810. He moved to the town of Murray in the winter of 1815.

For some years after he came to Murray, he served as a constable. Being a good talker, he practiced pettifogging or acted as counsel in Justice's courts. For a number of years until professional lawyers came in, he did a large business.

After the Erie Canal was made navigable, Austin Day engaged in buying wheat, which he followed for some years, shipping large quantities chiefly from Holley.

He was appointed Judge in the Old Court of Common Pleas of Orleans County, an office he held five years.

He was elected sheriff of Orleans County in November 1847 and held the office for three years. In January 1848, he moved to Albion, where he has since resided. He was Supervisor of Barre in 1852.

His wife died on October 15th, 1858, which broke up his family. Since then, he has resided in the family of his son, F. A. Day, in Albion, and lately with his daughter, Mrs. Buell, in Holley, relieved from the cares and anxieties of business.

ELIJAH W. WOOD

Elijah W. Wood was born in Pelham, Mass., April 22, 1782. He moved to the town of Murray at an early day, where for many years he served as Constable and Justice of the Peace, and during one term of five years he was Judge in the Old Court of Common Pleas of Orleans County.

He was a *clever* and successful lawyer in lower courts, relying on wit and natural insight rather than extensive legal knowledge. He died in Murray at the age of eighty years.

RECOLLECTIONS OF MRS. SALLY SMITH

"I was born in St. Johnsbury, Vermont, in 1795. My father moved with his family, including myself, to Leroy, New York, in 1816. We were twenty-one days on the journey.

I came to Murray in 1817, and taught school in district No. 8, in a log house in which a family resided at the time. My wages was nine shillings a week and I boarded among my patrons. I taught eight months during which time I was happy and fared well.

While I was boarding at the house of David Gould, in the winter time, his stock of fodder for his cattle gave out, and he was obliged to feed them with browse, and to save them from starving on such fare, he went to Victor, Ontario County, and bought a load of corn for his cattle. His brother-in-law brought the corn to Murray on a sleigh with two horses and arrived at Mr. Gould's house late in the evening of a cold and stormy night.

There was no stable nearer than Sandy Creek, three miles, where the horses could be sheltered. Mr. Gould's house had but one room, but it was concluded to keep the horses there overnight. Mr. Gould and his wife occupied a bed in a corner of the room; two girls and myself had our bed with its foot at the side of Mr. Gould's bed, and the horses stood in the other corner and ate their corn, and thus we all slept that night as we could.

I married Artemas Daggett, February 14th, 1819, and commenced house-keeping on the farm where I now reside, September 1870.

Mr. Daggett died in 1831 and left me with three small children and one hundred acres of land, owing about nine hundred dollars. In two years, I raised the money, paid our debts, and took a deed of the land.

About this time, I married Isaac Smith, with whom I lived in peace and plenty until his death in August 1866.

During a great sickness at Sandy Creek, Mr. Brace, his wife, and six children resided there. One of his daughters fell sick and went to the house of a *doctress* in town to be treated. Others of the children were taken ill. Mr. Brace was notified that his daughter under the doctress' care was much worse and he went to see her. She died, and he was taken down sick and could not go home. In the meantime, a son at home died. Mrs. Brace had taken sole care of him in his sickness, and while watching his corpse, the dead body of Mr. Brace was brought home, and father and son were buried at the same time. The other sick ones recovered.

At this time, Mr. Aretas Pierce, Sr., who lived four miles away, came and found the Brace family miserably poor and destitute of all the comforts and most of the necessaries of life. He went about and got a contribution, and next day the pressing wants of the family were supplied, by the benevolent settlers around.

SALLY SMITH."

Murray, September, 1870.

ALANSON MANSFIELD

Alanson Mansfield was born in Vermont, March 9th, 1793.

With an ax, which constituted his whole personal estate, he came into the town of Murray in the year 1814 and hired out to work, chopping until he earned enough to take an article of lot number two hundred and nineteen, a little north of Hindsburgh. He then returned to Vermont to bring his father's family to settle on his land. They started from Vermont, his father and mother, and six children, Alanson being the oldest of the children, with a pair of horses and a sleigh, in which was a barrel of pork and some meal, a few household goods, and the family. A milk cow was led behind. The pork and meal and milk of the cow supplied most of their provisions on the road and helped sustain them after arriving in Murray until they could otherwise be supplied.

They arrived in the winter of 1815, put up a log house for a dwelling, and began clearing the timber from a piece of land. In the first season, they planted corn from four ears among the logs, from which they raised a good crop.

He married Polly Hart, in Murray, October 14th, 1817. Her father settled near where Murray Depot now stands in 1816.

He united with the Baptist church in Holley in 1831. The next year, the Gaines and Murray Baptist church on the Transit was formed, and Mr. Mansfield united with them and was chosen deacon. He was a worthy, honored, and good man and died respected by all who knew him on September 30th, 1850.

ABNER BALCOM

Abner Balcom was born in Richfield, Otsego Co., N.Y., September 15, 1796, and brought up in Hopewell, Ontario County.

He married Ruth Williams, of Hopewell, March, 1816. She died in March, 1822.

In the fall of 1822, he married Philotheta Baker. She died February 7th, 1865, and for his third wife, he married Mrs. Philena Waring.

In the fall of 1812, in company with his older brother, Horace, and two other men, he chopped over twenty-two acres on lot one hundred and ninety-two, which Horace had purchased and on which he settled in the spring of 1816 and where he died. This was the first clearing in Murray, on this line between the Ridge and Clarendon.

Mr. Abner Balcom first settled in the town of Ridgeway, on the farm now or lately owned by Grosvenor Daniels, to whom he sold it and moved to Murray before the canal was made.

In the company with Mr. Hiel Brockway he built the dam and mills on the west branch of Sandy Creek, on lot one hundred and ninety-five, near which he has ever since resided.

These mills, a sawmill and gristmill, are known as Balcom's Mills, and in them Mr. Balcom has always retained an interest.

Mr. Balcom has always been much respected among his fellow townsmen. He has held all the town offices except clerk. He served as Supervisor of Murray in 1847-48. He is an influential and consistent member of the Transit Baptist church, in which he has been deacon.

His son, Francis Balcom, was among the volunteers who went into the Union Army in the first years of the Great Rebellion. He was killed in battle while gallantly fighting to save the country, which the instructions of his father and the instincts of his own nature had taught him to love.

REUBEN BRYANT

Reuben Bryant was born at Templeton, Worcester County, Massachusetts, July 13th, 1792. He graduated from *Brown University*, Rhode Island, about the year 1815.

After some time spent in teaching, he moved to Livingston County, N.Y., and studied law in the office of the late Judge Smith, in Caledonia. Having been *admitted to the bar* of the Supreme Court, he settled to practice his profession in Holley about the year 1823, in which village he was the pioneer lawyer.

In the fall of 1849 he moved to Albion, and in 1855 he moved to Buffalo to aid his only son, William C. Bryant, a rising young lawyer just getting into practice in that city.

He was appointed Master in Chancery by Governor Silas Wright, an office he held when the *Court of Chancery* was abolished under the Constitution of 1846.

He was a thorough *classical scholar* and had his mind well stored with *Greek and Latin lore*, which he delighted to quote in social moments with his friends when circumstances made it proper.

As a lawyer, he had a clear perception of the law and the facts and of their bearing in his cases, but he was too exact, cautious, and *diffident* of himself to be an advocate. All his life, he suffered from a malady which was a perpetual burden and cross to him and annoyed him in his business. He died in Buffalo in January 1863.

CHAPTER 22.

VILLAGE OF HOLLEY

Holley, situated in the town of Murray, is a village that owes its existence to the Erie Canal. The site of this village was originally covered with a heavy growth of hemlock trees. These were mostly standing when the canal was surveyed through. But it became apparent that a town must grow up at this site, and so a vigorous settlement was begun when work on the great embankment was commenced.

VILLAGE OF HOLLEY

Areovester Hamlin took up one hundred acres of land of the State of Connecticut, which included most of the present village of Holley, about the year 1820 and immediately commenced clearing off the timber and laid out a village.

Col. Ezra Brainard was the contractor who built the embankment for the canal over Sandy Creek. While that work was progressing, settlers came in and began to build up the place.

Mr. Hamlin erected a store in which he traded. He built an ashery and carried on that business; he also built the first warehouse on the canal.

To help his village and accommodate the settlers who were coming in, he got a post office established, of which he was the first postmaster. He was an enterprising, active businessman but attempted to do more business than his means would permit and failed. All his property was sold out by the Sheriff about the year 1828 or 1829.

Mr. John W. Strong opened a store here a little after Mr. Hamlin, and he also failed about the time Mr. Hamlin did. Hiram Frisbie and James Seymour purchased all the real estate that Hamlin had not sold to other settlers.

Mr. Frisbie came here in 1828, opened a store, and commenced selling goods, a business in which he has more or less been engaged ever since.

Mr. Frisbie bought out the interest of Mr. Seymour many years ago, and he has sold out the greater part of his tract of land into village lots.

Among the early merchants, after those named, were Mower and Wardwell and Selby & Newell. Alva Hamlin, George A. Porter, S. Stedman, and E. Taylor were carpenters and joiners who settled here in an early day. John Avery and brother were the first blacksmiths. Samuel Cone was the first shoemaker. Dr. McClough first physician.

Harley N. Bushnell built a sawmill on the creek north of the canal in 1824.

Reuben Bryant settled as a lawyer in Holley about the time the canal was made and was the first lawyer. John Onderdonk was the first tailor.

A man by the name of Samuel Cone built and kept a tavern where the Mansion House now stands, and a Mr. Barr built and kept another tavern house a little west of the Mansion House. Both of these taverns were kept before the Canal was navigable.

Mr. Turner was the first Justice of the Peace.

The Presbyterian and Baptist meeting houses were built in 1831.

Major William Allis came here as a clerk in the store of John W. Strong. After the closing out of Mr. Strong's business, Maj. Allis carried on business as a produce dealer and served a term as Sheriff of Orleans County.

Salt was found in the ravine on the bank of the creek south of the canal. A brine spring was located near where the railroad crosses the creek. In its natural state, this was known as a deer lick. When the State of Connecticut sold the land on which this spring was found, in the deed given, they reserved all mines, minerals, and salt springs. The State afterwards agreed with Mr. John Reed that he should open the spring, test the water, and share half the avails with the State.

Mr. Reed dug out the spring, set two kettles near the creek in the ravine, and commenced boiling the water for salt. When the water was pumped from the well it appeared limpid and clear, after boiling it became red colored, and if then boiled down to salt it remained red colored salt. To remedy this he boiled the water, then drew it off in vats to settle, the coloring matter fell to the bottom, the clear brine was then returned to the kettles, and made white salt.

Reed commenced boiling in 1814. After a time, sixteen kettles were set here to make salt and used until navigation was opened in the canal, when Onondaga salt could be furnished here so cheaply these works were abandoned. Indeed, they never afforded a profit to those working them.

The wood for the fires was cut on the west side of the creek mainly, and drawn upon the top of the bank, of proper length to put under the kettles, and thrown down the bank through a spout made of timber. A load of wood was sold at the works for a bushel of salt or one dollar. Although the brine so obtained was comparatively weak, they made hundreds of bushels of salt, which was sold to settlers in this vicinity and carried away in bags.

Some years after the canal was dug, Erastus Cone bored for stronger brine to a depth of nearly one hundred feet near the old spring, but the result did not warrant his making salt there, and none has been made since.

The first schoolhouse in the village of Holley was made of logs, about the year 1815, and stood not far from the present railroad depot. It had no arrangement for making a fire in it and was used for a school only in the summer for several years. The first teacher in this school was Lydia Thomas, afterwards Mrs. Henry Hill.

When laborers were excavating and building the canal embankment, a tooth of some huge animal, a mammoth, perhaps, was dug up. The tooth was a grinder and weighed two pounds and two ounces. No other bones of such a creature have been found, and it has been conjectured this tooth must have been shed there by the animal to which it belonged when it came after salt. It is now in the State collection in Albany.

Holley was sometimes called Salt Port by the boatmen, but that name was soon dropped for Holley, a name given to the village in honor of Myron Holley, one of the Canal Commissioners, when the canal was dug.

On the 5th of January, 1819, a Congregational Church was organized at the village of Sandy Creek in Murray, which was distinguished as the *Congregation Church of Sandy Creek*. July 13, 1831, by act of the Presbytery of Rochester, this church was united with the Presbyterian Church in Clarendon, and moved to Holley, where the new organization was thereafter known as the *Church of Murray*.

The village of Holley was incorporated under the General Act of the Legislature on July 1, 1850.

CHAPTER 23.

THE VILLAGE OF HULBERTON

The village of Hulberton is a *canal village* in the town of Murray. Joseph Budd, from the county of Rensselaer, New York, settled here in May, 1826, and purchased of a former proprietor about one hundred acres of land lying on both sides of the canal.

At first, Mr. Budd resided in a log house standing a little south of the Methodist Meetinghouse. He afterwards erected a substantial stone dwelling in which he resided, now occupied by Mr. Marcus H. Phillips.

Mr. Budd was a large-hearted, generous, and public-spirited man. He had the sagacity to see that a village would exist if the advantages were properly improved, and he set to work accordingly.

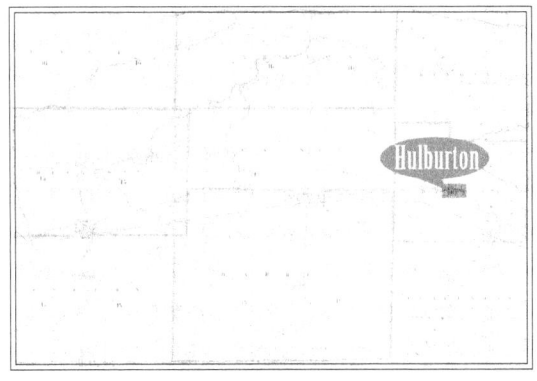

In 1828, he dug a basin in the south bank of the canal west of the bridge. It was large enough for canal boats to turn around in, and he started selling village lots to those he could persuade to buy from him. Settlers soon located here.

In 1830, Dr. Frisbie built a warehouse on the basin Budd had dug out. This was the first warehouse.

Isaac H. S. Hulburt opened a grocery on the towpath east of the bridge in 1830, being the first grocery.

Orsamus Squire built and occupied a store on the lot now used for a hotel in 1828. This was the first store. This store was altered over and fitted up for a tavern, and the first tavern was kept here by Timothy Tuttle in 1832.

In 1833, Mr. Budd had his land next to the highway and canal laid out into village lots by A. Cantine, a surveyor. The village was then built according to this plan.

I. H. S. Hulburt was an active businessman who sold goods, bought farm produce, staves, and lumber, drove a brisk trade with the boatmen, and served as justice of the peace.

Finding it inconvenient to go over to Sandy Creek, on the Ridge, for all their mail business, he applied for a post office here.

The village was named Scio at an early day by Mr. George Squire.

On examining the new post office's name, it was found that there was already one post office named

Scio in New York. And so the village name of Scio was changed to Hulberton in honor of Mr. Hulburt, by which name the village and the post office have ever since been called.

The post office was established in 1835. I. H. S. Hulburt, first postmaster.

Mr. Joseph Budd was a religious man. Desiring to promote the cause of religion and good morals among the people in his settlement, he invited Elders Wooster and Hemenway of the Methodist Episcopal Church to make this one of their preaching stations. Through these instrumentalities, a society and church of Methodists were organized. This society erected its meeting house in 1835. Its trustees at that time were I. H. S. Hulburt, Samuel Copeland, Hiram Hibbard, Joseph Budd, and George Squire.

Among the prominent businessmen whose wealth and industry aided largely in building up Hulberton were the Reed family, consisting of Abijah Reed and his sons Epenetus, Hercules, and Jacob, and his son-in-law Edward Mulford. They were merchants, upright, honorable, and fair, who came here from Greene County, N.Y. They enjoyed the confidence of the community and carried on a large business while they lived.

Gilbert Turner was the first blacksmith and Wm. Perrigo was the first shoemaker.

Among the early settlers in and near Hulberton were Remember S. Wheeler, George Squire, and Hanford Phillips, who bought the farm on which Mr. Budd formerly resided and on which he set out the apple orchard, which has since become justly celebrated, now owned by Mr. Phillips.

Mr. Joseph Budd, who is worthy to be called the Pioneer of Hulberton, died in May 1856.

CHAPTER 24.

VILLAGE OF HINDSBURGH

Hindsburgh, a little village in the town of Murray, is situated on land which was first settled by Jacob Luttenton, who built the first house here. Mr. Luttenton sold out to Jacob Hinds in 1829, and Mr. Hinds commenced building up a village. He built the first warehouse in 1830, and the first tavern in 1835.

Mr. Hinds, in connection with his brother Joel, built the first store for selling dry goods and groceries in 1835 and opened it for trade in 1836.

VILLAGE OF HINDSBURGH

In 1832, with growing trade and increased emigration to Kendall and other northern areas, Hindsburgh was established as the main point of departure from the canal. The Hinds Brothers and their neighbors held a public meeting and decided to name their village Hindsburgh, anticipating the location of a small village.

The produce trade was successful. In 1836, Mr. W. Whitney from Rochester constructed another warehouse in the area.

Hindsburgh has always been a good place from which to ship the abundant crops of grain, apples, and farm produce raised in this neighborhood. As long as passengers traveled by canal, boats stopping here made business lively with the help of local trade.

Several grocery stores were located here, several mechanics were employed, and a significant trade in dry goods was maintained by the Hinds Brothers and others.

The deaths of Joel and Darius Hinds, the relocation of their younger brother Franklin to Iowa, and the passing of Jabez Allison, an early settler who was involved in the produce trade, appeared to slow down business activities. As a result, Hindsburgh has not experienced growth in trade or population for some time.

Mr. Jabez Allison was for many years a justice of the peace, and Supervisor of the town.

CHAPTER 25.

THE TOWN OF RIDGEWAY

Ridgeway was formed from the town of Batavia on June 8th, 1812, and included in its original limits what now comprises Ridgeway, Gaines, Barre, Shelby, Yates, and Carlton.

In 1830, the west tier of lots in the town of Gaines, and three lots lying next south of them in Barre, being part of the most western tier of lots in the 15th township, second range of the Holland Purchase, were added to the east side of Ridgeway, in order to include the whole village of Knowlesville in one town.

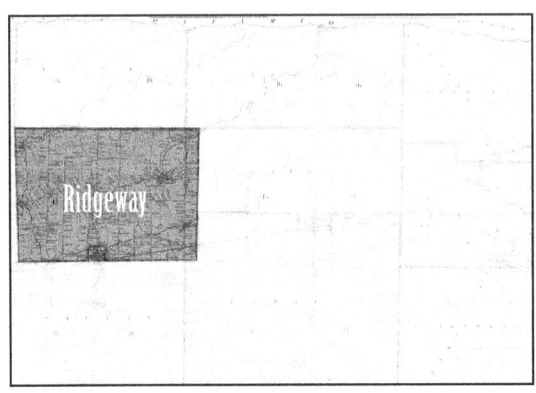

TOWN OF MURRAY

351

This town was named from the Ridge Road, or natural embankment called The Ridge, which runs through the county, parallel with the shore of Lake Ontario, and was the first town incorporated in Orleans County.

The first town meeting in this county was held at Oak Orchard in Ridgeway on April 6th, 1813. At this meeting, Oliver Booth of Gaines Corners was elected Supervisor.

A bounty of five dollars on each wolf killed in town was voted yearly at several town meetings.

Judge Otis Turner moved with his family from Palmyra, N.Y., and settled at Oak Orchard in November 1811. His brother-in-law, Dr. Wm. White, came from Palmyra shortly after and settled near Mr. Turner.

Turner, White & Hooker built a grist mill on Oak Orchard Creek, between the Ridge and Medina in 1812. The Holland Company built a sawmill on the same creek near Medina the same year.

Dr. William White was the first physician who settled in Orleans Co. After a few years he moved to Albion and built a sawmill there on Sandy Creek.

As settlers came in, Dr. White gave more attention to the practice of his profession and did a large business. About the time of the digging and opening of the canal, he kept a small drug store in connection with his other business, practicing medicine in partnership with Dr. O. Nichoson.

When Orleans County was organized, he was appointed the first Surrogate.

He was afterwards engaged in boating on the canal, then carried on a farm in Carlton. About 1842, he returned to Albion and resumed the practice of medicine, adopting the homeopathic system. Not getting much practice, he moved to Holley, where he served several years as justice of the peace of Murray and died a few years after.

The Holland Company cut out roads to the brine springs north of Medina and built works for making salt. But little salt was made until the works passed into the possession of Isaac Bennett in 1818. He bored about one hundred and fifty feet and obtained brine which he boiled into salt, having at one time as many as seventy kettles in use, furnishing a large portion of all the salt used in this portion of the country. At the time of opening the canal, these salt works were superseded by Onondaga salt and discontinued.

Mr. James H. Perry of Ridgeway has furnished the following additional history of his town:

"The first permanent settlement in this town was made by Seymour Murdock. In the spring of 1810, he moved with his family to western New York to settle where he might find a place to suit. Arriving at Avon, he left his family there, which consisted of twelve besides himself, and with his oldest son, went to the land office at Batavia. He there learned that the Ridge Road had been opened and a few settlements made on it.

From Batavia, he went to Buffalo, followed the river north to Lewiston, then went east along the Ridge Road, and when about two miles east of the western boundary of Orleans County, he came to two men by the name of Lampson, eating their dinner by a tree they had just cut down.

These men had contracted with the Holland Company to buy part of lot twenty-four, township fifteen, range four, and Mr. Murdock purchased of them their rights to the land they had selected. This done he returned to Avon after his family, going by way of Batavia, while his son went east on the Ridge to find the best route to get through.

His eldest daughter declared she would go no farther into the woods and was left at Avon. Taking the remainder of the family he started for Ridgeway, traveling through a dense forest to Clarkson, thence west on the Ridge Road, they reached their new home June 1st, 1810.

A Mr. William Davis began to build a log house on the lot next west of Murdock's about this time, but did not move his family there till September, 1810.

Soon after this, two men located at the Salt Works one and one-half miles south of the Ridge on the bank of Oak Orchard Creek in a log house erected by the Land Company.

Erza D. Barnes came the same summer and boarded at Murdock's while he was building his house two and a half miles east and working two days each week for Mr. Murdock to pay for his board. At that time there were in the present town of Ridgeway five horses, two yoke of oxen, and three cows, all the animals of the kind in town. These were brought in by Seymour Murdock.

Eli Moore moved to Ridgeway Corners in the spring of 1811 and built a block house, which he opened as a tavern the same season and which still comprises part of the large hotel standing there.

The same season he opened a small store for the sale of dry goods and groceries, which makes him no doubt the pioneer landlord and merchant of Ridgeway, if not of Orleans County.

Sholes and Cheeney were the first blacksmiths; Isaac A. Bullard the first tanner, *currier*, and shoemaker, Dr. Wm. White the first physician, Israel Douglass the first justice of the peace, Cyrus Harwood the first lawyer, and Elijah Hawley the first postmaster.

In 1814, the town was divided into school districts by William White, Micah Harrington, and Gideon Freeman, three Commissioners of Common Schools.

District No. 2 extended on the Ridge from the County Line on the west to Oak Orchard Creek on the east, a distance of about seven miles. The boundaries north and south were unlimited.

The first schoolhouse was built of logs in 1815 on the northwest corner of lot number twenty-four, on the south side of Ridge Road.

The first school in town was taught by Betsey Murdock in 1814 in a barn built by her father, Seymour Murdock. This barn is still standing.

A daughter of William Davis was the first person who died in town. She was buried about a mile west of the Corners, in what is probably the oldest burying ground in town and by some said to be the oldest in the County.

The first birth in town was a daughter of John Murdock.

The first Universalist Society was organized Dec. 14, 1833. Mrs. Julia A. Perry gave them a site on which their present church edifice was erected and dedicated in June 1835. Rev. Charles Hammond was the first pastor of that church.

Mr. Hildreth, of Vienna, drove the first public conveyance for carrying passengers and the mail between Rochester and Lewiston, being a covered wagon drawn by two horses.

When Isaac Bennett commenced salt boiling at Oak Orchard, Israel and Seymour B. Murdock, contracted to furnish him sixty-five *cauldron kettles* by a day set. They bought the kettles near Utica and sent them by lake to the mouth of Oak Orchard Creek, where they did not arrive until the day before the contract expired. They raised teams enough to transport all the kettles to the Salt Works, at one trip in time to perform their contract and get their pay in gold."

BIOGRAPHIES OF EARLY SETTLERS

ISRAEL DOUGLASS

Mr. Douglass was born in New Milford, Connecticut, November 20, 1777. He moved to Scottsville, Monroe County, N.Y., in 1806. In 1810, he moved to the town of Batavia, now Ridgway, Orleans Co. He was the first Justice of the Peace in Orleans Co., having been appointed previous to 1812, for the town of Batavia.

At the first town meeting held in and for the town of Ridgeway, after that town was set off from Batavia, at the house of John G. Brown, at Oak Orchard, April 6, 1813, he was elected town clerk. This was the first town officer elected by the people residing in what is now Orleans County.

There being no magistrate to preside at town meetings in the new town of Ridgeway, a Justice by the name of Smith was sent from Batavia for that purpose. The other town officers were elected afterwards at the same meeting.

Mr. Douglass held the office of Justice of the Peace for three terms in Ridgeway; he also held various other town offices and, at one time, was Justice, Overseer of the Poor, and Supervisor.

He was generally and justly regarded as an honest, fair-minded man and one of the best businessmen in the county. He always resided on the Ridge Road, near Oak Orchard Creek. Mr. Douglass died January 2, 1864, aged 86 years.

WILLIAM C. TANNER

"I was born in Clarendon, Rutland County, Vermont, April 30, 1793. My father gave me a good common school education, with a few months study at an academy.

On the first day of May 1815, I left home with a friend and spent most of the next summer exploring the western country. We bought land in the town of Ridgeway, then nearly three miles away from any settlement. I returned to Vermont to prepare for permanent settlement on my land the next spring.

When the time came to go back, my friend was sick and could not go, and my father permitted my younger brother Josias, not then twenty-one years of age, to accompany me.

We began our journey February 14, 1816, with a good yoke of oxen and wagon, and in company with another team, we went on our weary way.

We bought two barrels of pork at Skaneateles, which completed our outfit. We arrived at our new home March 6, 1816, being twenty-one days on the road. I cut the first tree that was cut on the farm on which I now live, lot seventeen, township fifteen, range three. We, my brother and I, kept *bachelor's hall* on my land for two years.

In October 1816, my brother went to Vermont, leaving me in the woods alone, out of sight and hearing of my neighbors. I suffered many hardships that winter, principally for want of proper food. I cut all the trees I could and fed our oxen on the tops, for we had raised little in that *cold season* for the sustenance of man or beast. I enjoyed my work well, but the nights were long and lonesome.

On leaving home, my mother gave me her bible, and I read it through that winter by firelight.

My brother returned in February. The next winter, I left him to keep house, but in comparative comfort, for we had plenty of provisions.

I went to Vermont in the fall of 1817, and returned in March following, bringing with me my younger sister for a housekeeper. She still resides near me, as the wife of Avery V. Andrews, is the mother of a large family, and in good circumstances.

My sister and I left my father's on the last day of February in a *cutter* and arrived in Ridgeway on March 12, 1818. Her bed, bedding, and clothing we brought were packed in a box, which contained all her worldly effects, with which she commenced life as an independent housekeeper.

She was a tall, slim girl, active and cheerful, carrying sunshine in her countenance and manners where she was. She left a large circle of young friends and associates, the pleasures of a father's house and mother's care, to obscure herself in the woods for the benefit of her brothers. She found a respectable circle of young people here, although rather widely scattered.

We brought with us at that time a favorite dog, concluding our sister would feel greater security in her wilderness home when we were absent at our work. He fully justified our conclusions, for he soon learned to consider himself as her special protector in our absence, and nothing could induce him to leave her when we were away from home.

If she went for an afternoon's visit through the woods to a neighbor's, the dog was sure to accompany her, lie down by the door, and be ready to attend her home. She always felt secure in his presence.

As cold weather approached, our season for evening parties commenced. Most of the houses in town were cheerfully opened for our accommodation, and the young folks, with a few couple of young married people, formed a company quite respectable in terms of numbers. We were quite democratic; there were no exclusions. Many a time did we spend our evening dancing on a split plank floor, traveling several miles to the place appointed, walking on logs, over brooks and wet grounds, some of the company carrying a torch to light the way.

We sometimes went four or five miles to an evening party, on an ox sled drawn by two yoke of oxen, with as many passengers as could pile on, and as far as appearances would prove, all enjoyed both the ride and the dance first rate.

The first regular ball we attended was held at what is now Millville, in Shelby, July 4, 1819, and as it was quite a primitive one and perhaps the first one ever held in this county, it may justify an imperfect description.

There were no carriages, and but few horses in the country. The young men would bring their girls behind them, both riding the same horse. Others would be in waiting to take the horse and go after their girls, and so on until the company had assembled. The same course was pursued on their return home.

At the time of which I write, we met in the upper room of a new building made for a store. The floor was good, but the ceiling overhead was low at the sides where the seats were placed, and it caused much polite bowing to prevent our heads from coming in contact with the rafters.

Our table was spread in the street in front of the store, and it was well supplied with substantial fare. We had a fine social time and formed many pleasant acquaintances and friendships, which were destined to endure through life. It is presumed there are few persons to whom it does not give pleasure when the thought of such gatherings in which they have participated recurs to mind. Of more than twenty young ladies, who attended that party, but three are known to be living at this time (1863.)

As bear stories are sometimes entertaining to pioneers, I will relate one with which my sister was somewhat connected:

A respectable young man of the neighborhood called to visit her one evening, and continued his stay into the small hours of the night. His way home lay for a mile and half through the woods. He reported the next day that as he was returning through these woods, he treed a bear, but men who were alarmed by his outcries were so uncharitable as to report that, the bear treed him. He was never very communicative on the subject, and it was generally believed the latter was the fact.

Our first religious meetings were held in a log schoolhouse half a mile west of Millville. The people would assemble from quite a distance and the house would be well filled.

Elder Gregory, a Methodist, was our preacher. He resided nearby, was a good man, and practiced what he taught.

A Mr. Fairbanks preached occasionally. He organized the first Presbyterian Church in Shelby, at that schoolhouse, in 1820.

Judge William Penniman, a popular school teacher in those days, taught a school in that schoolhouse several terms.

My sister Anna was a pupil in his school out there in the winter of 1820. The old schoolhouse has long since disappeared. An academy and fine church buildings have arisen in Millville in its stead. There are, however, associations connected with that old schoolhouse that will cause it to be remembered by the old settlers.

I received a lieutenant's commission in the militia service, dated March 4th, 1817, which I believe to be the oldest commission granted to anyone now a resident of Orleans County. I was promoted in regular gradation to other military offices, and was finally elected Brigadier General, my commission being dated April 30th, 1826. I was the first officer of that rank ever commissioned in this county. I discharged its duties as well as I was able for two years, and then resigned my commission.

I appointed the following named gentlemen my *brigade staff officers*: William Allis, Brigade Inspector; Samuel B. Ayers; Paymaster; John Fish, *Aide-de-Camp*; Harmon Goodrich, Quartermaster; Orson Nichoson, Surgeon; Alexis Ward, Judge Advocate.

I was married on March 15th, 1821, to Esther Lee, daughter of Judge John Lee of Barre. My wife died in August 1835.

I married my second wife, Julia A. Flagler, daughter of Rev. J. S. Flagler of Genesee County, N.Y.

WILLIAM C. TANNER."

Ridgeway, Dec 5th, 1863.

Gen. Wm. C. Tanner died July 8th, 1869

"I was born in Wardsborough, Vermont, in 1793. My father was a revolutionary soldier. My father afterwards moved with his family to New Salem, Mass., at which place I was married in November 1816 to Miss Lorana Hunt.

In 1814, I served a short time as a soldier in the war with England.

Soon after I was married, in company with two other families, I moved my wife and a few articles of furniture with a yoke of oxen and wagon to Ellicott, Chautauqua County, N.Y., a journey it took us thirty-five days to perform, during which snow fell almost every day.

After passing Canandaigua, we entered a forest with few settlers, and even these residing from three to ten miles apart; and in one case, we traveled fourteen miles without passing a single house. The road most of the way was only marked trees, with the underbrush cut out, and no bridges over the streams except the ice.

On our way we exchanged our wagons for sleds, and how any of us lived through the last perilous day of fourteen miles travel through the woods, God only knows.

We started as early as possible in the morning, overturned one load of goods, and fearing we should all perish in the woods, we unhitched our teams from the sleds some time in the night, putting our oxen before us. The women being supported by holding fast to the tails of the oxen, we thus pursued our way through the trackless forest four miles. We arrived at a log house about four o'clock in the morning. The house had been partially chinked but not plastered. Here, we tarried the next day and night, during which time we went back, shod our sleds, and got them out of the forest.

We had to pay one dollar each for a yoke of oxen, one night at hay, and one dollar a bushel for oats. So in about forty days, like the Israelites of old, we reached the promised land.

In October, before this time, I had been to Chautauqua County and contracted for a piece of land there, to do which I traveled out there from Massachusetts, and back again with my knapsack on my back, on foot, averaging fifty miles travel per day on the journey.

The third day after arriving on my land, I procured some boards and built a shanty twelve feet square, nailing two of the corners to two standing trees, making a board roof, with not a tree cut down near it.

The year 1816 was the *cold season*; corn was cut off by frost, and it was almost impossible to get bread. For three weeks before harvest, we had nothing to eat but some very small new potatoes, butter, and milk. By changing the order of having these dishes, we made quite a variety, lived high, with hope buoyant, and worked hard. Here we cleared up a new farm, raised an orchard from apple seeds brought out from Massachusetts, and also raised eight children.

I went into the lumbering business in 1832 and took my lumber to Cincinnati to sell, but the stagnation in trade and scarcity of money, owing to the course taken by the Old United States Bank after its renewed charter was vetoed by President Jackson, made it impossible for me to dispose of my lumber without great loss, which obliged me to sell my property in Chautauqua County to pay my debts, and I found even then I had not enough by $500 to pay up. That deficiency I afterwards earned by work at mason business and paid up in full.

I moved to Orleans County in 1833 and worked as a mason for several years.

Previous to the opening of the Erie Canal, I have paid seventy-five cents per yard for calico for my wife's dress. I have also paid fifteen dollars a barrel for salt.

I have laid the corners of over fifty log buildings, and have helped raise as many frames. I have spent more than six months of my labor gratuitously in opening new public highways and building causeways.

LEVI DAVIS."

Ridgeway, February, 1862.

JEREMIAH BROWN

"I was born in Cheshire, Massachusetts, July 7, 1780. My father, who was an officer in the Revolutionary War, died when I was seven years old. I lived with my eldest brother until I was sixteen years old, and then ran away from him and worked out by the month the next seven years.

When I was nineteen years old, I traveled with my knapsack on my back on foot from Massachusetts to Farmington, Ontario County, N.Y., spent a short time there, then returned as I came, most of the way alone.

Again, in 1807, I traveled the same ground over in the same way.

JEREMIAH BROWN

In 1809 I was married to Abigail Davis, daughter of the Rev. Paul Davis, of New Salem, Massachusetts.

The winter after I was married I came on horseback to Farmington, to seek a home in the wilderness of Western New York, and located a piece of land for that purpose. I went back to Massachusetts and worked by the month to earn the means to move my family to my new farm.

I arrived in Farmington in February 1811 and built me a log house in the woods one mile from any inhabitant. I was then the happy possessor of a wife and one child, six dollars in money, a dog, and a gun. I exchanged my gun for a cow, which was the best trade I ever made, except when I got my wife. The next spring I cleared my land, and raised over one hundred bushels of corn the same season.

In 1812, the war broke out. I was called to the lines to defend my country. I received notice on Friday night, about nine o'clock, to be in Canandaigua on the next Monday morning at ten o'clock to march to Buffalo. I hired a man and woman to take care of my sick wife and child during my absence while I responded to the call. I was then an officer in the militia, and I marched on foot with the rest of the officers and men to Buffalo, where we arrived the second day after the battle. Our company was the first that arrived and assisted in collecting the dead.

On receiving an honorable discharge, I returned home. The two summers following, myself and wife were sick with the ague and fever, almost constantly.

In the winter of 1815, the ague having left me and having regained my health enough to move, I sold my land and returned to Massachusetts. The next spring I came to Ridgeway, in Orleans County, and bought me some land, and in May brought on my family.

About the first of the next September, myself and my wife and one child were taken sick, and until December following, we suffered everything but death. Often during that time while myself and wife were confined to our beds, our children were crying for food, and neither of us had strength sufficient to enable us to get to the cupboard to help them.

In the month of June next, Israel Murdock informed me of several families who were destitute of bread and asked if I thought it could be had for them at Farmington. I told him I thought it could, and taking his horse and wagon, I went there and got a load of corn for which I paid one dollar a bushel. This, together with some rye, which Israel Murdock had then growing, and which the neighbors commenced cutting as soon as it was out of the milk, sufficed for all of us to live on until after the harvest.

The favorite, because the only way to replenish our meat barrels, was to hunt raccoons, using their flesh in place of pork, and their fat to fry doughnuts in. The next winter (1816), I went to Farmington, and bought two tons of pork, paying ten dollars per hundred for it, and one dollar and fifty cents each for barrels, and three dollars per barrel for salt. I brought my pork to Ridgeway with my oxen, and sold it to the inhabitants for from twenty-six to thirty dollars per barrel, trusting it out to such as could not then pay, and some of those old pork accounts remaining unsettled, I am beginning to consider them rather doubtful demands.

In the spring of 1816, we held our first town meeting, and elected our first town officers. There not being *freeholders* enough in town to fill the offices to which we had chosen our candidates, Mr. Joseph Ellicott sent Andrew Ellicott to our town to notify the town officers elect, to go to Batavia and take deeds of their lands and give their mortgages, in order to become legal town officers, and they went and did so. I, having been chosen commissioner of highways, went with the others.

In my official capacity, I assisted in laying out five highways from the Ridge to the lake. We would lay a road, following the lines between lots to the lake, keeping us busy all day. At night, we would make a fire, cut some hemlock boughs for a bed, and sleep on them before our fire soundly till morning. Then, making our breakfast, we would take another line back to the Ridge, and by the time we could get back to the settlement, it would be afternoon, and when we could get something to eat, we generally had excellent appetites.

We were, however, amply compensated, our pay being two dollars for every twenty-four hours we spent in this kind of labor to apply on our taxes. Who would not desire to be a commissioner of highways under such circumstances!

Since then I have held all the town offices in the gift of the people except clerk, collector, and constable. I was once a candidate for the last-named office, but to my great grief and mortification, I was defeated.

Our county was very unhealthy until 1828. That I think of as the last sickly season, and during that season, my health was good, and for eight weeks in that summer, I never undressed myself to go to bed at night, being constantly watching with and taking care of, the sick either in my own family or among my neighbors. Since that time, this county has been as healthy as any other section I ever knew.

In 1822, I built the first furnace and cast the first plow ever made in this State west of Rochester.

When I first settled in Ridgeway, the town of Ridgeway extended from Niagara County eastward to the Transit Line, having originally been the north part of Batavia, from which it was taken.

Such is some of my experience as a pioneer of Western New York. I have lived to see 'the wilderness blossom like the rose' and to see many of my early companions

369

in the hardships of this new county depart before me to 'that bourne from whence no traveler returns.'

JEREMIAH BROWN."

Ridgeway, July, 1862.

Mr. Jeremiah Brown died Nov. 17, 1863. He was a man of large frame, strong and vigorous constitution, a farmer by occupation, but sometimes varied his employment by buying cattle and driving them to Philadelphia to market and in other speculations in trade.

Albert F. Brown, late Mayor of Lockport, and Col. Edwin F. Brown, late of the Union Army, are his sons.

JOSEPH L. PERRY

Joseph L. Perry was born in Huntington, Connecticut, November 30th, 1794. In 1804, his father moved his family to Aurelius, Cayuga County, N.Y., to a farm near Auburn.

Joseph L. Perry married Julia Ann Reed, daughter of Jesse Reed, of Aurelius, July 15th, 1819, and in March, 1820, moved to Ridgeway, Orleans County, and located half a mile west of Ridgeway Corners, on the Ridge Road, on lot twenty-four.

He was town collector and clerk of Ridgeway, and deputy sheriff while this county was part of Genesee County, and deputy sheriff of Orleans County afterwards.

In 1825 he purchased the store and hotel at Ridgeway Corners, and carried on the mercantile business for a number of years, then moved into the hotel and kept tavern there many years. He also carried on the ashery business and, at one time, ran ten miles of the old pioneer lines of stages on the Ridge Road in company with Champion, Bissell, and Walbridge. He was postmaster a number of years, and mail contractor between Ridgeway and Shelby, several years. He was extensively engaged in buying and shipping grain on the Erie Canal, running two boats of his own, which he sometimes commanded in person. He was a shrewd, sharp, quick-witted man, a good judge of human nature, always jovial and abounding in fun.

He never lacked for expedients to extricate himself from any perplexity, and his sagacity and energy always carried him safely through, or over, every impediment which interfered with his purposes. He died September 17th, 1845, at his residence in the town of Ridgeway.

CHARLES D. BURLINGHAM

"I was born in Greenfield, Saratoga Co., N.Y., February 8th, 1810, being the fifth of my father's eleven children.

In 1818, my father moved with his family to Perry, now in Wyoming County, on what is known as The Cotringer Tract. The western line of our farm was the eastern bound of the Holland Purchase. The farm contained one hundred acres, fifteen of which had been cleared and a log house and barn erected when we came on.

In clearing our land, we were accustomed to making black salts for sale, as these, with pot and pearl ash, were the principal articles of export that brought money into the settlement.

In common with our neighbors, we sometimes suffered some hardships for lack of the necessaries of life. My father, at one time, went to the *Genesee Flats*, twelve or fifteen miles distant, and bought corn that was nearly spoiled by the flood of the previous season, paying one dollar and twenty-five cents a bushel to help us along in the spring.

I remember one pleasant incident of our pioneer history. After getting along as best we could at one time, without any bread for several weeks, we sat down to a meal of boiled new unground wheat and maple molasses, all the product of our own farm, the most delicious dinner, it seemed to me, I ever ate. Ah, that was a dinner a little boy could not easily forget, and that was the crisis, the turning point in the pinch.

Not long after this, we had grain to sell, wheat at the nominal price of thirty-one cents, and corn at eighteen cents per bushel, with very limited sales at those prices.

Our house stood, as I then thought, in about the center of the world, and having joined to it an addition of another house of about the like size, we were frequently favored with social gatherings of people there of all classes during the winter evenings. Those were occasions never to be forgotten by me. The children and young people would amuse themselves in harmless play and gossip, and the parents enjoy themselves in planning and storytelling, while a few of the venerable mothers were intent on preparing the invariable accompaniment of every gathering, a good supper.

Starch, prim, and upper ten were unknown there. Liberty, equality, and fraternity reigned supreme in those *halcyon days*. Ah me, but those were days of *Auld Lang Syne*, the memory of which is exceedingly pleasant.

In those times our religious meetings were held in a private house about half a mile from ours. Elder Luther, a man of more than ordinary ability, was the preacher who visited the place occasionally. He was a little eccentric in his manners and language but quite well adapted to the times and character of his congregations.

As a specimen of pioneer preaching, it is remembered of Elder Luther, as he was in the midst of a sermon, urging some topic, and wishing to adduce authority to sustain some point, he stopped a moment, then said, 'John, what do you say?' Then, changing his tone of voice to imitate a fancied reply, he repeated what the apostle said on that subject. And then he called out, 'Paul, what are your views?' Giving a reply as before in like manner thus interrogating other apostles and our Savior, and giving their answers, closing up with 'And now, old Ben, Luther, what have you to say to all this?' and then he gave his own conclusions, making the point deeply impressive upon his hearers.

Our *chorister* was the blacksmith of the settlement, 'Uncle Seava,' as he was called by everybody; a white-haired, tall, slim, straight, and solemn old gentleman. He would rise and give the pitch for New Durham, Exhortation, Northfield or Majesty, or some such tune in which the whole congregation who could sing would join, taking their style from the chorister, giving to the words and the music that peculiar nasal twang common in those days, which was designed to be especially impressive upon the hearers, and it had its intended effect, at least upon me, for I have not forgotten those auspicious occasions witnessed when I was a little boy. Although some of the young people seemed to be amused by the queer preaching and nasal singing, and some who attended failed to be profited, apparently, by the services, yet those religious meetings were really the green spots in our early pioneer life and were doubtless of great moral value to the settlement.

Though district schools were established at an early day around us, my early advantages for attending school were quite limited. However, at the age of eighteen years, I went before the board of inspectors for examination, and being found by them of sufficient capacity, I was installed into office as a schoolmaster in a district school, which calling I alternated with mercantile business until I was thirty years old.

I embraced religion while teaching school in Portageville, Wyoming County, in April 1831, and soon after became a member of the Methodist Episcopal Church.

I married Adeline C. Miller, in New Berlin, N.Y., in September, 1834.

In 1840 I was received as a member of the Genesee Conference of the M. E. Church, and began preaching, in which service I have ever since been engaged, moving to Knowlesville in 1862.

CHARLES D. BURLINGHAM."

Knowlesville, April, 1864.

JOSIAS TANNER

"I was born in Clarendon, Vermont, August 17th, 1795. I received a fair, common school education like other farmers' sons in that neighborhood. I came to the town of Ridgeway, N.Y., with my brother, William C. Tanner, in March 1816, where I have resided ever since. I was married November 28th, 1825, to Miss Lucy Baldwin. I have lived on my farm forty-eight years. I have had four children. My youngest son, Benjamin B. Tanner was a Lieutenant in the 151st Regiment N.Y. Volunteers and died in the service of his country in the War of the Rebellion.

JOSIAS TANNER."

Ridgeway, April, 1864.

LUCIUS BARRETT

"I was born in Fabius, N.Y., April 13th, 1807. I was son of Amos Barrett. My father moved with his family to Ridgway, N.Y., in March 1812 and settled on the Ridge Road, one mile west of Ridgeway Corners. We moved into the house of Jonathan Cobb and resided with his family until my father got his house ready for his family. Mr. Cobb was an old neighbor of my father and had moved to Ridgeway the year before we came.

I well remember the house my father first built with the help of the settlers in that vicinity. The walls were logs, the floor basswood logs split and hewed, the roof covered with long shingles split from black ash, not a door about the premises, nor a board. A blanket hung at the entrance served as a door and kept off the cold and wild beasts. The fireplace was some stones against

375

the logs at one end of the house, and the chimney was a hole through the roof. This sheltered us from the rain, but the snow sifted in plentifully.

Farming has been my business. I bought the farm on which I have since resided in 1831.

I was married to Electa B. Chase, of Clarkson, N.Y., April 23, 1833.

I have lived to see the various changes through which this section of country has passed. I have known by experience the pinching pain of poverty, and I have enjoyed the comforts of competence. I have seen broad fields, smiling with a harvest of plenty, emerge from the wild forests. I have not only seen this but I have realized it. I have lived it, and I trust my claim will not be disallowed when I assert that, in a humble manner perhaps, I have contributed my part to bring about these happy results.

LUCIUS BARRETT."

Ridgeway, 1864.

SEYMOUR B. MURDOCK

"I was born in Dutchess County, N.Y., April 8th, 1796.

My father, Seymour Murdock, emigrated to Orleans County in 1810, when I was fourteen years of age, and located on a part of the farm now owned and occupied by me on the Ridge in Ridgeway.

In the transit from Dutchess County, we had a hard time, traveling with an ox team, with a family of twelve persons. We were a little over a month on the way and reached our place of destination June 1st, 1810, and dwelt in our wagons nearly six weeks until we had time to erect a house in which we could reside.

From the Genesee River to Clarkson Corners was one dense wilderness, with only an occasional commencement of clearing made by a few settlers. At Clarkson was a log tavern at which we stopped. From Clarkson to our first stopping place, there was then, I think, but three houses, and they were cheaply erected log cabins.

We were two days in journeying from Clarkson to Ridgeway. The roads, if roads they could properly be called, were almost impassable.

At the crossing of Otter Creek in Gaines, fire had consumed the logs, which had been thrown into the bank to form a sort of dugway up the ascent from the stream, which left an almost perpendicular ascent for us to rise. To accomplish this, we took off our oxen and drove them up the old road, and then, with teams on the hill and chains extending from them to the tongues of the wagon below, we drew our wagon up. In doing this, at one time, the draft appeared too much for the team; the oxen fell and were drawn back by the load, and the horn of one of the oxen catching under a root was torn entirely off.

The next difficulty we encountered was at a slashing about two miles east of Oak Orchard Creek. A man by the name of Sibley had cut down timber along the track and just then set it on fire, rendering our path both difficult and dangerous as we were obliged to go through the midst of the fire.

The next difficulty was at Oak Orchard Creek. A dugway had been made down the bank only to accommodate the Yankee wagons, and ours, being a Pennsylvania wagon with a longer axle, was seriously endangered by its liability to be thrown down the bank.

On ascending the bank out of the creek on the west side, one of my brothers, then a little fellow, fell off the wagon and might have been left if he had not screamed lustily for help.

On arriving at our journey's end, our first business was to eat from the stock of prepared provisions we brought with us. The food was laid out in order around a large stump which stood conveniently by, and I well remember the relish with which we all partook of this our first meal, at our new home in the woods.

The scenery here, as I now remember it, was truly magnificent, one dense forest composed of large, sturdy oaks that extended as far as the eye could see, east and west, and on the south side of the Ridge Road. On the north side, the forest was more dense and composed of a greater variety of timber. The nearest opening east of us was the one alluded to above, where we encountered the fire two miles east of Oak Orchard Creek. The nearest one west was at Johnson's Creek, although Mr. Dunn had erected the body of a log house but had made no clearing at the place on which he has since resided, two miles east from Johnson's Creek.

At Johnson's Creek, which was about five miles west from our then home, there was one log house built and a small clearing. This was our nearest neighbor, as north of us was an unbroken forest extending to Lake

Ontario, with no mark of human habitation west of Oak Orchard Creek.

At the head of Stillwater, in Carlton, lived a widow Brown, and I have heard of residents at the mouth of Johnson's Creek, but of this, we knew nothing then. South of us were no families, so far as we knew, except two families by the name of Coon, who I think came in the same season we did, and one family by the name of Walsworth, residing near Tonawanda Swamp, which was our only stopping place between our place and Batavia, on this side of the swamp. We had no necessity then for the law we now have called the *cattle law*.

The store nearest to us then was at Batavia, thirty miles distant.

Our nearest post office was also at Batavia, and there also was the nearest church, and so far as I know, that was the nearest place to us where religious meetings were held.

There was also the nearest schoolhouse known to me unless there was one at what is called Slater's Settlement, near Lockport.

The nearest gristmill was at Niagara Falls, forty miles distant.

The health of our family continued good during the first year, and yet the season was so far advanced before we could be prepared to put in seed, that we raised nothing the first year except some potatoes and a few turnips.

I remember a man called at our house that summer, and knowing the family he kindly offered to make my mother a garden gate, there being then no fence around the garden, or within five miles of it. The general health of our family and of those who became our neighbors continued good, with trifling exceptions in the form of ague and fevers, etc., until after the war of 1812.

During this war, much suffering prevailed, as no provisions had been laid by, and the war necessarily took the time of many who would have otherwise been raising all necessary food, thus ceasing to be producers and yet remaining consumers. This produced a great dearth of provisions, and much suffering, consequently in some instances whole families left the county, some on foot; in some instances women went away carrying their children in their arms, in hopes of reaching a land of plenty and safety.

At the taking of Fort Niagara, I, most of our family, and our neighbors of sufficient age and size to bear arms went to the defense of our country. During our absence, a band of Tuscarora Indians on a retreat passed through our neighborhood and greatly frightened our women and children before they could be made to understand that these Indians were our friends.

Up to this time, the settlers were sparse and poorly prepared to encounter the horrors of war in our midst, and they were constantly preparing for immediate flight.

The hardships, privations, and sufferings of our people, which were a result of the war, were speedily followed by fearful sickness.

About this time, emigrants coming to this region were many and frequent, and as the population increased, so the sickness increased. Great and almost universal suffering among the inhabitants followed. If any were so fortunate as to escape sickness themselves, their physical abilities were overtaxed with the care of those who were sick, and still, the improvement of the county continued; perfect harmony abounded among the people, and contentment, founded on hope, was universal.

On June 1st, 1825, just fifteen years after dining off that stump above referred to, I was married to Miss Eliza Reed of Cayuga County, N.Y., and we took up our residence within a stone's throw of the log hut first erected by my father. I have resided in the place ever since and am happy and contented in the realization of the hopes entertained when I was a boy fighting mosquitoes and felling trees in the then wilderness, which is now a good flourishing neighborhood of inhabitants.

SEYMOUR B. MURDOCK."

Ridgeway, June, 1864

GLYMAN BATES

Lyman Bates was born in Palmyra, N.Y., January 16th, 1798. In November 1819, he came to Ridgeway and commenced clearing a new farm.

In January 1821, he married Miss Abinerva Kingman, who was born in Palmyra in June 1796.

When not employed in discharging the duties of public office, in which much of his life has been spent, he has labored on his farm. He has served nine years as Supervisor of the town of Ridgeway, been several terms justice of the peace, and held other town offices. He served one term of five years as a Judge of the Old Court of Common Pleas of Orleans County. He was a member of the *Assembly for Orleans County* in 1828. He was President of the Farmer's Bank of Orleans and has always been deeply engaged in business.

Coming here when everything was new and unsettled, he identified himself with every movement made to develop the resources of the country and to establish and maintain good order and prosperity. Of a plausible address and sound mind, honorable, fair, impartial, and honest in all he did, his party, his friends, and all who knew him have ever made him the prominent man in his town and neighborhood, whose opinions have been sought, whose counsel has been followed, and whose influence for good has been seen and felt.

DAVID HOOKER

David Hooker was born in Connecticut, July 9th, 1771. He married Betsey Saunders in 1795.

Mr. Hooker settled in Ridgeway, on lot thirty-seven, township fifteen, range three, in February 1812.

Soon afterward, in company with Dr. William White and Otis Turner, he was engaged in building the mills on Oak Orchard Creek, since known as Morris Mills, which are now destroyed. He served in the war against Great Britain and was at the taking of Fort Erie.

His first wife died March 1813. He married his second wife, Polly Pixley, February 1814.

He built the framed house now occupied by his son, Perley H. Hooker, in 1816.

Besides his son Perley, he left one daughter, who still survives him as widow of the late Harvey Francis, of Middleport N.Y.

David Hooker died August 6th, 1847.

OTIS TURNER

Otis Turner moved from Wayne County, and settled on the Ridge, east of Ridgeway Corners, in the year 1811. He was a farmer by occupation, but possessing intelligence and aptitude for business, he was frequently employed in public, official stations. With his brother-in-law, Dr. White, and David Hooker, he built a sawmill on the Oak Orchard Creek, between Medina and the Ridge, the second in town.

He was a Judge of the Old Court of Common Pleas of Genesee County before Orleans was set off, and he represented Genesee County as one of her Members of Assembly in 1823.

He was for many years a prominent member of the Baptist Church at Medina, being one of the few who took part in its organization. He died in Rochester, N.Y., August 14th, 1865.

THOMAS WELD

Thomas Weld, father of a large family who bear his name, was born in Connecticut in 1771. He married Lorana Levins.

They first settled in Vermont and moved to North Ridgeway in 1817.

Mrs. Weld died in 1820, and Mr. Weld, November, 18th, 1852.

They had five sons and two daughters. The sons were Elisha, Jacob, Andrew, Elias, and Marston. They all settled near their father. Elias now lives where his father did. They were industrious and thrifty farmers.

SAMUEL CHURCH

Samuel Church was born in Brookfield, Massachusetts, in 1781. He married Ann Daniels. They settled in North Ridgeway in 1816. Mrs. Church died in 1855. They had four sons.

WILLIAM N. PRESTON

William N. Preston was born in Lyme, N.H., in 1781. His wife, Sarah Daniels, was born in Pembroke, N.H., in 1785.

They settled in North Ridgeway, a mile and a half north of the Ridge, in 1819.

His wife died October 3rd, 1831. He died December 29th, 1841. He had three sons, Isaac, Samuel, and Williston.

JAMES DANIELS

James Daniels was born in Pembroke, N.H., in 1783. He settled in North Ridgeway, on the town line. A few years later, he moved to Michigan. He was brother of Grosvenor Daniels. He had four sons.

WILLIAM COCHRANE

William Cochrane was born in Pembroke, N.H., in 1781. He married Rhoda Mudgett of Pembroke. They settled in Ridgeway in 1819. They had four sons and three daughters. William Cochrane, of Waterport, is eldest of the sons.

WILLIAM COBB

William Cobb was born in Massachusetts. He married Hannah Hemenway. They settled in Ridgeway in 1817. They had four sons and one daughter. He died on the farm where he settled, April 1st, 1855, aged sixty-six years.

SEYMOUR MURDOCK

Seymour Murdock was born in Dutchess County, N.Y., in 1764.

He married Catharine Buck of Amenia. She was born in 1768.

They moved from Greene County to Ridgeway in 1810 and located on the Ridge Road, about five miles east of Johnson's Creek. At that time, there was no settler between Mr. Murdock's settlement and Lake Ontario on the north; none south to the swamp but Coon and Walsworth in Shelby, and east and west on the Ridge it was several miles to any neighbors

The nearest post office, store, or church was at Batavia, thirty miles distant.

The nearest gristmill was at Niagara Falls, forty miles distant.

Mr. Murdock was one of the first settlers on the Ridge in Ridgeway.

He had eight sons and four daughters. His sons' names were Israel, John, Seymour B., Henry, Zimri, Jasper, Hiram, and William.

Israel kept public house some fifteen years on the Ridge Road. He was one of the best businessmen in town. He died in 1831.

John died in Gaines, September 19th, 1866. Mr. Seymour Murdock died April 14th, 1833, and his wife died September 7th, 1823.

GROSVENOR DANIELS

Grosvenor Daniels was born in Pembroke, Rockingham County, N.H., May 3, 1793.

He married Sally Palmer of Vermont in April 1813. She died in July 1854, and he married Florinda Hicks in 1855.

Leaving his family in Vermont, Mr. Daniels came to Ridgeway in the spring of 1815 and took an article of part of lot forty-seven, township fifteen, range three.

Robert Simpson came with Mr. Daniels and took one hundred acres adjoining his land. At that time, there was no settlement between Ridgeway Corners and Lyndonville in Yates.

Simpson and Daniels built for themselves a camp and began cutting the trees on their lands, getting their washing done and bread baked at Eli Moore's, on the Ridge. After cutting the trees on five or six acres, Mr. Daniels went over to Canada to work a few weeks to get money, as he could get none in Ridgeway. After a few days, he was taken sick with fever and ague, of which he did not get cured until the next spring. Being unable to work, he returned to Vermont, where he arrived in December 1815.

The next winter, he moved his family to his western home on an ox sled. He had sixty dollars in money and thirty dollars worth of leather. On arriving at Rome N.Y., the snow went off, and he bought a wagon, on which he made the remainder of his journey. On arriving at his log cabin home, he had spent all his leather and money but six cents and owed six dollars for money he borrowed from a friend on the journey.

The next summer, 1816, was the **cold season**. He had not got his land fitted for crops; produce through the country was cut off by the frost, and Mr. Daniels found great difficulty in getting food for his family, but having recovered from his long sickness of the former year and being strong and resolute, he worked with a will and got through until he had raised something on his land.

Being among the first settlers in his neighborhood, he had raised produce and had it to sell to settlers, who came in abundantly for several years next after and soon found himself in affluence, a condition in which he has ever since remained.

After a few years on the lot he first took up, he bought from Abner Balcom the farm he now lives on. Having taste and ability for military service, he was commissioned Ensign not many years after he came here and rose by regular promotions to Brigadier General in the militia.

He has been a prominent man in public affairs, and though he has never sought official distinction in civil life, he has been honored with various town and local offices.

Mrs. Laura Baker was born in Bristol, Vermont. March 16th, 1799, and married Samuel Bostwick, December 4th, 1816.

In January 1817, they emigrated from Fairfield, Vermont, in a wagon drawn by a yoke of three-year-old steers to Shelby, N.Y.

While at Whitesboro, on their journey, their trunks were broken by thieves and robbed of everything valuable. This obliged them to sell part of their clothing to pay expenses by the way. They traveled in company with another ox team with another family of emigrants, averaging from eight to nineteen miles a day.

They remained the last night on the road at Gaines. The snow fell that night, a foot deep. The road was so bad and the steers so exhausted by travel and hard work, that Mrs. Bostwick was obliged to walk the last six miles of the way on foot, as she had done half the way from Vermont.

The house into which they, with the other wagon load of emigrants, moved, was a nice log building with one door, no window or light except what came down the chimney or between the logs. It was then occupied by another family from Vermont, former acquaintances.

A few weeks later another family of acquaintances came on from Vermont and moved into the same house, where they all resided until other houses could be built.

The inmates of this cabin now numbered twenty-five persons. Their furniture was two chairs, a spinning wheel, and a few pieces of ironware. Their table was a chest, their bedsteads were round poles bottomed with bark, one on each side of the room, the other beds were made on the floor. Holes bored in the logs, in which pins were driven, supported shelves against the walls.

The next spring, while making sap troughs, Mr. Bostwick cut his foot and was disabled from work for four weeks. Mrs. Bostwick hired a few trees tapped, gathered the sap herself, boiled it in the house in a twelve-quart kettle, a six-quart pot, and a small tea kettle, and made one hundred and sixty pounds of sugar.

When the snow went off, she made a garden in which she set gooseberry, raspberry, and blackberry roots that she found in the woods. She never feared wild animals that roamed in the forest, but she used to admit her fear of the Indians who frequently came along and remained all night. She would watch and tremble with fear while they slept like logs on the floor, with their feet to the fire.

Having worn out the clothing they brought from the east, Mrs. B bought a loom and made cloth for her family and others. She took in the weaving of her neighbors and received pay in wheat at six shillings a bushel, though the best she could do with it was to take it to Ridgeway Corners and sell it for four shillings a bushel, paid for in goods at a high price.

Mr. Samuel Bostwick died many years ago, and in the year 1833 his widow married Mr. Otis Baker, a thriving farmer of Shelby.

In 1853 he disposed of his farm and moved to Medina, where they reside.

Married at the age of seventeen years, Mrs. Baker has passed a stirring and eventful life in things which belong to the settlement of a new country. She has passed through it all in triumph. From pinching poverty to the possession of abundance, she has traveled every step, and surrounded by kind friends and present plenty; she yet remains one of the best specimens of the noble women who did their part in bringing this county out of the woods.

NAHUM BARRETT

Nahum Barrett was born in Hinsdale, N.H. He married Sally Bennett of Westmoreland, N.H., in 1805.

In March 1815, he moved with his family to Tioga County. His wife died there in 1820. In January 1828, he moved to Ridgeway and died there a few months later, on April 13th, aged fifty-one years. He had nine children.

LUTHER BARRETT

Luther Barrett was born in Windham County, Vt., in 1806. While living with his father's family in Tioga Co. for three years of the time it was five miles from his father's to any school, and when a school was opened nearer, young Luther never had much opportunity to attend it.

In May 1825, he left his father's family and came to Ridgeway and labored for his uncle, Amos Barrett, on his farm. He continued to work out by the month until the year 1831, when he purchased the farm three-fourths of a mile west of Ridgeway Corners, on which he has since resided.

He married Miss Almira Flood, February 18th, 1835. She was born in Londonderry, Vermont, January 2, 1807.

They have four children: Sylvester F., Elsie A., who married Henry Tanner, Medora P., and Lodema A., who married Andrew Weld and now resides in Paxton, Illinois.

Mr. Barrett is a farmer who, by a life of persistent industry and prudence, has accumulated a fair property and, by a life of honesty and integrity, has secured a fair character. He now enjoys the confidence of his townsmen and represented them as Supervisor of Ridgeway in the years 1857-58.

CHRISTOPHER WHALEY

Christopher Whaley was born in Montville, Connecticut, June 16th, 1798. With his parents, he moved to Verona, N.Y., in 1803.

He was educated as a physician at the medical institution at Fairfield, Herkimer County, and graduated as Doctor of Medicine, June 18th, 1819. In September, 1819, he settled in the practice of his profession at Shelby Center.

In February 1832, he moved to Medina, where he resided until his death on October 26th, 1867.

Dr. Whaley married Mary Ann S. Coffin, March 20th 1824. After her death, he married Sophronia Martin in 1841. After Sophronia died he married Carrie E. Perry, July 16th, 1863. His widow and three children survived him.

Dr. Whaley devoted his life zealously to the practice of his profession, in which he had a large ride and eminent success. It is truly said of him 'he never refused his services to any one in need of them, whether they were rich or poor, and without taking into consideration the possibility of losing his fee.'

ANDREW WELD

Andrew Weld was born in Reading, Vermont, August 6th, 1804. He came to Ridgeway in the fall of 1817 in the family of his father, Thomas Weld. They came in a wagon drawn by three yoke of oxen, being twenty-seven days on their journey. Mr. Weld settled on lot nine, township fifteen, range four.

Andrew resided with his father until he was twenty years old, then labored one year for his brother, Elisha, on a farm for one hundred dollars.

In February 1828, he married Roxy Stockwell. She died May 9th, 1839. He married Clarissa Root as his second wife. She died December 22nd, 1866, and he married Mrs. Susan Downs for his third wife.

Mr. Weld is a farmer, industrious and frugal who, in the honest pursuit of his chosen calling, has laid up a competence for his support and comfort while he lives.

WILLIAM JACKSON

William Jackson was born in Duanesburg, N.Y., October 21st, 1799.

He bought an article for one hundred acres of land in Ridgeway, part of lot twenty-one, township fifteen, range four, in September 1826. After building a log house on his lot, he returned to Onondaga County after his family and brought them to their new home the next February. His house was without a door or window or floor when he moved into it, but blankets for a few days were good substitutes. Prosperity attended his labor. In a short time, he bought more land, which he has fitted and cultivated into one of the finest farms in the county.

Mr. Jackson married Martha Comstock, January 20th 1822. They have had eleven children, seven of whom are living. His father, James Jackson, was born in London, England, and emigrated to America in early life.

ELIJAH HAWLEY

Elijah Hawley was born in Bridgeport, Connecticut, June 2, 1792.

He married Rhoda Spencer in May 1805. In May 1815, he settled near Ridgeway Corners.

Mr. Hawley was a practical surveyor, and many lines of lands in Ridgeway and Shelby were traced and settled by his surveys.

From memoranda found among Mr. Hawley's papers after his death, made by himself, in 1814, the town of Ridgeway, which then comprised the present county of Orleans, contained six hundred and eighty-one inhabitants, one hundred and thirty electors and but five freeholders worth two hundred and fifty dollars each.

He was appointed justice of the peace by the council in March 1816 and Judge of Genesee County Common

Pleas on May 23rd, 1818, which office he held until his death.

He was Supervisor of Ridgeway in 1818. He was appointed postmaster at Ridgeway Corners in 1816.

He died April 29th, 1820, leaving his widow and six children surviving. Merwin S. Hawley of Buffalo is his son.

JAMES JACKSON

James Jackson, eldest son of James Jackson, was born in Duanesburg, N.Y., March 29th, 1798. He married Maria Marlatte February 21st, 1819. He settled on part of lot twenty, township fifteen, range four, in Ridgeway in February 1823, where he has since resided.

He has been a successful farmer, overcoming by sturdy industry the obstacles of sickness, hardships, and the privations of a new country by which he has been beset.

He has had ten children, nine of whom survive. His wife died December 13th, 1870.

JOHN LE VALLEY

John LeValley was born at Paris Hill, N.Y., May 31st, 1810.

His parents moved to Holland, Niagara County, when he was nine years old. His father died poor, leaving a widow and five minor children, of whom John was eldest.

At the age of eighteen, he commenced the battle of life on his own account, with a resolute will his only capital, and his father's family on his hands to provide for.

He first bought seventy rods of land adjoining the place on which his father had resided and paid for it in work at seventy-five cents a day and boarded himself. On this, he built a small house into which he moved his mother and her children. He then bought on credit one hundred acres of land. On this, he cleared and fenced seventy acres, built a house and barn, dug wells, and made other improvements, and at the end of three years, sold his farm for three thousand six hundred dollars.

This he accomplished, though, to begin with, he had not a dollar in money, no team, or stock or seed, but he did have good health, a strong will, and a noble mother's wise counsel and encouragement, to which he was ready to listen and follow, in whose welfare he has always felt the most tender solicitude, who has always shared his house and home, and still survives at the age of eighty years, enjoying in the family of her son all that filial affection and abundant means can supply to make her old age happy.

In 1835, he purchased the farm he now occupies, parts of lots twenty-nine and thirty, township fifteen, range four, in Ridgeway, containing one hundred and ninety-two acres.

He has built mills, worked a stone quarry, and cultivated his large farm with eminent success and become wealthy.

In 1852, he was appointed one of the Commissioners by the Legislature to re-survey the Ridge Road.

He has held various civil offices in the gift of his fellow citizens.

He has been three times married and is now living with his third wife, Seraphine M., daughter of the late Joseph Davis of Ridgeway, to whom he was married January 13th, 1856.

AMOS BARRETT

Amos Barrett was born in Chesterfield, N.H., May 10th, 1778.

In 1802, he married Lucy Thayer and soon after settled in Fabius, Onondaga County, N.Y. His wife having died, he married Huldah Winegar, December 20th, 1807.

In 1811, he bought fifty acres of land, part of lot fifteen, lying one mile west of Ridgeway Corners, on the Ridge Road.

He moved his family to their new home with a sleigh, horses, and an ox team. One of his oxen broke his leg while being shod. He made a single yoke for his remaining ox, hitched him in the team beside a horse, and thus performed his journey, his team attracting much notice in passing. The yoke is preserved as a valued relic by his children.

He crossed Genesee River on the ice and arrived at his lot in Ridgeway March 14th, 1812, and stopped with his neighbor, Jonathan Cobb, in his log house, eighteen by twenty-four feet square, which on this occasion contained twenty-six inmates.

Mr. Barrett soon built a log house on his lot and moved into that. Snow was deep that spring. He had no hay; as a substitute, he dug up a few brakes on low land near and felled trees, on which his animals browsed, the poor horses hardly surviving on such a diet.

In June 1813, war with Great Britain was declared, and Mr. Barrett went with his neighbors under Capt. McCarty, to the defense of the frontier.

During this war, Mr. Barrett's family remained while many others fled from the country.

Beginning in the woods, with fields to be cleared of timber before they could be made productive, with fever and ague to contend with, and privations of so many of the necessaries and comforts of civilized life to be born, it was sometimes hard for Mr. Barrett to meet the wants of his somewhat numerous family with the needed supplies. Food sometimes ran short, and but for the fish in the streams, and game from the forest, they might have had more suffering.

Mr. Barrett had a *fowling piece* with which he was a dead shot (he never had a rifle) and a trusty steel trap, which did good service on occasion; he once detained a wolf who happened to put his foot in it. Numerous deer and occasionally a bear yielded to his prowess as a hunter and furnished meat for the family.

Mr. Barrett paid three dollars per acre for the first fifty acres of land he bought. He had the sagacity to foresee that the price of lands would rise as settlements increased, and he secured to himself titles to a number of other parcels of land, and realized the rise in value as he had expected.

Mr. Barrett had seven sons and one daughter, all of whom he lived to see married and settled around him, with twenty-two grandchildren to perpetuate the family.

He took pleasure in the last years of his life visiting the homes of his children. His social qualities made him a welcome guest always among all his acquaintances, by whom he was familiarly known and addressed as Uncle Amos.

He was generous and kind to worthy objects of his bounty, but the profligate, dishonest, and idle found no favor at his hands.

He was a pioneer in introducing improved modes and implements in agriculture. He was the first in his vicinity to use cast iron plows in place of the old Dutch plow. A threshing machine took the place of the flail in his barn at an early day, a rude, imperfect machine, but it was an advance in the right direction, and his neighbors were induced to draw their grain to his machine and thus taught its labor-saving power.

Mr. Barrett died in 1860, in the eighty-second year of his age.

SIDNEY S. BARRETT

Sidney S. Barrett, eldest son of Amos Barrett, was born in Fabius, N.Y., May 8th, 1804. He came to Ridgeway with his father's family in March, 1812, and resided in that family until he was twenty-four years old, then with two younger brothers he bought part of lot twenty-four, township fifteen, range four, in Ridgeway. He worked his land in company with these brothers for five or six years when it was divided, and he took a part to himself, on which he has ever since resided.

He married Lydia H. Fox, February 23, 1832, by whom he had two sons and two daughters, all of whom lived to adult age.

WILLIAM KNOWLES

Mr. Knowles was born in Sandersfield, Berkshire County, Massachusetts, on July 19, 1790. For several generations, his ancestors had lived on Cape Cod and were of the true New England Puritan stock.

They were God-fearing, deeply religious, and strict in their habits. His parents raised their family of nine children according to the notions prevalent among the descendants of the old Puritans at the time.

WILLIAM KNOWLES

The schoolhouse and the church were prominent institutions in New England civilization, and Mr. Knowles had the advantages of both, as they were enjoyed seventy years ago. His schooling was restricted to the district school of that time.

In December 1813, Mr. Knowles collected his effects together, purchased a span of horses and wagon and a quantity of iron and steel for loading, and started to go to the Genesee country, where three of his brothers had already located.

On his way west, he stopped at Schenectady and bought eight kegs of oysters to add to his load. He arrived safely at the house of his brother in Riga on January 5th, 1814.

In January 1815, he came to Ridgeway and stopped at the house of an old friend, Eleazer Slater. He took an article of lot three, township fifteen, range three, containing 341 acres, on which the village of Knowlesville (so named in his honor) now stands on the Erie Canal.

In March 1815, he began to cut down the trees on his land so purchased to build a house, then more than a mile from any house, highway, or footpath.

The spot on which he cut the first tree is where the residence of Mr. R. P. Wood now stands. In due time, his cabin was raised, with sides of logs, roof of staves, or shakes, as they were called, fastened to their places by poles bound crosswise, with a floor of basswood logs roughly hewed on one side.

Mr. John Canifee, having a wife and one child and no house, moved into Mr. Knowles's new house before it was completed, with the floor only half laid down and a blanket used for a door, and lived in it in that condition for two weeks.

Mr. Knowles hired two men to work for him, one of whom had a wife who was their housekeeper. During the first summer, this woman, Mrs. Hill, was taken sick and died.

At that time there were no roads, no barns, no pastures, and none of the modern conveniences for living in the settlement. Mr. Knowles had obtained some cows, which he kept two miles from his house. He would work hard in his clearing all day, then go two miles to milk his cows and bring the milk home in pails through the woods.

The death of Mrs. Hill was a sad event in the wilderness. It rendered the log cabin desolate. The men Mr. Knowles had hired soon left him.

In November 1815, he returned to Massachusetts and, in January 1816, married Miss Mary Baldwin. They moved into the house Mr. Knowles had built. Mrs. Knowles soon accustomed herself to the inconveniences and difficulties of her new situation, cheerfully went to work, and became a model housekeeper. The inconveniences of housekeeping were not few.

Mr. Knowles, on his way home with his wife, had purchased a set of chairs with splint seats. These were regarded at first by the neighbors as a great luxury, and frequent comments were made by them about the extravagance, as they regarded it of the Knowles family. But if they did indulge a little in the matter of chairs, their other furniture of the house at first was sufficiently primitive to satisfy the most fastidious of their friends, for they had at first no table but a board put on the top of a barrel. Their first bedstead was made by boring holes in the logs in the side of the house, and putting in rods fastened to pole bedposts, with side pieces of like material.

In the cold summer of 1816, frost in June killed the corn, rendering the prospect gloomy and sad for the new settlers, but the wheat crop proved good in quality, though less than an average yield in quantity. In the summer of 1816, the engineers surveying for the Erie Canal came along and pitched their tent on Mr. Knowles's farm, on the spot where Abell & Brace now have a store, stopping there a week and finally establishing the line for the canal through the center of his farm.

The canal was completed to Lockport from the east in 1824.

Mr. Knowles built one section of the canal a little east of Holley.

In 1825, he built the first framed house in Knowlesville on the south side of the canal, in which he kept a hotel for several years. Afterwards, he built the brick house near the canal on the west side of Main Street, in which he kept a temperance hotel for several years until he finally closed the house as a tavern.

Mr. Knowles built the first warehouse in Knowlesville in 1825, and he bought and shipped the first boatload of wheat from Orleans County.

Mr. Knowles was always among the first engaged in all public enterprises for the benefit of the community in which he lived.

He helped build the first schoolhouse in his district, which was made of logs. This served also as a place of public worship. Here, ministers of various denominations preached the gospel, and the people flocked to hear them without regard to sectarian prejudice or partiality.

In 1838, Mr. Knowles built his late place of residence on the beautiful eminence in the west part of the village and north of the canal.

In 1830 the brick church in Knowlesville was erected, Mr. K. furnishing one-half or more of the funds for that purpose.

Mr. and Mrs. Knowles united with the Presbyterian church in 1820, the first religious society organized in Ridgeway. For nearly forty years, he has been a ruling elder in that church.

He never had children of his own, yet he has taken into his family and brought up and educated seven or eight children of others. To one of these, Rev. I. O. Fillmore, he gave a liberal education, sending him to college and theological schools to fit for the gospel ministry, besides granting him a generous allowance of means to establish himself with comfort in life, in grateful remembrance of which favors, so bountifully and disinterestedly bestowed by Mr. Knowles and his family, Mr. Fillmore acknowledges his obligation and devotes himself with filial duty to make the last days of his kind benefactor as happy as possible.

Mr. Knowles has been twice married. His first wife died April 2, 1861. He married Mrs. Mary Crippen as his second wife.

He has sold his large farm and other real estate, reserving only a house and lot in Knowlesville, where he resides, relieved from the cares and perplexities of business, calmly awaiting the approach of death, enjoying the full assurance of the good man's hope.

The foregoing is the substance of a sketch of Mr. Knowles furnished for the Orleans County Pioneer Association by his adopted son, Rev. I. O. Fillmore.

AVERY V. ANDREWS

"I was born in Claremont, New Hampshire, July 25th, 1798.

In 1802, my father moved to Waterbury, Vermont.

In October 1817, he started with two yoke of oxen and a wagon to move his family to western New York. After traveling thirty days, he arrived at Gaines, then Genesee County, N.Y. I was then eighteen years of age.

In the fall of 1819, I bought an article for fifty acres of land in Ridgeway, and in 1821, I bought an article for sixty-two acres with a small log house on it. All my personal estate then consisted of one yoke of steers and a cow.

I lived in my log house seventeen years, then built a dwelling house of stone in which I now reside.

AVERY V. ANDREWS."

Ridgeway, June, 1866.

NANCY G. MASTEN

"I was born in Warwick, Massachusetts, September 20th, 1796.

I was married to Ephraim G. Masten, at Albany N.Y., November 15th, 1815. We settled in Bethlehem, Albany County N.Y.

In 1819 my husband came to Ridgeway, Orleans Co., and bought an article for one hundred and thirty acres of land on lot seventeen, township fifteen, range three, then in a wild state, cleared three acres and sowed it with wheat, and in November, 1819, moved upon his land with his family.

We lived in a log house until in 1831 we built a dwelling of stone on the site of the old log house. Mr. Masten died March 20th, 1840.

NANCY G. MASTEN."

Ridgeway, September, 1866.

LYSANDER C. GROVER

"I was born in Deerfield, Massachusetts, January 22, 1802.

In the fall of 1807, my father moved to Phelps, Ontario County, I being then in my sixth year. Here, I spent my boyhood working on farm summers and attending district school winters. When I was twelve years old, my father sent me with his hired man a mile and a half into the woods to chop *cordwood*, and on my twelfth birthday, I chopped and piled one cord of wood, and well, do I remember bragging of my exploit when I returned home. But strategy, of which we hear occasionally, had something to do with it, for I got the hired man to fell an old basswood tree with a dead top for me, and this helped materially to make out my pile.

My father being of **Green Mountain origin**, where men were born with iron constitutions, required more work of me than my constitution could endure, consequently when I was about nineteen years old, I became physically unable to labor.

In 1823, I went to school at an academy in Geneva, and in the fall of that year, I obtained a teacher's certificate. Thus accoutered, and with little knowledge of the world and still less of its lucre, I emerged as a pedagogue, which occupation I followed with an increase in both success and wages.

Finding this business irksome and by no means desirable for life, I resolved upon a profession. When consulting with friends for a choice it was thought my piety did not come up to the ministerial standard, and I had neither the confidence nor impudence to warrant success as a lawyer, therefore the only alternative was I must be a physician, which I resolved to be.

I studied medicine with Dr. James Carter, of Geneva, and attended medical lectures in the city of New York in the winter of 1827–28, and returned in the spring to Geneva, with just six cents capital in my pocket with which to start in business.

In January 1829, I located for practice in the village of Alloway, in the town of Lyons. There, with a capital all borrowed, except the aforesaid six cents which I had not encroached upon, did I start out with saddlebags well filled, full of confidence of success. I stuck up my tin and was ready for business.

It was in the healthy season of the year, and nobody would get sick to accommodate me, or test the efficiency of my drugs, or my ability in prescribing them. And it was even more than hinted that the blues were lurking about me.

But at length by patient industry I eventually acquired a good and lucrative practice as a physician, and how well I have acquitted myself in my profession, and in such other business as I have been engaged in, I leave for others to decide.

I had not physical stamina sufficient to enable me to enter the wilderness and lay low its primeval forests, supplant the ferocious bears and prowling and howling wolves, or to build log houses and occupy them, therefore I am scarcely entitled to have my name enrolled among the real settlers and early pioneers of Orleans County fifty years ago, my only claim being that I swung the ax in my boyhood days in Ontario County, and also that I have cleared some land by proxy in Orleans County.

October 3rd, 1831, I married a daughter of Henry Howard, of Alloway, Wayne County, N.Y. I carried on my professional business in connection with merchandising, until in 1844, I moved to Alexander, Genesee County, and in February, 1845, I moved to Knowlesville, on the farm on which I now reside. Here I have practiced medicine but little, keeping a drug and bookstore, and superintending my farm.

My wife died April 8th, 1847, and I married for a second wife, Mrs. Eliza Ann Brown, August 12th, 1858.

I have failed to get rich, being too timid to make any bold and great business strikes, having too great a development of the organ of cautiousness to secure the avails of any great far-reaching enterprise.

To sum up the events of my history in short, in my boyhood I was a farmer, then a teacher, then a clerk, next a student of medicine, after that a doctor, then a merchant.

I have run an ashery and a distillery, for which latter business I trust I am now sufficiently penitent. I have kept a drug and book store and am now living quietly on my farm in Knowlesville.

LYSANDER C. GROVER."

Knowlesville, January 21, 1867.

EDWIN P. HEALY

"My father moved from Massachusetts to Marcellus, N.Y., in 1805.

I was born in Marcellus, Onondaga County, N.Y., April 14th, 1812, and was brought up in labor on my father's farm until I became a man.

I taught school four years, then studied medicine, and graduated in my profession in 1837 and settled to practice in Cortlandville, N.Y. In 1838 I was married to miss Maria Thomas, of Skaneatelas, and began housekeeping immediately.

I practiced my profession eighteen years, then from failing health was compelled to abandon the practice of medicine and moved to Medina N.Y., in 1856, and engaged in the business of selling drugs and medicines, which I still follow.

EDWIN P. HEALY."

Medina, April, 1867.

MILO COON

Milo Coon was born in DeRuyter, N.Y., November 4th, 1799.

His father, Hezekiah Coon, was a native of Rhode Island. He came to Ridgeway in 1809 and took an article for one hundred acres of land one mile east of Ridgeway Corners, upon which he moved with his family September 29th, 1811.

When he settled here, his neighbors were Ezra D. Barnes, Israel Douglass, and Seymour Murdock.

Milo Coon married Edith L. Willets, August 31st, 1823.

PETER HOAG

Peter Hoag was born at Independence, New Jersey, December 3rd, 1794.

In 1804, he came with his family to Farmington, Ontario County, N.Y. From that time until October 1815, he labored on a farm, went to school, or kept school. In October 1815, he took up a lot of land in Ridgeway and built a log house on it, into which he moved his family in March 1816.

About the year 1838 he disposed of his lot, bought part of lot nineteen, township fifteen, range three, on which he resides with his son Lewis.

Mr. Hoag married Hannah Vanduser, March 15th, 1815. She died August 18th, 1831.

He married Maria Douglass, January 5th, 1832. She died March 20th, 1866.

His children are Mary, who died in infancy. Zachariah married Maria Temple and resides in Michigan. James, who married Elizabeth Slade, resides in Kendall. Ransom, who married Melvina Porter, resides in Medina. Mary, who married Sylvester Gillett, resides in Bergen. Lyman died in infancy. William L., who married Clara Bigford, resides in Wisconsin. Charles Henry, who married Minerva Powers, resides in Wayne County, N.Y., and Lewis H., who married Sarah Hoag and resides on his paternal homestead.

DAVID HOOD

"I was born in the town of Tarbot, Pennsylvania, August 2, 1794.

In 1797 my parents moved to Seneca, N.Y., the town of Romulus. We had many hardships and privations to endure, the country being new and we so far from school and religious meetings. Our land was heavily timbered and required a great deal of hard work to get it in a condition to till. We had to go ten miles to mill.

I went to school after I was nine or ten years old, what I could, and worked on the farm summers until in September 1813, I was drafted as a soldier, being then nineteen years old, and went to *Fort George*, in Canada, which had been taken by our forces in the spring before.

I was three months in the army, and was then discharged.

I continued with my parents until 1816, when I came to the town of Ridgeway and worked in summer for a brother of mine who had located one mile south of Knowlesville. The next spring, I bought an article for one hundred and nineteen acres of land, upon which I went to work clearing.

The title to the farm on which my father had resided and labored for twenty years in Seneca County proved bad, and he was compelled to abandon it, leaving him almost penniless. He came to the town of Shelby and began anew.

I built a house on my land in Ridgeway in October 1818.

In May, 1819, I was married to Miss Elizabeth Burroughs, daughter of David Burroughs, of Shelby, and in June after, we moved into my house upon my farm, on which farm I have resided now forty-seven years.

I worked my farm and my wife took good care of things about the house, and so we prospered as well as any of our neighbors. I built my first barn in 1820.

Presbyterian churches were organized at Oak Orchard Creek and at Millville at an early day. In the year 1831, a Church edifice was erected by the Presbyterians at Knowlesville.

During these years so long ago, although our labor was hard and fatiguing, yet we performed it with cheerfulness and in hope. Our neighbors knew no broils, families were all peaceful and friendly with each other, kind and attentive in sickness, even unto death.

Thus we toiled on from year to year, the forest gradually retiring before us, and giving place to fruitful fields, and garden, and orchard, yielding a generous reward for our labors.

I built a new house which I finished in 1835, but our old log house was like a sacred spot, cherished in our memories.

Since occupying my present residence I have seen the present wilderness exchanged for cultivated land, filled with the habitations of industry. I have witnessed the introduction into our county of those great works of improvement, the Erie Canal, the Railroad, and the Electric Telegraph, and now, in the evening of my days, I am enjoying a competence of this world's goods for my comfort, expecting soon to pass over the river, where I hope to meet not only the pioneers of the woods here, but all who are here seeking a better country.

DAVID HOOD."

Ridgeway, January, 1865.

CHAPTER 26.

VILLAGE OF MEDINA

The territory included in the village of "Medina" was mainly covered with forest trees when work was begun here on the Erie canal.

Mr. Joseph Ellicott had, at an early day, set aside a large tract of land here for the Holland Land Company, including the rapids in the Oak Orchard Creek. But nobody else then expected a village to grow in this area, so the settlement started at Shelby Center instead.

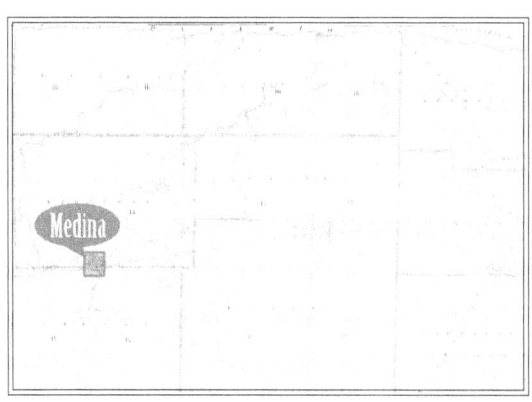

VILLAGE OF MEDINA

In 1805, the Salt Works were established at the brine springs north of the village. And about that same time Mr. Samuel F. Gear built a sawmill for the Holland

Company (or Mr. Ellicott) on the falls of the Oak Orchard Creek.

The sawmill was cheaply constructed and had no roads leading to it. A few settlers lived here between 1805 and the War of 1812, but they could not transport their logs to the mill due to the distance and bad roads. As a result, the sawmill was not kept in repair and soon tumbled into ruins.

Mr. Ellicott rented out the salt works, but working them was impractical, and not much salt was made there until Isaac Bennett took possession of the springs in 1818.

Mr. John B. Ellicott, a relative of Joseph Ellicott, was sent here by the proprietors to superintend their interests, as local agent.

Mr. Artemas Allen, a mason, arrived in 1822. He was a master mason for the aqueduct of the Erie Canal along Oak Orchard Creek. The stones for this work were mainly obtained from the bank of the creek north of the canal. The remaining stones were from Shelby Center, Clarendon, and a few from Lockport.

With these same stones, Mr. Allen built a large brick tannery, a dwelling house for Justus Ingersoll, and a large stone building called the Eagle Hotel.

Mr. Allen claims he first discovered the quarry of *flagging stone* near the creek, got out the first flags, and laid a number of rods of sidewalk in front of the residence of David E. Evans in Batavia.

The stone from which water lime was made was obtained between here and Shelby Center. The rock was then burned on log heaps and ground with an upright revolving stone.

After the Erie Canal was located and surveyed through the area, it seemed more likely that settlement would thrive here, and so, in 1823, Mr. Ebenezer Mix surveyed and laid out the village for the proprietors.

Mr. Sylvanus Coan opened the first store in 1824, before the canal was finished, and some stall establishments selling goods to those working on the canal soon followed. When the canal was finished and opened to navigation, it became clear that they needed to improve the water power on the creek, and that was the signal to develop the town.

And so it grew up steadily. Uriah D. Moor kept the first hotel, on Shelby Street, in 1824.

Simeon Down, blacksmith, arrived in 1825; The first attorney was Nathan Sawyer. The first iron founder was Simeon Bathgate.

In May 1825, David E. Evans laid the foundations of his large flouring mill on the race near the railroad. John Ryan, a master mason, built it of stone and finished it in 1826.

The State of New York had built a dam in the creek when the canal was dug and made a raceway to carry creek water into the canal as a feeder. But the race proved too low for the purpose and was soon abandoned.

Mr. Evans made another arrangement with the State, under which he raised a dam higher up the stream and connected this by a raceway to the canal. This proved more successful. Evans drew water from this raceway to turn his mill and sold water power to others to be drawn from it.

Justus Ingersoll, a tanner from Shelby, moved here in 1826 and built a large brick building for a tannery west of the creek, near the canal. Over the years Mr. Ingersoll served the village as justice of the peace, postmaster, Indian agent, and Judge of the Court of Common Pleas of the county, and was an active man in village affairs.

Ashael Woodruff and his brother became merchants here in 1826.

Joseph Nixon built a **brewery** about 1827. After a few years, it was turned into a distillery, and malt liquors or whisky were made there for several years. The brewery was burned three times, and this site is now occupied by Bignall & Co. as a foundry.

Dr. Rumsey became the first regular physician in 1827. Dr. Lathrop followed soon after.

The post office was established in 1829, and Justus Ingersoll was the first postmaster.

David Ford and John Parsons were tinsmiths. Otis Turner, and Chase and Britt were grocers. Clark and Fariman were early merchants.

On March 3, 1832, about 27 years after the first settlers arrived, the village was incorporated and the first fire company was organized on August 16th the same year.

The first printing press in the village was set up in the fall of 1832, and soon the first newspaper called the "Medina Herald," was published by D. P. Adams.

The first religious society organized in the village was the Episcopalian. On November 12th, 1827, the "St. John's Church in Medina" filed a certificate of incorporation in the county clerk's office under that name.

Rev. Richard Salmon, a missionary, was then in charge, and about a year later, Bishop Hobart held the first Episcopal service by a Bishop in Orleans County.

The corporate officers of the church for its first year were Justus Ingersoll and Richard Van Dyke, who were Wardens, and the Vestrymen were Christopher Whaley, Elijah Beech, John B. Ellicott, and Joseph Nixon. Additional Vestrymen were Henry Yerrington, Benjamin W. Van Dyke, Jonas S. Billings and Hezekiah R. Warner.

Mr. David E. Evans gave the church a piece of land on which to erect a building, the foundations of which were laid in 1831. On Christmas Eve, 1832, the first religious services, led by minister Joshua M. Rogers, were held in the basement of the unfinished building.

The house was finally finished and consecrated by Bishop Onderdonk on September 30th, 1836, where it now stands on Center Street.

Six years earlier, in 1830, the Presbyterians had built the first timber building designed for religious worship on the north side of Cross, near the corner of West Street. Deacon Theophilus Cook had commenced, alone and unaided, getting out the timber for this house. Seeing his zeal showing itself in faith and works, Mr. Ephraim Scovill joined him in the work. Others followed with their labor and contributions till a building about thirty by forty-five feet was erected. Presbyterians worshiped in the timber building from about 1830 to February 17th, 1836, when their new church edifice was dedicated.

The Presbyterian Church had been organized with seventeen members on March 19th, 1829, and the Presbyterian Society was incorporated the following year on August 27th, 1831.

The Methodists filed a certificate to incorporate their society as "The first Methodist Episcopal Society in Medina" on October 1st, 1830. Four years later, on April 7th, 1834, they filed another certificate altering their name, among other things.

They commenced building their house of worship of stone, in 1833. In raising the roof, the timbers gave way, and eleven men fell in the ruins. No one was killed, but some bones were broken. The basement of this house was finished and used in 1834, but it was several years before the whole house was completed. It was later taken down and rebuilt in 1850 and then again thoroughly repaired in 1869.

The Baptists filed a certificate to incorporate "The First Baptist Church and Society in Medina," March 14th, 1831.

Their first house of worship was a building put up for a barn in the rear of the brick hotel, on the southwest corner of Center and Shelby streets. This was lathed and plastered and seated, and used for religious meetings until their first meeting house was dedicated in the winter of 1832.

Their new church on the corner of West and Center streets commenced in the fall of 1870. When the new church was finished, the original building was converted into a school and, several years later, sold to the Roman Catholics. They moved it to the same lot as the Catholic church, built an addition to it, and it is now their schoolhouse.

The first bell in a steeple was raised at the "Presbyterian" church in 1836.

This was the first bell in the village and the only church bell between Albion and Lockport for several years. It was rung a number of times every day! to regulate the hours of labor and rest of the inhabitants.

Later, a town clock was procured and placed in the steeple of the Methodist church to replace so much bell ringing! The clock, which proved to be a poor machine, was soon abandoned.

CHAPTER 27.

THE VILLAGE OF KNOWLESVILLE

Knowlesville, situated on the eastern bounds of the town of Ridgeway, owes its existence to the Erie Canal. When work was begun on the canal, only two or three families had located on the ground now covered by the village.

Mr. William Knowles, the pioneer and founder of the village, was the first settler. He took up an article and settled upon lot three, township fifteen, range three, in the winter of 1815.

Shortly after, John Caniff took up one hundred acres of the north part of lot fifty-nine, in township fifteen, range three, adjoining Mr. Knowles' land and east of it.

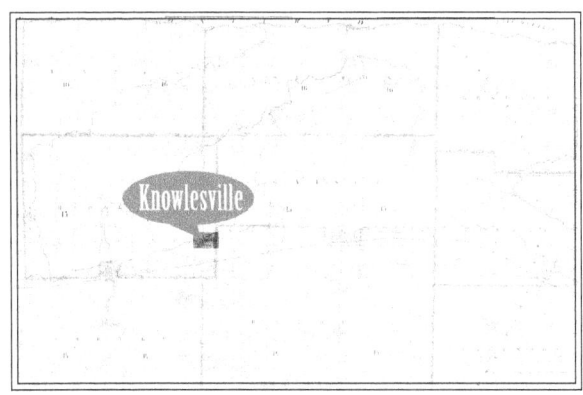

VILLAGE OF KNOWLESVILLE

The first tree cut on the site of Knowlesville stood where the residence of R. P. Wood now stands and was felled in March 1815. There Mr. Knowles built the first log cabin, in which he resided. He hired a Mr. Hill to work for him in clearing land, and his wife was their housekeeper. In the course of that season, 1815, Mrs. Hill died, being the first person who died in what is now Knowlesville.

Mr. Knowles built an ashery in 1816, and there he manufactured a little potash; afterward, for about four years, he used his works solely for making black salts, which he sold to James Mather and others at Gaines.

The first schoolhouse, built of logs in 1817, stood a little north of where a brick schoolhouse was later built, on the west side of the street, north of the canal.

The Erie Canal was finished from Lockport to Rochester a year or two before it was completed from Lockport to Buffalo; but as this long level had to be fed mainly by water let into it from Genesee River, it was impossible to raise the water in the western part more than two or three feet deep; but even then some little flat-bottomed boats were run through to Rochester regularly to carry passengers and light parcels before the water was let in from lake Erie to fill the canal.

In 1825, Mr. Knowles built the first framed house on the south side of the canal on the west side of Main Street. The house is still standing. It was there that he operated the first tavern for several years. Later, he built the first brick house near the canal, north of his old tavern, and ran a tavern there for some time.

Mr. Knowles also built the first warehouse in 1825, and Mr. Wm. Van Dorn kept the first store in Knowles' warehouse. Nathan S. Wood opened the second store in 1825-26.

Moses Huxley kept the first grocery store on the canal in 1825. Philo Dewey kept a grocery here in 1830.

The first tanner and shoemaker was Andrew Betts. The first blacksmith was Daniel Batty. The first carpenter and joiner was Andrew Ryan.

In 1827 Mr. Knowles bought twenty thousand bushels of wheat at Knowlesville. The first boat he loaded with this wheat is said to have been the first boatload of grain shipped from Orleans County by canal.

The post office was established here in 1826. It became necessary to give the village and post office a name. The inhabitants met together and requested Mr. Knowles to give the name, and he called it Portville. It was afterwards ascertained that there was already a post office in New York named Portville, and the name was then changed to Knowlesville.

The Presbyterian Church was first organized after the Congregational form by Rev. Eleazer Fairbanks, with eleven members, Aug. 27, 1817. In June 1820, it united with the Presbytery of Rochester and, since then, has been Presbyterian in its form of Government.

This was the first religious society organized in the present town of Ridgeway and, as such, received the deed of the "Gospel Lot," so-called, of one hundred acres given by the Holland Land Company. The first fourteen years of its existence, its meetings for worship were held in the schoolhouses and sometimes in the dwellings of its members in this part of the town.

Their first public house of worship, now standing in Knowlesville, was built of brick, and dedicated in 1832.

The first Baptist meeting house, and the first Methodist meeting house, which was afterwards burned, were erected in 1833.

The village of Oak Orchard, on the Ridge Road, in Ridgeway, was the principal village in town before the Erie Canal was made. After the canal was completed, Oak Orchard began to decline, and Knowlesville took the trade, population, and business.

CHAPTER 28.

THE TOWN OF SHELBY

Shelby was set off from Ridgeway on March 6th, 1818, and was named in honor of Governor Shelby of Kentucky.

In surveying the Holland Purchase for the proprietors, Mr. Joseph Ellicott noticed which tracts of land seemed to possess peculiar advantages and located some of the best for himself.

The falls on Oak Orchard Creek caught his attention as a great location for mills.

TOWN OF SHELBY

He acquired 700 acres of land, including the water power, for himself. In the early days, he settled some of his relatives in this area and provided the assets to develop the water resources and establish a community. In 1812, he constructed a sawmill, followed by a gristmill in 1813, with his nephew, Col. Andrew A. Ellicott, supervising the projects.

To facilitate the growth of this settlement, the Ellicotts, with the aid of the Holland Company, opened the first highway from Shelby Center east to intersect the Oak Orchard Road in Barre The Holland Company built the Salt Works Road from the Brine Springs, North of Medina, one branch of which led south-west through Shelby, to the Lewiston Road.

The mills first built at Shelby Center were small, coarse, and clumsy affairs, which, when driven to their utmost capacity for work, could not supply all the wants of the settlers.

The little grist mill was generally crowded with customers at all seasons of the year, some coming many miles. And in seasons when the water was low it could not do half the grinding required, and grists sometimes lay weeks at the mill before they were ground.

Late in the summer one year when the water was lowest in the creek, Luther Porter of Barre, then a boy fifteen years of age, was sent there, some ten miles, to mill with two bags of grain on horseback and told by his father to stay till he got his grist.

Arriving at the mill, Luther hitched his horse and went in. He saw the mill full of bags, unground, and a number of men waiting their turns, and concluding at the rate things moved it was likely to be several days before his turn would come, he resolved to try a little strategy to get his meal sooner.

Saying nothing to anybody, he unloaded his bags on some lumber and watched for his opportunity. When the miller had put in a fresh grist and gone out to wait upon his customers at a little grocery he carried on nearby in connection with his mill, Luther carried his bags in. Nobody seeing him, he set the bags back in a retired place among the most dusty bags in the mill, collected some mill dust and sifted it carefully over and about his bags and the place where he set them.

This done, he waited for the return of the miller and, going to him, asked very innocently if his grist was ground. "When did you bring it here?" said the miller. "Oh, a great while ago," says Luther.

The miller had forgotten and said he would look. Luther went and helped find the bags. The miller, seeing the dust, said they had accidentally been overlooked, but if Luther would put out his horse and stop at his house, he would try and put them through before the next morning.

Luther stayed, of course; the work was done, and by daylight the next morning, he started for home with his meal.

Col. Andrew A. Ellicott was the patron of Shelby Village. He is remembered for his many acts of kindness to the new settlers and especially for the interest he took in the welfare of the Indians at Tonawanda. He was adopted into their nation under the Indian name of "Kiawana," which means "a good man." He often helped them to bread in seasons of scarcity.

Col. Ellicott moved from Batavia with his family to reside in Shelby in 1817. He had been employed with his uncle, Joseph Ellicott, in surveying the Holland Purchase.

He built a second grist mill at Shelby Center, or Barnegat, as it was then called, about the year 1819. It was afterwards burned. When this mill was finished it contained the largest and best floor for dancing then in town, and the young people of Shelby and vicinity used it for the first ball in town. It was several times afterwards used by dancing parties, a man by the name of Hackett, who resided in Shelby, furnishing the music on a violin.

The young people were very fond of dancing, and got up parties to enjoy that amusement frequently whenever they could find a floor, and whenever they could secure the services of Hackett with his violin. If he was not to be had they managed with such other music as they could get, and some of the old people yet remember attending parties at an early day in this neighborhood, and dancing right merrily to the music of a Jews Harp.

Col. Ellicott died in September 1839.

The first birth in Shelby was that of Asa Coon, son of Alexander Coon, senior, February 14th, 1811.

The first death was that of William Bennett, October 4th, 1812.

The first tavern was kept by Daniel Timmerman in 1816, and the first store by Christian Groff in 1818.

The first school was taught by Cornelius Ashton in the winter of 1815-16.

In the winter of 1819, in order to get money to pay his taxes, Abner Hunt threshed wheat for John Burt for every tenth bushel.

The work was done on the floor of a log barn ten by eighteen feet, and the chaff was separated from the wheat with a hand fan made of boards. Mr. Hunt carried his share of the wheat on his back two miles and sold it to Micah Harrington for twenty-five cents a bushel.

The first regular physician who settled in Shelby was Dr. Christopher Whaley, who came in 1819. Dr. George Norton came soon after.

The first post office in town was at Shelby Center, and the first postmaster was Colonel Andrew A. Ellicott.

Justus Ingersoll built and carried on a tannery in Shelby about 1821.

John Van Brocklin built and carried on a small iron foundry about 1821-22, which is said to be the first iron foundry established in the county of Orleans.

THE GREGORY FAMILY

Among the old families in Orleans County, none are better or more favorably considered than the Gregory family of Shelby. Of Scotch descent, Ralph Gregory moved from Fairfield, Vermont, to Shelby in 1816, where he followed the occupation of a farmer and brought up his six sons to the same calling.

Mr. Gregory, the father, died in 1837. His six sons still survive and live in or near Shelby, except Philo, who moved to Michigan ten years ago.

Brought up in habits of industry and strict economy, they have each acquired a competence of property and are enjoying a serene and quiet old age, honored and respected by all who know them. It is rare that so large a family of brothers live together so long, and the Gregory Brothers may be referred to for proof that in this good land of ours, perseverance and energy will achieve success, and health and long life made happy will very surely be attained by those who live worthy of such rewards. Extracts from the local history of two of the brothers are as follows:

AMOS GREGORY

"I am fourth son of Ralph Gregory. I was born in Fairfield, Franklin County, Vermont, April 18th, 1796.

In the winter of 1817, my father, with his family, moved to what is now Shelby, Orleans County, N.Y. On that journey, it fell to my lot to drive the team of two yoke of Oxen attached to a wooden shod sled. We were on the road from February 5th to April 3rd, making some stops, waiting for snow and to recruit. The greatest distance traveled in any one day was twenty miles, and that was on the ice on Lake Champlain. But in the closing up of our journey we were three days getting from four or five miles north of Batavia to our stopping place.

I married Betsey Wyman, April 5th, 1818.

AMOS GREGORY."

MATTHEW GREGORY

"I was born in Fairfield, Vermont, April 10, 1802, being the youngest of seven sons. I was a cripple in my feet and ankles from birth. I did not walk until I was four years old. My crippled condition and my extraordinary birth, being a seventh son, occasioned my being called, while a boy, doctor. This title was peculiarly annoying to me. This and the drunkenness, profanity, and infidelity which characterized some of the faculty with whom I was early acquainted prejudiced my mind strongly against the medical profession. I have lived to find honorable exceptions to this character among some of the professions I have since known.

My only sister died before she was quite five years old.

In the early part of September 1815, there were severe frosts destroying the crops before they had matured. This so discouraged my two oldest brothers, who then had families living a few miles distant from each other, that they told my father they were done with Vermont, and had determined to seek their fortunes in the west.

At their suggestion, and in order to keep his family together, my father, then fifty years old, consented to go with them, patriarch-like, to seek for himself and his family a better country. He accordingly took a saddle horse and visited the Genesee country, and spent some six weeks in viewing the entire region. He returned home bringing in a favorable report of the land.

This was hailed with joy by us all except my mother, who was much attached to her old home. Houses and lands, and everything else too cumbersome to carry were disposed of, so that by the first of February, 1816, we were on our way to the far famed Genesee.

Our *caravan* consisted of two four-ox teams, each attached to heavy wooden shod sleds, starting on the 5th, and a two-horse team starting on the 6th. We had good teams, but we had a tedious journey. Most of the way, the sleighing was bad. From Whitehall to near Auburn, our sleds had to be newly shod every other morning, and from Auburn west we had to mount our sleds on wheels.

After refreshing ourselves awhile with friends in Gorham, Ontario County, we went on to Batavia and there made another stop. It was now about the middle of March, and the younger boys went to work, while my father and the two eldest of his sons went out to look for land. The place where we stopped was about four miles north from Batavia, and is now called Dawes Corners.

My father located a farm for himself on Maple Ridge, in Shelby, paying one hundred dollars for his chance on one hundred acres, and buying articles of land in the vicinity for his sons.

On the third of April we again started on our journey, and arrived at our new home near the close of the third day, a short journey this last, but a very wearisome one. I was then about thirteen years old.

When we arrived at our future residence, we had no shelter for men or beast. Orange Wells and Samuel Wyman had located in that neighborhood in the spring previous and made small improvements, and built log houses.

Through the hospitality of Mr. Wells, we were kindly sheltered for a week, by which time we had built a cabin for ourselves.

Our oxen could very well live on browse, but our horses after standing one night tied to a brush heap, looked so sorry that my father took them back to Batavia.

We were all happy when we got into our new house, not a costly edifice like those dwellings of some of our rich neighbors of the present day, but made of rough unhewn logs, notched down together at the corners, shingled with rough hemlock boards, with joints broken and battened with slabs round side up, the floor made of split basswood logs spotted upon the sleepers, and flattened on the top, leaving an open space at one end for the fireplace on the ground, the end of the floor planks affording a convenient seat for the children around the fire, in the absence of chairs and sofas.

Our first work was to fell trees around our dwelling, burn off the brush and logs, and enclose a patch of land for a garden and a fruit nursery, my father having brought a small bag of apple seeds from Vermont.

We procured peach stones in Ontario County. This was in the spring of 1816. Four families had wintered near our location, but on the opening of spring neighbors came in frequently, and the forest resounded with the sound of the woodman's ax and the crash of falling trees.

Among the names of settlers who had located in our neighborhood about the time of which I have spoken, I remember Elijah Bent, Alexander Coon, Oliver R. Bennett, James Mason, Leonard Dresser, Andrew Stevens, William Knowles, William C. Tanner, Josias Tanner, Elijah Foot, Peter Hoag, Stephen Hill, Franklin Bennett, Micah Harrington, Daniel Fuller, Daniel Timmerman, William Dunlap and Elizur Frary.

There was a will and indomitable courage entertained on the part of the settlers, but it was exceedingly difficult for them to obtain money for the common necessaries of life.

Mr. Hiel Brockway bought a lot in this vicinity, and sent on Mr. Calvin C. Phelps (now of Barre) to chop, clear, and sow with wheat ten acres of land. He boarded with Mr. Wells. To him Mr. Brockway would send barrels of pork, flour, and whisky, the last of which was considered in those days about as much of a necessity as pork or flour, for him to sell to the inhabitants.

This was a relief to many, and saved the buyers much time in looking up their supplies and transporting them home.

At one time my father paid Mr. Phelps eleven dollars for as much pork as he could carry away in a peck measure. I don't recollect the number of pounds.

At another time he bought pork from Elijah Bent for twenty-five cents a pound.

By the first of June in the year we came, we had driven the woods back from the house in one direction thirty or forty rods. The brush was burned off and the ground planted with corn among the logs.

This was in 1816, known as the *cold season*, when snow fell in every month in the year but two, with frost every month.

Consequently, we raised but little corn, and even that was saved in an unmatured condition. We were, however, with much care, able to make a passable meal from some of it.

The little wheat sown the fall before yielded bountifully, but the supply not being equal to the demand, owing to the large emigration of people into the country, scarcity and high prices prevailed before the next harvest.

With so small a supply to be obtained, roads so new and rough, prices high, settlers poor, and their best and almost only means of conveyance an ox team, it is no wonder much suffering and want prevailed.

My father had one horse, and he assumed the office of *commissary of subsistence* in part for the whole settlement, and acted as mill boy for the family. He would ride about the country to find grain, sometimes getting a grist near Batavia, the next on the Ridge

Road, between home and Rochester. Notwithstanding my father's faithful efforts, we would sometimes come short of food, then our good mother would put us on *half rations*.

At one time our supplies were completely exhausted. We had been expecting our father home all day, with his bushel grist perhaps, but he did not come and we went nearly supperless to bed, expecting he would arrive before morning.

Morning came but father did not. We hoped he would come soon, and took our axes and went to work, but our axes were unusually heavy. Faint and slow were the blows we struck that morning. While we boys were trying to chop, mother sifted a bag of bran we had and made a cake of the finest, which she brought out to us during the forenoon. We ate this which stayed us up till noon, when father came and brought us plenty to eat, such as it was. Variety was not to be had in those times.

In the course of this season most of the lands near my fathers were located by a hardy and energetic population, mostly from New England. By the fall most of the occupied farms had their fallows, of from three to twenty acres in extent, ready for sowing. This crop, though sowed among roots and stumps of trees, produced a yield of from thirty to fifty bushels per acre.

This bountiful return, together with a fair corn crop, placed us above want and fully satisfied us with the country we had adopted as our home. Pending this harvest there was great scarcity of provisions, but neighbor lent to neighbor; the half layer of meat and loaf of bread was divided, while for weeks many families subsisted on boiled potatoes and milk, and such vegetables as the forest afforded.

When the earliest patches of wheat were cut and threshed, there was no mill to grind nearer than Rochester. There were mills on the Oak Orchard Creek, but they were of such construction there was not water at that season sufficient to turn them. Neighbors would join together and send a team to Rochester to carry grists to mill for them all at once.

In many instances green wheat was boiled whole and eaten with milk. I ate of it and thought it good. The products of this harvest exceeded the wants of the producers for their bread, and as we had no highways on which we could send our grain to market, we were restricted in our sales mainly to newcomers who had not time to raise a crop. A bushel of wheat was the price of a day's work of a man, and he was considered lucky who had an opportunity to sell wheat for money, at even a low price.

On the first day of July, 1817, wheat was worth two dollars and fifty cents a bushel in Orleans County. In the winter next, farmers drew their wheat to Rochester with ox teams (a round trip taking three days or more) and sold it for from twenty-five to thirty-one cents a bushel in money. We felt that was better than to go home hungry.

In consequence of my lameness my parents did not design that I should be a farmer, but Providence seemed to order otherwise. My privileges and means for obtaining an education were limited, and to the business of felling the forest, clearing land, and reaping the harvest I became much attached, so that even to the present day, the axe and the sickle are my favorite tools.

At one time I came close to entering as a clerk in a drug store, but the proprietor proved to be a worthless character, broke down and ran away. No other business appearing to offer for me, I accepted the occupation of a farmer, which I have followed ever since, now residing on the homestead of my father.

The first school taught in our neighborhood was by Miss Caroline Fuller, of Batavia, in the summer of 1817. The next winter we had a full school taught by Mr. J. N. Frost, of Riga. And I taught school myself two terms before I was twenty-one years old.

When I was twenty-one years old I was elected constable, which office I held three years in succession. Since then I have held a few offices both in town and county, but never depended upon the fees of office for my support.

I was married April 20th, 1828, to Mary A Potter, daughter of Wm. C. Potter, of Shelby.

My mother died April 4th, 1832, aged 65 years, and my father died April 20th, 1837, aged seventy-two years.

My father was a local preacher of the Methodist Episcopal Church, and in connection with Rev. J. Carpenter of the Baptist denomination, he labored faithfully to plant and foster the principles of *evangelical truth* in the minds of a people otherwise mostly destitute of religious instruction.

I have been connected with the temperance organizations of all sorts that have been established here in the last thirty years.

At the age of eighteen years, I was led to embrace the Savior of the world as my Savior, and from that time through much unworthiness, I have been endeavoring to hold on my way, trusting that the merits of Christ will avail for my shortcomings.

MATTHEW GREGORY."

Millville, January, 1863.

DAVID DEMARA

David Demara was born in Albany County, October 26th, 1808, and moved with his father's family to Shelby, in 1811. His father first located in the woods two miles from any house, built a log house fourteen by sixteen feet, covered it with bark and moved into it, without floors, doors, or windows. He left the county in 1813, on account of the war, and returned in 1815.

David Demara married Maria Upham, April 12th, 1837. She was born in Ward, Massachusetts, March 29th, 1814.

ABRAM BIDELMAN

"I was born March 10, 1800, in Manheim, Montgomery County, N.Y.

In January, 1817, I moved with my father's family to Ridgeway, Orleans County. We built a log house and moved into it in the month of March. While building our house, and just previous to putting on the roof, a large tree fell upon the building, and cost us much labor to remove it and repair damages.

Cornelius Ashton and John Timmerman had settled within half a mile of my father's location when we came in.

My father's family consisted of my father and mother and ten children. When he moved here, he was to all intents and purposes, poor. I do not think, besides a pair of old ordinary horses and a cow, my father could boast he was worth other property worth fifty dollars. I worked out to help support the family until I was twenty-one years of age.

I married Miss Lucinda Michael in 1824. My father, Henry Bidelman, died in 1860, aged eighty-two years.

In March 1818, snow fell about two feet deep; the next day it thawed, and a frost following made a hard crust on the snow. On this James Woodward and myself resolved to have a day hunting deer. We made snow shoes from a seasoned board, which enabled us to walk on the crust with ease. We were attended by a small dog, and armed each with a common pocket knife.

We soon started a fine buck from his browse in a fallen tree top, the dog gave chase, and after a few bounds, in which the deer broke through the crust to the ground, he stood at bay. We rushed upon the deer with our knives and cut his throat. We soon started another deer, which we killed in the same manner. So we brought in two deer in about an hour.

Our success so animated George Holsenburgh, a neighbor, that he joined us in another hunt. In our second hunt we had not gone far into the woods before we started as large a buck as I ever saw. The dog soon brought him to a bay. Holsenburgh, who was a quick, athletic man, rushed up to the head of the deer with intent to seize his horns, when he received a blow from the fore foot of the animal which laid open his clothing from his chin down, as if cut by a knife. The hoof took the skin off upon his breast, and left a visible mark down his body.

Holsenburgh was terribly alarmed at this change in affairs. He turned pale, and retired from the contest he was so prompt to commence. Woodard and myself went to the rescue, and quickly dispatched the deer as we had done the others. Our friend Holsenburgh had had sufficient experience of that kind of deer hunting to satisfy him, and we went in with our game. Woodward and myself went out again the third time and brought in two more deer, making five in all killed by us in one day.

In March 1822, I helped the contractor, who had taken a section of canal to dig, build a log cabin where Medina now stands.

We cut our trees for the building on the ground, now the site of the village. We finished our cabin in five and a half days. I then engaged to work for the contractor half a month for six dollars and fifty cents, and be boarded. Our work was digging for the canal. The first two days we had fifteen hands, and the third day about fifty. We were allowed a liquor ration. Mr. Eggleston, the contractor, brought in, on an ox cart from Rochester, three barrels of whisky, among other stores, to use on his job. Of this, each man was allowed one *gill* a day.

At this time I was unacquainted with the nature of whisky, and I with the others, drank my first allowance. I will not here attempt to describe its effects. Suffice it to say, it was the first and last liquor ration I ever drank. I sold the remainder of my whiskey rations to those who were familiar with their use, at three cents each.

In the year 1828 I built for myself a log house twenty feet square, into which I moved my family, having but one room which we used for kitchen and parlor, dining room, bedroom, etc. Our furniture was such as pioneer farmers in this country usually possessed: a loom, quill wheel and swifts, great wheel and little wheel for spinning, necessary bedding, seven chairs, a table and a cradle, with a few exceedingly plain culinary utensils, which were indispensable to our comfort.

For many years, my wife manufactured our clothing, both woolen and linen, wove our own coverlets and blankets, and hundreds of yards for our neighbors.

ABRAM BIDELMAN"
Shelby, October, 1866.

Mr. Abram Bidelman died June 8th, 1868.

JOTHAM MORSE

"I was born in Providence, Saratoga County, N.Y., June 14th, 1793.

I was married to Dorcas Ferris, August 15th, 1814. I hired a man to move me to Ridgeway, agreeing to pay him forty dollars for it. Our outfit consisted of a good team of horses and wagon, as there was no snow then. My family consisted of my mother, my wife and two children.

After we had been two or three days on the road, a thaw came that compelled us to stop a week. The earth then became frozen, and we went to Palmyra when one horse gave out. I bought another horse for forty-five dollars, paid for my watch, a fur hat, and a pair of boots for thirty-two dollars, gave my note for thirteen dollars, and with my three-horse team went on to Rochester, which then consisted only of a few log buildings, one of which was a tavern where we stopped.

On examining our load here, I found our only bed had been stolen. I afterwards found it pawned at Palmyra by the thief and had to pay two dollars and a half to get it again. We came by the Ridge Road to West Gaines, where we found an empty shanty and moved into it. I went to Batavia through Shelby and procured an article of a piece of land west of Eagle Harbor, and returned in one day as far as Millville.

It snowed hard all that day, and I think I did a good day's work, traveling so far through the woods on foot. I acknowledge my steps were some hurried by seeing tracks of wolves in the snow, and seeing some evidence of a bloody encounter they had had.

I bought a three-year-old heifer and paid for her by chopping three acres of timber, and fitting it for logging, going three miles to the place where I did my work.

In time of haying and harvest I walked to Palmyra and worked there three weeks to buy pork and wheat for my family. The next fall I moved into a log house I had built, and felt at home. The next year I had a little trial such as was common to pioneer settlers in those days. It was before harvest. My cow had lost her bell, and had been gone in the woods eight days. We were destitute of provisions, except a small piece of bread, some sugar, and some vinegar.

I went to the nearest place where flour was sold and could get none. On my return we gave the last morsel of bread to our children. I picked some potato tops which my wife boiled and we ate, dressing them with vinegar. Our empty stomachs would not retain this diet. We speedily vomited them up and retired supperless to bed.

Early next morning I arose and went to my neighbors a mile away, and they divided their small store of flour with me. I carried it home and my wife speedily salted some water and made some pudding, which we ate with maple sugar, and this seemed to me to be truly the best meal I ever ate.

I felt, even in this straight, the words of Solomon to be true: 'Better is a dinner of herbs where love is, than a stalled ox, and contention therewith.'

Another incident. Myself and immediate neighbors were destitute of flour. I had money which I had taken in exchange of land, so a neighbor took me with his team and wagon to Hanford's Landing, at the mouth of the Genesee river, to purchase flour.

I bought six barrels of flour and one barrel of salt and took out my money to pay for it. Mr. Hanford, the man of whom I had made my purchase, divided the money I handed him into piles of about thirty-six dollars in each pile, after doing which I was astonished to hear him accuse me, in an angry tone, of being a dealer in counterfeit money, and to learn that he had condemned about one-half of what I had paid him.

He ordered a man in his employ to go immediately to Rochester and procure a precept for my arrest. I felt alarmed, and that I was in trouble. I knew not what to do, but God who is ever watchful over those who put their trust in him, was with me. While things were growing more threatening a gentleman whom I had never seen but once before came up, and after learning the facts, strongly condemned Mr. Hanford's course.

The money was again examined, and only about nineteen dollars were found bad. This was replaced by current funds, and we were then allowed to return to our homes in peace.

This supply carried the settlement through until harvest, and by the blessing of Heaven and our own industry and economy, we have been saved from such destitution until the present time.

I have seen the wilderness disappear, and beauty and civilization spring up in its place around me. I have, in common with mankind, drank of the cup of affliction, perhaps more deeply than many others. I have been called to mourn over the graves of two loved companions and four children, from a family of fourteen.

I now reside with my third wife, in West Shelby, and preach every Sunday at the Christian Church in Barre, N.Y., where I labored in the ministry, more or less, for fifty years.

JOTHAM MORSE."

West Shelby, May 1868.

DAVID BURROUGHS

David Burroughs was born near Trenton, New Jersey, and died in the town of Shelby, Orleans Co., N.Y., in 1822, aged 46 years.

Mr. Burroughs moved to Ovid, Seneca County, about the year 1798, where he resided, working a farm and keeping hotel until the year 1818, when he moved to Shelby, and settled on a farm about two miles south-west from Shelby Center.

Mr. Burroughs took first rank among his townsmen for his capacity and intelligence. He was the first Supervisor of Shelby, while it belonged to Genesee County, and was appointed justice of the peace about the year 1820, an office he held till his death. He was a member of the Convention that framed the Constitution for the State in the year 1821. He took an article of his farm from the Holland Company a year or two before he moved his family to Shelby. He had a few acres cleared and a log house built, ready for his family when they came in. He left two sons, I. K. Burroughs, formerly a merchant and business man in Medina, where he now resides, and Hon. Silas M. Burroughs, who began life for himself as a merchant. He afterwards abandoned merchandise for the practice of law. He represented the county of Orleans four years in the lower House, in the legislature of the State, and was twice elected member of Congress, and died before the end of his second term. He also resided in Medina.

DARIUS SOUTHWORTH

Darius Southworth was born in Palmyra, N.Y., on March 18th, 1800. He worked some at the trade of a carpenter while a minor, but since the year 1825, he has made that his principal business.

He married Mercy Mason, daughter of James Mason, of Millville, in Shelby, where he has ever since resided. They have four children, Elvira A., Albert, Dexter L, and George J. H., all now living.

NEWMAN CURTIS

Newman Curtis was born in Dalton, Massachusetts, September 9th, 1797.

He married Maria Van Bergen, of Kattskill N.Y., June 9th, 1818. In September, 1824, he settled on a farm in Shelby, one mile south of Millville. Mr. Curtis had fourteen children, eight sons and six daughters, all of whom lived to become men and women, and all of whom received their education at Millville Academy.

In 1854 Mr. Curtis sold his farm in Shelby and moved to the town of Independence, in Iowa, where he purchased two hundred and fifty acres for his own farm, and located a large quantity of wild land of the Government, for his children. Mr. Curtis became wealthy from the rise in the value of these lands, and the practice of industry and economy. He died in the year 1858. His widow and twelve children survived him.

HORATIO N. HEWES

Horatio N. Hewes settled in Shelby in the year 1825, as a partner in business with L. A. G. B Grant. He was engaged in selling goods, running mills, and dealing in produce with Mr. Grant for some years, and after that became a large contractor to do public work, and had large jobs of work on the Erie canal. He moved to Medina to reside about the year 1854, where he died June 17th, 1862.

He was an energetic businessman, and was extensively known in this part of the State. He married a daughter of Col. A. A. Ellicott.

LATHROP A. G. B. GRANT

Lathrop Grant settled in Shelby about the year 1824, as a merchant. He married a daughter of Col. A. A. Ellicott.

Mr. Grant gradually extended his business operations, and at length became a large dealer in farmer's produce.

About the year 1851, he built the large stone mills at Shelby Center and ran them for a time. He was an active and influential man in public affairs of his town and county, and was the representative of Orleans County in the State legislature in 1826, being the first member elected after the county was organized.

Twelve or fifteen years ago he sold out his property in Shelby, and moved to Oswego, N.Y., where he has since resided engaged in extensive business.

ANDREW A. ELLICOTT

Andrew A. Ellicott was born in Lancaster, Pennsylvania.

He married Sarah A. Williams, of Elizabethtown, New Jersey. He came to Batavia in May, 1803.

In July 1817, he moved to Shelby, Orleans County, where his uncle, Joseph Ellicott, had given him eight hundred acres of land, which included the water power at Shelby Center. He settled at Shelby Center, where he built mills, officiated as justice of the peace, and postmaster. He was the first postmaster in that town.

His influence, along with his wealthy and numerous family connections, as well as his own benevolence and willingness to aid those in need, endeared him to the pioneers in Shelby. He always generously helped those in need whenever he had the opportunity, which contributed greatly to the inducement of settlements in the area. He passed away on September 7th, 1839.

His wife died August 26th, 1850. His daughter Sarah, widow of the late Horatio N. Hewes, resides in Medina.

ALEXANDER COON

Alexander Coon was the first, or among the first settlers in Shelby. He came from Rensselaer County, N.Y., and located about two miles west of Shelby Center, in 1810.

In a statement furnished by Mr. Alexander Coon, Jr., for Turner's History of the Holland Purchase, he says:

"My father's family left the Lewiston Road at Walsworths, and arriving upon our land, four crotches

449

were set in the ground, sticks laid across, the whole covered with elm bark, making a sleeping place. The cooking was done in the open air. A very comfortable log house was then built in five days, without boards, nails, or shingles. Our cattle were fed the first winter on browse, the next winter on browse and cornstalks.

Our nearest neighbor south, was Walsworth; west, the nearest was in Hartland; north one family on the Ridge Road."

Mr. Alexander Coon, senior. Left several sons, and the family became among the most respectable in the community.

Alexander Coon, Jr., was afterward a prominent public man, well and favorably known in the affairs of his town and county. For eleven years he represented the town of Shelby in the Board of Supervisors of Orleans County, a longer time than any other man ever served as a member of that Board. He also held many other town offices. He said when he was collector of taxes in Shelby, he had a tax of less than a dollar against a man who, to pay it, made black salts, drew them to Gaines on a *handsled*, and sold them for the money.

JACOB A. ZIMMERMAN

Jacob A. Zimmerman was born in Manheim, N.Y., August 23, 1795.

In 1817 he came to Shelby with John B. Snell, who moved from the same town.

In the summer of 1817, he married Nancy Snell. In the spring of 1819, they commenced keeping house in Shelby, on the farm they ever afterwards occupied.

Mr. Zimmerman says:

"I made a table (we had no chairs) and three stools, two for ourselves and one for company. Our window lights were white paper; no window glass could be had then. Our cooking utensils were a four-quart kettle and a black earthen teapot. I gave a dollar for six cast iron knives and forks and six cups and saucers, which completed our eating tools.

Times were very hard. I was eleven months without a sixpence in money; two months without any shoes. When we saw shoes tied up with bark, we called them *half worn out*. I gave five bushels of wheat for a pair of poor coarse shoes, made of *flank leather*.

In 1821 my log house was burned. The neighbors helped me build another house, and in two weeks after the fire we moved to the new house. In November, 1826, I had bought and paid for eighty-seven acres of land. I afterwards increased my farm to one hundred sixteen acres."

Mr. Zimmerman's children are Morris, who married Phebe Bent; Eleanor, unmarried; Gilbert, who married Janette Sanderson; John A., who married Mary Powers; Arvilla, who married Egbert B. Simonds; and Andrew L., who married Jennie Bartsom.

Jacob A. Zimmerman, died December 6th, 1864.

JOHN GRINNELL

John Grinnell was born in Edinburgh, Saratoga County, December 4th, 1796.

His father, Josiah Grinnell, was a native of Rhode Island. He settled in Saratoga County and moved from there to Oneida County, where he died.

John Grinnell purchased a farm in Barre, in 1820, on which in the fall of that year he built a log house into which he moved in April, 1821. He cleared his farm and resided there till 1854, when he moved to Shelby.

He was three times married. First, to Roxana Kirkham; second, to Lucy Babcock; she died January 25th, 1846; third, to Mrs. Julia Ann Abbott, October 27th, 1847.

His children, Cyrene and Daniel, are dead. Paul, married Sarah Butler; Peter, married Eliza Berry; Lyman, married Leonora Rooker; Andrew J., married Mary Rodman; J. Wesley, married Alice Haines; Mahala, married William J. Caldwell; Harley, married Maria Kelsey; John Jr., married Margaret Root; Ella J., married Frederick Hopkins.

His brothers, Ezra, major and Amos, and his sister, Betsey, wife of Alanson Tinkham; Eliza, wife of William Tyler; Chloe, wife of Relly Tinkham, and Anna, wife of Weston Wetherby, all settled in Orleans County soon after Mr. John Grinnell came in.

These families, so early settled here, have been prosperous in business. Being upright in purpose, and honorable in character, they have become among the most respected families in the county.

CHAPTER 29.

THE TOWN OF YATES

Yates was formed from Ridgeway, April 17, 1822, by the name of Northton. The next year the name was changed to Yates, in honor of Governor Yates.

George Houseman, from Adams, Jefferson County, came into this town and settled in 1809. John Eaton came in 1810.

Only a small number of settlers arrived before or during the War of 1812. The challenge of transporting farm goods to a market, and the expectation that this challenge would persist for a long time due to the area's remote location, discouraged emigrants from settling here, and very little land was claimed before 1817.

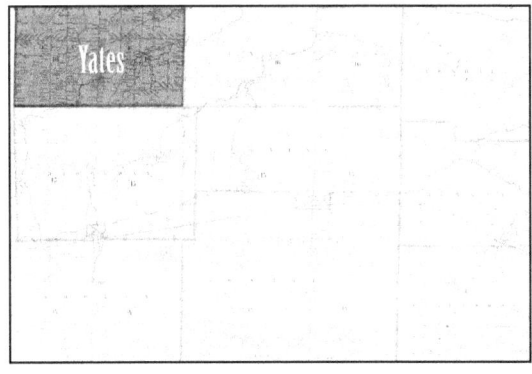

TOWN OF YATES

Persons coming to this county to look for a place for their home, generally sought a locality in the vicinity of neighbors, where roads were opened, and where the social enjoyments of human life could in some degree be realized. It required considerable heroism for a man to go back five or eight miles from any settlement into the thick, heavy forest, and begin with the intention there to clear for himself a farm.

A few hardy, resolute men were located in Yates, regardless of every discouragement, but no considerable settlement was affected until after the *cold season* of 1816–17 when the country rapidly filled up with settlers.

The first deed of land given by the Holland Land Company, in this town, was to Preserved Greenman, June 18th, 1810. Almost the whole of this town was deeded by the Holland Company between the years 1831 and 1835.

The first tavern was kept by Samuel Tappan, at Yates Center, in the year 1825. The population of the town at that time was less than eight hundred, yet Judge Tappan, in a biographical sketch of himself says:

"In the thirteen months in which I kept this tavern, I retailed fifty-three barrels of spirituous liquors."

The first marriage in town was that of George Houseman, Jr., and Sally Covert, in 1817. The first death that of Mrs. George Houseman, senior, December 1813.

The first store was kept by Moor & Hughes, at Yates Center, in 1824.

The first school was taught by Josiah Perry, in the year 1819, in the district including Yates Center.

A sawmill was built on Johnson's Creek, below Lyndonville, by Gardner and Irons, about the year 1819, and a gristmill on the same dam in 1821. These mills, at a later day, have been known as Bullock's Mills, named from a subsequent owner. The mills and dam are now gone.

Chamberlain & Simpson built the warehouse on the Lake shore, north from Yates Center.

A family by the name of Wilkeson lived in the east part of the town in 1811 or '12. In the summer season of that year, Miss Eliza Wilkeson saw a young cub bear near the house, among some vines they had planted. She was alone in the house, but seizing the old-fashioned fire shovel, she went and killed the bear with it.

Mr. Preserved Greenman took up about six hundred acres of land lying east from Lyndonville, before the war of 1812. Mr. Greenman did not occupy his land himself, but settled his sons Daniel and Enos there, giving the neighborhood the name of the "Greenman Settlement."

Some years after, Mr. P. Greenman moved from Montgomery County to Yates, to reside. After a few years he moved to Genesee County, and died there.

Mr. P. Greenman was noted for being set in his way, and having made up his mind, it was hard to turn him. Having sold his farm in Montgomery Co., while preparing to move to Yates, he had a valuable ox-cart to dispose of. He named a price for his cart. A man offered him a less price and would give no more. Greenman declared he would not abate a cent, and would burn his cart before he would sell for less. No better offer was made, and when he came away he piled his cart in a heap and burnt it.

A rule he made was, that a pail of water must be left standing in his house every night, and the last person who retired must see that it was done, under the penalty of being horse-whipped by Mr. Greenman next morning, in case of neglect. It happened once his daughter had a beau who made her a rather long evening visit, and she was the last in the family to retire for the night, and forgot the pail of water. Her father rose first, as usual, in the morning, and finding the water pail empty, called up his daughter and gave her a sound thrashing to maintain the rule he had established.

Amos Spencer was the first justice of the peace within the territory now called Yates. He was appointed by the Council in 1819.

The first schoolhouse in town stood three-fourths of a mile north of Yates Center, and was built in 1818. Mr. Josiah Perry kept the first school there in 1819.

YATES CENTER

At first, Yates Center seemed to be the site where the village would be built. Samuel Tappan opened a hotel here, and Moore & Hughes opened a store, the first in town. Several dwelling houses were built.

Here the first post office was located, Wm. Hughes first postmaster.

When population and trade began to settle at Lyndonville, Yates Center ceased to enlarge, but its inhabitants were not discouraged. About this time Peter Saxe, from Vermont, a brother of John G. Saxe, the poet, located here as a merchant. He may be considered the founder of Yates Academy, for through his influence and energy it was planned, the stock subscribed, and the institution incorporated. Mr. Saxe traded here a few years then moved to Troy, N.Y.

After the canal was made navigable, much of the produce of the town of Yates found a market that way; this trade, and the mills at Lyndonville, operated in favor of that place, and against the Center.

The Methodist Chapel at Lyndonville, which was the first house of worship built in town, was soon followed by the building of the Baptist and Presbyterian churches at that place.

Considerable oak timber grew in Yates. This was cut down long since, squared for ship building, or riven into staves, and sent down the lake to market.

The following is a lenthy list of names of persons who, if not the first, were among the first who settled on the road in the center of the town from the lake to Ridgeway, beginning on the lake:

On the west side of the highway, Amos Spencer settled here on the lake shore in 1818. Next south, Simeon Gilbert settled in 1818, Baruch H. Gilbert in 1817, Luther St. John, and Isaiah Lewis in 1818.

Next, a man by the name of Wing sold to Dr. Elisha Bowen, who resided there many years. Next, Zenas Conger, Mr. Nellis, Thomas Stafford, Moses Wheeler, Mr. Nichols, Mr. Rowley then Samuel and O. Whipple.

Next, Mr. Peck, Mr. Collins, Josiah Cambell and, Elisha Sawyer.

On the east side of the highway, beginning at the lake. First, Robert Simpson, then Elisha Gilbert, Nathan Skellinger, Zacheus Swift, and Comfort Joy, in 1817.

Next Lemuel L. Downs, and Isaac Hurd who took two hundred acres. Then Stephen Austin, Benjamin Drake, Truman Austin, Jacob Winegar and Stephen B. Johnson in 1817.

The next two hundred acres were owned by several different parties under article, but the deed from the Land Company was taken by Samuel Clark Esq., Mr. Peck, Abner Balcom, Harvey Clark, and Elisha Sawyer. These settlements were chiefly made between the years 1816 and 1819.

VILLAGE OF LYNDONVILLE

Mr. Stephen W. Mudgett, who had carried on tanning and shoemaking in Ridgeway, purchased fifty acres of land, part of lot two, section seven, on the east side of the north and south road in Lyndonville, and moved there and set up tanning and shoemaking.

Samuel Clark took a deed of two hundred acres next north of S. W. Mudgett, on the east side of the road.

About the year 1817, a man by the name of Peck took up one hundred acres on the west side where William Mudgett afterwards resided. Samuel and Oliver Whipple took up land next north of Peck.

Soon after the county of Orleans was organized, settlers began to gather here. Mechanics and tradesmen came in and a village began to be formed. Samuel Tappan, who was postmaster, and kept his office at

Yates Center, moved it here, much to the disgust of those living at the Center.

L. & N. Martin, from Peacham, Vermont, kept the first store in 1830. Smith & Babcock soon followed, and Royal Chamberlain was an early merchant. C. Peabody was the first blacksmith.

Blanchard and Chamberlain built the tavern which stands there yet, which was kept by Miner Sherwin, in 1830.

To settle the post office satisfactorily to the people, Yates post office was transferred to the Center, and application was made to the department for a new post office, to be called Lyndon, that being the name that had been agreed on at a public meeting of the inhabitants, several of whom came from Lyndon, Vermont. The post office department established the post office by the name of Lyndonville, to distinguish it from Linden, in Genesee County.

S. W. Mudgett, Samuel Tappan, Richard Barry and others, built the first flouring Mills at Lyndonville, in 1836. The Union School house was built in 1843.

Royal Chamberlain, from Vermont, settled here as a merchant about the time the village began to be established.

As there was no lawyer by profession in town, Mr. Chamberlain being a ready talker and possessed of some education and sufficient self assurance, engaged in trying suits in justice's courts, and continued the practice several years, until he became a noted pettifogger through several towns around. He was a judge of the Court of Common Pleas one term. He moved from Yates several years ago, and now resides in Lockport where he has edited a newspaper. He did considerable to build up a village at Lyndonville.

Dr. Horace Phippany was the first regular physician who settled in Lyndonville and Rev. Jeremiah Irons was the first Baptist minister who resided in Yates.

BIOGRAPHIES OF EARLY SETTLERS

REUBEN ROOT

"I was born in Cooperstown, Otsego County, N.Y., December 28th, 1792. My father moved with his family, then consisting of his wife and five sons, to Big Sodus Bay, in 1801 or '02. In April 1804, we moved by way of Irondequoit Bay and Lake Ontario, to the mouth of Johnson's Creek, in Carlton, near which place my father took an article of land from the Holland Land Company, and located on it to make him a farm.

The party that came consisted of my father's family and the Dunham family, of six or seven persons, and these constituted the whole white population north of the Ridge, between the Niagara and Genesee rivers, except a family by the name of Walsworth, who had settled at the mouth of Oak Orchard Creek.

My father built a house of such poles as we could carry, as we had no team to draw logs, and covered it with elm bark, in which we lived without a floor for one or two years, then a floor was made of split basswood logs.

After building a shelter for the family, the next thing in order was to get supplied with food and clothing, the stock we brought with us getting low. We cleared a small piece of land and planted it with corn; from this we made our bread. Our meat consisted of fish, venison, bear, raccoon and hedgehog. We pounded our corn for meal two or three years, by which time we began to raise wheat, which we took to Norton's mill, in Lima, to be ground. It was about seventy miles by way of Irondequoit Bay and the lake. The country was so infested with bears and wolves at that time we could not keep domestic animals.

In the summer of 1806 or '07, my father got a cow from Canada, but the following fall she was killed by wolves.

Our clothing was made from hemp of our own raising. We could not raise flax on account of the rust that destroyed the fiber.

For several years we had no boots or shoes for want of material to make them.

My father built the first frame barn in what is now Orleans County. The lumber and nails he brought from Canada.

Turner, in his *History of the Holland Purchase*, is in error when he says that 'James Mather built the first frame barn, and got part of his lumber from Dunham's mill.' Our barn was built before Dunham's sawmill was built. The barn was torn down by Daniel Gates twenty-two or twenty-three years since, who then owned the place, and some of the flooring can now be seen on the premises. They were split and hewn from whitewood logs. The nails used were all wrought nails.

In September, 1814, my father and myself being the only ones in our family liable to do military duty, were ordered to meet at Batavia, and go from there to Buffalo to serve in the United States army, in the war then being carried on against Great Britain.

On our arrival at Buffalo, there was a call made for volunteers to go to Fort Erie, under General Porter, to take the British batteries that were then besieging Fort Erie. My father and myself volunteered and went over and assisted in taking the batteries and capturing some five hundred prisoners. This was on the 17th of September, 1814. After this we were discharged, receiving at the rate of $8 per month for our services.

In 1814, I took an article from the Holland Land Company of the land on which I now reside, on lot one, section three, township sixteen, range three.

In April, 1815, I went to Canada and worked on a farm during the summer. The winter following I returned and chopped over twenty-five acres on my farm, and in March, 1816, I went to Toronto and took command of a vessel and sailed on Lake Ontario during the season of navigation until the year 1820.

On January 28th, 1819, I was married to Miss Elizabeth Hastings, of Toronto. We moved upon my farm in Yates, in December, 1820, where we still reside. We have raised a family of ten children, five sons and five daughters. My eldest and youngest sons are now serving in the armies of their country in the war of the great rebellion.

REUBEN ROOT."

Yates, June, 1864

SAMUEL TAPPAN

Samuel Tappan was born in Saco, Maine, November 19, 1781. When nine years old he went to reside with an uncle in Massachusetts. His father was a Quaker in religious opinion, a zealous advocate of their peculiar principles until his death. On the death of his father Samuel was placed with a man in Saco, to learn the tailor's trade. Disliking this business he was soon after bound as an apprentice to a shoemaker, and commenced his servitude, as he called it, August, 1793.

His master belonged to the sect of Quakers, hard and exacting, he made no allowance for the faults and failings, or the weakness or feelings of others. He obliged his apprentice to assume the dress, and conform to the mode of worship of the Quakers, both of which were repugnant to the feelings of the young man.

His master had no books but the Bible, and a few religious works on subjects connected with the Quakers. Samuel was inclined to read whatever came in his way His inclinations, however, were strictly restrained by his master, by whom all books of poetry and romance were absolutely forbidden, and the range of other books to which he was admitted, was exceedingly limited.

After several years spent in this manner, a friendly Congregational minister kindly supplied him with books, and gave him discreet counsel, which rendered his servitude more tolerable and happy. He had no benefit of schooling, never having attended school as a scholar but three days in his life.

In 1801, with the help of friends he purchased his freedom from his apprenticeship, and returned to Saco and worked at his trade about two years, studying what he could in the mean time to fit himself for a school teacher.

In 1803 he taught his first school, in which occupation he was mainly employed for a number of years, occasionally working at his trade, and studying when he could without a teacher.

For several years he supplied the poets corner in a village newspaper, and became considerably interested in politics, on the Republican side, under the lead of Mr. Jefferson.

In 1809 he was appointed deputy sheriff for York and Oxford counties, which office he held for two years.

In 1811 he moved to Pittstown, Rensselaer County, N.Y. The troubles between the United States and Great Britain thickening at this time, on his application he was appointed an Ensign in the Infantry in the United States Army, and assigned to duty in the 18th Regiment, and stationed in the recruiting service at Hoosic, N.Y.

After war was declared in 1812, he was transferred to the 23rd regiment.

In May, 1813, he was ordered with his company to the Niagara frontier. Fort George, at the mouth of Niagara river, on the Canada side, was taken by our forces, and Ensign Tappan was sent with forty men to plant the American flag on the fort, which was the first time that flag was raised over conquered British territory in that war. Ensign Tappan was now appointed adjutant. In September he was sent with a convoy of prisoners to Greenbush, being twenty-one days on the road. He remained in Greenbush the next autumn and winter, teaching school in the meantime.

In June, 1814, he was again ordered to the frontier and assigned to the command of a company, and served at the capture of Fort Erie. He was engaged in the battles of Chippewa and Lundy's Lane. In this last battle his company lost seventeen out of forty-five in killed and wounded.

In this battle Lieutenant Tappan, at the head of his company, captured Capt. Frazier, of the Royal Scotts, with twenty of his men. The American army afterwards retired to Fort Erie, and was besieged there by the British, but they were finally compelled to raise the siege.

Afterwards, a shell thrown by the British into our camp exploded, breaking his knee. This confined him to the hospital for a long time, and on account of this, he received a pension for the remainder of his life. After he became sufficiently recovered to return to duty, he was retained in the peace establishment, and the war with England ended. He resigned his commission in February 1816.

He then returned to Pittstown, and there taught school the next seven years, serving in the meantime as inspector and commissioner of schools, commissioner of deeds, auctioneer and coroner. In 1823 he moved to Ridgeway, moving in October, his family consisting of a wife and five children, with all his effects on two *Dutch Wagons*, reaching Ridgeway, November 10th.

After fitting a log cabin for his family he took a school for the winter. In the spring he went to work clearing land, but as he said his farming was not a success. Tappan once said, "My fruit trees would fall down and my forest trees would stand up; my crops were light but my bills were heavy, and one year's experience taught me I was not born to be a farmer."

In the spring of 1825, he moved to Yates and opened the first tavern in Yates Center. After running the tavern for a year and selling fifty-three barrels of liquor during that time, he sold the tavern. He was then elected constable, inspector of schools, and commissioner of deed. He held the position of commissioner of deed for twenty years.

He was elected as a justice of the peace in 1828. In the winter of 1827, he taught school for the last time, concluding his nineteen years of service in that capacity. In 1829, he was appointed as postmaster, a position he held for thirteen years. In 1832, he was appointed as one of the Judges of the Orleans County Court of Common Pleas, which he held for five years.

In 1846 he was elected town superintendent of common schools. The later years of his life were spent in quiet at home with his books, and enjoying the society of family and friends. He was constitutionally frail in body, but energetic and active in his habits of life.

Being ready with his pen, and having considerable experience in business, he was frequently employed to draft deeds, wills and contracts for his neighbors, and had some practice in trying suits in justices' courts, as counsel for parties.

Of a cheerful and lively turn of mind and easy flow of language, and having an inexhaustible fund of anecdotes and stories at his command, he would make himself exceedingly interesting in conversation, and give zest and enjoyment to society where he was.

His character as a man is aptly described by his daughter in a memoir of him prepared by her, from which we extract as follows:

"Judge Tappan may be described as a man of more than ordinary intellect, and well acquainted with the leading events of the day. He was of the strictest integrity in his business relations, noted for punctuality, a public-spirited citizen, and ready to bear his full share of responsibility. In his social relations, his keen perceptions and ready wit made him an instructive companion.

Although many eccentricities mingled in his character, yet those who knew him best overlooked these, knowing his heart was right, though his words might sometimes wound."

He was married four times and had nineteen children.

Many stories could be told about him that illustrate his different character traits. He had no mechanical ability and often recounted one of his experiments in this area.

After he moved to Ridgeway and became a farmer, he found that a well-curb was needed and decided to make one without any help. He determined the necessary size, gathered the materials, and built it at home in the evenings while working as a teacher during the day. However, after finishing it, he discovered that it was several inches wider than the doorway when he tried to take it through.

He was a great pedestrian, often making excursions on foot, showing greater powers of endurance than many younger and stronger men.

In the spring of 1844, when starting on one of his eastern journeys, he tells us in his journal that arriving in Albion and not finding the water let into the canal as he expected, he managed to get as far as Rochester, and walked most of the distance to Geneva. After he was seventy years old he walked from Medina to Daw's Corners, near Batavia, at one time. While postmaster, he often left two horses in his stable and walked from Yates to Ridgeway with the mail bag on his arm!

He died February 8th, 1868, aged eighty-six years.

JOHN H. TYLER

John H. Tyler was born in Randolph, Orange Co., Vermont, November 30th, 1793. He attended the academy in Randolph a short time and moved to Massena, N.Y., in 1810. On war with Great Britain being declared in 1812, he volunteered as a soldier and served near Ogdensburg six months.

In 1817 he moved to the Holland Purchase, and March 22 took an article for one hundred seventy-six acres of land in Yates, part of lot two, section two, range three, on Johnson's Creek, on which he afterwards resided and labored as a farmer. He was Supervisor of the town of Yates nine years, justice of the peace a number of years, and represented the county of Orleans in the Assembly of the State in 1830 and '31. He was man of vigorous intellect and good judgment, and enjoyed the confidence of all who knew him.

He married Selina Gilbert, daughter of Simeon Gilbert, of Yates, in 1819. She died October 7th, 1842. He married Saloma Gates, daughter of Daniel Gates, of Carlton, in 1843.

He died in August, 1856.

HORACE O. GOOLD

Horace O. Goold was born in Lyme, New London County, Connecticut, August 12th, 1800. In March 1818, in company with two other men in a one horse wagon, he came to Bloomfield, N.Y., after a journey of fifteen days. He labored on a farm the next summer, taught school the next winter, and in the spring of 1819, moved to Carlton, N.Y., and located about two miles west of the head of Stillwater.

The first year of his settlement here he raised thirty bushels of corn and as many bushels of potatoes.

Mr. Goold said, "During the first season, we were sometimes rather short of food, especially meat, but some of the boys would often kill some wild animal, and we were not very particular what name it bore, as hunger had driven us to 'esteem nothing unclean, but to receive it with thanksgiving.'"

Mr. Goold married Laurenda Fuller, of Carlton, November 15th, 1820.

Several years before his death, Mr. Goold moved to Lyndonville, in Yates, where he died October 5th, 1865, and his wife died a few weeks later on October 24th, 1865.

JOSIAH PERRY

Josiah Perry was born in Shaftesbury, Vermont, September 6th, 1787. He moved to Yates in April, 1817, and commenced clearing a farm, and planted and raised corn and potatoes among the logs and sowed some wheat, all the first year.

The people in Yates, in those days, generally went to Dunham's gristmill, at Kuckville, in Carlton, to get grain ground, and Mr. Perry relates of his carrying a bushel of wheat on his back a half dozen miles to that mill to be ground, going through the woods by marked trees, no road being cut out.

Mr. Perry taught the first school that was kept in town. He held office as justice of the peace a short time. He is yet living in Yates.

ALFRED BULLARD

Alfred Bullard was born in Barre, Massachusetts, February 19th, 1793.

He moved with his parents to Shrewsbury, Vermont, and there received a fair common school education, with the addition of a knowledge of field surveying.

In 1817 he came to Batavia, Genesee County, and in 1818 he moved to Barre, Orleans County, and he finally settled in Yates in 1824, where he has ever since resided.

For many years after coming into this county, his principal employment consisted in surveying land, and he was known to almost everybody in Orleans County as Surveyor Bullard. When he was not surveying he worked on a farm. He married Cynthia Peck in 1821. She died and he married Sally Smith, who is dead also.

Mr. Bullard has not engaged in surveying for a number of years on account of lameness, which compelled him to use one, and sometimes two canes in walking. He is considered the pioneer surveyor located in Orleans County.

HENRY MCNEAL

Henry McNeal was born in Pittstown, Rensselaer County, N. Y., in 1792. He married Lucy Sternberg in 1814. They moved to Yates in 1817. Mr. McNeal was the first Captain of a militia company in Yates.

AMOS SPENCER

Amos Spencer was born in Connecticut in 1787. He married Jerusha Murdock, September 10th, 1811. They moved to Yates and settled on the lake shore in 1818.

After a few years they moved to Hartland, Niagara County, where he was living in 1870. The first year he resided in Yates, he cleared the land and sowed the acres with winter wheat. On this the next year he harvested three hundred and thirty bushels of wheat.

He drew forty bushels to Ridgeway Corners, hired Amos Barrett to carry it to Rochester with his team, gave him five dollars for drawing and paid his expenses on the road. He sold his wheat for fifty-four cents per bushel. They were gone four days, and on getting home found they had only five dollars of the money received for their wheat left, all the remainder having been spent in paying necessary expenses.

ELISHA SAWYER

Elisha Sawyer was born in Reading, Vermont, September 30th, 1785. He settled in Yates in 1816. He took up four hundred acres of land on the south line of the town. After some years he moved to Lyndonville on a small place. He later moved to Paxton, Illinois, and died there December 8th, 1868.

BARUCH H. GILBERT

Baruch H. Gilbert was born in the town of Northeast, Dutchess County, New York, August 24th, 1795.

His father, Simeon Gilbert, came to Yates in the fall of 1816, and took an article of land on the west side of the line between ranges three and four, about a mile and a half south from Lake Ontario, and returned to his eastern home without making any improvement on his lands, to which he did not return until the spring of 1818.

Baruch H. Gilbert settled on the south part of the land so taken by his father in the spring of 1817, and cleared a farm there on which he resided about fifty years.

Mr. Gilbert was of fair education, of considerable spirit and energy of character, and settling in this town among the very first, he interested himself in every movement made to improve the country, introduce and maintain the institution of civilized society and induce people to settle in Yates. He soon took a prominent position in the business of his town and neighborhood, and as long as he resided here he was one of the leading men in all public affairs. He officiated as justice of the peace for thirty years. He married Miss Fanny Skellenger in 1821. His children are Simeon, who married Olive Skellinger, and resides in Illinois; Stephen B., married Ann Watkins, resides in California; Nathan S., married Mary E. Lane, resides in Lockport; and Cordelia, who is unmarried.

ELISHA BOWEN

Dr. Elisha Bowen was born in Reading, Windsor County, Vermont, in the year 1791.

He received a diploma from Dartmouth College. He was first married and moved to Palmyra, N.Y., in 1817, where his wife died.

In the year 1820 he moved to the town of Yates, and settled on a farm between Yates Center and the lake.

He was the first, and for several years the only regular physician residing and practicing in the town of Yates.

He married his second wife Miss Adeline Rawson. After her death he married his third wife Miss Mary Ann Clark. She died in 1861.

Dr. Bowen had twelve children, of whom nine are living: Francis W., married a daughter of Dr. Whaley, resides in Sacramento, California; Samuel C., married Kate, daughter of James Jackson, of Ridgeway, resides in Medina;

Adeline, unmarried, resides in Wisconsin; Charles C., married Julia Hard, resides in Detroit; Edgar J., married Mary Winn, resides in Chicago; Susan, married H. L. Achilles, Jr., resides in Rochester; Cornelia, married Samuel Boyd, resides in Appleton, Wisconsin; Mary, unmarried resides in Appleton, Wisconsin; Theodore E., married Mary Loomis, resides in Chicago.

Dr. Bowen was one of thirteen persons who united to form the Baptist Church in Yates, in 1822, of which church he continued an active member until his death. He was a strong advocate of temperance, and among the first who united in the town of Yates to form a society to promote that cause.

Dr. Bowen was conscientious and correct in all the habits of his life, and had the confidence and respect of all who knew him. In the later years of his life he did not practice his profession. He died April 6, 1863, aged 72 years.

CHAPTER 30
BIOGRAPHICAL NOTICES OF
JOSEPH ELLICOTT AND EBENEZER MIX

JOSEPH ELLICOTT

M r. Ellicott never lived in Orleans County, so he is not considered one of its pioneers, which is the main focus of this work. However, as the agent of the Holland Land Company for many years, he played a significant role in organizing and settling the county. He also contributed to planning and implementing the development of the diverse resources of Western New York.

The ancestors of Mr. Ellicott came from Wales to America at an early day, and were among the early pioneers of Bucks county, Pennsylvania.

Mr. Joseph Ellicott received a comprehensive education in surveying from his older brother, Andrew. His initial hands-on experience came from assisting his brother in surveying the city of Washington after it was chosen as the site for the National Capitol. In 1791, he was tasked with marking the boundary between Georgia and the Creek Indians. Following this, he surveyed lands for the Holland Company in Pennsylvania before being

475

assigned to survey the company's holdings in Western New York once the Pennsylvania project was finished.

He spent many years in the woods as a surveyor and when he left to work as a local agent for the Company, his hard work continued. During this time, he maintained a significant correspondence with the general office in Philadelphia regarding the entrusted business, as well as with prominent men of his time and country on public affairs. He is particularly well-known for his involvement in promoting the Erie Canal, a major work of internal improvement. He played a significant role in its inception, progress, and eventual success, and will always be remembered alongside the great minds who conceived and propelled the canal to completion.

By engaging in active pursuits and business endeavors, he amassed a considerable fortune without being accused of engaging in office speculation or mismanaging the extensive business entrusted to him.

The settlers on the Holland Purchase were starting to show signs of discontent. This was due to the fact that they owed a significant amount of money to the company from which they had bought their land on credit. Although the company's agents had not forced the settlers to pay back their debts, the interest that had been accruing over time had significantly increased the amount owed.

Feeling overwhelmed by the heavy workload and aware of the prevailing discontent, which he hoped would be allayed if directed by other counsels, Mr. Ellicott resigned from his position. After this, he suffered from a fixation on real and imagined diseases and was taken by his friends to New York and placed in the hospital at Bellevue, where, about August 1826, he committed suicide.

Joseph Ellicott never married, but he made ample provision for his numerous relatives by selecting and securing some of the best lands on the Holland Purchase for the Ellicott family.

His remains were brought to Batavia and buried in the village cemetery. A beautiful monument, supervised by David E. Evans, his nephew and successor as the local agent of the Holland Company, now marks the spot.

From his intimate acquaintance as surveyor with the Holland Purchase lands in Western New York, he was able to make some judicious selections of lands for himself.

In the original survey of Buffalo, he laid off for himself one hundred acres, now included in the best part of that city.

In the county of Orleans he bought seven hundred acres, including the water power at Shelby Center, and afterwards fourteen hundred acres farther down the Oak Orchard Creek, which included the village of Medina, and the best water power on that creek.

About the year 1824 he made his will, in which he devised a large part of his great landed estate in special gifts to his favorite relatives. The residue was devised to others of his kindred, nearly one hundred in number, share and share alike, with a few exceptions.

His property at the time of his death, even at the low price lands then bore, was estimated at six hundred thousand dollars. From the great advance in value at this time, this property is worth many millions of dollars.

He was the first Judge appointed in and for Genesee County courts.

EBENEZER MIX

Ebenezer Mix is a name familiar as household words to old settlers on the Holland Purchase, and no history of the pioneers, or of the early settlement, could be made complete without reference to him.

Mr. Mix was born at New Haven, Connecticut. He died at Cleveland, Ohio, January 12th, 1869, aged 81 years.

In his native New England he learned and worked at the trade of a mason.

He came to Batavia, Genesee County, to seek his fortune in the year 1809. There he worked first at his trade as a mason. He afterwards taught school; was for a time a student in a law office, and finally went into the service of the Holland Land Company as a clerk in their office at Batavia, in 1811, where he remained twenty-seven years.

Being a good theoretical and practical surveyor, and a clear headed and competent business man, in a short time he was made contracting clerk in the Batavia office, in which capacity it was his duty to make, renew and modify contracts for the sale of land, calculate quantities of land, make sub-divisions of tracts of land, and act as salesman generally.

In this way he became intimately connected with every transaction of the Company relating to gifts of land to churches and school districts, and took part in all business matters between the company and the people who settled on their lands. And few men could be found who would have done the business as well.

He excelled as a mathematician, was a practical surveyor and possessed a remarkable memory of boundaries, localities, dates and distances. Indeed the whole transactions of the Land Company, and the map of their territory seemed to be pictured on his mind with singular fidelity, making it a treasury of facts, exceedingly convenient for reference in settling conflicting questions concerning highways, boundaries and original surveys, which arise among the people.

Naturally of a somewhat irritable temperament, when aroused by the perplexities of business, he was sometimes rather sour and rough in manner towards persons by whom he was annoyed, but his wish and aim was to do right and justice, and however austere and crabbed his manner, his conclusions and final settlement of matters he had in hand was kind and benevolent to those with whom he had to do.

Many a time has the unfortunate settler who had been unable to make the payments on his article, and whom sickness and calamity had driven almost to despair of ever paying for his land, had reason to be grateful for the humanity and generous treatment he received from Mr. Mix in extending his payments, renewing his article, and abating his interest money.

In the war of 1812 he served for a time as volunteer aid to Gen. P. B. Porter, and was at the sortie at Fort Erie. And for twenty years in succession he was the Surrogate of Genesee County.

CHAPTER 31.

ORLEANS COUNTY PIONEER ASSOCIATION

This Association was organized June, 1859. Its members are persons who at any time previous to January, 1826, were residents of Western New York, who signed its Constitution. The objects of the Association, as contained in its constitution, are to promote social intercourse by meeting together statedly, in order to preserve and perpetuate the remembrance of interesting facts connected with the early history of the settlement of Orleans County and its vicinity. The annual meetings are held at the CourtHouse, in Albion, on the third Saturday in June.

It has been an object of the Association to collect and preserve as much of the history of the early settlement of Orleans County as possible. The local history of many of the early pioneers has been obtained and written out in books kept for that purpose, and several photograph albums have been filled with the pictures of the men and women who came here at an early day.

At these yearly gatherings, and at occasional special meetings held from time to time in various places in the county, the old people are accustomed to meet together and recount their adventures while subduing the wilderness, and have a good time generally.

It is intended to obtain as much of such history of "'ye olden time" as possible, and when the actors in these old scenes are no more, and the last of the log houses shall exist only in the memory and records of the times gone by, these old manuscripts and relics, laid up in some public depository, shall remain for the information of posterity of the things that were here, memories of the hardships, labors, and privations of the pioneers of Orleans County.

ADDRESS

DELIVERED BEFORE THE ORLEANS COUNTY PIONEER ASSOCIATION ON SEPTEMBER 10TH, 1859

By ARAD THOMAS

Mr. President and Members of the Orleans County Pioneer Association: —

In discharging the pleasant duty of addressing you on the present occasion, I am desirous to devote my thoughts to the consideration of topics kindred to the sentiments which led to the formation of this association.

This seems no fit time to indulge in abstruse speculations or idle rhetoric. I address a practical company —men who have been trained to meet the stern realities of life and accomplish their destiny with unflinching labor, and having achieved a good work, well, may they enjoy the triumph it affords! Let us then contemplate the past and learn wisdom for the future.

A stranger, who now for the first time should come into our county, judging from appearances, would be apt to think this an old settlement, where generation after generation of men had lived and died and where their accumulated labor had been expended upon those works, of enlightened civilization which cover the land. But we know scarcely fifty years since the first acre of this territory was cleared of its native forest, and the men are now living who recollect when there was nothing but a dark, unbroken wilderness.

Many of the first settlers of this county have passed away from among the living. Others following in the tide of emigration are now inhabitants of some Western States. A few survivors and representatives of a generation rapidly passing away remain quiet possessors of the soil their hands first subjected to cultivation, and today they have assembled to talk over the trials and privations, the hardships and the sufferings, the varied events of fortune, prosperous and adverse, which have fallen to their lot since first they came into this county.

The occasion is replete with interest to us All... To the aged veterans, it brings up memories of events, which in passing, thrilled their hearts with intensest emotion.

To the more youthful spectator ... it affords encouragement to labor, in view of these examples of success over every opposition, obtained by resolute and continued exertion. And to us all, it shows convincing proof that honest and laudable industry will reap its rewards in due time.

Our theme embraces the consideration of subjects connected with the early settlement of Orleans County. In tracing the history of mankind, in their migrations since their memorable dispersion on the plains of Shinar, we find a variety of causes which have impelled men to move from the places of their nativity. The venerable founder of the Jewish nation went Down to

Egypt to save his family from Death by famine, and his descendants came out of Egypt to save themselves from a terrible bondage.

The builders of ancient Rome were the scattered fragments of various nations, who assembled there as a common asylum of outcasts from everywhere and raised their walls for mutual protection and support; and by encouraging immigration from abroad and the gradual accretion of power by treaty, and conquest of foreign nations, in time they became the mightiest empire on earth, in their turn to be overrun by swarms from the northern hive, who, deserting their inhospitable homes, came down with all their moveable possessions by fire and sword to drive out the inhabitants of the fair provinces of Italy and so give themselves a better land.

The Spaniards, who first settled in America, were attracted there by their cupidity for gold. And the ranks of the settlers in most new countries have been swelled by adventurers who had been obliged to leave their native land to escape the consequences of their crimes.

A nobler impulse prompted our ancestors in their migrations from Europe.

The discovery of America, the invention of printing, and the Protestant Reformation had roused the minds of the most intelligent nations of the world to a more exalted sense of the value of liberty and a keen perception of those natural and inalienable rights of conscience, which form the richest possession of a free people. Persecuted for conscience's sake in their native country, England, they had borne for years the cruel oppression which religious intolerance and political tyranny forced upon them there, borne with Christian endurance till overcome by suffering too grievous to be borne. And hopeless of relief, they solemnly withdrew from their national church and from the land of their birth to Holland, where some years after, they formed and carried out the resolution to emigrate to America. There, under the protection of the King of England, they thought to worship God in peace, as they believed to be right.

Piety and love of liberty furnished them sufficient motives for removal and armed them with fortitude required to meet the perils and hardships of their new home.

With all proper admiration which we ought to feel for the early New England Puritans, the ancestors of so many of those who hear me, we may admit they had their failings. In the austerity of their faith, they often forgot the mild spirit of charity which pervades the gospel they revered, and in the ardor of their zeal, they made and sought to enforce laws of great severity against those professing religious beliefs at variance with the dogmas of their stern creed, and punished and persecuted with a strange infatuation, those charged with the crime of witchcraft.

But in reviewing this portion of the history of our forefathers, we should remember not to judge them by the lights of the present age. Toleration to faith and worship, contrary to the forms declared by the civil government for a thousand years, had then not been known in Europe, and the opinion of good men had before then always been that such religious freedom would destroy the best institutions of society. A belief in witchcraft was as old as history itself and was a common superstition of the times. The excellent and pious Baxter held the existence of witches as certain as the punishment of the wicked, and the great and good Sir Matthew Hale, the able judge and profound luminary of the law, believed in witchcraft as sincerely as did Cotton Mather.

The superstitions of the dark ages were then entertained by the most enlightened and liberal-minded men everywhere, and it would be requiring too much to expect our forefathers to have freed themselves from opinions we may deem absurd, but which up to that time, and by all other men then, were held worthy of acceptation.

I know we are sometimes charged with using extravagant eulogium in speaking of the New England Puritans of the olden time. But making due allowance for their eccentricities of character and conduct, resulting from circumstances with which they stood connected, we may look in vain to find in the early history of any other people such noble patriotism, fervent piety, sound wisdom, and incorruptible honesty as in the case before us.

They had all been trained in the same school of adversity and possessed in a wonderful degree identity of sentiment, sympathy, and character in all their conduct and opinions, which impressed itself upon all their laws, their individual and social arrangements, and upon every institution and action which found place among them.

Inflexible and steadfast in their cherished principles, they trained their children in the faith and practices of their fathers, and the combined influence of such faith and works, we may see in their effects upon the energy and enterprise, the love of liberty, the respect for law and order, good morals, religion, learning and true patriotism, which, inspired by such examples, has ever distinguished their descendants down through the period of more than two hundred years.

We need not sounding eulogy or words of windy panegyric to prove the value of New England intelligence, integrity, and power in molding and guiding the rising destinies of our country. The wisdom of her statesmen, the heroism of her soldiers, and the spirit and conduct of her people secured our national independence, and established our national federation of independent States upon the broad basis of constitutional liberty. And even up to now, this element has always been prominent, I had almost said controlling, in the legislation of most of the States and in Washington.

A few years since, some curious individual ascertained on inquiry that thirty-six of the members of the two Houses of Congress, then in session, were born in the single State of Connecticut.

In the language of Mr. Malthus, man coming up to take upon himself his place and the responsibilities of life finds no cover laid for him on nature's table, and so, he goes out to spread a table for Himself, where he deems the prospect most inviting. The rich treasures of experience and wisdom and the abundant stores of material good things the past has garnered up afford him capital with which to work out the fulfillment of his own and his country's hopes.

These magnificent results of the skill and enterprise of the present-day are only other phases and demonstrations of the same spirit which led to the first settlement in America and which has attended every step of our progress since, as well exemplified in the resolution of the solitary emigrant who sets his stake in the wilderness and determines there to dig up for himself a farm, as in that mightier work of a statesman, or a nation, which makes a canal or a railroad across a continent, lays a telegraph wire across an ocean, or solves the deepest problem of state policy for the world.

Soon after the Revolutionary War had ended, the settlements of New England were extended over the principal part of those States suitable for tillage, and multitudes of their active and adventurous young men went out to seek their fortunes among the borderers, who were pushing the bounds of civilizations and improvement back into the new territories, skirting the old Atlantic States upon the West.

A large majority of the first settlers of Orleans County were either emigrants from New England or descended from the Puritan stock, who traced their origin back to those who, in December 1620, landed from the May Flower upon Plymouth Rock.

It is admitted that as a class, they were poor but honest, possessing strong moral convictions of effective force of intellect and will; they determined to plant and grow up the institutions of religion, order, and civilization in this wilderness, such as prevailed in their New England homes. Such views, habits, and purposes characterized the emigrants who first settled in Western New York. Here was Not the hiding place of a population of whom it might justly be said they had left the homes of their youth as a measure of prudent care for their personal safety or from a kind regard for the good of the place they had left. Neither did they come here to buy choice lots and leave them until the toil of others on adjoining farms should add value to their purchases. Here were few non-resident landholders at an early day.

The Holland Land Company had purchased the Western part of the State of New York, bounded on the east by a line extending north from Pennsylvania to Lake Ontario, known as the Transit Line.

Before the last war with Great Britain, a portion of this tract which has been distinguished as the Holland Purchase, had been surveyed by the Company and offered for sale to settlers. The wonderful fertility of the Genesee country had been reported abroad, and before the war, a few emigrants had begun to make their homes among the heavy forests which covered this country, some of whom had located themselves in what is now Orleans County.

The possibility of such a work as the Erie Canal had not then entered the great mind of Dewitt Clinton or been dreamed of even by the great men of that day.

The most favorable means in prospect, then far in the future, for communicating with the old settlements in the east was by wagons on the highways or boats down the Mohawk or St. Lawrence. But the pioneer settlers of the Holland Purchase belonged to a bold and fearless race who did not stop to enquire whether the trail of civilization had extended to the new country, by which they could retreat with ease and safety to the homes of their fathers if life in the woods should happen to prove uncongenial to their tastes. They expected to overcome the formidable obstacles before them by their own strong arms and stout hearts. They knew that wealth was in their farms, not perhaps in the shape of the golden nuggets such as fire the imagination of emigrants to Pike's Peak or the other El Dorados of the West, but rather in the golden product of well-tilled fields, which honest hard work was sure to raise in abundance in time to come, and they meant to have it.

It is really not as great an undertaking for the emigrant, who at this day, goes from the Atlantic States to settle in Kansas or California as it was fifty years ago to make a settlement in Western New York. Railroads and telegraphs have made communication easy and rapid between places most distant, and modern improvements in the economy and arts of domestic life are such that most of the necessaries and comforts enjoyed by residents in older towns can readily be procured everywhere.

The farmer who locates on a prairie in the West begins his work by plowing the primitive sod, and the next year he reaps his crop and finds his field as clean and mellow as plow land along the Connecticut River, and he can sell his products for almost New York prices. But beginning a farm on the Holland Purchase fifty years ago was quite a different business.

Indeed, we who have not learned by experience can hardly imagine the obstacles and difficulties to be surmounted by the first settlers of Orleans County. Roads from Albany westward were bad; merchants and mechanics had not yet arrived. A dense and heavy forest of hard, huge trees covered the land, to be felled and cleared away before the plow of the farmer could turn up the genial soil. Pestilential fevers racked the nerves and prostrated the vigor of the stoutest, as well as the weakest among them. The ague, that pest indigenous to all new countries, came up from every clearing, usually in the best days of summer, to seize upon the settler, his wife, and children, some or all of them, and shake out all their strength and energy.

Though the noblest timber trees for their buildings existed in troublesome abundance, sawmills had not then been erected.

Though their lands produced the finest of wheat whenever it could be sown, it cost more than its market price to take it to the distant grist mills to be ground. Sales of farm produce were limited to home consumption.

Before the War of 1812 but few settlers had located in Orleans County.

From Canandaigua to Lewiston, along the Ridge Road, and from the mouth of Oak Orchard Creek, along an Indian Trail to Batavia, the trees had principally been cut wide enough for a highway. A few log cabins had been erected, and the sturdy emigrants had begun by felling the trees to open little patches of cleared land around their dwellings to form the nucleus of their farms.

War was declared. The regular pursuits of peaceful industry were broken up. The settler was summoned to become a soldier, and at the call of his country, at times, almost every able-bodied man in the settlement was away in the ranks of the army, leaving their scattered, unprotected families to risk the chances of hostile *forays* of the enemy, often threatened from the west along the lake. The courage and spirit of the women of those days was equal to the best examples to be found in American border warfare. Neither the frightful rumors of the massacre of their husbands and brothers in the fight or the terrible announcements that the Indians, with murder and pillage, were sweeping down the Ridge Road or coming up the Creek, could drive them to abandon the homes they had chosen in the woods, or make them turn a point from the performance of what their duty required.

Perhaps the gloomiest time in the experience of the pioneers was during and after the war, before the commencement of work on the Erie Canal. Considerable wheat was annually grown, but beyond what the farmer wanted for his own consumption, it was of little value, bearing a nominal price of about twenty-five cents a bushel.

A kind of crude potash, made by leaching wood ashes and known as black salts, was almost the only product which brought money, and became, in fact, almost a lawful tender for value in trade, and this had to be taken to market for miles upon ox sleds or hand sleds, or on the backs of the makers, through woods and swamps, following a line of marked trees. After the war came the memorable *cold seasons* of 1816–17. About these years, a contemporary says, "from half to two-thirds of all the people were down sick in the summertime."

Without a supply of physicians or nurses, or medicines, or even **bread**, how were such sick men to secure their crops or clear their land, endure storm, and want, and trouble and distress, which beset them at every turn? Surely nothing but an iron will which no impediment could break or bend, an abiding faith and hope which no disasters or discouragements could overcome or crush out, sustained them through these dark days. Like heroes of another time, "through the thick gloom of the present, they beheld the brightness of the future." and they struggled on.

It has been playfully said that you may place a Yankee in the woods with an ax, an augur, and a knife, his only tools, and with the trees his only material for use, and he will build a palace, if need be, wanting perhaps in the finish which other tools, and the aid of iron trimmings, nails, and glass would afford, but possessing the substantial requisites of convenience, and fitness and strength.

The first log houses built in this county proved almost literally the truth of this remark. They were the dwelling places of the best families in the land, made by their owners, where the latch string was always out at the call of the stranger, and the best of their plain and scanty store was always generously shared with the weary and destitute, whoever he might be.

The builders and occupants of those rude tenements were then probably poor, as can well be imagined, sick and suffering, with none of the luxuries, and few even of the necessaries of their former experience, but withal contented and happy.

How often do we hear these persons, now occupying their noble mansions, fitted and furnished and adorned with all the elegance and profusion which the abundant means of their owners, and the taste and fashion of the times command, refer to the little, old log cabin first built upon their farm, and count their residence there the happiest in their lives. These buildings belong to the time gone by, and the last of the log houses will soon have gone down with their builders to that destruction which awaits all things earthly.

For some years, none new have been erected in this county, and but rarely now can the traveler see one left standing in dilapidated humility behind the great new house, maintaining to the last its character for usefulness, as a shelter for the grindstone, the salt barrel, the swill tub, the workbench, and all the hand tools there carefully treasured up for use on the extensive domain of their wealthy owner.

Among these primitive settlers, the advent of a new family to locate among them was an occasion of joy through the town. The acquaintance of the strangers was promptly sought, a cordial welcome extended, and the more material aid of all the force in the neighborhood kindly volunteered to help the newcomer roll the logs to begin his clearing or pile them into the walls of his cabin home. Such friendly feeling prevailed in all their social affairs. Relations of acquaintance and friendship were sustained between all the families for miles around, and no distinctions of wealth or party, sect, or condition were known.

It is true there was no such visionary scheme of community of goods as was attempted by the old Plymouth Colony, or by the Fourierites of a later day, with all its attendant idleness and discontent obtained among them, but a most generous spirit to lend to and help the needy was a prominent trait in their character. They were not speculators who entered upon the lands to secure a title, trusting by a fortunate sale or by the rise in the market price to derive large profits on their investment. The fever for land speculation had not then set in.

The policy of the Holland Company was to get their lands taken up and occupied as fast as possible. With this in view they gave contracts for deeds of conveyance on payment of a small portion of the purchase money, giving the purchaser some years of credit in which to pay the residue. This policy brought in settlers, and the liberality of the company in extending contracts where prompt payment could not be made, kept them on their lots.

A portion, however, of the first inhabitants of this county, like a portion of the first inhabitants in every new settlement, became charmed with their life of vicissitude and hardship, and the varied advantages of pioneer settlement, and soon as the farms were mostly taken up and occupied, and the progress of cultivation have driven away the game and introduced in some degree the order of civilized society, they became uneasy and discontented, and longed for the freedom and excitements of wilder life on the border. Like Cooper's hero, "Leather Stocking," they would "get lost among the clearings," and moved to the West to begin again in the forests of Michigan or Ohio.

To those who remained and labored through every affliction and discouragement, using such means as their own sagacity and industry afforded them to assist their efforts, we are indebted for such successful results as we now see.

And I may repeat, what but an intelligent and confiding hope in "the good time coming" could have sustained these men under all discouragements they endured? What but that indomitable spirit of the race, which never falters at perils or hindrances in the way, when a desirable object is to be gained, under the wise ordering of a mysterious good Providence, nerved them for their work, and cheered them on to its successful accomplishment?

In the ardent imagination, the young emigrant, who had selected and contracted for his farm, looked over his future abode and traced the boundaries of orchard and meadow, and pasture, and plain, and saw the shadowy outlines of his houses and his barns, his fences and his fields, looming into being where then the gray old trees stood in solemn grandeur, the sturdy sentinels of nature for centuries keeping watch over the primitive wilderness. He saw in vision of the future his crops of waving corn and his granaries bursting out with plenty, and himself the happy possessor of a home blessed with comforts and luxuries of life in abundance, and seizing his ax, then perhaps his only *chattel*, he went to work with a will, to prove the scenes his fancy had portrayed.

It is a remarkable fact that the English settlements in America were, in the main, first made at points the most inhospitable and uninviting, thus bringing every part of our country to be settled and improved. The Puritans, who came over in the May Flower, intended to have gone to Virginia, but through the treachery of the captain of their ship, as some assert, they were landed at Plymouth.

The first emigrants westward from New England, located in the forests of New York, Michigan and Ohio, because they came from a forest country and were not afraid of the woods, and because they could not get to the fertile prairies of the West. There were no roads by land and no communication by water to these beautiful territories. They were compelled by necessity to clear up and settle the country as they went through it.

Had the Puritans reached their intended destination in the sunny South, and located along those noble rivers and fertile plains, they would never have moved to the hard, cold, ironbound hills of New England. When then would New England have been settled? Never by emigrants from the West. And had the southern and middle States been first settled, and the application of steam to motive machinery been made, and the railroad and the telegraph and the knowledge of the useful arts we now possess were known 200 years ago, Maine, New Hampshire and Vermont, would be to-day like parts of Lower Canada, a vast and dreary wilderness, and as such to remain until the more inviting regions of the West had all been settled. And had railroads and telegraphs, and steam power, as now used, been known even fifty years ago, I fancy some of these venerable pioneers would be now rejoicing in homes made happy upon the banks of the Missouri, or perhaps west of the Rocky Mountains.

The interesting details of *border settlement* in this country have so often been the theme of remark that they have become trite matters of history. The solemn and deepening shade of antiquity is beginning to clothe them with its mysterious interest. And as the immediate actors leave us, slowly and silently fading away from among the living, their memory is cherished as the pride of their kindred, and they come to be regarded as the benefactors of their country. The Pioneers of Orleans County are not all dead, but the times of their trouble have gone by. The Holland Purchase is settled, subdued, and made the cheerful home of an industrious and thriving population, now in their turn, sending out their caravans of emigrants, with the fervent spirit of their fathers, carrying the arts and institutions of our favored country to those new States so rapidly growing up in the regions of the West. All the improvements in science and the arts are brought to aid the swift progress of our people in spreading themselves over our entire national territory.

If the earlier march of emigration and settlement from the Atlantic westward has been toilsome and slow, and two hundred years scarcely brought settlers to the great lakes and the slopes of the *Alleghenies*, what shall we say of the advances of the last fifty years, and which are now going forward!

Since the first tree fell here under the ax of the white man, the triumphs of steam power have appeared. By the help of this tremendous agent, a voyage across the Atlantic, which took the May Flower months to accomplish, is now made in a week. A trip to Boston, which once cost these pioneers a month to perform, is now the business of a day. Steam drives our mills, carries our burdens, plows our fields, warms our houses, digs our canals, and furnishes a motive power to effect the mightiest and minutest work attempted by the ingenuity of man.

But steam, though admitted to be strong, is voted slow, in this fast age, and electricity is sent out to run the errands of our ordinary business.

Excelsior! Higher! is the motto of our noble **Empire State**, and Forward is the cry of encouragement with which Young America stimulates its ardor in the race for victory.

My friends, we who are the juniors of these noble men, whose praise we have thus faintly endeavored to celebrate, should never forget that we are building upon foundations they have laid for us. That we inherit the lands their hands have cleared; that we enjoy the liberties they have achieved.

We shall, ever admire their enterprise, patience and fortitude. We shall justly feel proud to claim acquaintance, perhaps relationship with such worthy predecessors.

We shall teach our children the story of their labors and success as examples to be imitated, and from every memorial they have left us of strenuous effort in a good cause, take courage and gain strength to help our resolution in the performance of all the duties, which have fallen to our lot. And when we look about us upon the broad patrimony we have derived from them and take an inventory of the abundant good things they have bequeathed to us as the fruits of their labors, let us not forget our duty of gratitude to the memory of these our benefactors, to whom we owe so much, nor fail to improve as we ought, the rich inheritance we enjoy.

Venerable Pioneers—you have not met on the present occasion to gratify your vanity by publishing to the world the exploits you have performed or boasting for the wonder of others of the marvelous adventures you may have achieved; but, like a company of weary travelers, life's toilsome journey almost done, you are here to spend an evening hour in social converse, on scenes you have witnessed by the way, to bring to mind again the stirring events in which you have been called to mingle; and to soothe your spirits by a grateful recollection of that kind Providence which has sustained you in all your toils and brought you in old age to the abundant enjoyment and realization of the most ardent hopes of your youth.

You have seen the country of your choice a gloomy wilderness. You now behold it, by your exertions changed to cultivated fields, and dotted over with noble houses, interspersed with thriving villages and connected by public highways.

Where a few years ago you hunted the savage bear, your splendid herds and numerous flocks now roam and feed in safety. Where but lately you were compelled to grope your way from town to town through pathless woods, by marked trees, or Indian trails, the railroad or telegraph afford you means of communication, in which time and distance are scarcely items in the account of delay.

The rich produce of your fields, instead of rotting in your hands, valueless because no buyer could be found, commands at all times the highest price in the markets of the world.

The howl of the wolf is exchanged for the scream of the steam whistle, and though you live as far inland, the gallant steam vessel is made to float by your very doors.

How astonishing, how stupendous the change! We have read of the Wonderful Lamp of Aladdin, and stories of Oriental Necromancy, whereby the superhuman power of magic, and the agency of demons, the loftiest works of art, and the noblest productions of industry and skill were made to appear or vanish at a word, but the magic which wrought the works we celebrate, was the power of indomitable energy, applied with strong hands and stubborn perseverance. The mighty improvements which excite our admiration are only the happy results of your steady, well-directed industry overcoming its early discouragements and trials, the honorable testimonials of the sternest conflict and most complete success.

Fortunate men and women! Long, long may you live, enjoying the rich fruits of your early toils. And may you be permitted to witness the return of many anniversaries of your present association, happy in the consciousness that you have accomplished the objects of your youthful ambition, and leaving, when at last you shall be called to your rest, a noble history, and a worthy example embalmed in the memory of your grateful posterity.

END

APPENDIX

Visit *pioneerhistory.us* to view the accompanying online reference material and notices of updates when they occur.

Online reference material includes high-resolution historical maps, statistics related to the emigration of settlers from New England to New York and extended information on key events such as the construction of the Erie Canal and the "Year without a summer."

And if you have not already done so, check out the two companion volumes "*Pioneer Handbook: Mastering Frontier Life in Orleans County, New York*" and "*Pioneer Cookbook: Wilderness Recipes of Orleans County.*" These two books provide a wealth of information to help you

LIST OF ILLUSTRATIONS

Gibson, J. & Baldwin, R. (1754) A map of the western parts of the colony of Virginia. [London: Printed for R. Baldwin, in Pater Noster Row] [Map] Retrieved from the Library of Congress, https://www.loc.gov/item/2013593293/.

Lea, P. (1685) North America divided into its III principall sic parts. [S.l] [Map] Retrieved from the Library of Congress, https://www.loc.gov/item/99446209/.

The Miriam and Ira D. Wallach Division of Art, Prints and Photographs: Print Collection, The New York Public Library. (1759 - 1885). A view of Niagara Fort, taken by Sir William Johnson, on the 25th of July 1759, drawn on the spot in 1758. Retrieved from https://digitalcollections.nypl.org/items/510d47da-244e-a3d9-e040-e00a18064a99

Bowen, J. T., Greenough, F. W., McKenney, T. L. & Hall, J. (ca. 1838) Thayendanegea, the great captain of the Six Nations / R.T. ; drawn, printed & coloured at I.T. Bowen's Lithographic Establishment No. 94 Walnut St. , ca. 1838. [Philadelphia: Published by F.W. Greenough] [Photograph] Retrieved from the Library of Congress, https://www.loc.gov/item/2013645356/.

The Miriam and Ira D. Wallach Division of Art, Prints and Photographs: Print Collection, The New York Public Library. (1777 - 1890). Sr. William Johnson Bart., major general of the English forces in North America. Retrieved from https://digitalcollections.nypl.org/items/510d47da-22ab-a3d9-e040-e00a18064a99

(1776) Major general John Sullivan, a distinguish'd officer in the Continental sic Army. United States, 1776. [London: Publish'd as the Act directs by Thos. Hart, Augt. 22] [Photograph] Retrieved from the Library of Congress, https://www.loc.gov/item/2004666644/.

Danforth, M. J. & Weir, R. W. Sa-go-ye-wat-ha Seneca chief Red Jacket / painted by R.W. Weir ; eng'd. by M.J. Danforth. United States, None. [Between 1830 and 1880] [Photograph] Retrieved from the Library of Congress, https://www.loc.gov/item/2002695258/.

The Miriam and Ira D. Wallach Division of Art, Prints and Photographs: Print Collection, The New York Public Library. (1825). DeWitt Clinton [mingling the waters of Lake Erie with the Atlantic]. Retrieved from https://digitalcollections.nypl.org/items/510d47d9-7f5e-a3d9-e040-e00a18064a99

GLOSSARY

100,000 Acre Tract
A large area of land in Western New York that was part of a land purchase known as the Holland Purchase. It was jointly owned by the State of Connecticut and the Pulteney Estate, and its lands were surveyed and sold to settlers over time.

Academy
A secondary school offering advanced education beyond the elementary level. In the 19th century, academies were often private institutions providing instruction in a range of subjects, including classical languages, sciences, and the arts.

Accessory
(in the context of a crime)
A person who helps commit a crime but is not present during the crime.

Acclimating fever
(Fever & Ague)
An illness that early settlers often experienced when they moved to new regions with different climates or environments. It often included symptoms similar to malaria or other fever-inducing diseases and was a significant cause of early deaths among settlers.

Actual Settlers
Refers to individuals who settled on and developed land, as opposed to speculators who bought land with the intention of selling it later for a profit without making improvements.

Act of Legislature
A law passed by the legislative body of a government.

Admitted to the bar
This refers to the process by which a lawyer is officially allowed to practice law before the courts. Being admitted to the bar means they completed the necessary legal education and passed the required examinations to become a licensed attorney.

Adoption by the Indians
A custom in some Native American tribes where a captured person could be adopted into the tribe, often to replace a deceased family member.

Ague
A fever, often with alternating chills and sweating, commonly associated with malaria. In the early settlement period, "fever and ague" was a common affliction for pioneers, especially when they first arrived in a new area.

Aide-de-Camp
A military officer acting as a confidential assistant to a senior officer. The Aide-de-Camp helps with administrative tasks, communication, and other duties as assigned by the commanding officer.

Algonquins

A group of Native American tribes originally from the northeastern part of North America, particularly in the region of what is now Canada. They were allies of the French during the conflicts with the Iroquois.

Alleghenies (Allegheny Mountains)

A range of the Appalachian Mountains running through the eastern United States, often referenced in historical accounts of early American expansion westward.

Allopathic

A term used to describe the conventional medical practice of treating symptoms with remedies that produce effects opposite to those caused by the disease. In the early 19th century, this was the dominant form of medical treatment, characterized by the use of strong medicines like quinine and blue pill.

Amherst, General (Jeffery Amherst)

A British general who led military campaigns during the French and Indian War. He played a key role in the British conquest of Canada, including the defeat of French forces and the acquisition of their territories.

Anterior lobe

The front part of the brain's cerebral hemisphere. In this context, it refers to the skulls found at the site, noting that the anterior lobe was well-developed, indicating intelligence or a certain level of mental capacity.

Anti-Masonic Excitement

Refers to a period in the early 19th century when there was widespread suspicion and opposition to Freemasonry, particularly after the abduction and presumed murder of William Morgan in 1826, who had threatened to expose Masonic secrets. This event led to the formation of the Anti-Masonic Party and widespread anti-Masonic sentiment in the United States.

Antiquity

The ancient past, especially the period before the Middle Ages. Here, it is used to describe the growing historical interest and reverence for the pioneer era.

Apprenticeship

The system under which Samuel Tappan learned the shoemaking trade, a common practice in the 18th and 19th centuries where young people learned a trade by working for a master.

Aquafortis

An old term for nitric acid, which was commonly used in early chemical processes, including metalworking.

Ardent temperament

Describes someone with a passionate and enthusiastic personality. They would have intense feelings and strong opinions, especially on topics like slavery and temperance.

Arrowheads

Sharpened points, usually made of stone, attached to arrows and used as weapons or hunting tools by Indigenous peoples.

Arsenic

A toxic substance that was historically used in small doses as a treatment for various illnesses, such as fever and ague. Its use was dangerous, and it was often administered with caution by early doctors.

Article

A written contract provided by the Holland Land Company to settlers, specifying the terms of land purchase, including payment schedules and conditions. The "Article" allowed settlers to take possession of the land while paying off the purchase price over time.

Ashery

A facility where wood ashes were processed to produce potash or perlash, which were valuable commodities in the early 19th century. Asheries were common in areas where land clearing created large amounts of wood ash. Potash was an important commodity for trade, especially in rural and frontier areas.

Assembly's Catechism

A reference to the Westminster Assembly's Shorter Catechism, a set of religious doctrines used by Presbyterian and Congregational churches. It was an essential part of the religious education for many early settlers.

Assembly for Orleans County

Refers to the New York State Assembly, the lower house of the New York State Legislature. Representatives (Assembly members) are elected from various districts, including Orleans County, to serve in the Assembly and participate in making state laws.

Assignee in Bankruptcy

A person appointed to handle the assets of a bankrupt individual or entity.

Assigning (an Article)

The process by which a settler could transfer their interest in a land purchase contract (Article) to another person. This practice was common among settlers, tradesmen, and speculators.

Aqueduct

A structure built to carry water over obstacles, such as rivers or valleys. In the context of the Erie Canal, aqueducts were used to carry the canal over streams and rivers.

Auld Lang Syne

A Scottish phrase meaning old long since or days gone by, often used to express nostalgia for the past. The term is famously associated with the song of the same name, traditionally sung at New Year's Eve.

Bachelor's Hall
A term used to describe the living arrangement of unmarried men sharing a cabin or house, often in pioneer settings.

Backlog
A large log placed at the back of a fireplace, often used as the primary source of fuel in a log house. It would burn slowly, providing heat and light for several days.

Bake Pan (Cast Iron)
A heavy iron pan with a moveable lid and legs, used for baking before stoves became common. The pan could be placed over coals, with additional coals placed on top of the lid to cook the contents evenly.

Baptist Church
A Christian denomination characterized by the practice of baptism by full immersion. In early Orleans County, Baptists were among the first to establish formal religious organizations.

Bark Roof
A roof made from strips of bark, typically from basswood or other trees, used in the construction of early log cabins

Barre
A town in Orleans County, New York, named after Barre, Massachusetts, by Judge John Lee. The town was officially separated from Gaines in 1818.

Barrel Head
The flat top surface of a barrel, which early settlers sometimes used as a makeshift table. This was a practical solution in the absence of more formal furniture.

Basin
A basin in the context of a canal is an artificial body of water created by digging out the bank, allowing boats to turn around or dock. It serves as a small harbor within a canal.

Basswood
A type of tree, also known as linden, commonly found in the forests of New York. The wood was often used by early settlers for building floors, furniture, and other wooden items due to its soft and workable wood.

Batavia
A city in Western New York that served as the administrative center for the Holland Land Company. The company's main land office was located here, managing land sales and other business activities related to the Holland Purchase.

Battle of Fort Erie
A key battle in the War of 1812, fought near present-day Buffalo, New York.

Bee (as in "house raising bee")
Social gatherings where neighbors came together to help each other with large tasks, such as building barns, houses, or other communal projects where everyone contributes labor without expectation of

payment. These were common in frontier and rural communities where labor-intensive tasks needed to be completed quickly.

Benefactors

Those who give aid, particularly in the form of money or resources. The term here refers to the pioneers who established the foundations for future generations.

Bible

A significant religious text for Christians. In the context of the time, it was common for families to pass down a family Bible, which often contained records of births, marriages, and deaths.

Black Ash Swamp

A type of wetland habitat commonly found in New York State, particularly in low-lying areas. The term here refers to a specific swamp area in what later became Rochester, noted for its difficult terrain.

Black Earthenware Teapot

A small, black ceramic teapot commonly used by early settlers. These teapots were highly valued for making tea, whether from store-bought tea leaves or herbs collected from the wild.

Black North

A term referring to a remote and wild area that was sparsely settled, often associated with difficult living conditions such as harsh weather, thick forests, and the prevalence of diseases like fever and ague.

Black Salts

A crude form of potash, produced by leaching ashes from burned wood. Black salts were an important product for early settlers, as they could be further refined into potash or used in trade. It was often sold to asheries for further refinement.

Blacksmith

A craftsman who works with iron and steel, forging and shaping metal objects, such as tools, horseshoes, and other items. They were essential in early American towns for maintaining tools and equipment.

Block House Fort

A small, fortified structure used during the American Revolutionary War to provide protection against attacks.

Blocks of Logs

Simple, rough-cut sections of logs used as makeshift stools or seats in early log houses. These were often used in place of chairs.

Blue-edged Plates

Crockery with a distinctive blue rim, often found in households of the 18th and 19th centuries. These plates were part of the minimal tableware owned by many early settlers.

Blue Pill

A type of pill containing mercury, used in the 19th century to treat various ailments, including syphilis and digestive issues. It was a common medication among early settlers but is now recognized as toxic.

Body Maple
Refers to the solid, central part of a maple tree.

Bond and Mortgage
A financial agreement where the land buyer received the deed to the land but provided a bond (a promise to pay) and a mortgage (a lien on the property) to secure the remaining balance owed to the Holland Land Company.

Bonfire
A large, controlled outdoor fire used for warmth, light, or celebration.

Border Settlement
The process of settling land on the frontier, often at the edges of established territories or in newly acquired regions.

Boughs
Branches of a tree, often used as feed for livestock when other fodder was scarce. Early settlers would cut down trees to provide boughs for their cattle during harsh winters.

Booked (in context of land ownership)
In this context, booked refers to the practice of informally claiming land by having it noted in an agent's records before it was officially put on the market. This was a way for settlers to secure their rights to the land before purchasing it.

Bran Bread
Bread made from the outer layers of grain, known as bran, which was often less desirable but used when resources were scarce.

Brant, Joseph
A Mohawk military and political leader who was closely associated with the British during the American Revolutionary War. He was instrumental in persuading many of the Iroquois nations to side with the British against the American colonists.

Break-even financial situation
A situation where one's income or revenue is equal to their expenses, meaning they are not gaining or losing money. It implies that an individual was not able to save money despite his efforts.

Brewery/Distillery
A brewery is a facility where beer is produced, while a distillery is where spirits like whiskey are made. Both were common in early American towns, providing local beverages and often serving as social hubs.

Brick Oven (Scotch Oven)
An oven made of brick, often used for baking, that marked a significant improvement in the domestic facilities of early settlers. The term "Scotch oven" refers to outdoor brick ovens raised on a frame, commonly used before the widespread introduction of kitchen ovens inside the house.

Brigadier-General

A rank in the military hierarchy, typically commanding a brigade or being responsible for a specific task or operation. A Brigadier General is a senior rank, usually the first rank of General Officer in the U.S. military.

Brigade Staff Officers

Military officers who assist a Brigadier General in managing the various functions of a brigade, including logistics, administration, and medical services.

Brine

A strong solution of salt in water. Brine springs were natural sources of salty water used to produce salt, an important preservative and seasoning in the 19th century.

Broadcast

A method of sowing seeds by scattering them widely over the surface of the soil rather than planting them in rows. This was a common technique for planting wheat in the early days of settlement.

Brown University

An Ivy League research university located in Providence, Rhode Island. Founded in 1764, it is one of the oldest institutions of higher education in the United States.

Browse (as in browse his cattle)

Refers to the twigs, leaves, and shoots of trees and shrubs that are eaten by livestock, particularly during the winter months when other forage is scarce. It indicates a time of scarcity when livestock had to be fed on less nutritious or less conventional fodder.

Buggy

A light, horse-drawn carriage with four wheels, commonly used for personal transportation in the 19th century. Buggies became popular as roads improved and transportation needs grew.

Bunker Hill

A significant early battle in the American Revolutionary War, fought on June 17, 1775, in Charlestown, Massachusetts. John Anderson, the ancestor of the Anderson family in Gaines, fought in this battle.

Burying Ground

An old-fashioned term for a cemetery or burial site. It was common for early American settlements to have a designated area for burying the dead.

Bush Shanty

A temporary shelter constructed using branches and foliage.

Busti, Mr. Paul

A key agent for the Holland Land Company, who managed many of its affairs from Philadelphia. He was involved in decisions regarding land donations to religious societies and other important matters related to the company's operations.

Butler, Colonel John

A British Loyalist who led a group of irregular fighters known as Butler's Rangers during the American Revolutionary War. He was known for his role in leading raids against American frontier settlements.

Calico

A type of inexpensive, printed cotton fabric that was widely used for clothing and household items in the 19th century.

Campaign on the Niagara Frontier

Refers to the military actions that took place along the Niagara River during the War of 1812 between the United States and Britain. Many settlers in Western New York volunteered to defend the region.

Canada West

Refers to the region of Canada that is now Ontario.

Canal Appraiser

A position responsible for assessing and valuing properties and lands impacted by the construction of the Erie Canal. This role was crucial in the development and expansion of the canal system in New York.

Canal Village

A village located along a canal, which often grew due to the commerce and transportation the canal provided.

Caravan

A group of people, especially traders or settlers, traveling together across a region, often for safety. In this context, it refers to groups of emigrants moving westward.

Cast

To form a material, such as metal, into a specific shape by pouring it into a mold and allowing it to harden. This process was used to create tools, parts, and other items.

Cattle Law

Local regulations that governed the grazing and movement of cattle. In early settlements, such laws were important for preventing livestock from straying and damaging crops.

Cauldron Kettles

Large iron pots used for boiling substances, in this case, brine to make salt. These kettles were essential for the salt production industry.

Causeway

Raised roads or paths, often constructed over wet or low-lying ground. In early settlements, causeways were important for making roads passable in areas prone to flooding or marshy conditions.

Cemetery Association

An organized group responsible for managing and maintaining a cemetery. Many of the old rural burial places in Orleans County were placed under the care of Cemetery Associations, which were incorporated under general law.

Cemetery Lot

A specific parcel of land within a cemetery where an individual or family can be buried. Cemetery lots in places like Hillside Cemetery are carefully numbered and mapped, with ownership transferred through deeds.

Champlain Canal

A canal in New York State that connects the southern end of Lake Champlain to the Hudson River. It was constructed concurrently with the Erie Canal and allowed boats to travel between Lake Champlain and Albany.

Chattel

Personal property or belongings. In this text, it refers to the few possessions, like an ax, that a pioneer might own.

Chest Cover

The flat top of a storage chest, which could be used as a makeshift table by early settlers. Chests were multifunctional, providing storage and serving as furniture.

Chinked

The process of filling gaps between the logs in a log house with materials such as clay, splints, or moss to insulate the structure and keep out wind and rain.

Chorister

A person who leads the singing in a church or congregation, often responsible for selecting hymns and setting the pitch.

Classical scholar

A person who has extensively studied the languages, literature, and culture of ancient Greece and Rome. Reuben Bryant, being described as a classical scholar, indicates his deep knowledge of Greek and Latin, which he enjoyed discussing and quoting.

Clearing

The process of removing trees and underbrush from land to prepare it for cultivation. The term also refers to the area of land that has been cleared of trees.

Clever

Clever refers to being skillful or ingenious in one's actions. One might rely on wit and natural ability to navigate challenges rather than formal education.

Clothier

A person or business that makes, sells, or deals in clothes. In the 19th century, this often involved the processing of wool and other fabrics, as well as the tailoring of garments.

Cold Season

A reference to the "Year Without a Summer" in 1816, when volcanic activity led to severe climate anomalies, including frost and snow in summer months which devastated crops, leading to widespread food shortages. This event significantly impacted early settlers and delayed settlement in many areas.

Collector of Canal Revenue

An official responsible for collecting tolls and other revenues from canal users.

Collector of Taxes

An official responsible for collecting taxes within a designated area.

Colonial government of New York

Refers to the government established by the British in the New York Colony prior to American independence. The colonial government was responsible for managing relations with Native American tribes and defending the colony from external threats.

Commissary of Subsistence

A role or responsibility typically involving the provision and distribution of food and supplies, especially in a military or pioneer context.

Commission

Commissions were formalized orders given by a governing authority or military command.

Commissioners

Officials appointed by the government or a company to oversee specific projects, such as the surveying, laying out, and maintaining of public highways.

Common School Education

A basic education typically provided by local schools in early American settlements. This term reflects the emphasis on fundamental literacy and numeracy skills, often taught in one-room schoolhouses.

Competence of this World's Goods

A phrase used to describe having enough material wealth or resources to live comfortably.

Comptroller of the State of New York

A high-ranking official responsible for overseeing financial operations, including audits and financial management of the state.

Condensed

To reduce something in size, volume, or extent, often while retaining essential elements. In this context, the author has condensed the histories to focus on what would be most interesting to the general reader.

Congregational Church

A Protestant Christian denomination where each congregation independently and autonomously runs its own affairs.

Connexional

Refers to a church organization that is structured as a connection of congregations under one administration, a term often used by Wesleyan and Methodist groups.

Constable

A public officer responsible for maintaining order and enforcing the law in a town or township. In early American communities, constables often handled minor legal matters and served as the primary law enforcement officer.

Corduroy Road

A road made by placing logs transversely side by side to create a stable surface over muddy or swampy ground. These roads were labor-intensive but essential for travel in areas with poor drainage and were common in early American settlements.

Cordwood

Wood cut and stacked for use as firewood, traditionally measured in cords, where a cord is a stack of wood 4 feet high, 4 feet wide, and 8 feet long. Cutting and stacking cordwood was a common task for settlers.

Corn

A staple crop planted by early settlers, often among the felled logs of a newly cleared field. In this context, "corn" refers to maize, a key food source for the pioneers.

Cornstalks

The stalks of corn plants, used as feed for livestock. In the early days of settlement, cornstalks were one of the few sources of fodder available.

Coronal region

The top part of the skull. The term is used here to describe the shape and structure of the ancient skulls found at the archaeological site.

Council

Refers to the local governing body or the New York State Council of Appointment, which appointed officials like Justices of the Peace before certain positions became elected roles.

Court House

A building where legal cases are heard and government functions are carried out. The decision to locate the courthouse in Albion instead of Gaines had a significant impact on the development and prosperity of the surrounding areas.

Court of Chancery

A court with jurisdiction over equity cases, which typically involve matters such as trusts, estates, contracts, and guardianships. This court operated separately from courts of law, which dealt more with criminal and civil cases. The New York Court of Chancery was abolished in 1847, with its duties being absorbed by other courts.

Court of Common Pleas

A local court in the 19th century United States that handled civil cases, such as disputes over contracts, land, and other non-criminal matters. Judges in this court often had more practical experience than formal legal training.

Cranberry Marsh

A wetland area that was once flooded by beaver dams, later becoming a marsh suitable for cranberry growth after the water receded. These marshes were found in places like the head of Otter Creek in Barre.

Credit System

A method of purchasing goods where payment is deferred to a later date. This system was common among early settlers, who often bought goods on credit and paid when they were able to sell crops or other products.

Crotches of Trees

The forked or Y-shaped part of a tree, often used as posts or supports in primitive structures, such as sheds or temporary shelters.

Cultivation

The preparation of land for growing crops. In the context of early settlers, cultivation involved clearing land of trees and stumps, followed by planting and tending crops.

Currier

A craftsman who finishes leather after it has been tanned, preparing it for use in making goods like shoes, saddles, and belts.

Cutter

A lightweight, open, horse-drawn sleigh, typically used in winter. It was a common means of transportation in rural areas during the 19th century.

Deacon

An ordained minister in a Christian church, particularly within Baptist, Congregational, and other Protestant denominations, who assists the pastor with the ministry's duties and serves the congregation in various capacities.

Dedication

The formal ceremony marking the opening or consecration of a cemetery or other significant site. For example, Mount Albion Cemetery was dedicated on September 7, 1843.

Deeds

Legal documents that convey ownership of property from one person to another. As settlers paid off their land, they received deeds from the Holland Land Company, confirming their ownership.

Denomination

A recognized autonomous branch of the Christian Church. Early settlers in Orleans County came from various denominations, including Baptist, Methodist, and Presbyterian, but initially did not maintain strict denominational distinctions.

Diffident

A term meaning modest or shy because of a lack of self-confidence. Reuben Bryant being described as diffident in himself suggests that despite his legal knowledge and skills, he was hesitant or lacked confidence in his abilities as an advocate in court.

Digging In

A method of planting seeds by digging small holes or furrows in the soil, often with a hoe, and placing the seeds inside. This technique was used when plowing was not possible due to tree stumps or other obstacles.

Distillery

A facility where alcoholic beverages, such as whiskey or rum, are produced by fermenting and distilling grain, fruit, or other materials. Distilling was a common practice in early American settlements, both for personal use and for trade.

Dipped Tallow Candle

A homemade candle made by repeatedly dipping a wick (usually a piece of string) into melted tallow (animal fat) until the desired thickness is achieved. These candles were commonly used for lighting in early log houses.

Divine Injunction

A religious or moral command believed to be given by God. Asa Sanford refers to the Biblical commandment to "love thy neighbor as thyself," highlighting the cooperative spirit among early settlers.

Doctress

A now-archaic term used to refer to a female practitioner of medicine. In the 19th century, this term might have been used to describe a woman who provided medical care, especially in rural or frontier areas where formally trained doctors were scarce.

Double Log House

A type of log cabin construction with two separate sections, typically connected by a central chimney. These were common in early American frontier settlements and served as both homes and, in some cases, a tavern.

Drag (Triangular Harrow)

A simple agricultural tool used to break up and smooth out the soil after sowing seeds. The triangular harrow or drag was pulled over the field to cover the seeds with soil.

Draymen

Laborers who transport goods using a dray, a low, strong cart without sides. Draymen played an essential role in early transportation and commerce.

Dry Goods

Merchandise such as textiles, clothing, and other products that are not considered groceries or hardware. Dry goods stores were a key part of trade in early American villages.

Dutch Fireplace

A type of open fireplace, commonly used in early American homes, particularly those with Dutch influence.

Dutch Wagons
Likely refers to the Conestoga wagon which were heavy, covered wagons used by settlers during the 18th and 19th century to move their families and belongings across long distances.

Dyspepsia
A term for indigestion or an upset stomach. It was used commonly in the 19th century to describe digestive discomfort.

Earthenware
Pottery made from clay that is fired at a relatively low temperature, often used for making plates, dishes, and other items.

Embargo
A government order restricting commerce, particularly with foreign nations. In this context, it refers to the U.S. Embargo Act of 1807, which prohibited American ships from trading with foreign ports, including Great Britain, during the Napoleonic Wars.

Edifice
A large or imposing building or structure, often referring to a church. The word is also used somewhat humorously to describe the small and simple log houses built by early settlers.

Elder
A title used in some Christian denominations, particularly among Baptists, to refer to a church leader or minister. Early Baptist elders like Irons, Dutcher, and Carpenter were instrumental in establishing churches in Orleans County.

Ellicott, Joseph
The principal surveyor for the Holland Land Company, responsible for surveying the Holland Purchase. He later became the local agent overseeing the company's business in Western New York.

Embankment
This likely refers to an embankment, which is a raised structure typically used to support roads, railways, or canals. In the context of the Erie Canal, it would be an artificial bank of earth constructed to contain the canal or its adjacent waterways.

Embarkment
The act of passengers and crew getting aboard a ship.

Embark
The process of starting a journey or project.

Emigration
The act of leaving one's own country or area to settle in another. In this context, it refers to the movement of people into the northern parts of New York State.

Empire State

A nickname for the state of New York, reflecting its wealth, resources, and influence, particularly during the 19th century.

Encroachment

The act of gradually taking over or trespassing on someone's territory or rights. In this context, it refers to the English building a fort in territory claimed by the French, leading to conflict.

Engraft

To establish or incorporate one thing into another. In this context, settlers from New England sought to "engraft" their educational and social institutions into their new communities in Western New York.

Ensign

A junior rank in the military, often the lowest commissioned officer in the militia during this period. It was typically responsible for carrying the colors (flag) of the regiment.

Erie Canal

A man-made waterway completed in 1825, linking the Hudson River with Lake Erie. The canal transformed New York State's economy, shifting the focus of commerce away from areas like Gaines to towns along the canal. It was a significant route for trade and transportation.

Esquire (Esq.)

A title used in the United States to denote a man of social rank or one holding an office of authority, such as a Justice of the Peace.

Evangelical Truth

A term associated with the teachings and beliefs of evangelical Christianity, emphasizing the importance of the gospel and personal faith in Jesus Christ.

Excelsior

A Latin word meaning ever upward or higher. It is the motto of the state of New York and symbolizes striving for progress and improvement.

Exhumed

To dig up something buried, especially a body. In this text, it refers to the skeletons that were dug up from the ground in various states of preservation.

Extreme North

Refers to the northernmost regions of early European exploration and settlement in North America, particularly in what is now Canada.

Fallow

Land that has been cleared and left unplanted for a period to restore its fertility. In the early days of settlement, fallow land often referred to fields that were in the process of being cleared or prepared for future planting.

Farmers Bank of Orleans

A local bank established in Gaines, likely to support the agricultural community by providing loans and other financial services.

Feeder Canal
A canal built to direct water from a larger waterway into another, such as from Tonawanda Creek into Oak Orchard Creek, to help supply water to the Erie Canal.

Felled Trees
Trees that have been cut down.

Fever and Ague
A term used to describe the recurrent malarial-like symptoms of fever, chills, and sweating that afflicted many pioneers. It was a common condition in areas where the land was swampy or newly cleared. It was a significant cause of early deaths among settlers.
See the "Pioneer Handbook" for more detail.

Finishing School
A private school for girls that emphasizes cultural studies and prepares them for society.

Fire Sill
The bottom part of the opening for a fireplace or chimney.

Five Corners
A notable intersection in Gaines, about a mile north of Albion. It was a key point for settlers and a location where important decisions and actions took place. The Oak Orchard Road was surveyed from this point to the south, marking one of the first public highways in Barre.

Fir Tree Memorial
A fir tree planted in the Medina burial grounds by John Parsons in 1860 as a lasting memorial. Under the tree, a glass jar enclosed in lead was buried, containing mementos of the time.

Flagging Stone
A type of flat stone used for paving sidewalks, floors, or as flagstones. The discovery of flagging stone in Medina was significant for construction and infrastructure in the area.

Flail
A manual tool used to thresh grain, separating the edible part from the chaff. It consists of a long wooden handle attached to a shorter, free-swinging stick. Threshing machines eventually replaced the flail as a more efficient method.

Flank Leather
A type of leather that comes from the flank or side of an animal, typically of lower quality and used for less durable goods, such as the poor coarse shoes mentioned by Jacob A. Zimmerman.

Flintlock Gun
A type of firearm that uses flint striking steel to ignite the gunpowder.

Flouring Mill
A mill where grain is ground into flour. Flouring mills were central to the agricultural economy, turning locally grown wheat into flour for local use and export.

Fodder

Food for livestock, particularly during the winter months when fresh grass was not available. Fodder typically included hay, cornstalks, and other plant materials.

Foray

A sudden attack or incursion into enemy territory, especially to obtain something; mentioned in the context of hostile actions during the War of 1812.

Forehanded

An old term meaning financially secure or well-off.

Fort Erie

A fort in Canada that was the site of significant military action during the War of 1812.

Fort George

A fort at the mouth of the Niagara River in Canada, captured by American forces during the War of 1812.

Fortifications

Military constructions or buildings designed for defense in warfare. In this chapter, it refers to the ancient defensive structures found in Orleans County, which were likely used by the earlier inhabitants of the region.

Foundry

A workshop or factory where metal is melted and cast into shapes, such as tools, machinery parts, or decorative items. Foundries were critical for the industrial development of early towns.

Fowling Piece

A type of light shotgun used primarily for hunting birds but also effective for small game and, at times, larger animals like deer. It was a common tool among settlers for providing food.

Framed House

A house built with a wooden frame structure, as opposed to log houses. Framed houses were more durable and considered a step up in comfort and quality for early settlers.

Freeholders

Landowners who held their land outright, rather than leasing it. In early American towns, certain public offices required the holder to be a freeholder.

Freeman Settlement

A community founded by Gideon Freeman in the town of Gaines, named after him. This area was known for its early agricultural development, although it faced severe hardships, such as the crop failure in 1816.

Freemasons

A fraternal organization with roots in the medieval stonemasons' guilds. Freemasonry was widespread in early America and played a significant role in social and civic life.

Free thinker
A person who forms their own opinions rather than accepting those commonly accepted or promoted by others. This term often describes someone who challenges societal norms or traditional beliefs.

French's Gazetteer of New York
A geographical dictionary or directory that provides detailed information about places, typically including statistics and descriptions of their history. French's Gazetteer would have been a key reference work for understanding New York State's geography and history at the time.

Frying Pan
A basic cooking utensil with a long handle, used for frying food over an open fire. The long handle allowed the cook to hold the pan over the fire without getting too close to the heat.

Furnace
In this context, a furnace is a facility used for smelting or casting metal. Early furnaces were essential for producing tools, implements, and machinery, such as plows.

Gaines Academy
The first incorporated literary institution in Orleans County, established in 182It initially thrived but declined after rival academies were established in nearby towns.

General Muster
A military term for a full assembly of troops, often for training or inspection, which settlers were required to attend.

General Sullivan's Expedition
A military campaign led by General John Sullivan in 1779 during the American Revolutionary War. The campaign targeted the Iroquois Confederacy, who had sided with the British, and involved burning their villages and crops to weaken their support for the British forces.

General Winfield Scott
A United States Army general who played a major role in the War of 1812, the Mexican-American War, and the early stages of the American Civil War. He was also involved in maintaining peace during the Patriot War.

Genesee and Niagara Counties
Regions in Western New York where the Seneca tribe had their villages. These areas were part of the broader territory traditionally occupied by the Seneca people.

Genesee County
A county in Western New York. It was part of the territory inhabited by the Seneca tribe, and they had their villages there.

Genesee Country
A region in Western New York that was a popular destination for settlers moving westward in the early 19th

century. It was known for its fertile land and opportunities for farming and settlement.

Genesee Flats

A fertile agricultural area in the Genesee River Valley, New York. It was known for its productive farmland and was a source of food for settlers.

Genesee River

A major river in Western New York that served as a key geographical and cultural boundary during the early settlement of the region. It was central to the history and development of the Genesee Country and the Holland Purchase.

German Flats

A region in central New York State where American General Philip Schuyler met with Iroquois leaders during the Revolutionary War to negotiate neutrality. Schuyler met some Six Nations chiefs in council at German Flats to promise protection of Oneida lands against encroaching settlers. He pledged that the United States would honor the boundary line established by the 1768 Treaty of Fort Stanwix, In return, the attending chiefs renewed a friendly neutrality that endorsed Schuyler's military plans to defend the valley.

Gideon Hard

A prominent figure in Orleans County history, known for his service as a Congressman, State Senator, and County Judge. His contributions to law and governance in the area were significant.

Gill (as a unit of measure)

A unit of liquid measure, equal to one-fourth of a pint. In the context of this text, it refers to the amount of whiskey rationed to workers each day.

Gospel Land/Lot

A parcel of land, often reserved by land companies like the Holland Land Company, to support religious institutions and encourage settlement in a new area. The distribution of these lands was often contentious and managed carefully by company agents like Joseph Ellicott.

Gotham

A reference to a major city, used here to describe Batavia as the expected commercial hub of the Holland Purchase, an area in Western New York.

Gravelly Ridge

A naturally elevated area composed of gravel. The Ridge Road, an important highway in Orleans County, was built along such a ridge, which extended from the Genesee River to the Niagara River.

Great Eclipse (1806)

A significant solar eclipse that occurred on June 16, 1806 It was observed by Asa Sanford and others, and it caused a temporary darkening of the sky.

Great Rebellion

Another term for the American Civil War (1861–1865).

Greek and Latin lore

This refers to the body of knowledge, stories, myths, and literary works from ancient Greece and Rome. The use of lore suggests not just the languages but also the cultural and historical knowledge that comes with studying these classical civilizations.

Green Mountain Origin

Refers to the region of the Green Mountains in Vermont and the people from that area. The term is often associated with hardy, resilient individuals, reflecting the rugged terrain and self-reliant culture of the region.

Grindstone

A tool used for sharpening or grinding, typically in the context of agricultural or manual labor.

Grist

Grain that has been ground into flour or meal. The term can also refer to the quantity of grain taken to a mill for grinding.

Grist Mill

A mill where grains such as wheat, corn, or rye are ground into flour. Gristmills were essential in early American communities as they provided a means for settlers to process their crops into usable food products.

Half Rations

A term used to describe a reduced food allowance, often implemented during times of scarcity to make limited supplies last longer.

Half Worn Out (in reference to shoes)

A colloquial expression used to describe shoes that are already in poor condition. In the context provided by Jacob A. Zimmerman, it highlights the difficulty settlers faced in obtaining new footwear.

Halifax

The capital city of Nova Scotia, Canada. During the War of 1812, it served as a British military stronghold where American prisoners of war were held.

Halcyon Days

A term referring to a peaceful and happy period in the past. It is often used nostalgically to describe a time that seems idyllic compared to the present.

Handsled

A small sled used for transporting goods by hand, typically over snow or ice.

Handspike

A wooden lever used for lifting or prying heavy objects.

Hardscrabble

A term used to describe a rough or difficult area, often used to describe places with harsh living conditions.

Harrow

An agricultural tool used to break up and level soil, often used after sowing seeds to cover them with earth. The triangular harrow mentioned in the text was a basic version of this tool.

Hatchet

A small axe. The term "take up the hatchet" refers to engaging in warfare, often used in the context of Native American tribes.

Hemlock Boughs

Branches from hemlock trees, used as bedding by early settlers. They were spread on the floor and covered with blankets to create a makeshift bed.

Hewed

The process of shaping logs or wood by cutting with an axe. Hewed logs were often used to create flat surfaces for floors, doors, or other structural elements in a log house.

Hieroglyphics

Here, it refers humorously to the system of marks and symbols Oliver Booth used to keep track of his tavern accounts on the walls.

High-spirited horses

This refers to horses that are very lively or easily excited. Such horses can be difficult to control, especially when driving a carriage, and may cause accidents.

Highway

In the context of early settlement, a highway referred to any main road used for public travel. These were often simple dirt roads or paths cleared through forests and were critical for connecting communities.

Hillside Cemetery

A cemetery located south of Holley Village, established by The Holley Cemetery Association in 1866 The cemetery was formally dedicated on August 17, 1867, and has been carefully maintained and improved by the association.

Hoe

A hand tool used for digging, weeding, and planting. In the context of early farming, a hoe was often used to plant seeds among the stumps and logs left after clearing the land. It was a basic but essential implement for early settlers.

Hoe Cake

A type of simple bread made from cornmeal, water, and salt, traditionally baked on a flat surface, such as the blade of a hoe. This was a common food among early settlers.

Holland Purchase

A large tract of land in Western New York purchased by a group of Dutch investors, known as the Holland Land Company, in the late 18th century. This area was a significant part of the early settlement and development of New York State.

Homestead

A family's residence, typically including the house and surrounding land.

Honorary A.M. Degree

A Master of Arts degree awarded as an honor, without the usual academic requirements.

Hovel House
A small, simple dwelling often built from logs and other readily available materials. Bailey describes building a hovel house from logs to serve as his first home.

Hulled Corn/Wheat
Corn or wheat that has had its outer husk or hull removed, often by boiling. It was often boiled and eaten as a simple meal by early settlers when other food was scarce.

Hunger-driven foraging
During times of food scarcity settlers would eat whatever wild animals they could catch, regardless of the type of meat.

Hunter's Lodges
Secret societies formed by American sympathizers during the Patriot War in Canada (1837-1838). These lodges supported Canadian rebels fighting against British rule.

Hurons
A Native American tribe originally from the region surrounding the Great Lakes, particularly in what is now Ontario, Canada. The Hurons were allies of the French during their conflicts with the Iroquois.

Incorporated
The legal process of forming a corporation or association, giving it a separate legal identity and granting it certain legal rights and responsibilities.

Indian Agent
A government-appointed official responsible for managing interactions between Native American tribes and the U.S. government.

Indian Mill
A primitive milling method used by early settlers, involving a hollowed-out tree stump (mortar) and a heavy pestle attached to a springy sapling, used to grind corn or other grains into coarse meal.

Indian Road
A specific trail used by Native Americans, running from the Genesee River to Niagara County, and intersecting with other trails. It was later used by settlers and became part of the early road system in the area.

Indian Trail
Pathways originally used by Native Americans, later utilized by settlers for travel and trade.

Indomitable
Spirit A spirit that cannot be defeated or subdued, highlighting the determination and resilience of the pioneers.

Inn
A place offering lodging, food, and drink to travelers often serving as a social and commercial hub for the community.

Infinitesimal
A term used to describe something extremely small or minute. In

the context of medicine, it refers to the very small doses used in homeopathic treatment, which contrasts with the larger doses used in allopathic medicine.

Intellect
Refers to the capacity for thinking and reasoning, especially to a high degree. In this context, it highlights the natural intelligence of an individual who may not have had much formal schooling.

Iron Trammel
An adjustable iron bar with holes, hung over a fireplace. Kettles could be hung from it at different heights, allowing the cook to control the heat by raising or lowering the kettle.

Iroquois
A powerful confederation of six Native American nations (Mohawk, Oneida, Onondaga, Cayuga, Seneca, and Tuscarora) in what is now New York State. They played a significant role in the colonial history of North America, often allying with the British against the French and later the Americans.

Insolvency
Refers to the inability of a business or individual to meet their financial obligations, often leading to bankruptcy. In the context given, it indicates that some merchants were unable to continue their operations.

Inventory
A detailed list of possessions or property. Here, it refers to taking stock of the achievements and resources inherited from the pioneers.

Jack ("make his Jack")
A slang term for money or profit.

Jews Harp
A small musical instrument that produces a twanging sound when plucked. It was sometimes used as a substitute for more formal instruments like violins in early American settlements for entertainment.

Johnson's Creek
A creek in Orleans County, New York, named by Sir William Johnson during a military expedition. It was a significant waterway for early settlers and was used historically as a fishing site by Native Americans. It remains an important geographical feature.

Johnson, Sir William
A British colonial administrator who played a significant role in managing relations between the British and Native American tribes, particularly the Iroquois. He was influential in securing Iroquois support for the British during various conflicts.

Johnson, Sir John
A Loyalist leader during the American Revolutionary War who was the son of Sir William Johnson. He led Loyalist forces, including Native American allies, in raids against American settlers and American revolutionary forces.

Judge Advocate
A legal officer in the military responsible for overseeing legal proceedings, including courts-martial and other military justice matters.

Justice of the Peace
An official appointed to act as a judge in minor legal matters, such as small claims, minor criminal offenses, and performing marriages. This role was important in rural areas where more formal courts were not easily accessible.

Kettles
Large metal pots used for boiling liquid. In this text, kettles are used to boil brine to evaporate the water and leave behind the salt.

Knapsack
A type of bag or backpack used by early travelers to carry provisions and personal items.

Lake Ontario
One of the Great Lakes of North America. It forms part of the boundary between the United States and Canada and is mentioned in the context of the waterways that connect to the creeks in Orleans County.

Land Office
The office established by the Holland Land Company in Batavia (and other locations) to manage the sale and administration of lands within the Holland Purchase.

Latch-String
A string used to lift a latch from the outside of a door, symbolizing hospitality and openness. The phrase "latch-string was always out" indicates a welcoming home.

Leaching
The process of washing ashes with water to extract soluble substances, such as potash, which could be used for making soap or traded. Leaching was an important activity for early settlers in clearing land and making use of wood ashes.

Leather Stocking (Cooper's Hero)
A reference to a character in James Fenimore Cooper's series of novels known as the Leatherstocking Tales, which depict the life of a frontiersman. The term symbolizes the adventurous and rugged spirit of early pioneers.

Leeks
A type of wild onion that grows in the forest and can give a strong flavor to milk when cows graze on them. The settlers sometimes consumed fresh leeks to get accustomed to the taste.

Liberty Party
A political party in the United States during the 1840s that was primarily focused on the abolition of slavery.

Lieutenant's Commission
An official document granting a person the rank of lieutenant in

the military. Commissions were formalized orders given by a governing authority or military command.

Limpid
Clear, transparent. In this text, it describes the appearance of the water when first pumped from the spring before it was boiled to produce salt.

Livery Stable
A stable where horses and vehicles are kept for hire.

Log Causeway
A type of causeway constructed by laying logs side by side across a wet or swampy area to create a passable road. This method was commonly used in areas with abundant timber.

Logging Bees
Social gatherings in which neighbors helped each other clear land by cutting down trees and preparing logs.

Log House
A type of house built from logs, common among early settlers in Western New York. The log house was simple and sturdy, providing basic shelter in the wilderness.

Log Schoolhouse
A simple, rustic school building made of logs, similar in construction to the log houses in which early settlers lived. These early schoolhouses were often uncomfortable and lacked modern amenities but were crucial to the education of pioneer children.

Log Sled
A sled made from logs, used for transporting goods or people over snow-covered ground. In winter, log sleds were often the primary means of transportation in rural areas.

Loom
A device used to weave cloth. In pioneer settlements, women often wove cloth at home for clothing and other necessities, making the loom an essential household tool.

Lot
A parcel of land designated by surveyors for sale or settlement, often referenced by number, town, and range in historical records.

Lot and Range System
A method used in the surveying of land, particularly in the early 19th century. Lot refers to a specific parcel of land within a township, and Range refers to a specific row or line of townships. For example, lot three, township fifteen, range three is a specific location within a surveyed area.

Lower courts
Courts of limited jurisdiction that handle less serious criminal cases and smaller civil disputes. Success as a lawyer in these courts would have involved dealing with minor legal issues.

Lumbering Business
The industry of harvesting, processing, and selling timber. This was a common occupation in heavily forested areas.

Lundy's Lane
A significant battle of the War of 1812. It took place near Niagara Falls and was one of the bloodiest battles of the war.

Lye
A strong alkaline solution obtained by leaching wood ashes. Lye was commonly used in soap-making and other household tasks by early settlers.

Magic of Aladdin
A reference to the story of Aladdin and his magic lamp, from One Thousand and One Nights, where the lamp grants wishes and performs miracles. It is used metaphorically to describe the seemingly miraculous transformation of the land.

Mail Contractor
A person or company responsible for delivering mail along a specific route. In the early 19th century, mail contractors often also ran stagecoach services.

Main Street
The principal street of a village or town, often where most businesses, stores, and important buildings are located.

Malady
A disease or ailment. It sometimes refers to a chronic illness or condition that troubles the afflicted throughout their life, affecting their work and personal comfort.

Manuscript
A handwritten or typed document, especially one that contains an author's work before it is published. In this case, it refers to the original local histories written by members of the Orleans County Pioneer Association.

Marked Trees
Trees that were marked, often by notching or blazing, to guide travelers through the forest. Before formal roads were established, these markers helped people navigate through undeveloped areas.

Mason
A skilled craftsman who builds with stone, brick, or similar materials.

Mason Business
The trade of building structures with stone, brick, or concrete, such as walls, buildings, or chimneys. Masons are skilled craftsmen who work with these materials.

Massacre
Refers to the killing of settlers or soldiers, often used in the context of border warfare or conflicts with Native Americans during the early settlement period.

Master in Chancery

A judicial officer appointed to assist in equity cases, often dealing with complex legal matters, such as the administration of estates or the partition of land. This position would have involved duties beyond those of a typical judge.

Master in Chancery

A judicial officer in a court of equity, particularly under the old English legal system and the American legal systems that followed it. The Master in Chancery would oversee certain aspects of equity cases, such as conducting inquiries and managing the administration of justice in complex cases. The office was largely abolished in the U.S. with the adoption of new legal frameworks, such as the Constitution of 1846 in New York.

Mayflower

The ship that brought the Pilgrims from England to the New World in 1620, landing at Plymouth Rock. It is often referenced in discussions of early American history.

Medina Herald

The first newspaper published in Medina, established in 1832. Newspapers were vital for communication and spreading information in early American communities.

Merchandising

Refers to the buying and selling of goods, often in a general store or trading post. In rural or frontier areas, merchandising was an essential service, providing settlers with necessary supplies.

Mechanics

In this historical context, mechanics refers to skilled workers who worked with machinery or tools, such as blacksmiths, carpenters, and other tradespeople essential to village life.

Mechanic Shops

Workshops where skilled laborers, or mechanics, produced and repaired tools, machines, and other goods. These shops were essential to the economic development of early settlements.

Medina and Darien Railroad Company

A company incorporated in 1834 to build a railroad from Medina to Akron. The railroad was operated using horse-drawn cars but was ultimately unsuccessful and discontinued.

Medina and Ontario Railroad Company

A company incorporated in 1836 with the intent to build a railroad from Medina to Lake Ontario at the mouth of Oak Orchard Creek. However, the project never progressed beyond incorporation.

Meeting House

A building used for public worship. The first meeting house in Orleans County, built in Gaines, was shared by the Congregational and Baptist societies.

Melodeon
A small reed organ or harmonium, commonly used in the 19th century for musical performances.

Member of Assembly
A representative elected to the New York State Assembly, the lower house of the state legislature. Arba Chubb served as a Member of Assembly for Orleans County in 1848.

Methodist
A member of a Protestant Christian denomination known for its emphasis on personal faith, social justice, and methodical worship practices. The Methodist Church was one of the early religious influences in Orleans County, with preachers like Rev. Mr. Steele playing a key role in ministering to the settlers.

Militia
A military force composed of ordinary citizens to provide defense, emergency law enforcement, or service during times of crisis.

Militia Company
A military force composed of ordinary citizens to provide defense, emergency law enforcement, or paramilitary service. In early America, militias were essential for local defense and were organized at the state or local level.

Millerites/Second Adventists
Followers of William Miller, a preacher who predicted the Second Coming of Christ in the 1840s. Captain Miller, who commanded Samuel C. Lewis during the War of 1812, later became a founder of this religious movement.

Mill Boy
A term referring to someone who was responsible for taking grain to a mill to be ground into flour. This task was essential in pioneer communities where families relied on local mills for their food supply.

Mill pond
A body of water created by damming a stream to power a mill. The water stored in the pond would be used to drive the mill's machinery, which could be used for various purposes, including sawing wood or grinding grain.

Mill Stream
A stream of water used to power mills, such as sawmills and gristmills.

Millville Academy
A local educational institution where the children of Newman Curtis received their education. Academies were common in the 19th century as a higher level of schooling beyond the basic district schools.

Millwright
A craftsman who designs, constructs, and maintains mills, particularly those that involve moving parts such as as gears and belts.

Missionaries

Religious individuals sent on a religious mission, particularly to promote Christianity in foreign or remote regions. French missionaries were allowed to stay in Iroquois territory to spread Christianity. Rev. Mr. Steele served as a missionary in Orleans County, preaching to the settlers in Carlton.

Mohawk Valley

A region in New York State along the Mohawk River, historically significant as a center of trade and conflict during the colonial period and the American Revolutionary War.

Morass

A swamp or bog; in this context, it refers to a swampy area that was difficult to traverse, possibly an ancient lake or impassable marshland.

Morgan Affair

A reference to the abduction and presumed murder of William Morgan in 1826, which led to widespread anti-Masonic sentiment. Timothy C. Strong's newspaper was influenced by this event, leading him to change its name.

Morris Reserve

A tract of land in Western New York, named after Robert Morris, a financier of the American Revolution, who owned extensive lands in the region. The Morris Reserve was part of the larger land deals that shaped the settlement of Western New York.

Morris, Robert

An American financier who played a key role in funding the American Revolution. He later acquired large tracts of land in Western New York, including the land that became the Holland Purchase, before selling it to the Dutch investors.

Mortar and Pestle

A simple tool used to crush or grind substances. In the early settlement days, a large mortar could be made from a hollowed-out stump, with a heavy pestle used to pound corn into meal.

Mosquitoes

Insects that were a significant nuisance to early settlers, especially in areas with standing water. The clearing of forests and draining of swamps reduced mosquito populations, improving living conditions.

Motive Machinery

Refers to machinery driven by a power source, such as steam, used to move or operate mechanical systems.

Mount Albion Cemetery

The largest cemetery in Orleans County, located southeast of the village of Albion. Established in 1843, it is known for its natural beauty and has become the primary burial ground for the area.

Moveable Ladder

A simple ladder that could be moved from place to place, used to access the upper chamber or loft of a log house.

Nominal Price A price that is very low and often not reflective of the actual value of the goods.

Nasal Twang

A distinctive singing style, especially in early American religious music, characterized by a nasal resonance. This style was often used in hymns and spirituals of the time.

Necromancy

The practice of magic or sorcery, especially to communicate with the dead. It is often associated with legends and stories of supernatural events.

Neutrality
The state of not taking sides in a conflict. The Iroquois initially agreed to remain neutral in the American Revolutionary War, though this neutrality was later compromised.

New York Central Railroad

A major railroad company that absorbed the Rochester, Lockport, and Niagara Falls Railroad, providing significant transportation infrastructure in New York State, including Orleans County.

Niagara River

The river that connects Lake Erie to Lake Ontario, forming part of the U.S.-Canada border. Samuel Salsbury crossed the frozen Niagara River, a risky endeavor given the river's strong currents and the precarious ice.

Nine Mile Woods

A term referring to a heavily forested area in early Gaines, where settlers like John Proctor cleared land and built their first homes.

Norton, Zebulon

An early settler in Western New York who was known as a "backwoods doctor." He utilized natural remedies, such as rattlesnake oil and gall, to treat various ailments.

Notching

The technique of cutting notches in the ends of logs so they interlock at the corners of a log house, providing stability to the structure.

Norwegians

Refers to a group of settlers from Norway who established a community in Kendall in the mid-1820s. These settlers were part of a broader wave of Scandinavian immigration to the United States in the 19th century, and they initially settled in Kendall before moving on to Illinois.

Oak Orchard and Johnson's Creeks

These are specific waterways in Western New York that were important fishing grounds for both Native Americans and early settlers.

Oak Orchard Harbor
A reference to a location on Lake Ontario in New York, which early settlers believed would become a significant commercial port.

Oak Orchard Road
A significant early road in Orleans County, running from the mouth of Oak Orchard Creek. The road was originally an Indian trail and later improved by the Holland Land Company.

Oblivion
The state of being forgotten or unknown. In this context, the author expresses a desire to save historical facts and stories from being lost to oblivion.

Onondaga salt
Salt produced in the Onondaga region of New York State, known for its rich salt springs. The availability of cheaper Onondaga salt led to the decline of local salt production in places like Orleans County.

Ordained
The process by which someone is formally invested with the responsibilities and duties of a religious leader, such as a minister or elder.

O'Reilly's sketches of Rochester
Refers to historical sketches or descriptions of the city of Rochester, New York, written by Henry O'Reilly. This work was likely used as a reference for information about the region.

Orleans County
A county located in Western New York, where much of the historical context of this text is set. It was home to various Native American tribes and later to early European settlers.

Orleans County Pioneer Association
Orleans County Pioneer Association An organization established in June 1859, composed of individuals who lived in Western New York before January 1825. Its purpose was to preserve the history and memories of the early settlers of Orleans County.

Ornamental Branches
Subjects of study considered decorative or non-essential, often including the arts, music, and languages. These were often part of the curriculum in academies and seminaries, especially for girls.

Ornamenting
The process of enhancing a cemetery with decorative elements such as trees, shrubs, and other landscaping features. Ornamenting was a common practice in the development of cemeteries like Hillside Cemetery.

Oswego
A city in New York State located on the shore of Lake Ontario. It was the site of important forts and trading posts during the colonial period and was contested by both the French and English.

Otter Creek
A waterway in the Gaines area of Orleans County, New York, that was historically significant for its association with beaver dams and early settlements.

Outer Lines of the Road
Refers to the boundaries of a road or highway as defined by the land survey. When the Holland Company sold land adjacent to roads like Ridge Road, they often included the land up to the outer lines of the road, effectively donating the road space to the public.

Overseer of the Poor
A local official responsible for the care and relief of the poor in a town or parish. The role that involved managing poor relief and possibly administering local workhouses or distributing aid to the needy.

Oxen
Domesticated cattle used as draft animals for plowing fields, hauling loads, and other heavy work. Oxen were essential to early settlers, especially in areas where horses were scarce or the terrain was rough.

Ox Sled
A simple sled pulled by oxen, used by early settlers for transportation and hauling goods, especially in the absence of roads.

Ox Team
A pair of oxen used together to pull a plow, wagon, or other heavy loads. Oxen were commonly used by settlers for heavy labor due to their strength and endurance.

Pail Kettles
Metal containers used for cooking or carrying liquids.

Pastures
In this context, refers to the wild, often uncleared lands where settlers grazed their cattle. These areas were not like modern fenced pastures but rather open, forested lands.

Paternal homestead
Refers to the original family home or farm, usually inherited by the eldest son or another family member, where the family has lived for generations.
Patrimony Property or inheritance passed down from one's ancestors. In this context, it refers to the land and resources inherited from the pioneers.

Patriot War
A series of skirmishes in 1837-1838 involving American sympathizers who supported Canadian rebels in their fight against British colonial government.

Peace Establishment
Refers to the U.S. military organization after the War of 1812, when many officers were retained for peacetime service.

Pedestrian
A term that refers to frequent and long-distance walking.

Pension
A regular payment made by the government to veterans, the elderly, or the disabled. Moses Bacon received a pension from the United States government for his service and the injuries he sustained during the War of 1812.

Pettifogger
A derogatory term for a lawyer who engages in unethical or underhanded legal practices, particularly one who quibbles over insignificant details. Being known as a successful pettifogger might indicate they were a shrewd and often crafty lawyer in local legal matters.

Perlash
A refined form of potash, obtained by further processing black salts. Perlash was used in the production of glass, soap, and other industrial goods.

Pewter
A metal alloy primarily composed of tin, often used to make utensils, mugs, and plates in the 18th and 19th centuries. Pewter items were common in households before the widespread use of more durable materials.

Phelps and Gorham Purchase
A large tract of land in Western New York that was purchased in the late 18th century by Oliver Phelps and Nathaniel Gorham. This area was among the first to be sold to settlers, marking the beginning of the region's development. It is significant in the early settlement of the region and is often mentioned in historical texts about Western New York.

Phipps Union Seminary
A boarding and day school for girls in Albion, established in the early 1830s and incorporated in 1840. It offered a broad curriculum, including both academic and ornamental subjects, and was highly regarded in the region.

Pioneer Association
Refers to the Orleans County Pioneer Association, a group formed to preserve and document the history of the early settlers in the region. This association collected histories from its members, which formed the basis of the book.

Pioneer
A person who is among the first to settle in a new area, playing a significant role in its development. In this text the term refers to the early European settlers who moved into the area now known as Orleans County, New York, during the 18th and 19th centuries.

Pioneer Life

The lifestyle and experiences of early settlers who moved into undeveloped areas, often involving significant hardships, labor, and isolation.

Pioneer Lines of Stages

Early stagecoach routes used for transportation and mail delivery across regions before the widespread use of railroads. They were often operated by private companies or partnerships.

Pittsburgh

A city in Pennsylvania, originally founded as a French settlement known as Fort Duquesne. It played a strategic role in the French and Indian War.

Plank Road

A road constructed with wooden planks, commonly used in the 19th century.

Plat

A map or plan of a piece of land showing the divisions into lots.

Plausible Address

Refers to a person's demeanor or manner of speaking that is persuasive, credible, and acceptable to others. This quality was particularly valued in public figures and those holding office.

Pleurisy

An inflammation of the tissues that line the lungs and chest cavity, often causing sharp chest pain.

Plow (Plough)

An agricultural implement used to turn over and break up the soil, making it ready for planting. In the early days, plowing was difficult due to the presence of tree stumps, which had to rot away before the land could be fully plowed. The invention of the cast iron plow was a significant advancement in agricultural technology, making it easier for farmers to work the land.

Pocket Knife

A small folding knife with one or more blades that fit inside the handle. In this context, it was used by the settlers for hunting deer, showcasing their resourcefulness with limited tools.

Posterity

Future generations. This term is used to emphasize the lasting impact of the pioneers' efforts on those who come after them.

Post Coaches

Horse-drawn vehicles used to transport mail and passengers. They were a common sight along Ridge Road before the Erie Canal shifted much of the travel and trade to waterways.

Postmaster

The person in charge of a post office, responsible for managing the operations and ensuring mail is handled and delivered efficiently. Being a postmaster in the 19th century was often a significant community role.

Post Office

A place where mail was received, sorted, and distributed. Early post offices were few and far between, making communication difficult for settlers in remote areas.

Potash

A substance derived from wood ashes, used in making soap, glass, and other products. It was a valuable commodity in the early settlement period and was often produced from the ashes left after clearing land.

Pounding Corn

A process used by early settlers to grind corn into meal using a pestle driven by a water wheel. This method was slow but provided a way for settlers to produce meal before gristmills were established.

Practical Surveyor

A person who is trained in the techniques of surveying land, which involves measuring and mapping out plots of land. This was an important skill in the early days of settlement as land was divided and sold.

Prairie

A large, open, grassland area, especially in the Midwest of the United States, which was more easily settled by later pioneers due to its lack of dense forests.

Preaching Station

A designated place within a community where ministers would regularly come to preach, especially important in rural or newly settled areas without a permanent church building.

Presbyterian Church

A Protestant Christian denomination governed by elders and characterized by a tradition of Reformed theology. Although many early settlers were Presbyterian, formal denominational distinctions developed later.

Presbytery

A governing body in Presbyterian churches made up of ministers and elders from multiple congregations within a specific area.

Primitive

A term describing the basic, unrefined methods and materials used by early settlers to build homes and furniture. This included log cabins, rough-hewn furniture, and other handmade necessities of frontier life.

Printing Press

A machine used to produce printed material, such as newspapers and books. The establishment of a printing press in Gaines signified the community's ambition to become a center of trade and information.

Privations

Hardships or lack of basic necessities. The early settlers of Orleans County faced numerous privations, including food scarcity, disease, and isolation.

Produce Trade
The buying and selling of agricultural products, such as grains, fruits, and vegetables. This trade was essential to the economy of villages which were surrounded by farmland.

Promissory Notes
Legal instruments involving a written promise to pay a certain amount of money at a specified future date.

Provincial Americans
Colonists from the American colonies who participated in military campaigns under British command, particularly during the French and Indian War.

Public Conveyance
A vehicle or mode of transportation available for public use, such as a stagecoach or covered wagon, often used to transport passengers and mail.

Public House
Another term for an inn or tavern, a place where travelers could find food, drink, and lodging. These establishments were important social centers in early American communities.

Public Library Association
A group formed by early settlers in Kendall to establish a shared collection of books. This was an early example of community efforts to improve access to education and information in remote or newly settled areas.

Public Highway
A road or pathway that is open for use by the general public. Public highways were critical for transportation and communication in the early settlement period.

Public Work (in the context of construction)
Government-funded construction projects, such as roads, canals, and other infrastructure.

Public Worship
The act of religious worship performed by a community in a public setting, such as a church or meeting house. In the early days of Orleans County, public worship was held in log cabins and later in schoolhouses and dedicated church buildings.

Pulteney Estate
A landholding in Western New York named after Sir William Pulteney, a British investor who purchased large tracts of land in the area during the late 18th century. The estate's land was surveyed, then managed by agents who sold parcels to settlers beginning around 1821.

Quagmire Swamp
A type of swamp characterized by soft, muddy ground that can be difficult to traverse.

Quaker
A member of the Religious Society of Friends, known for their pacifist beliefs and simple living.

Quaker Training

A reference to the religious and ethical upbringing associated with the Quakers, a Christian group known for their principles of simplicity, pacifism, and integrity.

Quartermaster

A military officer responsible for providing supplies, transportation, and other logistical support to troops.

Quebec

A major city in Canada founded by the French. It was the center of French power in North America until it was captured by the British in 1759 during the French and Indian War.

Quilting Frolics

Social gatherings where women would come together to work on quilting projects. These events were also important social occasions, providing opportunities for community bonding.

Quinine

A medication derived from the bark of the cinchona tree, used to treat malaria and other fevers. It was commonly prescribed by doctors in the early 19th century to treat "fever and ague."

Raceway

A channel were built to harness water for mills and other enterprises, often used to generate power.

Rafters

The sloping beams that support the roof of a structure. In a log house, the rafters would hold up the bark or wooden shingles that formed the roof.

Ration (in the context of alcohol)

A fixed amount of alcohol, in this case, whiskey, provided to workers as part of their daily compensation. This was a common practice in the early 19th century, especially in labor-intensive jobs like canal construction.

Rattlesnake Oil

An oil extracted from rattlesnakes, believed by early settlers to have medicinal properties, particularly for treating stiff joints and bruises.

Rattlesnake Point

A location near the lower falls of the Genesee River, known for being a habitat for rattlesnakes. It was a notorious spot for these reptiles during the early settlement of the area.

Red Jacket

A prominent Seneca chief known for his oratory skills and efforts to preserve the rights of his people. His counsel was highly respected, and he played a significant role during the War of 1812.

Reformed Dutch Church

A Christian denomination that originated in the Netherlands and was brought to America by Dutch settlers.

Regents of the University

A governing body responsible for overseeing education in New York State, including the incorporation of educational institutions like academies and seminaries.

Reminiscence

A memory or the act of recalling past experiences. The author sought to collect personal reminiscences from the older inhabitants of Orleans County to include in the book.

Reservations

Tracts of land set aside for Native American tribes as part of treaties with the U.S. government. These areas were meant to be sovereign territories where tribes could maintain some autonomy.

Revolutionary Mothers

A term of honor given to women like Ray Marsh's widow, who supported the war effort during the American Civil War by providing essential supplies, such as knitted stockings for soldiers. It reflects the patriotic contributions of women during times of conflict.

Revolutionary Soldier

A person who served in the American Revolutionary War (1775-1783), which led to the independence of the United States from Great Britain.

Ridge Pole

The horizontal beam at the top of a roof that supports the rafters on either side. It is a key structural component in the roof of a log house.

Ridge Road

A historic road running along the Niagara Escarpment in Western New York, parallel to Lake Ontario. This road provided a dry and reliable route for settlers traveling to and from the old states. It was one of the earliest routes established and used by both Native Americans and early settlers. The Ridge Road became a key route for early settlers, leading to the establishment of many farms along its path.

Rochester

A city in Western New York that was an important center of commerce and settlement in the 19th century. The history of Rochester is closely tied to the broader history of the region.

Rochester, Lockport, and Niagara Falls Railroad Company

A railroad company organized in 1850, which built a railroad passing through Orleans County near the Erie Canal. The company was later consolidated into the New York Central Railroad.

Rod

A unit of length equal to 16.5 feet (5.03 meters). In this context, the Land Company cleared a path four rods wide (about 66 feet) along the Transit Line to serve as a guide for settlers.

Ruffle Shirt

A dress shirt with decorative ruffles along the front, popular in the 18th and early 19th centuries.

Ruling Elder

A lay member of a Presbyterian church who is elected to a governing body responsible for the spiritual and administrative oversight of the congregation. The position is one of significant respect and responsibility within the church community.

Running the Gauntlet

A form of punishment or trial by ordeal used by Native American tribes, where prisoners were forced to run between two rows of people who would strike them with clubs, stones, and other weapons.

Rust

A plant disease that affects crops like flax, which was a problem for early settlers attempting to grow flax for clothing.

Rye

A type of grain similar to wheat, often used in breadmaking. During hard times, settlers often relied on rye as a cheaper and more readily available grain.

Saddlebags

Bags draped over the back of a horse or carried by someone traveling on horseback, used to carry personal items, supplies, or, in the case of doctors, medical equipment and medicines.

Sagacity

The quality of being wise or having good judgment. It refers to the ability of the pioneers to make sound decisions despite difficult circumstances.

Salts of Lye (Black Salts)

A crude form of potash, derived from the ashes of burned hardwood. Settlers would trade these salts to obtain money or goods.

Saltwater (Brine)

Refers to water that contains a high concentration of salt, found naturally in some wells. The water was boiled down to produce salt, a valuable commodity before the Erie Canal made imported salt more accessible.

Salt Works Road

A road created by the Holland Land Company to provide access to salt works near Medina. Salt production was an important industry, and roads were built to facilitate transportation of the product.

Samp

A coarse ground meal made from corn, often boiled and eaten with milk. It was a staple food for many early settlers and Native Americans.

Sand hill

A natural elevation of sand, which in this context refers to a location near the ancient fortifications where many human skeletons were exhumed.

Sanguine

Optimistic or hopeful, especially in the face of adversity. The early settlers often felt sanguine about their prospects despite the hardships they faced.

Sap Troughs

Wooden containers used to collect sap from maple trees, which would then be boiled down to produce maple syrup or sugar. This was a common activity among settlers who had access to maple trees.

Saw Mill

A mill where logs are cut into lumber. The first sawmill in Barre was built by Dr. William White in 1816.

Sawyer

A person who operates a sawmill or is responsible for cutting timber into lumber. Sawmills were crucial in converting the abundant trees of the frontier into usable wood for building homes, barns, and other structures.

School District

A geographical area served by a particular public school system. Early school districts were often small, reflecting the scattered and rural nature of early settlements. School districts were often one of the first community services established in a new town.

Sea Biscuit (Hardtack)

A type of hard, dry bread that was commonly used as rations by soldiers and sailors due to its long shelf life.

Sectarian

Sectarian refers to something related to or characteristic of a sect, which is a subgroup within a larger religious, political, or ideological group.

Sectarianism often implies a focus on the specific beliefs, practices, or interests of that subgroup, sometimes leading to conflict, division, or prejudice against other groups. The term is often used in the context of religious or political conflicts where different sects within the same religion or political movement are in opposition to each other.

Seines

Large fishing nets that hang vertically in the water, with weights on the bottom edge and floats on the top. They are used to encircle and capture fish.

Seminary

An educational institution, often for advanced studies. In this context, it refers to Phipps Union Seminary, a girls' school in Albion known for its rigorous academic and ornamental education.

Senecas

One of the six nations of the Iroquois Confederacy, historically located in what is now New York State. The Senecas were known as the "Keepers of the Western Door," being the westernmost of the Iroquois tribes.

Shade Trees

Trees planted to provide shade and enhance the landscape. The planting of shade trees was a common practice in cemeteries, parks and other landscapes to create a peaceful and pleasant environment.

Shakes
Roughly split wooden shingles used for roofing in early log cabins. Levi Atwell's cabin had a roof made of shakes, held in place by poles.

Shanty
A small, roughly built shelter or dwelling, often made from simple materials like wood and used as a temporary residence by settlers or workers.

Sheriff
The chief law enforcement officer in a county, responsible for maintaining peace, serving court papers, and overseeing the county jail. In this context, the Sheriff was also involved in the sale of properties when owners defaulted on their debts.

Shillings
A former British coin and monetary unit that was used in the British Empire. In the context of early American settlements, it often referred to an amount of money equal to 1/20th of a pound. The use of shillings in the narrative reflects the period before the widespread adoption of the U.S. dollar.

Sickle
A hand-held agricultural tool with a curved blade, used for cutting wheat or other crops. It was commonly used by early settlers before more advanced harvesting tools were available.

Singing School
An early American institution where people learned to sing, particularly hymns and religious songs.

Six Nations
Refers to the Iroquois Confederacy, originally composed of five Native American nations the Mohawk, Oneida, Onondaga, Cayuga, and Seneca. The Tuscarora joined later, making it the Six Nations. They were a powerful and influential group in the northeastern part of what is now the United States.

Skeletons
The internal framework of bones in a body. The term is used to describe the remains of ancient people found in the region, including some of unusually large stature.

Slashing
A field where trees have been cut down and left to lie on the ground. This term describes the initial stage of clearing land, where the felled trees were left to dry before being burned.

Sled
A vehicle mounted on runners, used for transporting goods over snow or rough terrain. In the absence of roads, settlers often used sleds drawn by oxen to transport grain or other supplies.

Sleigh

A type of vehicle used for traveling over snow, typically drawn by horses. In the context of early 19th-century America, sleighs were crucial for transportation during winter months, especially in rural areas.

Slips

Refers to pews or benches in a church that were sold or rented to individuals or families. The sale of slips in the first church building in Gaines helped fund the construction of the meeting house and contributed to Gaines Academy.

Sluiceways

Channels or drains constructed to manage water flow under or across a road. Sluiceways were necessary to prevent roads from flooding, especially in areas with poor drainage.

Smuggling

The illegal transportation of goods across borders.

Snow Shoes

Footwear designed to enable walking on snow without sinking. They distribute the wearer's weight over a larger area. In the 1800s, snowshoes were often homemade, as described by

Social Intercourse

Interaction and communication between individuals during their meetings and gatherings.

Soft Water

Water that is free from minerals, particularly calcium and magnesium. Soft water was often preferred for washing clothes and other household tasks, but it was difficult to obtain in areas where only hard, mineral-rich water was available.

Solemn Seasons

A phrase used to describe deeply meaningful or sacred religious gatherings. Early settlers often recalled these solemn seasons of worship held in their simple log cabins.

Solid Branches

Academic subjects considered essential or fundamental, such as reading, writing, arithmetic, and the sciences. These were the core focus of education in both common schools and academies.

Sound judgment

The ability to make sensible and well-thought-out decisions based on experience and practical knowledge, even if the individual has not had extensive formal education.

Sortie

A military term for an attack made by troops coming out from a position of defense. John Proctor participated in a sortie from Fort Erie, successfully repelling British forces.

Span of Horses

Refers to a pair of horses used together for pulling a wagon, sleigh, or other vehicles. The term span indicates that the horses are matched in size and strength.

Speculators

Individuals or companies who bought large tracts of land with the intention of selling them later at a profit, often without developing the land themselves. Speculators were common during the early settlement of the United States.

Special Pleading

A legal term referring to a detailed and specific form of argument in court, involving multiple responses and counter-responses between the plaintiff and defendant.

Spinning Wheels

Devices used to spin fibers into thread or yarn.

Split Plank Floor

A simple and rough-hewn wooden floor made from split logs. Such flooring was common in the early log cabins of settlers.

Snow Shoes

Footwear designed to enable walking on snow without sinking. They distribute the wearer's weight over a larger area. In the 1800s, snowshoes were often homemade.

St. Lawrence River

A major river in North America that flows from the Great Lakes to the Atlantic Ocean. It was a key route for French exploration and settlement in Canada.

Stagecoach

Horse-drawn vehicle used for passenger travel and mail delivery before the advent of railroads and automobiles.

Stalled Ox

A well-fed, fattened ox. The phrase better is a dinner of herbs where love is, than a stalled ox and hatred therewith is a Biblical proverb (Proverbs 1517) implying that simple meals in a loving home are better than feasts where there is conflict.

Staves

Wooden planks or strips, typically used in making barrels or casks. Stave production was an important trade in areas with access to good timber and waterways for shipping.

State Road

A public highway established by the state, often with specific legislation and appointed commissioners. The State Road referenced in this chapter ran from Rochester to Lockport along or near the Erie Canal.

Steady, well-directed industry

Consistent and purposeful hard work.

Steeple

A tall, tower-like structure on top of a church, often containing a bell. The steeple of a church was often the tallest structure in early towns, serving as a landmark and a source of civic pride.

Stick Chimney

A chimney constructed of sticks and coated with clay, used in early log houses. It was a simple and affordable method for creating a vent for smoke in houses where stone or brick was not available.

Stillwater

A term referring to a part of a river or stream with very little current, often making it a good spot for fishing.

Stoga Boots

Sturdy, practical boots worn by settlers and frontiersmen. They were more affordable and durable compared to other types of footwear at the time.

Stools

Simple seating made from wood, often homemade, used in early log houses. Stools were usually small and had no backrest, making them easy to move and store.

Stump

The base of a tree that remains after the tree has been cut down. In early pioneer life, stumps were often left in fields and pastures because removing them was labor-intensive. They were sometimes used as tables or benches.

Stupendous

Extremely impressive or large.

Superintendent of Repairs

An official responsible for maintaining and overseeing repairs on a particular section of the canal. In this case, Jacob Hinds was responsible for repairs on the western section of the Erie Canal.

Sunday School Superintendent

An individual responsible for overseeing the operation of a Sunday School, which is a religious education program typically held on Sundays for children and sometimes adults. The superintendent would manage the curriculum, teachers, and other aspects of the program.

Supervisor

An elected official responsible for overseeing the administration of a town or township. The position involved managing public affairs, such as the maintenance of roads, the allocation of funds, and other local governance tasks.

Supreme Court Commissioner

A judicial officer with the authority to hear certain types of cases and make decisions in the state's Supreme Court system. This role indicates involvement in higher-level legal proceedings in New York State.

Surgeon

A medical officer in the military responsible for the health and medical treatment of soldiers. Surgeons were vital for treating injuries sustained in battle or during military operations.

Surrogate

A judicial officer who deals with matters of probate, including the validation of wills and the administration of estates.

Survey

The process of measuring and mapping land, often for the purpose of establishing roads or dividing land into lots.

Surveyor

A professional responsible for measuring and mapping land, often to establish property boundaries or to plan out a village, including the layout of roads and highways. Surveyors played a critical role in the development of transportation infrastructure in early America.

Susquehanna River

A river that flows through New York, Pennsylvania, and Maryland. It was a key area of conflict during the American Revolutionary War, particularly during raids by Loyalist and Native American forces.

Sycamore (Cotton Ball) Tree

A large deciduous tree known for its broad leaves and distinctive bark. In the text, it is referred to as a common tree in low areas of Orleans County during the early settlement period.

Swamp

A wetland area that is often forested. In this context, it refers to a swamp near the ancient fortifications in Orleans County.

Take up the hatchet

An expression meaning to engage in warfare. The phrase is derived from Native American customs, where burying the hatchet symbolized peace, and taking it up again meant a return to war.

Taking of Ticonderoga

A reference to the capture of Fort Ticonderoga on May 10, 1775, during the American Revolutionary War.

Tanner

A craftsman who processes animal hides into leather.

Tanning and Currying

The process of treating animal hides to produce leather (tanning) and then dressing, finishing, or coloring the leather (currying).

Tanyard

A place where animal hides are tanned to make leather.

Tavern

An establishment where travelers could eat, drink, and sleep. Taverns were important social and economic centers in early settlements. Taverns were central to social life in early American communities, serving as gathering places for news, business, and leisure.

Tavern Keeper
An owner or operator of a tavern, where travelers could get food, drink, and lodging.

Telegraph
An early communication system that used electrical signals to transmit messages over long distances via telegraph wires. The introduction of the telegraph was a major technological advancement in the 19th century, revolutionizing communication

Temperance
A social movement that promoted abstinence from alcoholic beverages. In the 19th century, temperance organizations were common, and many settlers were actively involved in them.

Temperance Hotel
A hotel that abstains from serving alcoholic beverages. The temperance movement was strong in the 19th century, and some establishments chose to align with its principles.

Temperance Organizations
Groups or movements that promoted abstinence from alcohol, which were popular in the 19th century.

The Creature
A colloquial term often used in the 19th century to refer to alcoholic beverages, especially whiskey or rum.

Theological Seminary
An institution for training ministers or clergy.

The Triangle
A tract of land in Western New York, located between the Holland Purchase and the 100,000 Acre Tract. It was another key area during the early settlement of the region.

The Union Company
A group of eight young men from Stockbridge, Massachusetts, who formed a cooperative company in 1810 to establish a settlement on the Holland Purchase in Carlton. They agreed to pool resources and labor to help each member clear land, and build a house and barn on their respective farms.

Threshing
The process of separating grain from the husks or straw. In the early 19th century, this was often done by hand, using tools like flails, or by animals trampling on the grain.

Tinder Box
A small container holding materials such as flint, steel, and tinder, used to start a fire. Before the invention of friction matches, a tinder box was essential for lighting fires in early settler homes.

Tinned Iron Spoons
Spoons made from iron that had been coated with a thin layer of tin to prevent rusting. These were common in households that could not afford more expensive silverware.

Tonawanda Swamp
A large wetland area covering parts of Genesee and Orleans Counties. It was a significant geographical feature that posed challenges for settlement and development, requiring extensive efforts to drain and manage.

Tories
American colonists who remained loyal to the British Crown during the American Revolutionary War. They often allied with British forces and Native American tribes against the American revolutionaries.

Tow Cloth
A coarse, strong cloth made from the rougher parts of flax or hemp fibers. It was commonly used for making work clothes in early American settlements.

Towing Path
A path alongside a canal where horses, mules, or oxen walked while towing boats through the canal. These paths were essential for the movement of goods before the advent of steam-powered boats.

Town Clerk
An official responsible for maintaining the public records and documents of the town, including minutes of town meetings, vital statistics, and other important municipal records.

Town Clock
A large, publicly visible clock, usually installed in a church steeple or town hall. Town clocks were important for regulating daily life in the community before the widespread availability of personal timepieces.

Town Meeting
A form of direct democratic rule where members of a town come together to legislate policy and budgets for local government. In early American towns, town meetings were crucial for making decisions on community issues.

Track
The rails on which trains run. In the early days of railroads, tracks could be built for horse-drawn cars or steam-powered trains.

Trailblazer
A term used to describe someone who is a pioneer or first to explore and settle in a new area.

Train as Soldiers
Refers to the requirement for able-bodied men to participate in militia training, a common practice in early America.

Transit Instrument
A precision instrument used by surveyors to measure angles in the horizontal and vertical planes. It was crucial in establishing accurate land boundaries, such as those in the Transit Line.

Transit Line

A boundary line that runs from Pennsylvania north to Lake Ontario along the eastern edge of the Holland Purchase. It was named "Transit" because it was originally surveyed with the aid of a transit instrument, which is a type of surveying tool.

Treading (Trod)

A method of threshing grain by having animals, such as oxen or horses, walk over it to separate the grain from the chaff. This was a common practice before the development of mechanical threshers.

Treaty

A formal agreement between two or more states or groups. The text mentions treaties between Native American tribes and the U.S. government regarding land rights.

Trenchers

Wooden plates or platters used for serving food. Trenchers were common in early settler households and were often made by hand.

Trite

Something that is overused and lacks originality, often used to describe stories or themes that have been extensively covered.

Trod

Previously defined, this refers to the method of threshing grain by having animals walk over it to separate the grain from the chaff.

Trustees

Individuals responsible for managing the affairs of a cemetery association or other organization. Trustees oversee the maintenance, improvement, and financial management of cemeteries.

Turner's History

Refers to the historical works by Orsamus Turner, particularly his histories of the Phelps and Gorham Purchase and the Holland Purchase which provide descriptions of ancient fortifications and historical events in Western New York. Turner's works were important sources for the author of *Pioneer History of Orleans County*.

Turning Shop

A workshop where wood was shaped and turned into products like chairs and bowls.

Tuscaroras

The sixth nation to join the Iroquois Confederacy. Originally from North Carolina they migrated to New York in the early 18th century. During the War of 1812, they were allied with the United States against the British and their Native American allies.

Union Schoolhouse

A type of public school that served multiple communities or religious denominations.

Universalist

Refers to someone who believes in universal salvation, the idea that all people will eventually be saved and that there is no eternal damnation.

It was a significant religious perspective at the time.

Universalist Society
A religious organization that follows Universalism, a Christian theological perspective that emphasizes universal salvation and the belief that all people will eventually be reconciled with God.

Valley Forge
A military camp in Pennsylvania where General George Washington's Continental Army spent the winter of 1777–1778 during the American Revolutionary War. It is known for the severe hardships the soldiers faced, including cold, hunger, and disease.

Variety Store
A type of retail store that sold a wide range of goods, including groceries and other essentials, to both local residents and travelers on the Erie Canal.

Vats
Large containers used for holding liquids. In salt production, brine would be placed in vats to allow impurities to settle before the clear liquid was boiled to extract the salt.

Venerable
Worthy of respect due to age, wisdom, or character.

Venison
Meat from deer, which was a common source of food for early settlers.

Vicissitude
A change or variation, typically one that is unwelcome or unpleasant. In this text, it refers to the unpredictable challenges and hardships faced by pioneers.

Victuals
An old term for food or provisions, especially as prepared for consumption.

Wagon Load
The amount of goods that could be carried in a single trip by a wagon. In the early settlement days, a wagon load of supplies from a distant city was a significant event.

Warehouse
A building used for storing goods. In the context of early American villages like Hindsburgh, warehouses were essential for storing farm produce, goods for trade, and supplies before they were shipped via canal or other means.

War with England (War of 1812)
A conflict fought between the United States and the United Kingdom from 1812 to 1815. It was caused by trade restrictions, impressment of American sailors, and British support of Native American attacks on American settlers.

Water Lime

A type of hydraulic lime used to make water-resistant cement or mortar. It was produced by burning limestone and was essential in construction, especially for projects near water like the Erie Canal.

Waterport

A location in Orleans County, New York, connected to the Ridge Road by a highway cleared by local settlers. Waterport served as an important hub for transportation and trade.

Water Power

The use of water flow to drive machinery, particularly mills. In the early 19th century, water power was crucial for operating sawmills and gristmills, which were essential for processing lumber and grain in new settlements.

Wedding the Waters

A symbolic ceremony performed by Governor Dewitt Clinton at the completion of the Erie Canal, in which water from Lake Erie was poured into New York Harbor to symbolize the connection between the Great Lakes and the Atlantic Ocean.

Weevil (Wheat Midge)

An insect pest that attacks wheat crops, causing significant damage. Its presence in Orleans County led to a decline in wheat cultivation and a shift to other crops like beans.

Wesleyan Methodist Connexion

A branch of the Methodist Church formed in the United States in the 19th century. This group emphasized abolitionism and social reforms.

Western fever

A term used to describe the strong desire many people had in the early 19th century to move westward into newly available lands in the United States, often referred to as the Genesee country or other frontier areas.

Western Possessions

Refers to the territories in North America west of the Appalachian Mountains that were claimed by European powers, particularly the French and British, during the colonial period.

Wheat

A key crop planted by early settlers, often sown in the fall to be harvested the following season. Wheat was a staple food and a primary focus of agricultural efforts in newly cleared land.

Whip in Hand

An expression used to describe someone actively driving a team of animals, such as oxen or horses.

Whisky

A distilled alcoholic beverage.

Whitewood

Also known as tulip tree or poplar, a type of tree commonly found in New York. Its wood was used for lumber in early construction projects, particularly for floors and finishing.

Whittier

Refers to John Greenleaf Whittier, an American Quaker poet and advocate of the abolition of slavery. The quoted lines at the end of the Preface are from Whittier's poetry, reflecting on the passage of time and the importance of remembering history.

Wigwam

A traditional dome-shaped dwelling used by Native American tribes, particularly the Algonquins and Iroquois. The log houses of early settlers were somewhat inspired by the wigwam in their use of bark for roofing and other construction methods.

Wild Land

Unsettled, undeveloped land that was often purchased from the government by early settlers or speculators.

Wild Plum Tree

A type of tree bearing small, tough, and often sour plums. These trees were sometimes found by early settlers in the forests of Orleans County.

Wild oats

A phrase used metaphorically to describe youthful misbehavior or reckless activities, typically before settling down into a more responsible lifestyle.

Withees

Flexible branches or twigs used to bind or fasten parts of a structure together. In log houses, withees might be used in place of nails to secure different elements.

Wool carding and cloth dressing

The process of preparing wool for spinning by untangling and cleaning the fibers (carding) and then treating the woven cloth to improve its appearance and durability (cloth dressing).

Wolves

A common predator in early Orleans County, wolves posed a threat to livestock, particularly sheep and young cattle and sometimes to settlers themselves, symbolizing the dangers of the untamed frontier. They were eventually hunted out as the area became more settled.

Wooden Latch

A simple wooden device used to secure a door. The latch could be lifted from the outside by a string, a common feature in early log houses.

Wrought Nails
Hand-forged nails used in construction before the advent of machine-made nails.

Yoke of Oxen
A pair of oxen harnessed together for plowing or pulling heavy loads.

Young America
A political and cultural movement in the mid-19th century that celebrated American nationalism, territorial expansion, and technological progress.

NAME INDEX

Gates, Dr. Richard W., 208

Gates, John, 234 258

Gates, Lewis W., 210

Gates, Matthew A., 210 258

Gates, Nehemiah F., 210

Gates, Saloma, 469

Gear, Samuel F., 413

Gibson, James, 74

Gilbert, Baruch H., 457 472

Gilbert, Elisha, 458

Gilbert, Mr., 230 472

Gilbert, Selina, 469

Gilbert, Simeon, 457 469 472

Gilbert, Widow, 42 230-231

Gillett, Sylvester, 410

Goodrich, Harmon, 362

Goodrich, Harvey, 77 114

Goodrich, Laura, 185

Goodrich, Zenas, 114

Goodsell, Dr. Pensfield, 118

Goold, Horace O., 469

Gould, David, 333

Graham, Ethan, 298

Graham, James, 98

Granger, Eli, 57

Grant, Lathrop A. G. B., 448

Gray, Carrie E., 254

Green, Andrew H., 109 323

Greenman, Preserved, 454-455

Gregory, Amos, 430-431

Gregory, Elder, 361

Gregory, Matthew, 431 439

Gregory, Philo, 430

Gregory, Ralph, 430

Grinnell Jr, John, 452

Grinnell, Amos, 452

Grinnell, Andrew J., 452

Grinnell, Anna, 452

Grinnell, Betsey, 452

Grinnell, Chloe, 452

Grinnell, Cyrene, 452

Grinnell, Daniel, 452

Grinnell, Eliza, 452

Grinnell, Ella J., 452

Grinnell, Ezra, 452

Grinnell, Harley, 452

Grinnell, J. Wesley, 452

Grinnell, John, 451-452

Grinnell, Josiah, 452

Grinnell, Lyman, 452

Grinnell, Mahala, 452

Grinnell, Paul, 452

Groff, Christian, 429

Grover, Lysander C., 405 408

Guernsey, Elizabeth, 164

Guller, Ezbon G., 273

Gwynn, William R., 72-73

H

Hackett, 428,

Hadley, Elizabeth, 253

Haines, Alice, 452

Haines, Jesse P., 60

Hall, Elder, 70

Hallock, Rufus, 142-143

Halsey, Polly, 174

Hamlin, 299, 309 321 330 339-341

Hamlin, Alva, 340

Hamlin, Areovester, 330 339

Hammond, Rev. Charles, 356

Hard, Hon. Gideon, 97 198

Hard, Samuel B., 99

Harrington, Micah, 355 429 434

Hart, Dea., 134 136 183

Hart, Elizur, 153 155

Risden, Orange, 194
Robinson, Chauncey, 218 221 328
Rodman, Mary, 452
Rogers, Dea. Ebenezer, 77 90 99
    133 170 183
Rogers, Joshua M., 417
Rooker, Leonora, 452
Root, Amos, 23 25-26 120
Root, Clarissa, 392
Root, Israel, 121
Root, Margaret, 452
Root, Moses, 204 206 208
Root, Reuben, 205 460 462
Rowena, 247,
Ruggles, Humphrey, 74
Ruggles, Seth, 291
Ruggles, William Oakley, 292
Ruggles, William W., 198 247 291
Ryan, Andrew, 423
Ryan, John, 415
S
S, Rev. J., 362
Salmon, Richard, 417
Salsbury, Samuel, 245
Samson, Amos S., 293
Sanderson, Janette, 451
Sanderson, Louisa, 155
Sanford, Asa, 100 109
Saunders, Betsey, 382
Sawyer, Elisha, 457-458 472
Sawyer, Nathan, 415
Saxe, John G., 456
Schuyler, Philip, x
Scoot, Capt. Justin, 172
Scoot, Lydia, 172
Scott, Amy, 231
Scovill, Ephraim, 417
Scovill, Samuel, 253

Seward, William H., 122
Seymour, James, 330 340
Shaw, Dr. Truman S., 263
Shaw, Elijah, 148
Shaw, Martha, 213
Shaw, Melinda, 254
Shelby, Governor, 425
Sheldon, Dr., 270
Shelley, Betsey, 251
Shelly, Nathan, 252
Shelly, Sylvia, 318
Sherwin, Miner, 459
Shipman, Israel, 214
Shipman, Jobe, 208 214
Sibley, William, 230 234
Sickels, Hiram, 77
Simonds, Abigail, 147
Simonds, Egbert B., 451
Simpson, Robert, 386 458
Skellenger, Miss Fanny, 473
Skellinger, Nathan, 458
Skinner, Jarvis M., 155-156
Slade, Elizabeth, 410
Slater Jr, Giles, 207
Slater, Eleazer, 400
Smith, Calvin, 196
Smith, Caroline, 290
Smith, David, 294-295
Smith, Harvey, 293
Smith, Isaac, 334
Smith, James P., 172
Smith, Judge, 338
Smith, Moses, 151
Smith, Russell, 207
Smith, Sally, 333 335 470
Snell, John B., 450
Snell, Joseph, 265

SUBJECT INDEX

589